SQL Server Services

- **Microsoft Distributed Transaction Coordinator (MS DTC):** SQL Server uses the MS DTC service to coordinate distributed transactions.

- **Microsoft Search:** SQL Server uses the Microsoft Search service to add support for full-text searches.

- **MSSQLServer:** This service is the database engine. It processes all your Transact-SQL queries, manages your databases and their files, verifies the integrity of your data, and allocates the server's resources.

- **SQLServerAgent:** This service makes it possible for you to automate many of your administrative tasks through alerts, jobs, and operators.

Database Objects

- **Tables:** Consist of both columns and rows. Each row represents one of the entities you're tracking in the table, and each column stores the individual pieces of information you want to track for each row.

- **Indexes:** Used to speed up your searches of a table. You can create a total of 250 indexes per table, of which only one index can be clustered, and the rest must be nonclustered.

- **Views:** Used to restrict the rows and columns your users can access in a table.

- **Stored procedures:** Enable you to save a series of Transact-SQL statements; SQL Server then compiles and caches the query execution plan for each stored procedure.

- **Triggers:** Used to configure SQL Server to perform specific tasks whenever a user adds, deletes, or modifies a row in a table.

System Databases

- **Distribution:** Stores history and transaction information used by SQL Server when replicating a database across multiple servers. You see this database only if you have configured replication on your server.

- **Master:** Contains information about the operation of SQL Server, including user database files, transaction logs, logon IDs, and environment variables.

- **Model:** Used by SQL Server to store template database objects, which SQL Server copies automatically to any new user database you create. For example, the model database contains a table for storing users' permissions. SQL Server then copies this table to every new database you create.

- **Msdb:** Stores information about all the jobs, alerts, and operators you have defined on your server. The SQLServerAgent service uses this database.

- **Tempdb:** Used by SQL Server to store temporary information generated during processing. SQL Server uses this database as its "scratchpad" for performing such tasks as sorting tables.

MCSE SQL Server 2000 Administration For Dummies®

Cheat Sheet

Server Roles

- **System Administrators (sysadmin):** Members can perform any task on the server.
- **Security Administrators (securityadmin):** Members can add, change, or delete the server's login IDs.
- **Server Administrators (serveradmin):** Members can manage server-wide configuration settings.
- **Setup Administrators (setupadmin):** Members can install and configure replication, execute some system stored procedures, and configure linked servers.
- **Process Administrators (processadmin):** Members can administer the processes running on a server.
- **Disk Administrators (diskadmin):** Members can manage database and transaction log files.
- **Database Creators (dbcreator):** Members can create and modify databases.
- **Bulk Insert Administrators (bulkadmin):** Its members can run the BULK INSERT SQL statement for importing a large amount of data into a table.

Database Roles

- **Public:** Members can perform any task permitted by the permissions you have assigned to this role.
- **Db_owner:** Members can perform any task in the database.
- **Db_accessadmin:** Its members can add or delete database users, groups, and user-defined roles.
- **Db_securityadmin:** Members can assign and manage users' permissions.
- **Db_ddladmin:** Members can add, change, or delete database objects.
- **Db_backupoperator:** Members can back up and restore the database.
- **Db_datareader:** Members can read data from any of the database's tables.
- **Db_datawriter:** Members can add, change, or delete data from any of the database's tables.
- **Db_denydatareader:** This role prevents members from reading data in any of the database's tables.
- **Db_denydatawriter:** This role restricts its members from adding, changing, or deleting data from any of the database's tables.

Hungry Minds™

For Dummies®: Bestselling Book Series for Beginners

MCSE SQL Server™ 2000 Administration FOR DUMMIES®

by Rozanne Murphy Whalen
and Daniel W. Whalen

Hungry Minds™

HUNGRY MINDS, INC.

New York, NY ◆ Cleveland, OH ◆ Indianapolis, IN

MCSE SQL Server™ 2000 Administration For Dummies®

Published by
Hungry Minds, Inc.
909 Third Avenue
New York, NY 10022
www.hungryminds.com
www.dummies.com

Library of Congress Control Number: 00-111130

ISBN: 0-7645-0480-0

Printed in the United States of America

10 9 8 7 6 5 4 3 2 1

1O/RS/QU/QR/IN

Distributed in the United States by Hungry Minds, Inc.

Distributed by CDG Books Canada Inc. for Canada; by Transworld Publishers Limited in the United Kingdom; by IDG Norge Books for Norway; by IDG Sweden Books for Sweden; by IDG Books Australia Publishing Corporation Pty. Ltd. for Australia and New Zealand; by TransQuest Publishers Pte Ltd. for Singapore, Malaysia, Thailand, Indonesia, and Hong Kong; by Gotop Information Inc. for Taiwan; by ICG Muse, Inc. for Japan; by Intersoft for South Africa; by Eyrolles for France; by International Thomson Publishing for Germany, Austria and Switzerland; by Distribuidora Cuspide for Argentina; by LR International for Brazil; by Galileo Libros for Chile; by Ediciones ZETA S.C.R. Ltda. for Peru; by WS Computer Publishing Corporation, Inc., for the Philippines; by Contemporanea de Ediciones for Venezuela; by Express Computer Distributors for the Caribbean and West Indies; by Micronesia Media Distributor, Inc. for Micronesia; by Chips Computadoras S.A. de C.V. for Mexico; by Editorial Norma de Panama S.A. for Panama; by American Bookshops for Finland.

For general information on Hungry Minds' products and services please contact our Customer Care Department within the U.S. at 800-762-2974, outside the U.S. at 317-572-3993 or fax 317-572-4002.

For sales inquiries and reseller information, including discounts, premium and bulk quantity sales, and foreign-language translations, please contact our Customer Care Department at 800-434-3422, fax 317-572-4002, or write to Hungry Minds, Inc., Attn: Customer Care Department, 10475 Crosspoint Boulevard, Indianapolis, IN 46256.

For information on licensing foreign or domestic rights, please contact our Sub-Rights Customer Care Department at 212-884-5000.

For information on using Hungry Minds' products and services in the classroom or for ordering examination copies, please contact our Educational Sales Department at 800-434-2086 or fax 317-572-4005.

Please contact our Public Relations Department at 212-884-5163 for press review copies or 212-884-5000 for author interviews and other publicity information or fax 212-884-5400.

For authorization to photocopy items for corporate, personal, or educational use, please contact Copyright Clearance Center, 222 Rosewood Drive, Danvers, MA 01923, or fax 978-750-4470.

Hungry Minds™ is a trademark of Hungry Minds, Inc.

About the Authors

Rozanne Murphy Whalen is the President of Software Solutions, Inc., in New Orleans, Louisiana. Unlike her husband Dan, Rozanne has pretty much always been a computer geek. In addition to an MBA, she holds the MCSE, MCDBA, and MCT certifications. She teaches instructor-led training courses to prepare students for the MCSE and MCDBA exams. Rozanne also writes instructor-led training manuals for Element K Press and is the editor of Element K's *Inside Microsoft Windows 2000* journal. In her spare time (what little there is of it), she enjoys photography and spending time with her family — and a little fishing. You can reach Rozanne via her e-mail address: Rozanne@softsol.com.

Daniel W. Whalen is the Vice President of Software Solutions, Inc., in New Orleans, Louisiana. Prior to becoming a computer geek, Dan flew F-14 Tomcats in the Navy, and he is a Gulf War veteran. After spending a tour of duty teaching Navy student pilots to fly jets, he decided to move on to teaching students who can't kill him if they don't learn. Dan holds the MCSE, MCDBA, and MCT certifications, and is also an Oracle8 DBA. Dan teaches instructor-led training to prepare students for the MCSE, MCDBA, and Oracle DBA exams. When it comes to spare time, Dan would rather be fishing. You can reach Dan via his e-mail address: flailn@hotmail.com.

Dedication

We would like to dedicate this book to our parents. (We figure this way we'll find out if they actually read it!)

Authors' Acknowledgments

We would like to begin by thanking Lisa Swayne, without whom we would not have had the opportunity to write this book. We also want to thank Nancy Maragioglio for her constant support and never-ending words of encouragement. Many, many thanks to John Pont, our project editor, for guiding us through the development of this book, putting up with endless questions, and providing words of wisdom. For their insights, attention to detail, and suggestions, we thank Paula Lowell, our copy editor, and Rob Scrimger, our technical reviewer. Finally, thanks to everyone in the Media Development department for their efforts in putting together the CD-ROM that comes with this book, and to the talented production people who transformed our manuscript into this finished product.

Publisher's Acknowledgments

We're proud of this book; please send us your comments through our Online Registration Form located at www.dummies.com.

Some of the people who helped bring this book to market include the following:

Acquisitions, Editorial, and Media Development

Project Editor: John W. Pont

Senior Acquisitions Editor: Nancy Maragioglio

Copy Editor: Paula Lowell

Technical Editor: Rob Scrimger, MCT, MCDBA, MCSE+I, CTT

Permissions Editor: Laura Moss

Media Development Specialist: Megan Decraene

Media Development Coordinator: Marisa Pearman

Editorial Manager: Constance Carlisle

Media Development Manager: Laura Carpenter

Media Development Supervisor: Richard Graves

Editorial Assistants: Amanda Foxworth, Jean Rogers

Production

Project Coordinator: Maridee Ennis

Layout and Graphics: LeAndra Johnson, Heather Pope, Jacque Schneider, Erin Zeltner, Jeremey Unger

Proofreaders: David Faust, Angel Perez

Indexer: York Production Services, Inc.

General and Administrative

Hungry Minds, Inc.: John Kilcullen, CEO; Bill Barry, President and COO; John Ball, Executive VP, Operations & Administration; John Harris, CFO

Hungry Minds Technology Publishing Group: Richard Swadley, Senior Vice President and Publisher; Mary Bednarek, Vice President and Publisher, Networking and Certification; Walter R. Bruce III, Vice President and Publisher, General User and Design Professional; Joseph Wikert, Vice President and Publisher, Programming; Mary C. Corder, Editorial Director, Branded Technology Editorial; Andy Cummings, Publishing Director, General User and Design Professional; Barry Pruett, Publishing Director, Visual

Hungry Minds Manufacturing: Ivor Parker, Vice President, Manufacturing

Hungry Minds Marketing: John Helmus, Assistant Vice President, Director of Marketing

Hungry Minds Online Management: Brenda McLaughlin, Executive Vice President, Chief Internet Officer

Hungry Minds Production for Branded Press: Debbie Stailey, Production Director

Hungry Minds Sales: Roland Elgey, Senior Vice President, Sales and Marketing; Michael Violano, Vice President, International Sales and Sub Rights

◆

The publisher would like to give special thanks to Patrick J. McGovern, without whom this book would not have been possible.

◆

Contents at a Glance

Cartoons at a Glance

By Rich Tennant

The 5th Wave — By Rich Tennant

"Our automated response policy to a large company wide data crash is to notify management, back up existing data and sell 90% of my shares in the company."

page 193

The 5th Wave — By Rich Tennant

"I'm not saying I believe in anything. All I know is since it's been there our server is running 50% faster."

page 31

The 5th Wave — By Rich Tennant

"We sort of have our own way of mentally preparing our people to take the MCSE SQL Server exam."

page 475

The 5th Wave — By Rich Tennant

"Your database is beyond repair, but before I tell you our backup recommendation, let me ask you a question. How many index cards do you think will fit on the walls of your computer room?"

page 305

The 5th Wave — By Rich Tennant

FELDMAN NOVELTY ITEMS

"We can monitor our entire operation from one central location. We know what the 'Wax Lips' people are doing; we know what the 'Whoopee Cushion' people are doing; we know what the 'Fly-in-the-Ice Cube' people are doing. But we don't know what the 'Plastic Vomit' people are doing. We don't *want* to know what the 'Plastic Vomit' people are doing."

page 111

The 5th Wave — By Rich Tennant

AFTER DISCOVERING THE LAND OF LOST FILES, BILL AND IRWIN RUN INTO A TRIBE OF SQL INDIANS.

THIS IS GONNA BE TRICKY. THEY PROBABLY ALL SPEAK A DIFFERENT LANGUAGE.

page 7

The 5th Wave — By Rich Tennant

MCSE Testing Center

"...and it doesn't appear that you'll have much trouble grasping some of the more 'alien' configuration concepts on this MCSE exam."

page 465

The 5th Wave — By Rich Tennant

"A centralized security management system sounds fine, but then what would we do with the dogs?"

page 373

The 5th Wave — By Rich Tennant

"You know, this was a situation question on my SQL Server exam, but I always thought it was just hypothetical."

page 421

Cartoon Information:
Fax: 978-546-7747
E-Mail: richtennant@the5thwave.com
World Wide Web: www.the5thwave.com

Table of Contents

Introduction

. . . .

So, you're chasing after the elusive MCSE (Microsoft Certified Systems Engineer) or MCDBA (Microsoft Certified Database Administrator) certification, and you're planning to take the SQL Server 2000 exam, are you? Well, you've opened the right book! This book provides you with everything you need to know for studying, practicing, and mastering the objectives for exam 70-228, Installing, Configuring, and Administering Microsoft SQL Server 2000 Enterprise Edition.

You should be prepared to spend lots of time studying and practicing with SQL Server 2000 in order to pass the exam. You also need to know what to focus on when preparing for the exam. Although you can find other resources for helping you administer SQL Server, this book focuses specifically on what you need to master for the exam. (We also give you hints about what you don't need to know for the exam!)

About This Book

We wrote this book to provide you with everything you need to prepare for the SQL Server 2000 exam. Of course, having experience with SQL Server helps make passing the exam easier. If at all possible, we strongly recommend that you install SQL Server 2000 and use it to practice the labs throughout this book. You should also give yourself time to work through the Quick Assessment and Prep Test we provide with each chapter.

This book is a step-by-step guide to preparing for the exam. We recommend that you go through the Table of Contents to identify the topics you need to study and then review the material in the chapters that cover those topics. At the beginning of each chapter, we tell you what you should focus on as you study for the exam.

Foolish Assumptions

We know, we know — we've just met, and yet we're already making some assumptions about you! Here's what we assumed when we wrote this book: First, that you're already familiar with SQL Server and its purpose. (After all, this isn't really a beginner book.) We also assume that you have some experience administering SQL Server 2000. Finally, we assume that you bought this book because you want to pass exam 70-228, so we focus solely on that goal throughout this book — and not on teaching you the ins and outs of administering SQL Server.

How This Book Is Organized

We designed this book to follow the order of Microsoft's published exam objectives. Each part of the book corresponds to a section of exam objectives; within each part, we have chapters that correspond to one or more exam objectives within that section.

Part 1: Getting Started

We use the two chapters in Part I to get your feet wet with the SQL Server 2000 exam. You find out what types of questions you can expect and what the exam covers. We also provide you with an overview of administering SQL Server 2000. If you need to brush up on SQL Server before you dig into the meat of the exam, Part I is where you should start.

Part II: Installing and Configuring SQL Server 2000

The fact that Microsoft includes the verbs "installing" and "configuring" in the exam title should give you a hint that the exam focuses on both installing and configuring SQL Server. We cover just that in Part II of this book. Specifically, we show you how to plan your installation, install SQL Server 2000, upgrade to SQL Server 2000 from an earlier version, and troubleshoot installation problems. This part also includes an overview of how to configure SQL Server to send and receive e-mail.

Part III: Creating SQL Server Databases

Because the key reason you use SQL Server is to implement a database, we use Part III of the book to explain everything you need to know about creating SQL Server databases. The chapters in this part focus on the topics you need to know for the exam, including how to design and create a database, manage the database, and create and manage database objects.

Part IV: Managing, Monitoring, and Troubleshooting Databases

For the exam, you need to know how to optimize the performance of SQL Server databases. In Part IV, we explore all the utilities and techniques you can use to manage, monitor, and troubleshoot databases. We focus on providing you with just the techniques you need to know both to optimize a database and for the exam. We also walk you through performing maintenance tasks such as backing up and restoring a database.

Part V: Transferring Data

No SQL server is an island. In other words, sooner or later you're probably going to have to configure SQL Server to import or export its data (or both). SQL Server includes several features that make exchanging data between SQL Server and a wide variety of systems easy for you. In Part V, we show you how to integrate SQL Server with Internet Information Services (IIS), transfer data by using Data Transformation Services, and configure replication between SQL servers.

Part VI: Securing SQL Server

One of your key administrative duties when implementing SQL Server is to secure it. In Part VI, we show you how to implement login security, permissions, and auditing to protect your SQL servers. Pay close attention to the material in these chapters because you can expect to see several security-related questions on your exam.

Part VII: Managing, Monitoring, and Troubleshooting SQL Server 2000

In Part VII, we explain everything you need to know to answer exam questions on managing, monitoring, and troubleshooting SQL Server. We show you how to automate administration of your server by configuring jobs and alerts. We also explain how you optimize SQL Server. Finally, we explore the utilities you can use to monitor and troubleshoot SQL Server. Because one of your main responsibilities as a SQL Server administrator is to make sure that everything runs smoothly, you can expect to see several questions on your exam that are based on the material in Part VII.

Part VIII: The Part of Tens

In Part VIII, we give you our top-ten lists of information that you can use to help you pass the exam. We give you our favorite test-taking tips based on our own experience with the exam. We also provide you with our top-ten list of resources that we found invaluable when we prepared for the exam.

Part IX: Appendix

The "About the CD" appendix explains what resources we've included on the CD-ROM that comes with this book. Turn to this appendix for installation instructions and descriptions of the test-prep tools you can find on the *MCSE SQL Server 2000 Administration For Dummies* CD-ROM.

About the CD-ROM

The CD-ROM included with this book has several great features to help you get ready for the SQL Server exam. Most importantly, the CD-ROM contains a practice test that you can use to see if you're ready for the real thing. In addition, the CD-ROM includes a QuickLearn game, a full-length Practice Exam, a bonus chapter on Microsoft's adaptive testing, a screen saver, and demo versions of practice test software.

Conventions Used in This Book

We want this book to guide you to mastering what you need to know for the exam. To accomplish this goal, we include straightforward labs to help you practice the topics that you're most likely to see on the exam. We also throw in plenty of tips along the way to help you identify what you should focus your studies on. Finally, we use tables as a way to streamline information that you should make sure you know for the exam. Any time you see information in a table, you should memorize that information for the exam.

As far as typographical conventions go, we use the `monotype font` to help you identify the Transact-SQL keywords and commands for performing the various administrative tasks that we describe throughout the book. In addition, we typically set series of Transact-SQL commands apart from the regular paragraphs of a chapter so that these commands are easier to read — for example:

```
SELECT *
FROM pubs.dbo.authors
```

In the hands-on labs, we use an arrow to indicate that you should choose an option from a menu. For example, you might see something like this in a lab:

In SQL Server Enterprise Manager, choose Tools⇨Replication. This statement means that you should choose the Tools menu first and then select the Replication option on the Tools menu. One other convention: We use bold-face type in the labs when we want you to type something exactly as shown.

Icons Used in This Book

Throughout the book, we use the following icons to highlight key points that can help you pass the SQL Server exam:

We use the Instant Answer icon to point out information you can use to respond to exam questions.

We use the Remember icon to help you identify the advantages to SQL Server that you should know for the exam.

Look for the Time Shaver icon for ways you can focus your studies for the exam.

We use the Tip icon to point out handy pieces of information for getting the most out of SQL Server. We also use this icon to tell you what to focus on when you study.

The Warning icon draws your attention to problems or pitfalls you can run into when installing, configuring, or administering SQL Server 2000.

Where to Go from Here

If you're new to SQL Server 2000, or you think you may have some holes in your knowledge, we recommend that you begin by reviewing the list of exam objectives in Chapter 1 and the primer on SQL Server in Chapter 2. When you move on to the remaining chapters in the book, take the time to work through the Quick Assessment questions at the beginning of each chapter. These questions help you identify what you don't know. After you find out what topics you need to review, move on to the heart of the chapter to study those topics. Use the Prep Test at the end of each chapter to make sure that you've mastered those topics.

Good luck!

Part I
Getting Started

In this part . . .

*B*efore you begin preparing for the Installing, Configuring, and Administering SQL Server exam, make sure that you're familiar with the basics of SQL Server 2000 and that you understand the focus of the exam. If you're concerned that you don't know the role SQL Server plays on a network, or if you're wondering what to expect on the exam, this part is for you.

In Chapter 1, we provide you with an overview of the forms of questions you can expect, the types of exams you might see, and what information you can expect on the exam. In Chapter 2, we explore the basic components of SQL Server, show you how you can integrate a SQL server into your network, and give you an overview of security.

Chapter 1

The Microsoft SQL Server 2000 System Administration Exam

··

In This Chapter

▶ Taking a look at exam 70-228

▶ Finding the content of the exam and what you'll be tested on

▶ Surviving exam day

··

*W*hether you're using exam 70-228, Installing, Configuring, and Administering Microsoft SQL Server 2000 Enterprise Edition, as one of your MCSE electives, or using it to fulfill the core requirements for your MCDBA, this book can help you prepare for the exam. Because SQL Server 2000 is Microsoft's premiere enterprise database management system, you'll find that its popularity is growing — and, as a result, the demand for SQL Server certified professionals is also growing. In this chapter, we help get you on your way to passing the exam by introducing you to the exam objectives. We also tell you what to expect from the exam and how to go about scheduling it. Finally, we give you some test-taking tips to help you survive the exam process.

What Can You Expect from the SQL Server 2000 Exam?

Before you take this exam, you should have an idea of what you're getting yourself into. We don't want to scare you off, but we also want you to know that you'll find this exam challenging. Make sure that you study both carefully and "smartly" in order to ensure that you pass the exam.

How will the exam work?

Microsoft tests you by using one of two types of exams: standard or adaptive. With a standard exam, you have a fixed number of questions. In contrast, with an adaptive exam, you see a varying number of questions. Although our exams both used the standard format, Microsoft states that the 70-228 exam may be adaptive — so you should be prepared for either format.

Standard exams

You may find that the Installing, Configuring, and Administering SQL Server exam is a *standard exam*, which means that you'll get a typical Microsoft exam with a fixed number of questions (usually in the neighborhood of 50 to 70), and that downloads to your testing center from a pool of questions. With standard exams, you can review any of the questions and change your answers.

You can expect to see questions that use any of the following formats:

- **Multiple-choice questions:** These questions can have one or more correct answers.

- **Scenario-based questions:** In these questions, Microsoft provides you with a detailed scenario or problem and then asks you for the best solution. You can expect to see questions that give you a scenario, a solution, and a series of objectives. You then must choose which objectives the proposed solution meets.

- **Simulation questions:** These questions show you a particular SQL Server utility and prompt you to perform a specific task.

Make sure that you're ready for the exam and all of these types of questions by using the practice exam on the CD-ROM for this book.

Adaptive exams

Instead of a standard exam, you may find that your SQL Server exam is *adaptive*, which means that the exam tailors itself to you as you take it. For example, if you miss a question on a particular topic, the exam will typically ask you additional questions on that same topic.

The adaptive exams tend to ask you more questions on the user interface. In contrast to standard exams, adaptive exams typically have a minimum of 15 questions — and a maximum of 25. Although fewer questions mean that you'll get through with the exam faster, you have a lot less room for making a mistake. In addition, in contrast to the standard exams, you can't go back and review any of the questions or change your answers.

You can find out more about adaptive exams by going to `www.microsoft. com/trainingandservices`. Look for the "Testing Innovations" topic.

What does the SQL Server exam cover?

In addition to this book, the Microsoft certification site at `www.microsoft. com/trainingandservices` is your other best friend when preparing for the SQL Server exam. Make sure that you also check out Microsoft's exam preparation guide for the SQL Server exam on this site.

Microsoft's exam preparation guides tell you exactly what they plan to test you on for each exam. To help you focus your studying time for the SQL Server exam, we divided this book into parts and chapters that closely correspond to Microsoft's exam objectives.

Make sure that you review these exam objectives as you study. Also be sure to check Microsoft's Web site regularly to make sure that they haven't changed. Keep in mind that Microsoft can change these objectives at any time — and without notice.

Microsoft's Installing, Configuring, and Administering SQL Server 2000 exam measures your ability to do just that: install, configure, and administer SQL Server. Microsoft divides the exam objectives into six main sections, each with its own objectives. We list these sections and objectives here. For each major exam objective in the following list, we also identify the corresponding part or chapter from this book.

Installing and configuring SQL Server 2000 (Part II)

✔ Install SQL Server 2000 (Chapters 3 and 4). Considerations include

- Clustered servers
- Collation
- File locations
- Number of instances
- Services accounts

✔ Upgrade to SQL Server 2000 (Chapter 5):

- Performing a custom upgrade
- Upgrading from SQL Server 6.5
- Upgrading from SQL Server 7.0

✔ Create a linked server (Chapter 18)

Because you use linked servers when querying multiple servers at the same time (heterogeneous queries), we cover how to create linked servers along with executing these types of queries in Chapter 18.

✔ Configure SQL Mail and SQLAgentMail (Chapter 7)

✔ Configure network libraries (Chapter 4)

✔ Troubleshoot failed installations (Chapter 6)

Creating SQL Server 2000 databases (Part III)

✔ Configure database options for performance (Chapter 8). Considerations include

- Capacity
- Network connectivity
- Physical drive configurations
- Storage locations

✔ Attach and detach databases (Chapter 10)

✔ Create and alter databases (Chapters 9 and 10):

- Add filegroups
- Configure filegroup usage
- Expand and shrink a database
- Set database options by using the ALTER DATABASE or CREATE DATABASE statements
- Size and place the transaction log

✔ Create and manage objects (Chapter 11). Objects include constraints, indexes, stored procedures, triggers, and views

Managing, monitoring, and troubleshooting SQL Server 2000 databases (Part IV)

✔ Optimize database performance (Chapter 12). Considerations include

- Indexing
- Locking
- Recompiling

✔ Optimize data storage (Chapter 13):

- Optimize files and filegroups
- Manage database fragmentation

- Modify the database schema (Chapter 12)
- Perform disaster recovery operations (Chapters 14 and 15):
    - Perform backups
    - Recover the system state and restore data
    - Configure, maintain, and troubleshoot log shipping
- Perform integrity checks (Chapter 16). Methods include
    - Configuring the Database Maintenance Plan Wizard
    - Using the Database Consistency Checker (DBCC)
- Troubleshoot transactions and locking by using SQL Profiler, SQL Server Enterprise Manager, or Transact-SQL (Chapter 16)

Extracting and transforming data with SQL Server 2000 (Part V)

- Set up Internet Information Services (IIS) virtual directories to support XML (Chapter 17)
- Import and export data (Chapter 18). Methods include
    - Bulk Insert task
    - Bulk Copy Program
    - Data Transformation Services
    - Heterogeneous Queries
- Develop and manage Data Transformation Services (DTS) packages (Chapter 18)
- Manage linked servers (Chapter 18):
    - Manage OLE DB Providers
    - Configure security mapping
- Convert data types (Chapter 18)
- Configure, maintain, and troubleshoot replication services (Chapter 19)

Managing and monitoring SQL Server 2000 security (Part VI)

- Configure mixed security modes or Windows Authentication (Chapter 20). Considerations include
    - Client connectivity
    - Client operating system
    - Security infrastructure
- Create and manage logins (Chapter 20)
- Create and manage database users (Chapter 21)

✔ Create and manage application, database, and server security roles (Chapter 21). Tasks include

- Add and remove users from roles

- Create roles in order to manage database security

✔ Enforce and manage security by using stored procedures, triggers, views, and user-defined functions (Chapter 21)

✔ Set permissions in a database (Chapter 21). Considerations include

- Object permissions

- Object ownership

- Statement permissions

✔ Manage security auditing (Chapter 22). Methods include

- SQL Profiler

- SQL Trace

- C2 Auditing

Managing, monitoring, and troubleshooting SQL Server 2000 (Part VII)

✔ Create, manage, and troubleshoot SQL Server Agent jobs (Chapter 23)

✔ Configure alerts and operators by using SQL Server Agent (Chapter 23)

✔ Optimize hardware resource usage such as the CPU, disk I/O, and memory (Chapter 24). Considerations include

- Monitor hardware resource usage by using the Windows System Monitor

- Resolve system bottlenecks by using the Windows System Monitor

✔ Optimize and troubleshoot SQL Server system (Chapter 25). Activities include cache hits, connections, locks, memory allocation, recompilation, and transactional throughput. Methods include

- Monitoring SQL Server system activity by using traces

- Monitoring SQL Server system activity by using System Monitor

Surviving the Exam Day

After studying this book and spending some time answering the practice exam questions, you should be ready to take your exam. Before you do so, though, we want you to understand a few things about scheduling your exam and what you can expect when you take it.

Scheduling your exam

Microsoft has authorized two testing providers with whom you can register to take your test: Prometric and Virtual University Enterprises (VUE). Both Prometric and VUE have testing centers throughout the United States and other parts of the world.

You can schedule your exam with Prometric by calling 800-755-EXAM or by visiting its Web site at www.2test.com. To schedule your exam with VUE, call 800-837-8734 or visit the VUE Web site at www.vue.com. The toll-free numbers work only in the United States and Canada. If you live in other regions, check each testing provider's Web site to find the appropriate method for registering for your exam.

You may want to go to each provider's Web site to see which testing center is closest to you.

You need to provide Prometric or VUE with the name of the exam (Installing, Configuring, and Administering Microsoft SQL Server 2000 Enterprise Edition) and its number (70-228) when you register for the test. In addition, you need to know the date and time you want to take the exam and your Social Security Number. Finally, you must pay for the exam when you register for it, so have your credit card handy.

The testing providers require that you show two forms of ID to take an exam. One of them must be a valid photo ID such as your driver's license, passport, or state identification card.

Some exam-taking advice

We want you to pass! (That's why we wrote this book.) We use the following strategies when we take the Microsoft exams — and we both find that they work for us.

We've found that our best, A-number-one strategy for taking a Microsoft test is to outline the material by hand. (And yes, we do mean write it out by hand. Don't cheat and type your outline on the computer.) We know it isn't fun, but we also know that your mind wanders when you're reading dry material. BUT, when you write something on paper, you pay attention to what you're writing — and it's the best memorization technique you'll ever find.

Pay very close attention to the information we put in tables. We use tables whenever we want to highlight material that you can expect to see on your exam. The exam focuses on the details for installing, configuring, and administering SQL Server 2000, and you need to know those details.

Also make sure that you use all the practice questions and practice exams throughout the book and on the CD-ROM. These hundreds of test preparation questions can help you make sure you're ready for the test, so make sure that you use them.

Make sure that you give yourself plenty of time on the day you schedule your test. You don't want to be distracted — and you also want to have time to relax before you take your test. Taking an exam is stressful enough, so don't overdo it!

Watch your time! You can expect to see several long scenario-based questions, so watch the time limit to make sure that you don't run out of time. Pace yourself so that any one question doesn't use up all of your time.

Finally, and most importantly, don't forget to pick up your score report (passing, of course) when you're done. Your testing center notarizes this report to make it official, and your testing provider informs Microsoft of your test score. Congratulations!

Chapter 2

Exam Prep Roadmap: A SQL Server 2000 Primer

*I*f you haven't spent a lot of time with SQL Server 2000, or you're a little bit rusty on what it is and what you can do with it, use this chapter to help you get up to speed quickly. We designed this chapter to give you a solid foundation in the basics of SQL Server — the stuff you need to understand before you can tackle the exam-specific material we cover throughout the rest of this book.

If you're sure you know all the basics about SQL Server 2000, you can skip this chapter.

What Is SQL Server Anyway?

Before you start reviewing how to install, configure, and administer SQL Server, you first need to make sure you understand what SQL Server is.

It's a relational database management system

First of all, SQL Server is a *relational database management system* (RDBMS), which means that you can use SQL Server to create tables to store data — and then define many different relationships between those tables. Because an RDBMS doesn't require specific relationships, these systems provide you with a lot of power and flexibility for retrieving your data.

By the way, you query your tables by using the Structured Query Language (SQL). SQL is a standard set of commands you use to work with your databases and their data. This language was originally developed by IBM and adopted as an American National Standards Institute (ANSI) standard. SQL Server 2000 uses Microsoft's enhanced version of the SQL language called *Transact-SQL*.

It's a client/server application

You may be asking yourself "Aren't other programs such as Microsoft Access also relational database management systems?" If so, you're right. So why do you need something as complicated as SQL Server? Well, in addition to being an RDBMS, SQL Server is also a *client/server application*. A client/server application has two components: one runs on a server, and the other on a client. The advantage to using a client/server database management system is that your database server can process most of the workload for your clients. And because most of the workload is processed on the server, client/server databases such as SQL Server enable you to reduce the traffic on your network.

To understand how SQL Server can reduce network traffic, take a look at two examples. In the first example, you've installed Microsoft Access on your network clients and configured them to use and share a 100MB customer database on a server. Each time a client queries this database, the server must send the entire 100MB database down to the client's computer for processing, as shown in Figure 2-1. In this scenario, if you have 20 clients accessing this same database, you could see up to 20 copies of this database being sent across the network simultaneously. Whew, that's a lot of traffic! And just imagine how much traffic a 10GB database (which isn't uncommon anymore) would put on your network.

Figure 2-1:
With a non-client/server database application, your server must send the entire database across the network to a client.

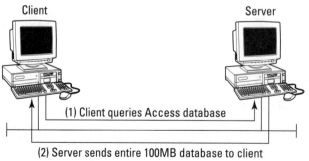

Client   Server

(1) Client queries Access database

(2) Server sends entire 100MB database to client

In the second example, you've installed SQL Server on your server and configured your network clients to access a 100MB customer SQL Server database. Each time a client queries the database, your server processes the query (not the client) and then sends only the results of the query to the client, as shown in Figure 2-2. And if the results of the query are only 20KB in size, you've saved yourself quite a lot of network traffic.

Figure 2-2:
With a client/server database application, your server must send only the results of a query across the network to a client.

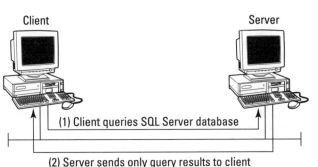

In addition to saving you network traffic, a client/server RDBMS offers you several other advantages. These include the following:

- ✔ You can upgrade the database application on a server more easily than you can upgrade an application on all of your client computers.

- ✔ You can improve the performance of your database environment simply by upgrading the server (and not a bunch of client computers).

- ✔ You won't have to use as high-performance client computers because your server does most of the processing, not the clients.

In the client/server database environment, you'll often hear the server portion of the environment referred to as the *back-end* or *database engine*. Conversely, the client portion is referred to as the *front-end*. SQL Server supports a variety of front-end applications, including off-the-shelf software such as Microsoft Access, as well as custom programs developed with languages such as Visual Basic.

It's whatever you want it to be

In case you haven't noticed, SQL Server 2000 comes in almost as many flavors as ice cream. One reason why so many editions exist is because SQL Server 2000 supports so many operating systems (including Windows 2000,

Windows NT, Windows 98/Me, and even Windows CE). We look more at which SQL Server edition supports which operating system (and vice versa), and the differences between the editions in detail in Chapter 3. But for now, here are the SQL Server flavors . . . er, editions:

- ✔ **Standard:** Designed for workgroup or departmental database servers.

- ✔ **Enterprise:** Designed for the enterprise database environment. In other words, this edition supports very large databases (VLDBs) and data warehousing.

- ✔ **Enterprise Evaluation:** Includes all the features in the Enterprise edition, but expires 120 days after you install it.

- ✔ **Developer:** Designed for programmers to develop and test applications.

- ✔ **Personal:** Designed for laptop users to work with a database both on and off the network.

- ✔ **Windows CE:** Designed for users with personal digital assistants (such as the Microsoft PocketPC) to access a database both on and off the network.

Exploring the Components of SQL Server

Before you tackle studying SQL Server, you need to make sure that you have an understanding of its components. At its core, SQL Server is made up of services, system and user databases, database objects, and utilities for managing its components.

Services

The components of SQL Server 2000 that do all the work are its services. In a Windows NT or Windows 2000 environment, SQL Server implements these services as just that — services. You can manage these services by using the Services icon in Control Panel on a Windows NT–based computer, or by using a Microsoft Management Console (MMC) such as Computer Management on a Windows 2000–based computer. In a Windows 98/Me environment, SQL Server implements these services as applications, which means that you must manually start these components each time you boot your computer (or add them to your computer's Startup group).

MSSQLServer

First and foremost, SQL Server's database engine is the MSSQLServer service. As the database engine, its main job is to process all of your Transact-SQL queries. In addition, MSSQLServer is responsible for the following tasks:

✔ Managing your databases and their files

✔ Verifying the integrity of your data

✔ Allocating the server's resources to its clients

SQLServerAgent

The SQLServerAgent service makes automating many of your administrative tasks possible. This service's main function is to manage alerts and jobs. You use alerts to notify you of problems such as when a database's transaction log is about to run out of space. You use jobs to automate such administrative tasks as backing up your database. You can even configure an alert to fire a job. For example, because one of the easier ways you can free up space in a transaction log is to back it up, you can create an alert to notify you when your transaction log is running out of disk space *and* call a job to back up the transaction log.

As part of automating administrative tasks, you can define operators (such as yourself). You then configure the SQLServerAgent service to notify your operators by e-mail or pager. We explore how to automate administrative tasks with jobs and alerts, and define operators, in Chapter 23.

Microsoft Distributed Transaction Coordinator (MS DTC)

SQL Server uses the MS DTC service to coordinate distributed transactions. Distributed transactions enable you to post a transaction to multiple databases simultaneously. These databases can be on the same or different servers, and the transaction can be made up of multiple parts.

We typically use the example of a bank's automatic teller machine to explain what happens with a transaction. When you use an ATM to transfer money from your checking account to your savings account, this transaction consists of two parts. First, your bank must reduce your checking account by the amount you specified. Second, your bank must increase your savings account by the same amount. Both of these steps must complete successfully, or your whole transaction must fail. SQL Server makes sure that all the transaction's steps complete — and if they don't, to make sure that the whole transaction fails. And keep in mind that each of a transaction's steps could be using a different database — and that those databases could be on the same or different servers. If the transaction accesses different databases on different servers, SQL Server uses the MS DTC service to coordinate the changes on those servers.

Microsoft Search

SQL Server uses the Microsoft Search service to add support for full-text searches. These searches enable you to query your databases in a much more flexible manner than with the standard SQL language. With this capability, you can search for any word in a character column — instead of searching for the exact contents of that column. For example, after you add support for full-text searches, you could query a movie database for any movie title that contains the word "alien."

Databases

SQL Server supports two types of databases: system and user. Setup automatically installs the system databases along with two sample user databases when you install your server. SQL Server uses the system databases to store information about the server itself and its configuration. For example, the master database keeps track of your user database files and user login IDs. Table 2-1 describes these databases and their use in SQL Server.

Table 2-1	System Databases
Database	*Contains*
Master	Information about the operation of SQL Server, including server configuration information, user login IDs, and environment variables.
Model	Template database objects that are automatically copied to any new user database you create. For example, the model database contains a table for storing users' permissions. This table is automatically copied to any new databases.
Tempdb	Temporary information generated during processing. SQL Server uses this database as its "scratchpad" for performing such tasks as sorting tables.
Msdb	Information about all the jobs, alerts, and operators you've defined on your server. This database is used by the SQLServerAgent service.
Distribution	History and transaction information used by SQL Server when replicating a database across multiple servers. You see this database only if you've configured replication on your server.

Make sure you know the system databases and the types of information they contain for the exam.

Database files

SQL Server uses a minimum of two files for each database: the primary data file and a transaction log file. You use the data file to store all of your database's objects, such as tables, indexes, views, and stored procedures. You can optionally create secondary data files in order to distribute a database across multiple files; you might then place each data file on a separate hard disk.

SQL Server uses the other file, the transaction log, to protect your database. SQL Server uses a two-step process to write information (in the form of a transaction) to a database. The first step occurs when SQL Server writes the data to the database's transaction log. The second step occurs when SQL Server takes the data from the transaction log and writes it to the log's associated database. This two-step process of writing to a transaction log and then to the database enables SQL Server to recover your data in the event of a problem.

User databases

You create user databases to store your own information. By default, SQL Server automatically copies all the objects in the model database to any new databases you create.

In order to protect your databases in the event of a system failure, SQL Server uses a two-step process whenever you write to a database (such as adding a new row to a table):

1. SQL Server first records any changes you make to the database's transaction log.

2. SQL Server then eventually posts those changes to your database's files.

This two-step process makes it possible for SQL Server to roll back or undo any incomplete transactions in the event your server fails. This means that for each user database you create, you must also create a transaction log. We explore how to create databases and their transaction logs in detail in Chapters 8 and 9.

Database objects

Within each database, you can create several different types of objects. Most importantly, you create tables within a database to store your data. A table consists of both columns and rows. Each row represents one of the entities you're tracking in the table. For example, if you create a table to store the inventory for a retail store, each row in that table would contain the information for one inventory item.

You use a table's columns to store the individual pieces of information you want to track for each row. Continuing with our inventory example, you might define columns such as item number, description, quantity on hand, wholesale price, and retail price in a table for storing inventory information.

Other types of objects you can create within a database include

- **Constraints,** for specifying rules as to the types of data users can enter into a column. For example, you might use a check constraint to force users to enter a date between 01/01/1990 and 01/01/2010. Types of constraints include check, default, primary key, foreign key, rule, and unique.

- **Data types,** for defining the values each column can support. SQL Server includes many system data types (such as character and numeric). In addition, you can create your own user-defined data types based on the system data types. (You use user-defined data types when you want to make sure that columns used in multiple tables use the same data types.)

- **Indexes,** for speeding up your searches of a table. For example, you may create an index based on last names for a table in which you're storing name information.

- **Stored procedures,** for automating a series of Transact-SQL statements. For example, you can create a stored procedure to automate updating an audit trail table whenever any of your users make changes to a table with sensitive information (such as a payroll table).

- **Triggers,** for configuring SQL Server to perform specific tasks whenever a user adds, deletes, or modifies a row in a table. For example, you may use a trigger to double-check the accuracy of the data a user enters into a table.

- **User-defined functions,** for creating subroutines of one or more Transact-SQL statements. User-defined functions can make performing frequently-executed statements easier for you.

- **Views,** for customizing the information other users can see within a table. For example, if you have an employee table that contains both address and salary information, you may create a view that enables users to see only the address information. In this way, a view makes "hiding" certain columns from your users possible. You can also use views to enable users to access data from a table without giving them permissions to that table. In addition, you can use views to combine multiple tables together to make it easier for your users to access their data.

Utilities

SQL Server 2000 includes a variety of utilities that you can use to administer your server. These include both graphical and command-line utilities, plus many different wizards for walking you through different administrative tasks. You can perform many of your administrative tasks by using any of these utilities. For example, you can create a database by using SQL Server Enterprise Manager (a graphical utility), executing a Transact-SQL statement in osql (a command-line utility), or by using the Create Database wizard. We look at all of these utilities in detail throughout the book, but we want to take a moment to hit the two you use most often.

SQL Server Enterprise Manager

SQL Server Enterprise Manager is the graphical utility you'll use most often when managing your servers. It's essentially your one-stop shopping place for performing administrative tasks. In fact, you can use it to manage multiple SQL servers. Like many of the utilities in Windows 2000 and other Microsoft Server applications, SQL Server Enterprise Manager uses the Microsoft Management Console (MMC) interface, as shown in Figure 2-3.

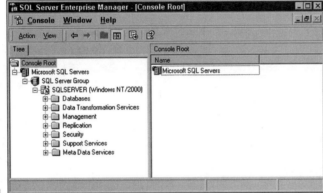

Figure 2-3:
The SQL
Server
Enterprise
Manager
interface.

Here are some of the tasks you can perform in SQL Server Enterprise Manager:

- ✔ Create, manage, and delete databases and their objects
- ✔ Configure server and database options
- ✔ Install and configure database replication
- ✔ Automate administrative tasks with jobs and alerts
- ✔ Configure your server to send and receive e-mail
- ✔ Manage security by configuring user login IDs, specifying database access, and defining permissions

SQL Server Query Analyzer

You use SQL Server Query Analyzer to query your databases by using Transact-SQL statements. Microsoft has significantly improved SQL Server Query Analyzer in SQL Server 2000 by adding an Object Browser pane that enables you to view your server's databases and objects, as shown in Figure 2-4. This pane makes finding object names when constructing your queries much easier.

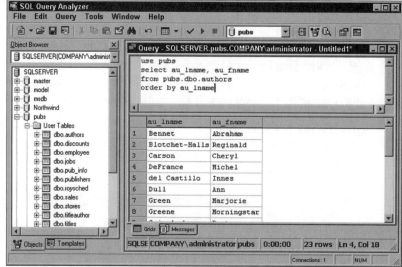

Figure 2-4:
The SQL
Server
Query
Analyzer
interface.

Integrating SQL Server with Other Software

Microsoft designed SQL Server so that it can easily slip into your existing environment. SQL Server is integrated with both a variety of operating systems and Microsoft Server (formerly BackOffice) applications.

Operating systems

You can run the server portion of SQL Server 2000 on the following operating systems:

- All versions of Windows 2000
- All versions of Windows NT 4.0
- Windows 98/Me
- Windows CE

Keep in mind that some of the components you can run on each operating system vary depending upon the edition of SQL Server 2000 you're running.

SQL Server 2000 is tightly integrated with both Windows 2000 and Windows NT. For example, you can configure your Windows 2000 Active Directory user accounts to access your SQL servers. Likewise, you can configure Windows NT domain accounts to log in to your servers as well. SQL Server is further integrated with both Windows NT and Windows 2000 security in that it enables pass-through authentication, which means that after your users have been authenticated by a domain controller, they can access your server (without having to retype their user names and passwords).

Many of the Windows NT/2000 utilities support SQL Server 2000, including Event Viewer, the Windows 2000 System Monitor, and the Windows NT Performance Monitor. SQL Server also supports features such as multitasking and multithreading, symmetric multiprocessing, and clustered servers. You can further integrate SQL Server with both the Windows 2000 Internet Information Services, and the Windows NT–based Internet Information Server.

Microsoft Server applications

To further extend SQL Server's capabilities, Microsoft designed SQL Server so that it integrates seamlessly with its other Microsoft Server products. For example, SQL Server can use Exchange Server to both send and receive e-mail messages. This capability enables your server to send you an e-mail message as part of an alert.

Microsoft Systems Management Server (SMS) uses SQL Server to store the information it uses to automate the management of client computers. For example, SMS stores your client workstations' inventory in a database on a SQL server.

Implementing Security in SQL Server

Make sure you know security in SQL Server backward and forward for the exam. You can expect to see several questions prompting you to choose the tasks a particular role enables a user to perform. (Keep in mind that we're giving you just an overview here — we cover security in detail in Part VI.)

Security in SQL Server consists of two layers. First, you use logins (also known as login IDs) to specify who can log in to your SQL server, and database users to define the databases these login IDs can access. Second, you use permissions to control what database users can do when they gain access to your server.

Creating login IDs and database users

Before we talk about login IDs, we want to talk about the login authentication methods SQL Server supports. SQL Server can use both Windows Authentication (where your server relies on either a Windows 2000 or Windows NT domain controller to authenticate logins) and SQL Authentication (where your SQL server itself authenticates logins). With Windows Authentication, you map a user's Windows NT/2000 account to a login ID, and the user can then access the SQL server without having to enter a login ID and password. With SQL Authentication, you must create your users' login IDs — and your users must specify their login IDs and passwords to access the server. You typically use SQL Authentication to provide login IDs for non-Windows–based clients such as those running UNIX.

By the way, Microsoft refers to users who log on to your server using their Windows accounts as using *trusted connections*. This simply means that your SQL server had to trust your Windows NT or Windows 2000 to authenticate these users. The phrase "log on to SQL Server with a trusted connection," means that you must log on to the server with a Windows NT or Windows 2000 user account.

You can configure your server to support either Windows authentication only, or both Windows and SQL authentication, as shown in Figure 2-5. Microsoft refers to the combination of both Windows and SQL authentication as *mixed mode*.

Figure 2-5:
You can configure your server to support only Windows logins, or both SQL Server and Windows logins.

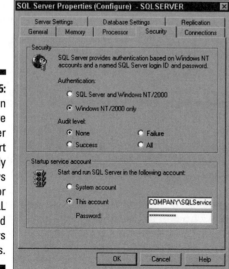

You may find a question or two on your test prompting you to choose your server's authentication mode based on the types of clients on your network. Make sure you choose both SQL Server and Windows Authentication if the clients are running operating systems such as UNIX.

You may think of login security as consisting of two sublayers: the login IDs themselves, and database access. After you've created a login ID for a user, she still can't access any of your server's databases until you make her a user of a database. For example, the user in Figure 2-6 has a login ID for the server but hasn't been made a user of any of the server's databases. In Chapter 20, you review the procedures for configuring your server's authentication mode and creating login IDs. In Chapter 20, you review defining database users.

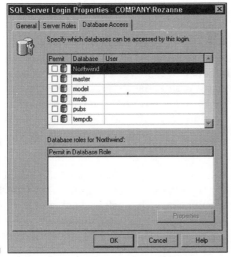

Figure 2-6:
A login ID that hasn't been made a user of a database.

Make sure you understand that a login ID and a database user account are two separate things. A *login ID* enables you to log in to a SQL server, but doesn't automatically permit you to access any of its databases. A *database user account* enables you to access a database on a SQL server.

Assigning permissions

After you create your users' login IDs and make them users of databases, your last task is to give them permissions. Although SQL Server enables you to assign individual permissions (such as the CREATE DATABASE permission) to specific users, implementing permissions is much easier if you use SQL

Server's predefined roles. SQL Server includes both server and database roles. You can also create your own user-defined database roles. We explore the server, database, and user-defined roles in detail in Chapter 21.

Server roles

You use the server roles included with SQL Server 2000 to assign different levels of administrative permissions to your users. (Of course, because these permissions are administrative, you want to be selective as to who you assign to these roles.) These roles are called "server" roles because they enable their members to perform administrative tasks that affect server-wide settings, not individual databases. Microsoft refers to the server roles as "fixed" because you can't make changes to the permissions associated with these roles.

Database roles

SQL Server uses its database roles to enable you to assign permissions to users for a specific database. Like server roles, database roles other than the public role are also fixed. Because SQL Server uses the public role to assign default permissions to users for a database, you can make changes to its permissions. You can use database roles to either grant or deny permissions. For example, you can use the db_datareader to assign users permissions for reading all data in the database. In contrast, you use the db_denydatareader role to prevent users from reading any data in the database.

Microsoft expects you to know the permissions associated with both the server and database roles for the exam. You can expect a few questions that provide you with a description of a specific task and ask you to choose the appropriate role to which you should add a user. Make sure that you study these roles and their associated permissions by reviewing Chapter 21.

Part II

Installing and Configuring SQL Server 2000

The 5th Wave   By Rich Tennant

"I'm not saying I believe in anything. All I know is since it's been there our server is running 50% faster."

In this part . . .

*A*s a database administrator, you can expect to spend a lot of your time installing and configuring SQL servers. The decisions you make when installing SQL Server can have a big impact on your SQL environment's performance — and the satisfaction of your users. Because a good installation is so important, Microsoft wants to be sure you know how to install and configure SQL Server properly. So you can expect to see quite a number of questions on the topics we cover in this part of the book.

In Chapter 3, we tell you everything you need to know about planning your SQL Server installation. In Chapter 4, we explore installing SQL Server itself and point out the types of installation questions you might see on your exam. We show you how to upgrade to SQL Server 2000 from older versions of the software in Chapter 5. You find our best installation troubleshooting tips in Chapter 6. And in Chapter 7, we show you how to configure your SQL server to both send and receive e-mail.

Chapter 3

Planning to Implement SQL Server 2000

* *

Exam Objectives

▶ Installing SQL Server: Selecting a SQL Server edition

▶ Installing SQL Server: Designing your server's hardware

▶ Installing SQL Server: Choosing configuration options such as instances, the services account, and collation settings

* *

*B*efore you begin your installation of SQL Server 2000, you need to first design your strategy for configuring its settings. Your strategy should take into consideration everything but the kitchen sink (just kidding). But we do mean it when we say you should plan your installation first — or you could end up having to redo a lot of work later. In this chapter, we cover the options you configure during installation, highlighting the installation topics you can expect to see on the SQL Server exam.

We cover the following important exam topics in this chapter:

✔ Installing multiple instances of SQL Server on the same computer

✔ Specifying file locations

✔ Designing the SQL Server services account

✔ Choosing your server's collation settings

✔ Configuring server and client network libraries

Quick Assessment

Selecting a
SQL Server
edition

Designing
your server's
hardware

Choosing
configura-
tion options

1 The SQL Server 2000 _____ edition can access up to 64GB of RAM.

2 You can install the Enterprise edition of SQL Server 2000 on the _____ and _____ operating systems.

3 The computer on which you install SQL Server must have at least a(n) _____ CPU.

4 _____ licensing in SQL Server 2000 is the most cost-effective choice for large companies.

5 Users can connect to the _____ instance of SQL Server by using only the server's computer name.

6 The SQL Server services use a(n) _____ to log on to a Windows NT or Windows 2000 domain.

7 If you change your server's collation settings, you must _____.

Answers

1 *Enterprise.* Read "Step 1: Selecting a SQL Server Edition."

2 *Windows NT Server and Windows 2000 Server.* Check out "Step 1: Selecting a SQL Server Edition."

3 *133 MHz Pentium.* See "Step 2: Selecting Your Server's Hardware."

4 *Per processor.* See "Licensing."

5 *Default.* Examine "SQL Server instances."

6 *Services account.* Study "Services account."

7 *Rebuild your server's databases.* Read "Collation settings."

Designing Your SQL Server Implementation Strategy

Having a plan in mind before you start your installation of SQL Server is important. That's because you can expect to be asked a lot of questions during the installation. In addition, some of the settings you choose during installation (such as your server's collation settings) require that you rebuild all of your databases if you want to change them. And rebuilding your databases means that you must first recreate them and then restore all of their data from backups — essentially the equivalent of open-heart surgery to a database administrator!

Inserting the SQL Server 2000 CD and starting the installation is the easy part. Designing your environment so that it meets your users' needs is the hard part. To help make the installation easier for you, we use the following sections to describe in detail the steps you should use to design your SQL Server environment.

You can expect to see several questions related to designing your SQL Server installation on the exam. These questions focus on topics such as designing your hard disk subsystem, selecting a SQL Server edition, choosing a service account, implementing multiple instances, and collation and sort orders. Pay close attention to these topics as you work through this chapter.

When you're ready to begin planning your SQL Server implementation strategy, make sure that you complete the following steps:

1. **Select an edition of SQL Server to install.**

2. **Choose your server's hardware.**

3. **Pick your server's configuration options.**

Step 1: Selecting a SQL Server Edition

SQL Server 2000 consists of five editions: Standard, Enterprise, Developer, Personal, and Windows CE. (SQL Server 2000 also includes the Enterprise Evaluation edition with all the same features as the Enterprise edition — so we aren't going to cover it separately here.) As an administrator, one of your first choices is to decide which edition you want to install in your environment. To be honest with you, you're really choosing between only the Standard and Enterprise editions if you want to implement a server. That's because Microsoft really designed the other editions for end-users, not for servers.

The exam is based on the Enterprise edition of SQL Server 2000.

The Standard edition

Microsoft designed the Standard edition of SQL Server 2000 as the solution for small workgroups and departmental servers. That's because this edition doesn't support the features required by large, enterprise database environments. For example, the Standard edition supports up to four CPUs and a maximum of 2GB of RAM. Because of these limitations, the Standard edition doesn't support very large databases.

The Enterprise edition

Microsoft designed the Enterprise edition of SQL Server 2000 with the scalability features necessary for supporting very large databases. For example, the Enterprise edition supports up to 32 CPUs and 64GB of RAM. In addition, the Enterprise edition also includes enhanced reliability features such as support for clustered servers and log shipping. The scalability and reliability features make the Enterprise edition your best choice for environments that require high performance, such as Web sites, online transaction processing systems (OLTP), and data warehousing applications.

Because many of the scalability and reliability features are new in SQL Server 2000, you can expect a few questions on the exam about these features.

Other editions

Microsoft designed the remaining SQL Server 2000 editions (Developer, Personal, and Windows CE) for end-users and not a production server environment. For example, the Developer edition contains all the features of the Enterprise edition, but its license agreement limits you to a single user. Likewise, the Personal and Windows CE editions are designed for mobile users who want to access a SQL database offline from your network. In fact, the Windows CE edition can replicate data between what's stored locally on the Windows CE device and a database on a Standard or Enterprise edition server.

Supported operating systems

In addition to the differences in features between the different versions, you should also consider the operating system on which you want to install SQL Server. Table 3-1 lists the various SQL Server editions and the operating systems on which you can install them.

Table 3-1	Supported Operating Systems		
Edition	2000 Server/ NT Server	2000 Professional/ NT Workstation	Windows 98/Me
Enterprise	Yes	No	No
Standard	Yes	No	No
Developer	Yes	Yes	Yes
Personal	Yes	Yes	Yes
Windows CE	No	No	No

Just because you can't install the server portion of SQL Server on a particular operating system doesn't mean you can't install the client software on it. You can install the SQL Server client software on Windows 9x, Windows Me, and all versions of Windows NT and Windows 2000.

Step 2: Selecting Your Server's Hardware

Your next decision before you install SQL Server is to make sure that your server has adequate hardware resources. Your server won't be able to function properly and meet the needs of your users unless you configure it with powerful enough hardware. One technique you can use to make sure your server can handle its workload is to make sure you don't overload it with too many applications. For example, Microsoft recommends that you don't install SQL Server on a computer you're already using as a domain controller.

Table 3-2 lists the minimum hardware requirements for the SQL Server 2000 Standard and Enterprise editions. But be warned, these hardware requirements are the absolute, bare-bones minimum. Although no easy formula exists for coming up with what you need, we can tell you that you will absolutely need more than these minimums — and what you'll need will vary depending on the number of users connecting to your server, the types of applications they use to work with the data, and the size of your databases. You can count on your server requiring much more RAM and CPU power than these minimum requirements. We consider these minimum requirements more for what you need to practice using SQL Server instead of what you need for a production server.

Always make sure that you check Microsoft's Hardware Compatibility List (HCL) to verify that your hardware is supported by SQL Server. You can find this list at www.microsoft.com/hcl.

Table 3-2	SQL Server Hardware Requirements
Hardware Component	*Minimum Requirements*
RAM	64MB
CPU	133 MHz Pentium or faster
Free disk space	95MB to 270MB

Use special consideration when designing your server's hard disk subsystem, because the performance of your server's hard disks can have a big impact on SQL Server's performance. One way you may be tempted to optimize your hard disks is to implement a write-caching disk controller — but don't yield to that temptation unless the controller is specifically designed for SQL Server. A write-caching disk controller can interfere with SQL Server's built-in mechanisms for protecting your database.

Remember that you shouldn't use a write-caching disk controller with SQL Server. You can expect to see a question or two on this topic on your exam.

One strategy you may consider implementing is to use a drive array in your server. A drive array enables your server to "stripe" data across multiple hard disks simultaneously. Windows NT Server, Windows 2000 Server, and SQL Server all support RAID levels 0, 1, 5, and 10. These levels offer you different combinations of performance and reliability, as described in Table 3-3.

Table 3-3	RAID Levels Supported in SQL Server
Level	*Description*
RAID 0 (Data Striping)	Enables your server to stripe data across all the disks in the array. Offers excellent read and write performance, but no built-in redundancy.
RAID 1 (Data Mirroring and Duplexing)	Enables your server to exactly duplicate the data on one disk onto another disk. Offers excellent data redundancy, but no enhancements to hard disk performance.
RAID 5 (Data Striping with Parity)	Enables your server to stripe data across all the disks in the array and to use parity to build in data redundancy. Offers excellent redundancy and enhanced read performance. However, RAID 5 also gives you slower write performance because your server must calculate the parity information.
RAID 10 (Data Mirroring with Data Striping)	Enables your server to use a combination of data striping (RAID 0) and mirroring (RAID 1). Enables you to have both the enhanced read and write performance of RAID 0, along with the enhanced redundancy of RAID 1.

Step 3: Choosing Your Server's Configuration Options

Your next step in designing your implementation strategy is to choose how you want to configure the server options during installation. By the way, we look at these options in the order you're prompted to configure them when you perform a custom installation of SQL Server 2000.

Licensing

One of the options you must configure during installation is your server's licensing mode. SQL Server 2000 supports two licensing modes: per processor and per seat. With per-processor licensing, you must buy a processor license for each CPU in the servers on which you're running SQL Server 2000. For example, if you plan to install SQL Server 2000 on two servers, each with two CPUs, you must buy a total of four processor licenses.

You can find out more about SQL Server's licensing and the retail price of both per-processor and per-seat licenses by going to Microsoft's SQL Server Web site at www.microsoft.com/sql.

Per-processor licensing

The big advantage to per-processor licensing is that once you've bought these licenses, you're done. You don't have to worry about buying any client licenses, and you can have an unlimited number of users connect to your server. Microsoft designed per-processor licensing for big companies, so this type of licensing is economical only if you have a lot of users.

Per-seat licensing

Your other choice when configuring your server's licensing mode is to use per-seat licensing. This option requires that you purchase a client access license (CAL) for each workstation on your network that connects to the SQL server. For example, you may have a network with 200 workstations, and of that, only 25 workstations actually connect to your SQL server. Per-seat licensing requires that you purchase a CAL for only those 25 workstations.

SQL Server instances

Another new change in SQL Server 2000 is that you can now install multiple named instances of SQL Server on the same computer. Each instance has its own set of system and user databases. You can use multiple instances, each with its own application, to isolate those applications from each other. That way, if one of the applications doesn't play well with others (in other words, it crashes), it won't crash any of your other applications running in other instances.

If you define multiple instances of SQL Server on a server, you connect to an instance by using the syntax *computer_name\instance_name*. For example, if your server's name is sqlserver with instances named sales and account-ing, you connect to the sales instance in utilities and programs by typing **sqlserver\sales**. You typically configure the first installation of SQL Server 2000 as your default instance. The default instance doesn't get its own name, so you connect to this default instance simply by using your server's name.

Any subsequent installations of SQL Server 2000 you perform enable you to define additional named instances. You can use instance names of up to 16 characters in length; these names must begin with either a letter, ampersand (&), underscore (_), or number sign (#). You must use both the computer and instance name to connect to a named instance other than the default.

Installation types

Setup enables you to choose from one of three installation types: typical, minimum, and custom. These types differ as to which of the SQL Server components they install by default. Take a look at Table 3-4 to compare the three installation types and the components each one installs. Notice that the custom installation type provides you with the most flexibility in choosing the SQL Server components for your environment Choose your installation type based on the features you want to install.

Table 3-4	Comparing SQL Server Installation Types		
Option	*Minimum*	*Typical*	*Custom*
Books Online	No	Yes	Optional
Client Connectivity	Yes	Yes	Yes (not optional)
Client Management Tools	No	Yes	Optional
Code Samples	None	None	Optional
Collation Settings	Yes (default)	Yes (default)	Your choice
Database Server	Yes	Yes	Optional
Development Tools	None	Debugger only	Optional
Full-text Search	Yes	Yes	Optional
Replication Support	Yes	Yes	Optional
Upgrade Tools	No	Yes	Optional

SQL Server 2000 also includes features that you install separately from the installation of SQL Server itself. For example, you must install Microsoft English Query by using its setup program on the SQL Server CD. By the way, Microsoft English Query makes it possible for you to query a database by using an English sentence such as "which customers live in New Orleans?" instead of using the equivalent SQL commands (SELECT * FROM customers WHERE city = 'New Orleans').

Services account

When you install SQL Server on a Windows NT- or Windows 2000-based computer, its services must log on just like a regular old user. The SQL Server services log on in order to gain access to your server. You can configure the services to log on by using either a special user account called the Local System account, or a domain user account. Microsoft refers to the account with which you configure your services to log on as the *services account*.

As you can see in Figure 3-1, Setup lets you configure each of the SQL Server services to log on with different domain user accounts, but it's simpler and easier for you if you configure all the SQL Server services to log on with the same account. You can also control whether or not your server's operating system automatically starts the services by choosing the Customize the Settings for Each Service option. By default, Setup configures the services to start automatically.

Figure 3-1:
Configure
the SQL
Server ser-
vices to use
either the
Local
System or a
domain user
account.

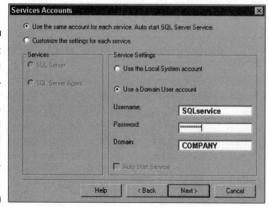

Using a domain user account

If your server is part of either a Windows NT or Windows 2000 domain, Microsoft strongly recommends that you use a domain user account as the services account instead of the Local System account. In fact, if you configure your SQL server to use the Local System account, it won't be able to interact with other SQL servers on the network. Further, you must configure your SQL server to use a domain user account if you want the server to perform the following tasks:

- ✔ Configure multiserver jobs
- ✔ Enable your SQL server to send e-mail notifications
- ✔ Configure your SQL server to communicate with other Microsoft Server applications such as Exchange Server and Systems Management Server

Microsoft expects you to know that you must use a domain user account in order for SQL Server to be able to do the preceding tasks. You can expect to see a question or two testing your knowledge of this fact.

By default, when your server is already a member of a domain, Setup attempts to use the user account with which you've logged on as the services account. For example, if you log on as Administrator and then start the SQL Server installation, Setup attempts to use Administrator as the services account. Don't use this account as the services account! You should never configure your server to use a regular user account for the services account, because if you change the password for this user, your SQL Server services can no longer log on successfully. Always create a separate user account specifically for your SQL Server services. Also configure this account so that its password never expires and that it's without any logon restrictions.

Assigning permissions to the services account

The SQL services not only need to log on to the server, but they also need permissions to do their jobs. As part of your installation of SQL Server, then, you need to make sure that the services account you choose has all the right stuff. One of the easiest ways you can give this account the permissions it needs is to make it a member of your SQL server's local Administrators group.

Now if adding the services account to the Administrators group gives you the heebie-jeebies, you can assign the necessary permissions to this account manually. To do so, first make sure that the services account can access and change files in the SQL Server directory (usually C:\Program Files\Microsoft SQL Server\Mssql), and then access and change all the database files (files with the extensions .mdf, .ndf, and .ldf). You also must grant this account Read and Write permissions to the following Registry keys:

- ✔ HKEY_LOCAL_MACHINE\Software\Microsoft\MSSQLServer
- ✔ HKEY_LOCAL_MACHINE\System\CurrentControlSet \Services\MSSQLServer
- ✔ HKEY_LOCAL_MACHINE\Software\Microsoft \Windows NT\CurrentVersion\Perflib
- ✔ HKEY_LOCAL_MACHINE\Software\Clients\Mail

If you install multiple instances of SQL Server, you must grant the services account to the following Registry keys as well:

✔ HKEY_LOCAL_MACHINE\Software\Microsoft\Microsoft SQL Server

✔ HKEY_LOCAL_MACHINE\System\CurrentControlSet \Services\MSSQL$*instance*

For the exam, be prepared for a question or two that test to see whether or not you understand that the services account must have the necessary permissions in order to function properly.

Supporting multiple Windows domains

You need to consider your implementation strategy carefully if your environment consists of multiple domains for two reasons:

✔ First, if you plan to install SQL Server on computers in more than one domain, Microsoft recommends that you configure these servers to use the same services account.

✔ Second, Windows Authentication makes it possible for your users to log on to a SQL server with their domain user accounts. But for this process to work, SQL Server must be able to talk to a domain controller to authenticate your users. And if your server is in one domain, and a user's account is in a different domain, your SQL server may not be able to authenticate the user.

The steps you take to coordinate SQL Server with multiple Windows domains vary depending on whether you're using Windows NT or Windows 2000.

For Windows NT domains, place your SQL servers in domains with access to all of your network's user accounts. To do so, you have to configure trust relationships between the domains. In Windows NT lingo, this means to implement the master domain model in which one domain contains all the user accounts (this is the master domain) and all other domains contain your network's resources (oddly enough, these are called resource domains). You then configure the resource domains to trust the master domain; this trust relationship enables the administrators of the resource domains to use the user accounts in the master domain. After you configure the trust relationships between your domains, put your SQL servers in the resource domains.

In Windows 2000 domains, one of the biggest advantages of the Active Directory is that it enables you to combine multiple domains into a *forest*. Once combined, as an administrator, you can administer users and resources in any of the domains within the forest. As long as you have only one forest, you can put your SQL server in any domain and still have access to all domains' users.

On the off chance that you have multiple Active Directory forests, and you want to place a SQL server in one forest and have users in another forest access that server, you must configure an external explicit trust between a domain in each forest. After you configure this trust, your SQL servers can authenticate users in any domain in any forest.

Authentication mode

SQL Server supports two authentication modes: Windows or Mixed. With the Windows Authentication mode, your users log on to SQL Server with their Windows NT or Windows 2000 user accounts. In fact, SQL Server actually communicates directly with either Windows NT or Windows 2000 to authenticate your users. That way your users don't have to retype their user names and passwords. With the Mixed Authentication mode, users can log on with either a Windows user account or a SQL Server login ID. You typically use SQL Server accounts for users on computers with non Windows–based operating systems such as UNIX.

If you select the Mixed Authentication mode, Setup prompts you to define a password for the *sa* (system administrator) SQL Server login ID. (This user can log on only if you configure your server to support SQL Authentication.) The sa user has full rights to administer your SQL server, so never leave it with a blank password.

Leaving the password for the sa user blank is just like leaving the front door to your house open when you're away from home. Don't do it! If you forget to set the sa user's password during installation, you can always assign one to this user by using SQL Server Enterprise Manager.

Collation settings

When you install SQL Server 2000, you must tell the server how you want it to compare and sort data. You do so by configuring its collation settings. You can use collation settings that consider not only case sensitivity, but also whether or not the characters have accents or include letters in Asian character sets (these are called kana characters).

Another new change in SQL Server 2000 is that you can configure your collation settings not only for your server, but also for individual databases, tables, and even each column within a table. For example, you can configure one collation setting for your server, yet still use a different setting for a specific database. Unless you specify otherwise, when you create a database, SQL Server uses your server's collation setting for that database. You configure your server's collation setting when you install SQL Server 2000; you configure a database, table, or column's collation setting when you create them.

SQL Server Setup enables you to choose between two major groups of collation settings for your server: Windows and SQL. Within these two groups, you find further choices for specifically controlling how your server handles character data, as shown in Figure 3-2.

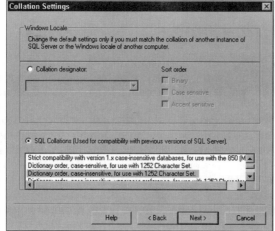

Figure 3-2:
SQL Server
uses colla-
tion settings
to determine
how to sort
character
data.

Windows collation

With Windows collation, your server's operating system determines the rules SQL Server uses for sorting and storing character data. Your server's operating system, in turn, determines these rules based on its Windows locale. You configure your server's locale when you install Windows 2000 and Windows NT, and this locale determines how your operating system displays numbers, dates, times, currency, and numbers with decimal places.

Windows collation sets the rules for dictionary sorting on your server based on your server's locale. Because many languages share the same alphabet and rules for dictionary sorting, you do find that many different languages can use the same Windows collation setting. For example, the default Windows collation, Latin1_General, supports 33 Windows locales. For example, you would use Latin1_General if your server's locale is any of the English locales (such as United States, Britain, and Canada), Dutch, German, Indonesian, Italian, and so on.

SQL collations

Like the Windows collations, SQL collations also set the rules for sorting and storing character data. Microsoft included SQL collations in SQL Server 2000 for compatibility with older versions of SQL Server. For example, in SQL Server 2000, the SQL collation named "Dictionary order, case-insensitive, for use with 1252 Character Set" exactly matches the default collation, sort order, and code page setting in SQL Server 7.0. You must use one of the SQL collation settings on your server if

✔ You want to configure replication between SQL Server 2000 and older versions of SQL Server.

✔ You want to use an application written for an older version of SQL Server on your SQL Server 2000 server.

If you install SQL Server 2000 by using the Typical or Minimum installation types, Setup automatically configures your server to use both a Windows collation setting and a SQL collation setting based on the Windows locale of the computer on which you're installing SQL Server. You can configure your server's collation settings yourself only if you perform a custom installation of SQL Server 2000.

If you change your server's collation settings, you must rebuild all of your server's databases and objects. For this reason, choose your collation settings carefully.

Network libraries

Both the SQL server and its clients use a network library to communicate with each other. This network library is essentially a driver that implements a specific network interprocess communication mechanism (IPC). IPCs, along with a network protocol, manage the communications between a client and a server. You can configure your SQL server to support more than one network library. This strategy makes communicating with a variety of clients, each using a different network library (and possibly a different network protocol) possible for your server.

What you need to realize about these network libraries is that they aren't transport protocols (such as TCP/IP and NWLink IPX/SPX). However, network libraries are closely linked to your transport protocols because not all protocols support all the network libraries, and vice versa. Table 3-5 describes the network libraries from which you can choose, along with the protocols they support.

Table 3-5	SQL Server 2000 Network Libraries
Network Library	*Supported by*
TCP/IP Sockets	TCP/IP
Named Pipes	NetBEUI, TCP/IP, NWLink
NWLink IPX/SPX	Novell clients running IPX/SPX

(continued)

Table 3-5 *(continued)*

Network Library	Supported by
VIA ServerNet II SAN	Clients connecting to a ServerNet II System Area Network (clustered servers)
Multiprotocol	NetBEUI, TCP/IP, NWLink
AppleTalk ADSP	AppleTalk
Banyan VINES	Banyan VINES IP

If you're like most people, you're probably wondering why you would choose one of these network libraries over the other. Well, first of all, you should install the network library that's supported by your network's transport protocol. For example, if you're using TCP/IP as the only transport protocol on your network, you can configure your SQL server to use the Named Pipes, TCP/IP Sockets, or Multiprotocol network libraries. Also consider the following factors when choosing a network library:

- ✔ You must use Named Pipes, TCP/IP Sockets, or Multiprotocol if you want to use the Windows Authentication mode on your server.

- ✔ You can't use the Multiprotocol network library if you plan to implement multiple instances of SQL Server on the same computer.

- ✔ You should use TCP/IP Sockets if you want to implement secure sockets layer (SSL) encryption on your network.

- ✔ You can use only the TCP/IP Sockets and Named Pipes network libraries on clustered servers.

You can also implement encryption with the Multiprotocol network library. SSL encryption is supported only in SQL Server 2000, so you should use Multiprotocol encryption if your server must communicate with older versions of SQL Server.

If you install SQL Server by using either the typical or minimum installation types, Setup automatically configures your server's network libraries as follows:

- ✔ It installs both Named Pipes and TCP/IP Sockets as the default network libraries on your server.

- ✔ It configures the TCP/IP Sockets client network library for all management tools.

- ✔ It requires that you configure the Named Pipes network library for all SQL servers running on Windows NT 4.0 or Windows 2000.

When you install SQL Server 2000, you can configure your server to use a nonstandard TCP/IP port number instead of the default port of 1433. (You might do this if you want to make it harder for someone to hack into your server using the TCP/IP protocol.) You can also change your server's port number later by using the Server Network Utility. Keep in mind that if you change your server's port number, you must also configure your clients to use this same port number by using the Client Network Utility. You may see a question on your exam that asks you how to configure your SQL environment to use a nonstandard TCP/IP port number.

Prep Test

1 You plan to install SQL Server 2000 on your department's file and print server. This server is using Windows 2000 Server as its operating system. What editions of SQL Server can you install on this computer? (Choose all that apply.)

A ❑ Enterprise

B ❑ Standard

C ❑ Developer

D ❑ Personal

2 You're responsible for planning the hardware for your company's SQL server. Your boss has asked you to make the server both as reliable and high performance as possible. Which RAID level should you use for the server's hard disk subsystem?

A ○ RAID 0

B ○ RAID 1

C ○ RAID 5

D ○ RAID 10

3 You have configured your SQL server (named "dbserver") with a default instance plus an instance named "accounting." You want to connect to the default instance to query its databases. What name should you use?

A ○ dbserver\default

B ○ dbserver\instance0

C ○ dbserver

D ○ dbserver\default_instance

4 You plan to run an application developed for SQL Server 6.5 on your new SQL Server 2000 server. In order to minimize compatibility problems, which group of collation settings should you use?

A ○ Windows collation.

B ○ SQL collation.

C ○ Latin1_General.

D ○ Any — which one you choose doesn't matter.

5 Your network consists of a Windows 2000 Active Directory domain. You've configured your servers and workstations to use TCP/IP. You're planning the installation of SQL Server 2000, and you would like your users to log on to the server with Windows authentication. Which network library (or libraries) should you use? (Choose all that apply.)

A ❏ TCP/IP Sockets

B ❏ Named Pipes

C ❏ Multiprotocol

D ❏ Banyan VINES IP

Answers

1 **All of them.** You can install all the SQL Server editions except the Windows CE edition on a computer running Windows 2000 Server as its operating system. *Review "Supported operating systems."*

2 **D.** Although it isn't the cheapest option, RAID 10 offers you both exceptional redundancy and performance. That's because it combines the best of both worlds: data striping without parity (RAID 0), so you don't have the additional overhead of writing parity information to the drives; and mirroring (RAID 1) for reliability. *See "Hard disk configuration."*

3 **C.** You connect to the default instance on a SQL server by using only the server's name. *See "SQL Server instances."*

4 **B.** Microsoft included this group of collation settings so that SQL Server 2000 can support legacy applications written to use the character set, sort order, and case-sensitivity settings defined in older versions of SQL Server. *See "SQL collations."*

5 **A, B,** and **C.** You must use Named Pipes, TCP/IP Sockets, or Multiprotocol if you want to support Windows authentication. In addition, SQL Server 2000 requires that you use the Named Pipes network library on all versions of both Windows NT and Windows 2000. *See "Network libraries."*

Chapter 4

Installing SQL Server 2000

• •

Exam Objectives

▶ Installing SQL Server 2000

▶ Performing unattended installations

• •

*H*old on to your hats, because it's time to jump in with both feet. As you know, installing software can be a leap of faith. Sometimes it goes very smoothly, and other times living through "Nightmare on Elm Street" seems easier than completing your installation.

In this chapter, we tell you what you need to know for the exam questions that relate to the installation of SQL Server 2000 — and how to install SQL Server successfully. In particular, you can expect to see exam questions on the following topics:

  ✔ Creating a services account

  ✔ Installing SQL Server 2000

Quick Assessment

Installing
SQL Server
2000

1 You should use _____ to create a Windows 2000 domain user account for your SQL Server services.

2 In order for the services account to have the permissions it needs, you should add it to the _____ group on the SQL Server.

3 You can use the SQL Server installation wizard to install the _____, _____, and _____ SQL Server 2000 components.

Performing
unattended
installations

4 You need a command file and a(n) _____ to perform an unattended installation of SQL Server 2000.

5 You start an unattended installation by using either _____ or _____.

Answers

1   *Active Directory Users and Computers.* Study "Creating a services account."

2   *Local Administrators.* Read "Creating a services account."

3   *Database Server, Analysis Services, and English Query.* Study "Running the installation."

4   *Setup initialization file.* Check out "Performing Unattended Installations."

5   *A command file or the setupsql.exe command.* See "Using the default unattended installation files" and "Creating your own setup initialization file."

Installing SQL Server 2000

After you plan your SQL Server installation, you can (at long last) start the installation. However, you must do one other thing before you start — create the services account.

You can skip creating a services account if you're installing SQL Server on a stand-alone server that isn't a member of a Windows NT or Windows 2000 domain. You use that special account, Local System account, for your services account on these types of computers.

Creating a services account

Before you start your SQL Server installation, create the account with which you want your SQL Services to log on to your domain. Remember, if you use a SQL server that's a member of a domain, Microsoft recommends that you use a domain user account for this services account. Use the Active Directory Users and Computers MMC to create this account on a Windows 2000 domain; use User Manager for Domains to create the services account on a Windows NT domain.

Make sure that you give this account the necessary permissions. You can do so by making it a member of the local Administrators group on your SQL server, or by assigning it the necessary permissions to the SQL Server keys in the Registry.

Lab 4-1 describes the steps you use to create a SQL Server services account when your server is a member of a Windows 2000 Active Directory domain.

Implementing SQL Server 2000 on a server that's part of a Windows 2000 domain enables you to take advantage of all the features in both SQL Server 2000 and Windows 2000. For this reason, and because you can expect questions on implementing SQL Server in a Windows 2000 domain environment, we use a Windows 2000 domain as the basis for this book.

Lab 4-1	Creating a SQL Server Services Account

1. **Choose Start⇨Programs⇨Administrative Tools⇨Active Directory Users and Computers.**

   You must run Active Directory Users and Computers on either a Windows 2000 domain controller or on a computer on which you've installed the Windows 2000 administrative tools.

2. **In Active Directory Users and Computers, choose Action⇨New⇨User.**

   Active Directory Users and Computers starts a wizard to walk you through creating a new user in your domain.

3. **Enter a first name and a user logon name for your services account.**

   Active Directory Users and Computers automatically defines this user's full name based on what you type in the First name, Initials, and Last name text boxes, as shown in Figure 4-1.

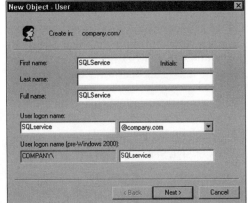

Figure 4-1:
Creating the
SQL Server
services
account.

4. **Click Next.**

5. **Enter a password, and then confirm the password.**

   Use a secure password for this user. Make sure that you don't check any of the options such as "User cannot change password."

6. **Click Next.**

7. **Click Finish.**

   Active Directory Users and Computers creates your new user account.

8. **Add your new user as a member of your SQL server's local Administrators group.**

   If you plan to run SQL Server on a computer that's a member of your domain but not a domain controller, use the Computer Management utility to add this user to the local Administrators group. On the other hand, if you plan to run SQL Server on a computer that's also a domain controller, use Active Directory Users and Computers to add this user to the local Administrators group.

9. **Close Active Directory Users and Computers.**

Running the installation

Just a few more words before you start the installation. When you insert the SQL Server 2000 CD into your CD-ROM drive, it automatically starts a wizard to walk you through the installation process. Not only does this wizard provide you with options for installing SQL Server itself, but you can also use this wizard to install any of the prerequisites your computer might need for SQL Server 2000 (such as Windows NT or Windows 2000 Service Packs), browse the online Help files for SQL Server Setup, read the SQL Server 2000 release notes, and connect to Microsoft's Web site. You can also use this wizard to install both the Analysis Services (for data warehousing) and English Query.

After you select the install SQL Server option in this wizard, it prompts you to choose either a local or remote install. Choose the local option to install SQL Server on the computer at which you're working; choose the remote option to install SQL Server across the network to another computer.

You need the following information to complete this installation:

✔ Licensing mode (per processor or per seat)

✔ The number of instances of SQL Server you want to create

✔ Installation type (typical, minimum, or custom)

✔ The services account user name and password

✔ Authentication mode (Windows or Mixed Mode authentication)

✔ Collation settings (you configure these settings only if you choose the custom installation option)

✔ Network libraries (Named Pipes, TCP/IP sockets, NWLink IPX/SPX, VIA GigaNet SAN, Multiprotocol, AppleTalk ADSP, or Banyan VINES)

We explain these installation options in detail in Chapter 3.

Follow the steps in Lab 4-2 to install SQL Server on your computer.

Lab 4-2   Installing SQL Server 2000

1. **Log on to Windows 2000 as a user with administrative privileges.**

2. **Insert the SQL Server 2000 Enterprise Edition CD into the CD-ROM drive.**

   Your computer should automatically launch the SQL Server Setup wizard from the CD. If it doesn't, access the SQL Server 2000 CD and double-click autorun.exe.

3. **When the wizard starts, click SQL Server 2000 Components.**

   You can also use this page of the Setup wizard to walk you through installing the prerequisites for SQL Server 2000.

4. **On the Install Components page, click Install Database Server.**

   SQL Server Setup enables you to install three components: the database server itself, Analysis Services, and English Query. Use this page to select the component you want to install.

5. **On the Welcome page, click Next to begin the installation.**

6. **On the Computer Name page, verify that Local Computer is selected and click Next.**

   You can install SQL Server on either your local computer (the computer you're sitting at) or on a remote computer. By default, Setup assumes that you want to install SQL Server on your local computer, as shown in Figure 4-2.

Figure 4-2:
You can install SQL Server on either the local or a remote computer.

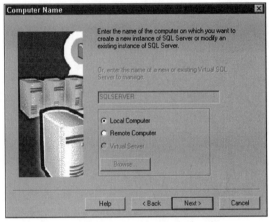

7. **On the Installation Selection page, verify that Create a new instance of SQL Server is selected, and then click Next.**

   You can use this page to choose between creating a new instance of SQL Server or configuring advanced options. By default, Setup assumes that you want to create a new instance of SQL Server.

8. **On the User Information page, enter your name and company name (if necessary), and then click Next.**

   Microsoft uses this information for the licensing agreement.

9. **Read Microsoft's Software License Agreement page, then click Yes to agree this agreement.**

10. **On the Installation Definition page, make sure that Server and Client Tools is selected and then click Next.**

    You can use this page to specify whether you want to install only the client tools, server and client tools, or only the connectivity components.

11. **On the Instance Name page, verify that Default is selected and then click Next.**

    You use this page to specify whether or not you want your current installation of SQL Server to be the default instance. If you don't, you can use this page to name an instance. For right now, keep things simple by installing only a default instance.

12. **On the Setup Type page, select the Custom installation type, and then click Next.**

    We want you to use the Custom installation type so that you can see all the options you can configure during installation. Notice that you can also use this page to choose the destination for SQL Server's program and data files, as shown in Figure 4-3.

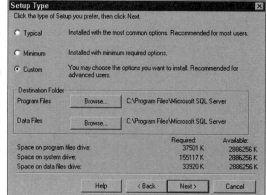

Figure 4-3:
Use the
Setup Type
page to
choose the
install-
ation type.

13. **Accept the default components installed with the Custom installation type by clicking Next.**

    You use this page to specify which of the SQL Server components you want to install on your server.

14. **On the Services Accounts page, enter the user name and password for the service account you created.**

    As shown in Figure 4-4, you use this page of the wizard to specify whether or not you want to use the same settings for all the services, and also whether you want to use the Local System account or a domain user account. Notice that Setup automatically chose the user you're logged on as (Administrator). Make sure you change this user name to the service account you created, and type the password for this user.

15. **Click Next.**

16. **On the Authentication Mode page, make sure that Windows Authentication Mode is selected and then click Next.**

    You use the Authentication Mode page to configure your server to use either the Windows Authentication or Mixed Authentication modes. If you choose Mixed Mode, you can define a password for the SQL login ID.

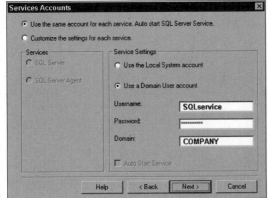

Figure 4-4:
Setup
prompts
you for the
name and
password of
the services
account.

17. **On the Collation Settings page, accept the default settings and click Next.**

    As shown in Figure 4-5, you use this page to configure your server's collation and sort order settings. By default, Setup configures your server to use the predefined SQL collation combination of dictionary order, case-insensitive, and the 1252 character set.

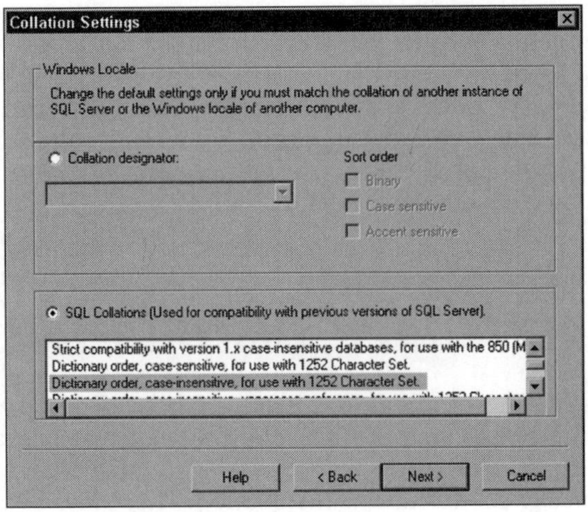

Figure 4-5:
Use colla-
tion settings
to control
how your
server
sorts data.

18. **Accept the default settings on the Network Libraries page by clicking Next.**

    By default, Setup configures your server to support both the Named Pipes and TCP/IP Sockets network libraries, as shown in Figure 4-6.

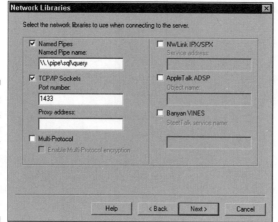

Figure 4-6:
Network libraries enable your server to communicate with clients.

19. **On the Choose Licensing Mode page, select the appropriate licensing option for your version of SQL Server.**

    You can choose either per-seat or per-processor licensing.

20. **Click Continue to begin the installation.**

    At long last, Setup has all the answers it needs to install your software! So kick back and relax while it copies the necessary files to your server, modifies your computer's Registry, and updates your program groups.

By default, Windows 2000 doesn't automatically re-sort your Program menus whenever you install a new software program. If you want to re-sort your menus so that they're in alphabetical order, choose Start➪Programs. Right-click the Program menu and choose Sort by Name.

Performing Unattended Installations

For your convenience, Microsoft has included files that you can use to perform an unattended installation of your SQL servers. You need two files: a command file to control the installation, and a setup initialization file to answer all the questions you typically answer during installation. These files come in pairs. For example, you use a specific command file (sqlins.bat) along with a specific setup initialization file (sqlins.iss) to perform a typical installation of SQL Server 2000. You can use any text editor (such as Notepad) to edit the contents of a setup initialization file to tailor it to your environment.

Using the default unattended installation files

Microsoft includes both command and setup initialization files in your SQL Server edition's folder on the SQL Server CD. (On a SQL Server 2000 Enterprise edition CD, you find these files in the folder named \SQLENT.) We describe these pairs of files for you in Table 4-1.

Table 4-1	Unattended Installation Files	
Command File	*Setup Initialization File*	*Automates*
Slqcli.bat	Sqlcli.iss	The installation of the SQL Server management tools.
Sqlins.bat	Sqlins.iss	A typical installation of SQL Server (uses the Local System Account for the services account).
Sqlcst.bat	Sqlcst.iss	A custom installation of SQL Server (also uses the Local System account for the services account). Use this option if you want to change options such as collation settings or network libraries as part of the installation.
Sqlrem.bat	Sqlrem.iss	The removal of SQL Server 2000.

You can use these installation files simply by running the appropriate command file. For example, to install only the SQL Server management tools, run the sqlcli.bat file — and it automatically calls the sqlcli.iss file.

Creating your own setup initialization file

You don't have to use the setup initialization files Microsoft included on the SQL Server CD. Instead, you can create your own. Now you can create this file the hard way (from scratch), or you can create it one of two easy ways.

Using another server's setup.iss file

Here's easy way number one: SQL Server Setup automatically creates a file named setup.iss with all the configuration settings you choose when you install SQL Server on a computer. If you want to configure another SQL server with the same settings as a server on which you've already installed SQL Server, use this server's setup.iss file to perform your unattended installation.

Keep in mind that the setup.iss file contains all the settings you specified when you installed a specific server. When you use this file to install a new server, you need to make sure that this file contains the appropriate settings for the new server. Most importantly, make sure that the services account information is correct for your new server. If you run the unattended installation with a setup.iss file that contains services account information that's invalid, the installation will fail.

Creating your own setup.iss file using Setup

Here's easy way number two for creating a custom setup initialization file: You can run SQL Server Setup to create the file without actually performing an installation. When you run the SQL Server Setup wizard, on the Installation Selection page, select Advanced Options. You then can choose to record an Unattended .ISS file, as shown in Figure 4-7. Once you select this option, Setup records all the options you choose in the Setup wizard into a setup initialization file named setup.iss and stores it in the path *windows_root* (typically \winnt).

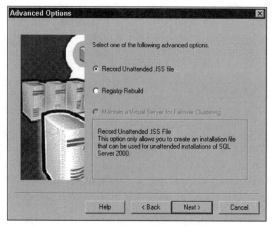

Figure 4-7:
Use SQL
Server
Setup to
create a
setup initial-
ization file.

Using a custom setup initialization file

When you create a custom setup initialization file, you must launch the unattended manually by using the setupsql.exe command-line utility instead of one of the predefined batch files. You find this file in the appropriate folder for your hardware platform on the SQL Server CD. For example, if you're installing on an Intel-based computer, use the setupsql.exe command in the \SQLENT\x86\Setup folder.

Setupsql.exe is a command-line utility, which means you must run it in a command-prompt window. Use the following syntax with setupsql.exe:

```
start /wait \SQLENT\x86\Setup\setupsql -sms -s -f1
        "setup.iss"
```

The `start /wait and -sms` in this command prevents Windows 2000 from returning control to the command-prompt window until Setup has completed installing SQL Server. Use `-s` to run the installation in silent mode so that you don't even see any messages on the screen, and the `-f1` parameter to specify the name of the setup initialization file.

Prep Test

1 Which of the following settings do you configure during the installation of SQL Server? (Choose all that apply.)

A ❑ Number of instances

B ❑ Services account

C ❑ Size of the master database

D ❑ Network libraries

2 Which of the following licensing options are available in SQL Server 2000? (Choose all that apply.)

A ❑ Per workstation

B ❑ Per server

C ❑ Per seat

D ❑ Per processor

3 You are planning to perform an unattended installation of the SQL Server management tools on your computer (which isn't the SQL server). Which pair of files should you use?

A ○ Sqlcli.bat and Sqlcli.iss.

B ○ Sqlins.bat and Sqlins.iss.

C ○ Sqlcst.bat and Sqlcst.iss.

D ○ None. You can't perform an unattended installation of only the management tools.

Answers

1 **A, B,** and **D.** You configure all the settings except the size of the master database when you install SQL Server. *See "Running the installation."*

2 **C** and **D.** SQL Server 2000 supports either per seat or per processor licensing. *See "Running the installation."*

3 **A.** You use the sqlcli.bat and sqlcli.iss files to install only the client management utilities on a computer. *See "Performing Unattended Installations."*

Chapter 5

Upgrading to SQL Server 2000

• •

Exam Objectives

▶ Upgrading to SQL Server 2000 from older versions of SQL Server
▶ Customizing your installation of SQL Server 2000

• •

Choices, choices, choices! When it comes to upgrading to SQL Server 2000, you have a lot of options from which to choose. For example, you can install SQL Server 2000 as a separate, named instance — and continue to run SQL Server 7.0 at the same time. Or you can overwrite SQL Server 7.0 altogether by installing SQL Server 2000 as the default instance. Here's another option: You can keep SQL Server 6.5 on your server, and then install SQL Server 2000 as either the default or a named instance on the same computer.

Regardless of the type of upgrade you perform, you also have to choose what you want to do with your old databases. The good news is that SQL Server 2000 includes wizards that make upgrading your databases easy. For example, you can use the Copy Database Wizard to copy a SQL Server 7.0 database to SQL Server 2000.

In this chapter, we explore how to upgrade from older versions of SQL Server to SQL Server 2000. In addition, we tell you what you can expect to see on the exam.

You can expect to see exam questions on the following topics:

   ✔ Upgrading to SQL Server 2000 from SQL Server 6.5

   ✔ Upgrading to SQL Server 2000 from SQL Server 7.0

   ✔ Performing a custom upgrade

Quick Assessment

Upgrading to
SQL Server
2000

1   You can directly upgrade to SQL Server 2000 from the _____ and _____ versions of SQL Server.

2   You must use the _____ network library when you upgrade an old version of SQL Server to SQL Server 2000.

3   You use the _____ to upgrade your SQL Server 7.0 databases to SQL Server 2000.

4   You use the _____ to upgrade your SQL Server 6.5 databases to SQL Server 2000.

Performing
custom
upgrades

5   Before you can upgrade multiple SQL Server 2000 instances, you must first select the _____ you want to upgrade.

1 6   2000."

2   r 7.0 upgrade."

3   our SQL Server 7.0 data-

     rming the SQL Server 6.5

     om Upgrades."

Upgrading to SQL Server 2000

Before we talk about upgrading to SQL Server 2000, we should first define what *upgrading* means, because Microsoft uses the term upgrading to refer to all the different types of upgrades you can do. These include

- ✔ Overwriting an installation of SQL Server 7.0
- ✔ Configuring a named instance of SQL Server 2000 to coexist with SQL Server 7.0
- ✔ Upgrading SQL Server 6.0 or SQL Server 6.5
- ✔ Adding or removing components from SQL Server 2000
- ✔ Upgrading to a newer release of SQL Server 2000

Upgrading from SQL Server 7.0

SQL Server 2000 offers you two choices for upgrading SQL Server 7.0: You can overwrite your existing SQL Server 7.0 installation, or you can keep your SQL Server 7.0 installation and install a separate instance of SQL Server 2000. Before you do either, though, make sure that your hardware and software support the upgrade. Also keep in mind that the edition of SQL Server 2000 you can upgrade to depends on the edition of SQL Server 7.0 you're currently running. For example, you can upgrade the Enterprise Edition of SQL Server 7.0 only to the Enterprise Edition of SQL Server 2000.

Performing the SQL Server 7.0 upgrade

Okay. So you have the necessary hardware and software to upgrade to SQL Server 2000, but where do you start? Well, you perform the upgrade from SQL Server 7.0 to SQL Server 2000 just like you install SQL Server 2000: Insert the CD-ROM. Keep in mind that just like a regular old installation of SQL Server 2000, you also need the following information:

- ✔ Licensing mode (per processor or per seat)
- ✔ Installation type (typical, minimum, or custom)
- ✔ The services account user name and password
- ✔ Authentication mode (Windows or Mixed Mode authentication)
- ✔ Collation settings (you configure these settings only if you choose the custom installation option)
- ✔ Network libraries (Named Pipes, TCP/IP sockets, NWLink IPX/SPX, VIA GigaNet SAN, multiprotocol, AppleTalk ADSP, or Banyan VINES)

We cover what these installation options are and why you need them in Chapter 3.

When you perform the upgrade, Setup prompts you to either create a new instance of SQL Server or upgrade an existing instance of SQL Server, as shown in Figure 5-1. Choose the "Create a new instance of SQL Server" option if you want to install a separate, named instance of SQL Server 2000 and keep your existing SQL Server 7.0 installation. Choose the "Upgrade, remove, or add components to an existing instance of SQL Server" option if you want to overwrite your SQL Server 7.0 installation.

Figure 5-1:
You can
install SQL
Server
2000 as a
separate
instance
or over-
write SQL
Server 7.0.

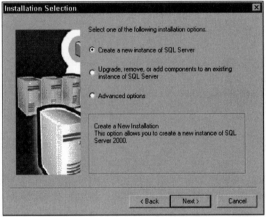

After the SQL Server 7.0 upgrade

You need to make sure that after you upgrade to SQL Server 2000 your data-bases are as efficient as possible. So, you have a little cleanup work to do. Microsoft recommends that you complete the following tasks after you upgrade SQL Server 7.0 databases to SQL Server 2000:

- ✔ **Repopulate full-text catalogs.** SQL Server uses these catalogs and their associated indexes to give you extra flexibility in querying a database.

- ✔ **Update index statistics.** SQL Server uses statistics to determine whether processing a query by scanning a table row-by-row or by using an index is faster.

Do both of these tasks regardless of whether you choose to overwrite your SQL Server 7.0 installation or install a separate instance of SQL Server 2000.

You may see a question or two on the exam about the types of cleanup tasks you need to do after upgrading to SQL Server 2000.

Overwriting SQL Server 7.0

If you choose the Upgrade, Remove, or Add Components to an Existing Instance of SQL Server option, Setup makes SQL Server 2000 your default installation. You won't be able to install SQL Server 2000 as a named instance during the upgrade. In addition, Setup prompts you to confirm that you want to upgrade your SQL Server tools and data, as shown in Figure 5-2. When you check this option, Setup upgrades all of your user databases and SQL Server utilities to SQL Server 2000.

Figure 5-2:
Setup auto-
matically
upgrades all
of your user
databases
and utilities
to SQL
Server
2000 when
you over-
write SQL
Server 7.0.

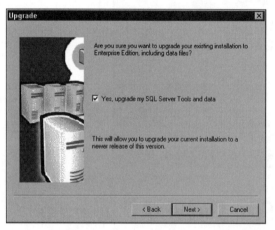

When you overwrite your SQL Server 7.0 installation, it's gone for good. For this reason, make sure that you give yourself a "safety net" before you leap into the installation: BACK UP FIRST! If you have a backup and anything goes wrong during the upgrade, you can go back to SQL Server 7.0 by reinstalling the software and restoring your backup.

Installing a separate instance of SQL Server 2000

If you choose to create a new instance of SQL Server 2000, both SQL Server 7.0 and 2000 can coexist on your server. Each instance of SQL Server can be running at the same time — and your users can access either instance. This kind-of-cool feature in SQL Server 2000 makes seeing how your applications work in SQL Server 2000 without having to abandon your SQL Server 7.0 environment possible.

Because each version of SQL Server is its own instance, you manage each instance individually. For example, when you install SQL Server 2000 as a named instance, you manage each version of SQL Server's services separately. In fact, if you look at the SQL Server-related services in a utility such as the Computer Management MMC, you find two sets of services. The SQL Server 7.0 services use the names MSSQLServer and SQLServerAgent. In contrast, the SQL Server 2000 services are part of a named instance, so they use the names MSSQL$*name_of_instance* and SQLAgent$*name_of_instance*.

Upgrading your SQL Server 7.0 databases

When you install SQL Server 2000 as a separate instance on a server with SQL Server 7.0, Setup doesn't upgrade any of your 7.0 databases automatically. So your next task in this upgrade trek is to decide whether or not you want to make your existing SQL Server 7.0 databases available under SQL Server 2000. You probably will want to upgrade your SQL Server 7.0 databases, and the Copy Database Wizard is the utility for you. (Although this wizard is called the "Copy Database" Wizard, you can use it to both copy and move a database to another server.)

You can use the Copy Database Wizard not only to upgrade SQL Server 7.0 databases, but also simply to copy or move SQL Server 2000 databases from one server to another, or from one instance of SQL Server to another.

The Copy Database Wizard makes upgrading user databases from SQL Server 7.0 to SQL Server 2000 easy. By the way, you can't upgrade any of the system databases (such as master or model) from SQL Server 7.0 to SQL Server 2000.

You can't use the Copy Database Wizard to upgrade a SQL Server 7.0 database if you already have a database with that same name on your SQL Server 2000 server. You must rename either the SQL Server 7.0 or SQL Server 2000 database before you attempt to upgrade the SQL Server 7.0 database.

Upgrading from SQL Server 6.5

If you're currently running SQL Server 6.5, you can install SQL Server 2000 as either the default or a named instance. Although you can install both versions on the same computer, only one version can be running at a time. You can change which version is active on your server by using the Microsoft SQL Server – Switch utility. This utility stops the currently running version of SQL

Server's services and then starts the other version's services. Just as with any upgrade, make sure that your hardware and software meet the minimum requirements before you start.

Before you start

Unlike the SQL Server 7.0 upgrade, you have some tasks you need to complete before you perform the upgrade from SQL Server 6.5. Here's what you need to do:

✔ Back up before you start, and make sure you include the SQL Server 6.5 master database in your backup set.

✔ Configure the SQL Server 6.5 tempdb database to be at least 10MB in size. If you have enough free disk space, you should make tempdb 25MB. Your server uses this database during the upgrade.

✔ Make sure that your SQL Server 6.5 master database has at least 3MB of free space. If it doesn't, expand the database.

✔ Stop replication before you start the upgrade.

After you complete these tasks, you're ready to upgrade!

Performing the SQL Server 6.5 upgrade

Begin your upgrade from SQL Server 6.5 to SQL Server 2000 by installing SQL Server 2000. You can install SQL Server 2000 on the same computer on which you're running SQL Server 6.5, or on a separate computer. After you complete the installation of SQL Server 2000, you can then upgrade your SQL Server 6.5 databases by using the SQL Server Upgrade Wizard.

The SQL Server Upgrade Wizard enables you to upgrade not only your user databases, but also replication settings and most of the SQL Server 6.5 configuration options. You launch the Upgrade Wizard from the Microsoft SQL Server – Switch menu.

You should make sure that you understand the difference between the Copy Database Wizard and the SQL Server Upgrade Wizard for the exam. You use the Copy Database Wizard to upgrade SQL Server 7.0 databases to SQL Server 2000. Use the SQL Server Upgrade Wizard to upgrade SQL Server 6.5 or 6.0 databases to SQL Server 2000.

After the SQL Server 6.5 upgrade

Like the SQL Server 7.0 upgrade, you also have some cleanup work to do when you upgrade SQL Server 6.5. First, this upgrade doesn't remove SQL Server 6.5 from your server. So when you're sure you have all of your databases transferred over to SQL Server 2000, you must manually remove SQL Server 6.5 from your computer.

Performing Custom Upgrades

In addition to upgrading from one version of SQL Server to another, you can also perform an upgrade simply to modify your installation of SQL Server 2000. You perform a custom upgrade by inserting the SQL Server 2000 CD-ROM and choosing the Upgrade, Remove, or Add Components to an Existing Instance of SQL Server option. Setup prompts you to choose an instance of SQL Server to update, and you can then choose to perform one of the following upgrade tasks:

- ✔ Add components to your existing installation.
- ✔ Uninstall your existing installation.
- ✔ Upgrade your existing installation (such as from the Standard edition to the Enterprise edition of SQL Server 2000).
- ✔ Upgrade your existing installation to a clustered installation.

Prep Test

1 You installed SQL Server 2000 as a separate instance on your existing SQL Server 7.0 server. You named your SQL Server 2000 instance "sales." You now want to start the SQL Server database engine. What service should you start?

A ○ MSSQLServer

B ○ MSSQLServer$sales

C ○ MSSQL$sales

D ○ MSSQLServer_sales

2 You installed SQL Server 2000 as a separate instance on your server. What utility should you use to upgrade your old SQL Server 7.0 databases?

A ○ SQL Server Enterprise Manager

B ○ Copy Database Wizard

C ○ SQL Server Upgrade Wizard

D ○ SQL Server Setup

3 You can install both SQL Server 6.5 and SQL Server 2000 on the same computer, and both instances can be running at the same time.

A ○ True

B ○ False

4 Which of the following tasks should you complete before upgrading SQL Server 6.5 to SQL Server 2000? (Choose all that apply.)

A ❑ Back up all databases, including master.

B ❑ Verify that you have at least 3MB of free space in the master database.

C ❑ Set the size of tempdb to at least 10MB.

D ❑ Delete all scheduled jobs on your server.

5 You're attempting to use the Copy Database Wizard to copy a SQL Server 7.0 user database to SQL Server 2000. However, you're unable to choose the database when you run the wizard. What could be the problem?

A ○ Your SQL Server 7.0 database is corrupt.

B ○ The name of the SQL Server 7.0 database is already in use for another database on the SQL Server 2000 server.

C ○ The SQL Server Agent service isn't running.

D ○ You don't have enough free space in the tempdb database to complete the copy.

Answers

1 **C.** MSSQL$sales. SQL Server Setup assigns the name of MSSQL$name_of_instance to the MSSQLServer service of a named instance. *See "Installing a separate instance of SQL Server 2000."*

2 **B.** Copy Database Wizard. You use the Copy Database Wizard to upgrade SQL Server 7.0 databases to SQL Server 2000 databases when you've installed SQL Server 2000 as a separate, named instance. *See "Upgrading your SQL Server 7.0 databases."*

3 **B.** False. Although you can install both SQL Server 6.5 and SQL Server 2000 on the same server, you can run only one version at a time. You use the Microsoft SQL Server – Switch utility to switch between the two versions. *See "Upgrading from SQL Server 6.5."*

4 **A, B,** and **C.** Before you upgrade SQL Server 6.5, make sure that you back up all of your databases, you have at least 3MB of free space in the master database, and that your tempdb database is at least 10MB in size. *See "Before you start."*

5 **B.** You can't upgrade a SQL Server 7.0 database if a database with the same name already exists on the SQL Server 2000 instance. *See "Upgrading your SQL Server 7.0 databases."*

Chapter 6

Troubleshooting Installation Problems

Exam Objectives

▶ Installing SQL Server

▶ Troubleshooting installation problems

*W*e know you've heard it before, but when it comes to computers, usually whatever can go wrong, will go wrong. In this chapter, we show you how you can find out what went wrong during installation — and how to fix it. After you review this chapter, you'll be ready for exam questions that involve troubleshooting failed installations.

Quick Assessment

Trouble-
shooting
installation
problems

1   You can use the _____ in Event Viewer to determine whether SQL Server has reported any information, warning, or error messages.

2   SQL Server stores the MSSQLServer service's error log in the _____ folder.

3   SQL Server keeps the current and archives the last _____ MSSQLServer service error logs.

4   You use _____ to view the Microsoft Search service's error log.

5   If you can't start the MSSQLServer service, you should verify that your server can communicate with a(n) _____.

6   You suspect the SQL Server entries in your computer's Registry are corrupt. You can fix them by running _____.

7   The services account you use for the SQLServerAgent service must be a member of _____ or _____, or it won't be able to start.

8   If you receive a communications error when attempting to connect to a SQL server in SQL Server Enterprise Manager, the problem might be that you don't have the necessary _____ to access the server.

Answers

1   *Application log.* Check out "Searching for Clues."

2   *\Program Files\Microsoft SQL Server\MSSQL\Log.* See "Searching for Clues."

3   *Six.* Study "Searching for Clues."

4   *Any text editor (such as Notepad).* Read "Searching for Clues."

5   *Domain controller.* See "Solving Common Installation Problems."

6   *Registry Rebuild in Setup.* See "Solving Common Installation Problems."

7   *The local Administrators group or the sysadmin server role.* See "Solving Common Installation Problems."

8   *Permissions.* Review "Solving Common Installation Problems."

Searching for Clues

Uh-oh. Your installation of SQL Server 2000 failed. It's time for you to take off your database administrator's hat and put on your Sherlock Holmes' hat to go searching for clues. When it comes to troubleshooting, your first step should always be to find out as much information as you can about the problem. The good news is that both SQL Server 2000 and Windows 2000 (or Windows NT) offer you a wealth of sources for these clues.

SQL Server Setup log

SQL Server 2000's Setup utility automatically creates an installation output file named Sqlstp.log and stores it in the *system_root* folder (typically C:\\ WINNT). This file contains the results of the scripts Setup runs when you install SQL Server. If your installation fails, you can use this file to figure out at what point your installation of SQL Server 2000 failed. You can use any text editor (such as Notepad) to view this file.

One of the first things you need to do if you get an error during installation is to write down the error message. Next, open Sqlstp.log and take a look at the last few lines of the log file. This log lets you see whether SQL Server's Setup utility recorded any problems with your installation before it displayed the error message. If you see an error in the log file, you can use its information to begin resolving the problem.

Application log

Regardless of whether you're using Windows 2000 or Windows NT, SQL Server 2000 records its information, warning, and error messages in the Application log. You can also troubleshoot a failed installation by taking a peek at this log in the Event Viewer utility. (In Windows 2000, Event Viewer is a Microsoft Management Console; in Windows NT, it's a regular old utility.) You find the Event Viewer on your Administrative Tools menu.

Don't forget that you can filter the Application log by types of messages (such as warning or error), event source (such as the MSSQLServer service), and dates.

MSSQLServer log

In addition to the Application log, SQL Server also keeps error logs for each of its services. The MSSQLServer service records its errors in a log file that's stored in the \\Program Files\\Microsoft SQL Server\\MSSQL\\Log folder. By default, SQL Server 2000 automatically creates a new log each time you start your server; it also maintains archived copies of its last six logs. You can use any text editor to view these logs, or you can examine them within SQL Server Enterprise Manager. Lab 6-1 shows you how to navigate SQL Server Enterprise Manager to view your MSSQLServer service's error log.

Lab 6-1   Examining the MSSQLServer Logs

1. **In SQL Server Enterprise Manager, navigate to SQL Server Group\ *your server*\Management\SQL Server Logs.**

   You should see at least a current log, and up to six archive logs, as shown in Figure 6-1.

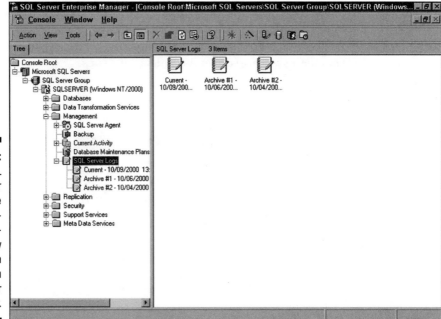

Figure 6-1: The MSSQL Server service automatically creates a new log each time you start your server.

2. **In the console tree, select your current log.**

   You now see the messages recorded by the SQL Server service in the details pane. Notice that unlike Event Viewer, SQL Server Enterprise Manager doesn't display different icons to indicate the severity of the messages.

3. **Double-click one of the messages to display it in a dialog box.**

   Reading the messages in the dialog box format instead of the list format you see in the details pane is easier.

SQLServerAgent log

Like the MSSQLServer service, the SQL Server Agent service also records messages in a log file. This file is named SQLAGENT.OUT, and it's also stored in the \Program Files\Microsoft SQL Server\MSSQL\Log folder. You can view its contents by using any text editor or SQL Server Enterprise Manager. Use the steps in Lab 6-2 to view this log file in SQL Server Enterprise Manager.

Lab 6-2	Viewing the SQLServerAgent Error Log

1. **In the console tree of SQL Server Enterprise Manager, expand your server's Management folder.**

2. **Right-click the SQL Server Agent object and choose Display Error Log.**

   By default, SQL Server Enterprise Manager automatically filters the messages displayed in the error log so that you see only the errors. (And hopefully you don't have any!)

3. **From the Type drop-down list, select All Types.**

   All the SQLServerAgent messages recorded by your server appear, as shown in Figure 6-2.

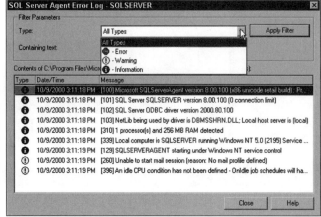

Figure 6-2: You can filter the SQLServer Agent service's error log.

4. **Double-click any of the messages to view it in a dialog box.**

SearchSetup log

If you install the Microsoft Search service as part of a custom installation, you can research any problems by looking at its error log. It's named SearchSetup log, and you find it in the \Temp folder. Use any text editor to examine the contents of the file.

Researching Installation Errors

So you've found the error messages — now what? You next need to find out what you can do to resolve the problem. We recommend that you use the following resources to research the error messages:

- ✔ **SQL Server 2000 Books Online.** Pay close attention to the Trouble-shooting topic in Books Online. You can also use the Index and Search tabs to search for a specific error message.

- ✔ **Microsoft TechNet.** When it comes to researching problems, you won't find a better resource than TechNet. In addition to product manuals and in-depth white papers, it also contains the Knowledge Base. The Knowledge Base is built based on technical support issues, so it contains documentation on problems, their causes, and how you can fix them. You can subscribe to TechNet on CD-ROM, or you can access it on Microsoft's Web site by going to www.microsoft.com/technet.

Solving Common Installation Problems

Although almost anything can (and will) go wrong when you install software, we've found that you can encounter one of a few common problems when you install SQL Server 2000.

The SQL Server services won't start

One of the more common causes of services not starting after installation is a problem with your SQL Server services account. If you see the following error message: "Error 1069: The service did not start due to a logon failure," then you have a problem with the services account.

SQL Server can't access a domain controller

If your services account can't log on to the domain, verify that your SQL server can communicate with a domain controller. When you configure SQL Server to use a domain user account as its service account, your server must be able to communicate with a domain controller in order to validate the logon attempts by your services. If your server can't communicate with a domain controller, it can't validate the service account — and thus can't start your services. As you probably already know, a bunch of reasons exist for why your server may not be able to communicate with a domain controller. These include

- ✔ Your domain controller is down.
- ✔ You have a problem with the network cabling system (such as a network card, cable, hub, or router failure).
- ✔ Your server's network properties such as the IP address, subnet mask, or default gateway aren't configured properly.

If you're desperate to get your SQL server up and running, and it's unable to communicate with a domain controller, you can reconfigure your SQL Server services to use the Local System account in the interim. You can change how your services log on by modifying their properties within the Computer Management MMC.

The services are using the wrong password

Another possible reason why your SQL Server services won't start is that they're configured to use the wrong password. This might happen if you (or another administrator) have changed the services account's password, or it has expired. Keep in mind that if you change the password for your service account, but don't change the password SQL Server uses to authenticate its services, the services will no longer be able to log on.

If you change your service account's password by using a utility such as the Active Directory Users and Computers MMC in Windows 2000, you must configure your SQL Server services to use this new password. You can do so by modifying the properties of the services within SQL Server Enterprise Manager, as shown in Figure 6-3, or by using a utility such as the Computer Management MMC.

The services account doesn't have permission

SQL Server 2000 requires that you configure its services to use an account that's either a member of the local Administrators group on your Windows 2000 (or Windows NT) server, or a member of the sysadmin server role in SQL Server. If you don't configure the services account this way, the SQL Server Agent service won't be able to start.

The Registry is corrupt

Another possible problem that can cause the SQL Server services not to start is a corrupted Registry. If you suspect that the SQL Server–related entries in the Registry are corrupt, you can use the Registry Rebuild option in Setup to rebuild your server's Registry information. You get to the Registry Rebuild option by clicking Advanced Options in Setup.

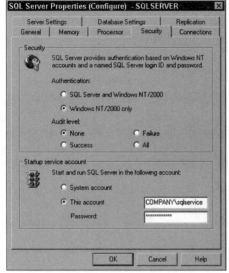

Figure 6-3:
You must reconfigure your services if you change the service account's password.

What we have is a failure to communicate

You've installed SQL Server — and it's running just fine. But now you want to connect to it from a client computer, and you can't. If you encounter this problem, odds are that it's due to one or all of the following:

- Your network itself
- The network library configuration
- Your permissions

Network problems

Before you drive yourself crazy, always make sure that your network is functional before you start troubleshooting in greater detail. And remember to start with the simple things first (such as "is everything plugged in?") before you move on to the hard stuff (like testing your entire cabling system).

Different network libraries

The first rule of communication in the SQL Server environment is that both your server and your clients must have a network library in common. (Well, actually that's the second rule. The first rule is that you must have a functioning network!) You can view and add to your server's network libraries by using the Server Network Utility; you configure your clients' network libraries by using the Client Network Utility. And remember, if you're using a nonstandard port instead of the default port for the TCP/IP Sockets network library, make sure you've configured both your server and its clients to use the same port.

Permissions

You also won't be able to connect to your server if you don't have the necessary permissions. In this case, you usually see this message "A connection could not be established to *server*." In order to connect to your server within a utility such as SQL Server Enterprise Manager, you must log on as a user with permissions to administer SQL Server.

Prep Test

1 **Which log should you check first when troubleshooting a failed SQL Server installation?**

A ○ MSSQLServer log

B ○ Application log

C ○ Sqlstp.log

D ○ SQLServerAgent log

2 **Which utility can you use to view the Application log?**

A ○ SQL Server Enterprise Manager

B ○ Event Viewer

C ○ Notepad

D ○ Computer Management

3 **Which utility can you use to view the MSSQLServer log? (Choose all that apply.)**

A ❑ SQL Server Enterprise Manager

B ❑ Event Viewer

C ❑ Notepad

D ❑ Computer Management

4 **Which of the following utilities can you use to view the Microsoft Search service's error log? (Choose all that apply.)**

A ❑ SQL Server Enterprise Manager

B ❑ Event Viewer

C ❑ Notepad

D ❑ Computer Management

5 **You are unable to start the MSSQLServer service. You've verified that this service is using the correct domain user account and password. What else should you check? (Choose all that apply.)**

A ❑ The status of your domain controller

B ❑ The service account's permissions

C ❑ Your server's network library configuration

D ❑ Your server's Registry

Answers

1 **C.** Although all of these logs give you information about the status of your server, always check the Setup log first to see whether you can determine at what point your installation is failing. *See "SQL Server Setup log."*

2 **B.** You can view the Application log only in Event Viewer. *See "Application log."*

3 **A** and **C.** You can use any text editor such as Notepad, or SQL Server Enterprise Manager, to view the contents of the MSSQLServer log — but doing so is a little easier in SQL Server Enterprise Manager. *Review "MSSQLServer log."*

4 **C.** You can view the Search service's error log only in a text editor such as Notepad. *Review "SearchSetup log."*

5 **A, B,** and **D.** Your server's network library doesn't have any effect on whether or not your services start. *See "The SQL Server services won't start."*

Chapter 7

Configuring SQL Server to Send E-Mail

*J*ust when you're used to the fact that you can exchange e-mail with anyone and everyone, including your grandmother, now SQL Server has joined the bandwagon. That's right — you can send e-mail to SQL Server, and it can send e-mail to you. (In fact, you can even configure SQL Server to page you if it's having a problem!)

In this chapter, we examine how you configure both the MSSQLServer and SQLServerAgent services to send e-mail. And, of course, we cover what you need to know for the exam.

Quick Assessment

1 The MSSQLServer service uses _____ to send e-mail.

2 SQL Server is a(n) _____-compliant application; this enables it to communicate with a messaging server.

3 The SQLServerAgent service uses _____ to send e-mail.

4 The SQLServerAgent service won't be able to send e-mail unless you configure it to log on with _____.

5 You must configure a(n) _____ for the SQL Server services account before you can configure SQL Mail and SQLAgentMail.

6 You configure SQLAgentMail by modifying the properties of the _____ object in SQL Server Enterprise Manager.

7 The _____ stored procedure enables your server to send you the results of a query by e-mail.

8 You configure SQL Server to use SQLAgentMail by defining a(n) _____ in SQL Server Enterprise Manager.

Answers

1 *SQL Mail.* See "Preparing SQL Server to Send E-Mail."

2 *MAPI.* Study "Preparing SQL Server to Send E-Mail."

3 *SQLAgentMail.* Check out "Preparing SQL Server to Send E-Mail."

4 *A domain user account.* Study "Configuring the SQLServerAgent Service."

5 *Messaging profile.* See "Configuring SQL Mail and SQLAgentMail."

6 *SQL Server Agent.* See "Configuring SQLAgentMail."

7 *xp_sendmail.* Study "Using SQL Mail."

8 *Operator.* Read "Using SQLAgentMail."

Preparing SQL Server to Send E-Mail

Before we dive into how you go about configuring the SQL Server services to send e-mail, we need to cover a little background first. Microsoft designed SQL Server as a MAPI-compliant application — which means that SQL Server can communicate with any e-mail server that's also MAPI-compliant (such as Microsoft Exchange Server).

The Messaging Application Programming Interface (MAPI) is a standardized messaging interface developed by Microsoft. A program (such as SQL Server) being MAPI-enabled means that it has the ability to communicate with any program that uses the same interface.

What are SQL Mail and SQLAgentMail?

In SQL Server, both the MSSQLServer and SQLServerAgent services can send e-mail. As you know, SQL Server uses the MSSQLServer service to perform all of its database work. In essence, the MSSQLServer service is SQL Server's database engine. SQL Server uses the SQLServerAgent service to handle alerts, jobs, and to notify you about the status of jobs and any problems on your server.

Because both the MSSQLServer and SQLServerAgent services perform different functions, it makes sense that you configure each service's e-mail capabilities independently. When you configure the MSSQLServer service to send e-mail, Microsoft calls it "SQL Mail." And when you configure the SQLServerAgent service to send e-mail, Microsoft calls it "SQLAgentMail."

The MSSQLServer service uses SQL Mail to process incoming e-mail messages in the form of queries and to send responses by e-mail. For example, you can use the `xp_sendmail` stored procedure to send a query to your server, and it can send you the results of that query in an e-mail message. You can also write applications that use SQL Mail. On the other hand, the SQLServerAgent service uses SQLAgentMail to notify you about the status of jobs and to alert you in the event of a problem.

Configuring the SQLServerAgent service

Before you configure the SQLServerAgent service to send e-mail, make sure that it's ready to go. And it isn't ready to go by default, because Setup doesn't configure this service to automatically start.

Here's what you need to do:

✔ Configure the SQLServerAgent service to log on with a domain user account that also has the necessary permissions.

✔ Verify that the SQLServerAgent services account is set to use the Windows Authentication mode and not SQL Server Authentication.

✔ Set the SQLServerAgent service to start automatically.

Make sure you understand why you must use a domain user account for your services for the exam. If you configure the SQLServerAgent service to use the Local System account, your SQL server won't be able to access network resources (including your e-mail server). So, you must configure the SQLServerAgent service to use a domain user account, or you won't be able to configure it to send e-mail. Further, you must configure the SQLServerAgent service to establish its connection by using Windows authentication, not SQL Server authentication, in order for the service to have access to network resources. (Unless the SQLServerAgent's services account is validated with Windows authentication, it won't be able to access other resources such as your Exchange server.) Finally, make sure you configure the SQLServerAgent service with a services account that's either a member of the local Administrators group or the sysadmin server role.

In addition to configuring the SQLServerAgent service to log on with an appropriate user account, configure the SQLServerAgent service to start not only whenever your server boots up, but also whenever it or the MSSQLServer service stops unexpectedly. (Stopping the MSSQLServer service automatically stops the SQLServerAgent service.)

Now that you know what you need to do, your next step is to do it. You have a lot of choices in utilities for the SQLServerAgent service. However, only SQL Server Enterprise Manager enables you to define the services account, specify its type of authentication, and configure the SQLServerAgent service to automatically restart if it's stopped unexpectedly. In Lab 7-1, we show you how to do all of these tasks for configuring the SQLServerAgent service.

Lab 7-1   Configuring the SQLServerAgent Service's Properties

1. **If necessary, log on as Administrator.**

2. **Open SQL Server Enterprise Manager.**

3. **In the console tree, expand your server's Management folder.**

   As shown in Figure 7-1, you see the SQLServerAgent service's object in this folder. You use this object to manage the properties of the service. If you see a red dot in the icon for the SQLServerAgent service, it isn't started; a green arrow in the icon indicates that the service is started.

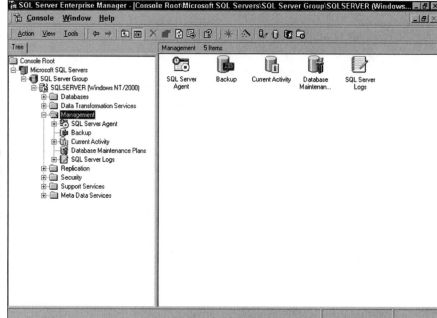

Figure 7-1:
By default,
SQL Server
doesn't
start the
SQLServer-
Agent
service
automati-
cally.

4. **Right-click the SQL Server Agent object and choose Properties.**

5. **Examine the Service Startup Account portion of the dialog box.**

   If necessary, use this portion of the dialog box to configure the SQLServerAgent service to log on with a domain user account, as shown in Figure 7-2. Specify a user account and password that's valid for your domain. You may not have to change any of the services account information, though, if you specified that you wanted the Setup utility to configure all of your services the same when you installed SQL Server.

6. **Select the Advanced tab, and take a look at the Restart Services portion of the dialog box.**

   Check the two auto restart check boxes, shown in Figure 7-3, to configure the SQLServerAgent service to automatically restart whenever it or the MSSQLServer service stops unexpectedly.

7. **Select the Connection tab, and examine the SQL Server Connection settings.**

   The SQLServerAgent service uses the Connection settings, shown in Figure 7-4, to determine whether it should use the Windows or SQL Server Authentication modes. By default, Setup configures your server to use Windows Authentication, so you shouldn't have to change anything here.

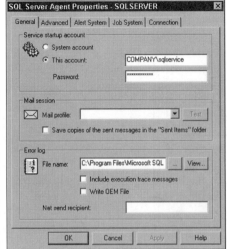

Figure 7-2:
Configure
the SQL-
ServerAgent
service to
log on with
a domain
user
account.

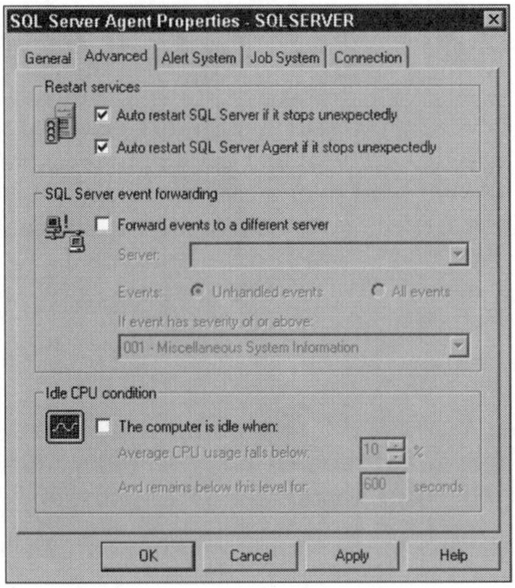

Figure 7-3:
Always con-
figure the
SQLServer-
Agent
service to
automati-
cally restart.

8. **Click OK to save your changes to the properties of the SQLServerAgent service.**

    You now have the SQLServerAgent service all set to go, so it's time to start it.

9. **Right-click the SQLServerAgent service object and choose Start.**

    You should now see a green arrow on the SQLServerAgent service's object instead of a red dot. (If necessary, press F5 to refresh SQL Server Enterprise Manager's display.)

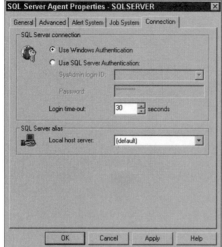

Figure 7-4:
Configure
the
SQLServer-
Agent
service to
use
Windows
Authentica-
tion.

Configuring SQL Mail and SQLAgentMail

After you configure the SQLServerAgent service, you're ready to move on to configuring both SQL Mail and SQLAgentMail. For the purpose of this book, we assume that you're using Microsoft Exchange Server 2000 as your e-mail server, and Microsoft Outlook 2000 as your e-mail client software. (Keep in mind that because SQL Server 2000 is MAPI-compliant, you can use any e-mail server and client software as long as they are both MAPI-compliant.)

Here's an overview of what you need to do:

1. **In the Active Directory Users and Computers, create a mailbox for the SQL Server services account. (If you're using an older version of Exchange Server, use Microsoft Exchange Administrator.)**

2. **Install Outlook 2000 (or any MAPI-compliant client application) on your SQL server.**

3. **On your SQL server, log on as your services account. (For example, if you named your services account "SQLservice," then log on as this user.) Define a messaging profile for the services account by configuring Outlook 2000 to connect to your services account's mailbox on the Exchange server.**

4. **Log back on as an administrator and configure the SQL Mail and SQLAgentMail to use the mailbox for the services account.**

Make sure you know the steps for configuring both SQL Mail and SQLAgentMail for the exam.

Step 1: Creating a mailbox for the services account

Now because SQL Server 2000 is MAPI-compliant, you can create the mailbox for the services account in any e-mail server written to use this interface. For example, you can create the mailbox on an Exchange server.

You will want to have SQL Mail and SQLAgentMail send e-mail messages to you, so you also need your own mailbox. If you don't have one already, go ahead and create a mailbox for yourself while you're creating one for the SQL Server services account.

Step 2: Installing a mail client

Your next task is to install a mail client on the SQL server. For example, you can use Microsoft Outlook as your server's mail client. Even though SQL Server doesn't actually open the mail client to send e-mail messages, you must still install it on your SQL server.

Step 3: Configuring Outlook 2000 for the SQL Server services account

Okay. So you've created the mailbox for the services account *and* installed Outlook 2000 on your SQL server. Now what? Your next move is to log on as the services account user on the SQL server itself and then configure Outlook 2000 for this user. When you're done, Outlook 2000 creates a messaging profile for the services account user (named MS Exchange Settings, by default); you use this profile to configure SQL Mail and SQLAgentMail.

Test the configuration of Outlook by sending an e-mail message (while you're logged on as the services account user) to another mailbox (such as yours). By testing the configuration this way, you know that Outlook and Exchange Server are communicating properly.

Step 4: Configuring SQL Mail and SQLAgentMail

Good news — this step is the last! You're now ready to configure both SQL Mail and SQLAgentMail in SQL Server Enterprise Manager. You configure both by specifying that you want them to use the services account's messaging profile.

Configuring SQL Mail

You configure SQL Mail by modifying the properties of the SQL Mail object in SQL Server Enterprise Manager. You find the SQL Mail object in the Support Services folder. Lab 7-2 takes you through the steps for configuring and testing SQL Mail.

Lab 7-2	Configuring SQL Mail

1. **If necessary, log on as Administrator.**

2. **Open SQL Server Enterprise Manager.**

3. **In the console tree, expand your server's Support Services folder.**

   You should see the SQL Mail object within this folder.

4. **Right-click the SQL Mail object and choose Properties.**

   This opens the SQL Mail Configuration dialog box. You use the Profile Name drop-down list to configure the MSSQLServer service to use the messaging profile you defined for the services account user.

5. **From the Profile Name drop-down list, select MS Exchange Settings.**

6. **Check Autostart SQL Mail when SQL Server Starts.**

   As shown in Figure 7-5, this option configures your server to automatically start SQL Mail whenever it starts the MSSQLServer service.

7. **Click Test.**

   SQL Server tests SQL Mail by verifying that it can use the messaging profile you specified.

8. **Click OK to close the message box.**

   You now receive a message stating that SQL Server successfully started and stopped a MAPI session with the services account messaging profile.

Figure 7-5:
Configure
SQL Mail to
use the
messaging
profile for
the services
account
user.

9. **Click OK to close the SQL Mail Configuration dialog box.**

10. **Stop and restart SQL Server. (In the console tree, right-click your server and choose Stop. When your server has stopped, right-click your server again and choose Start.)**

You can now communicate with the MSSQLServer service by e-mail!

Configuring SQLAgentMail

You configure SQLAgentMail by modifying the properties of the SQLServerAgent service in SQL Server Enterprise Manager. In Lab 7-3, we show you the steps for configuring and testing SQLAgentMail.

Lab 7-3	Configuring SQLAgentMail

1. **In SQL Server Enterprise Manager's console tree, expand your server's Management folder.**

2. **Right-click the SQL Server Agent object and choose Properties.**

   You use the General page of the SQL Server Agent Properties dialog box to configure SQLAgentMail.

3. **From the Mail Profile drop-down list, select MS Exchange Settings.**

   As shown in Figure 7-6, this option configures the SQLServerAgent service to use the messaging profile that you created for the SQL Server services account.

4. **Notice the Save copies of the sent messages check box.**

   If you check this option, the SQLServerAgent service will store copies of every e-mail message it sends in the Sent Items folder in the services account's mailbox. Because the services account won't delete any of these messages, you will have to manually delete them yourself. We recommend that you don't check this option unless you're troubleshooting a problem with SQLAgentMail.

5. **Click Test.**

   Like you just saw with SQL Mail, SQL Server tests SQLAgentMail by verifying that it can access the messaging profile for the services account user.

6. **Click OK to close the message box.**

7. **Click OK to close the Properties dialog box for the SQLServerAgent service.**

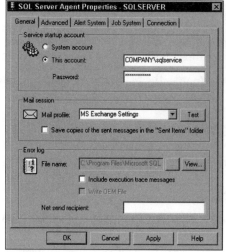

Figure 7-6:
Configure
SQLAgent-
Mail by
modifying
the proper-
ties of the
SQLServer-
Agent
service.

8. **Click Yes.**

   SQL Server must stop and restart the SQLServerAgent service in order
   for its new configuration to take effect.

9. **Click OK to close the message box.**

   A message box appears stating that SQL Server restarted the
   SQLServerAgent service successfully. The SQLServerAgent service is
   now ready to send e-mail.

Sending and Receiving E-Mail

Now that you have both SQL Mail and SQLAgentMail configured, how do you
use them? You use SQL Mail by executing stored procedures. On the other
hand, you use SQLAgentMail by configuring your server to notify you about
the status of jobs or alerts.

Using SQL Mail

One way that you can use SQL Mail is with the xp_sendmail stored procedure. This stored procedure enables you to send a query your server and
have it send the results by e-mail.

A stored procedure is a program that you create and store on the SQL server. For example, you might create a stored procedure to automate the update of multiple tables in a database. SQL Server comes with two types of predefined stored procedures: extended and system. An extended stored procedure is actually an external program in the form of a dynamic link library (DLL). Most of the system stored procedures have names that begin with sp_, and extended stored procedures begin with xp_.

Use the following syntax to query your server with the xp_sendmail stored procedure:

```
EXEC xp_sendmail 'your_mailbox_name',
@subject = 'subject',
query = 'SQL_query_statements'
```

In Lab 7-4, we show you how you can use xp_sendmail to have your SQL server e-mail you the number of authors in the pubs database who live in Utah. (The pubs database is one of the sample databases installed by SQL Server's Setup by default.)

Lab 7-4   Using xp_sendmail

1. **Make sure you're logged on as Administrator.**

2. **Open Outlook 2000.**

   You're going to query your server and have it send the results to you by e-mail. Leave Outlook open so that you can see this e-mail message.

3. **Click Start⇨Programs⇨Microsoft SQL Server⇨Query Analyzer.**

4. **In the Connect to SQL Server dialog box, make sure you're connecting to your SQL server with Windows NT authentication.**

5. **Click OK.**

6. **In the Query pane, type the following query:**

   ```
   SELECT *
   FROM pubs.dbo.authors
   WHERE state = 'UT'
   ```

7. **Choose Query⇨Execute.**

   SQL Server displays a list of the authors who live in Utah in the results pane. (We wanted you to see this list before you used the xp_sendmail stored procedure.)

8. **Choose Edit⇨Clear Window.**

   This clears your previous query out of the Query pane.

9. **Now type the following query:**

```
EXEC xp_sendmail 'administrator',
@subject = 'Utah authors',
query = "SELECT COUNT(*) FROM pubs.dbo.authors WHERE
        state = 'UT'"
```

Because you're using a `WHERE` clause with character data (`WHERE state = 'UT'`), you must enclose the character data (`UT` in this case) in single quotes. As a result, you must enclose your whole `query` statement in double quotes. If you were using a simpler `query` statement such as `SELECT * FROM pubs.dbo.authors`, you could enclose it in single quotes.

10. **Choose Query⇨Execute.**

SQL Server processes your query, and sends the results to you by e-mail.

11. **Switch to Outlook and double-click your e-mail message.**

As shown in Figure 7-7, the authors table contains two authors who live in Utah.

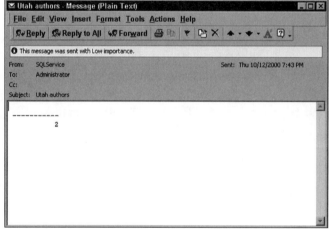

Figure 7-7: SQL Server sends the results of an xp_sendmail query to you by e-mail.

Using SQLAgentMail

The SQLServerAgent service uses SQLAgentMail to notify you about the status of jobs and alerts. Before it can notify you, though, you must be an operator on the server. SQL Server can contact you as an operator by a combination of methods, including e-mail, pager, and the `net send` Windows command. If you want to configure SQL Server to page you, you must have an e-mail server configured with paging support.

You can configure yourself as an operator on your SQL server by using the steps in Lab 7-5.

Lab 7-5   **Configuring an Operator**

1. **Switch to SQL Server Enterprise Manager, but leave Outlook running.**

2. **In the console tree, expand the SQL Server Agent object (in your server's Management folder).**

3. **Right-click the Operators object, and choose New Operator.**

   You use the New Operator Properties dialog box to add yourself as an operator on your server.

4. **Enter your name and mailbox name in the Name and E-mail Name text boxes, as shown in Figure 7-8.**

   You can click on the Browse button (...) to display a list of the mailboxes on your Exchange server. Notice that you can also configure the SQLServerAgent service to notify you by pager and by the `net send` command.

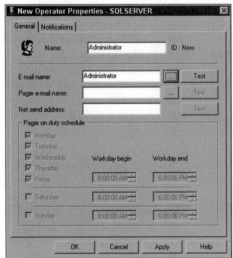

Figure 7-8: Defining an operator.

5. **Click Apply to save your changes.**

6. **Click Test to have SQL Server use SQLAgentMail send a test message to your mailbox.**

7. **Click OK to confirm that you want to send the test message, and then click OK in the message box stating that the message was sent successfully.**

8. **Switch to Outlook, and double-click your new message.**

   As shown in Figure 7-9, SQLServerAgent sends the test notification message.

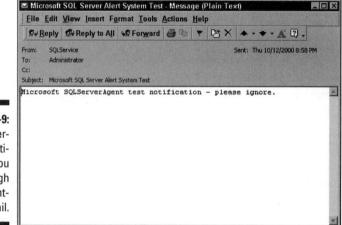

Figure 7-9:
SQLServer-
Agent noti-
fies you
through
SQLAgent-
Mail.

9. **Switch back to SQL Server Enterprise Manager, and then click OK to close the New Operator Properties dialog box.**

Now that you've defined yourself as an operator, you can configure the SQLServerAgent service to notify you about the status of jobs and alerts. We look at defining jobs and alerts, as well as how they can notify you, in detail in Chapter 23.

Prep Test

1 Which of the following steps should you complete when configuring the SQLServerAgent service? (Choose all that apply.)

A ❑ Set it to use SQL Server Authentication.

B ❑ Configure it to use the Local System account for the services account.

C ❑ Set it to start automatically.

D ❑ Configure it to use a domain user account for the services account.

2 You have created a mailbox for the services account user. What should you do next when configuring SQL Mail?

A ○ Create a messaging profile for the services account.

B ○ Install Outlook 2000 on the server.

C ○ Start and stop your SQL server.

D ○ Create a messaging profile for the administrator's account.

3 When you install Outlook 2000 on your SQL server, what configuration option should you choose?

A ○ Exchange Server

B ○ Internet

C ○ Corporate or Workgroup

D ○ SQL Server

4 What is the default name that Outlook 2000 assigns to the services account's messaging profile?

A ○ Outlook Settings

B ○ *Service_account_name* Settings

C ○ MS Exchange Settings

D ○ Messaging Settings

5 What does SQL Server use to respond to queries via e-mail?

A ○ SQL Mail

B ○ SQLAgentMail

C ○ SQL Server Enterprise Manager

D ○ SQL Server Query Analyzer

Answers

1 **C** and **D.** In addition to configuring the SQLServerAgent service to start automatically and to log on with a domain user account, you must also configure it to use Windows Authentication. *See "Configuring the SQLServerAgent service."*

2 **B.** You must install Outlook 2000 (or some other MAPI client) on your SQL server in order for it to send e-mail with SQL Mail or SQLAgentMail. *Review "Configuring SQL Mail and SQLAgentMail."*

3 **C.** Only the Corporate or Workgroup configuration option enables Outlook 2000 to communicate with an Exchange server. *See "Step 2: Installing Outlook 2000."*

4 **C.** Outlook 2000 defines the name "MS Exchange Settings" to the default messaging profile for each user, including the services account user. *Review "Step 3: Configuring Outlook 2000 for the SQL Server services account."*

5 **B.** SQL Server uses SQL Mail to respond to queries, whereas it uses SQLAgentMail to notify the operators you define about the status of jobs and alerts. *See "Sending and Receiving E-Mail."*

Part III
Creating SQL Server Databases

The 5th Wave   By Rich Tennant

"We can monitor our entire operation from one central location. We know what the 'Wax Lips' people are doing; we know what the 'Whoopee Cushion' people are doing; we know what the 'Fly-in-the-Ice Cube' people are doing. But we don't know what the 'Plastic Vomit' people are doing. We don't want to know what the 'Plastic Vomit' people are doing."

In this part . . .

After you have your server up and running, your next task is to create the databases you need for your environment. How you design these databases can have a tremendous impact on your server's performance, so investing the time to develop a strategy for implementing your databases is important. Because the heart and soul of SQL Server is its databases and their objects, you can expect to see many of your exam's questions based on the topics in this part of the book.

In Chapter 8, we explore all the factors you need to consider before you create a database. For example, how many files do you need? Do you want to spread the database across multiple disks? Then, in Chapter 9, we show you all the nuts and bolts for creating a database, both in SQL Server Enterprise Manager and with the CREATE DATABASE SQL statement. Next, we show you how to manage a database and its files in Chapter 10. And in Chapter 11, we explore how you create and manage database objects.

Chapter 8

Designing Databases

● ●

Exam Objectives

▶ Selecting storage locations

▶ Estimating capacity requirements for a database

▶ Sizing and placing the transaction log

▶ Choosing a physical drive configuration

● ●

*1*n SQL Server administration, the phrase "designing a database" actually means nothing more than deciding the ins and outs of the files that make up a database. (We don't actually get into what goes into a database until we look at designing and creating database objects in Chapter 10.) As a database administrator, when it comes to designing a database, you must complete the following tasks:

   ✔ Choose your filenames and locations.

   ✔ Decide on initial sizes of the database file and the transaction log.

   ✔ Optimize performance.

You need to consider many factors when designing a database. In this chapter, we explore how you go about naming a database's files, choosing an appropriate size, and optimizing the database's performance with files and filegroups. (And we make sure you review what you need to know for the exam.)

Quick Assessment

Selecting storage locations

1 By default, SQL Server assigns the extension of _____ to a database's primary data file.

2 SQL Server automatically creates databases and transaction logs in the _____ folder.

Estimating capacity requirements for a database

3 The smallest unit of disk space SQL Server uses is called a(n) _____.

4 An extent is made up of _____ pages.

5 The maximum width of a row is _____ bytes.

Sizing and placing the transaction log

6 For an online transaction processing system (OLTP), you should generally size a database's transaction log as being _____ percent of the database's size.

7 The general rule for sizing a database's transaction log for a decision support system (DSS) is _____ percent of the database's size.

Choosing a physical drive configuration

8 If you don't specify otherwise, SQL Server automatically places any database objects you create in the _____ filegroup.

9 SQL Server calls the first filegroup you create the _____ filegroup.

Answers

1 *.mdf.* Check out "Choosing Filenames and Locations."

2 *C:\Program Files\Microsoft SQL Server\MSSQL\Data.* Study "Choosing Filenames and Locations."

3 *Page.* See "Capacity Planning."

4 *Eight.* Study "Capacity Planning."

5 *8,060.* Check out "Capacity Planning."

6 *25.* See "Capacity Planning."

7 *10.* See "Capacity Planning."

8 *Default.* Take a look at "Optimizing Performance."

9 *Primary.* See "Optimizing Performance."

Choosing Filenames and Locations

A database consists of a minimum of two files: a primary data file and a transaction log file. When you create a database, you provide SQL Server with names for these files. You do so by assigning both a logical name and a physical filename to the data file and transaction log. You see the database's logical name in SQL Server Enterprise Manager. You also use the logical name whenever you query a database in SQL Server Query Analyzer. SQL Server assigns the physical name to the database's files.

Although you can use different names for the logical and physical names, using something similar for both is easier. If you create your database by using SQL Server Enterprise Manager (and not the Transact-SQL statements), SQL Server automatically generates the physical filenames for both the database and transaction log files based on the logical name you specify. For example, if you assign the logical name of "accounting" to your database, SQL Server names the primary data file "accounting_data" and the transaction log file "accounting_log." We show you how to create a database in Chapter 9.

In addition to generating the physical filenames based on the logical name you assign to the database, SQL Server also assigns specific extensions to each type of file. SQL Server assigns an extension of .mdf to the primary data file for a database. Likewise, it assigns the extension of .ldf to the transaction log file. Finally, if you create secondary data files for your database in order to fine-tune its performance, SQL Server assigns an extension of .ndf to them. Make sure you know these extensions for the exam.

By default, SQL Server 2000 places both a database's data file and its transaction log in the folder C:\Program Files\Microsoft SQL Server\MSSQL\Data. For performance reasons, mostly because SQL Server accesses these files continuously, you can get significant performance enhancements if you place these files in other locations. For example, one caveat Microsoft consistently recommends is that you place a database's transaction log on a separate hard drive from its data file(s). We address this strategy in the section "Optimizing Performance," later in this chapter.

Capacity Planning

One of the cool database options Microsoft introduced beginning with SQL Server 7.0 is that you can configure your databases to grow or shrink automatically. You can enable or disable these options when you create a database, and you can also change them later by modifying the database's properties. The advantage to the automatic growth option is that just like any old file you're used to, it enables SQL Server to increase the size of a data file as needed. In other words, if your users add thousands of rows to a table,

SQL Server can increase the size of the file proportionally to support those rows.

Previous versions of SQL Server couldn't automatically grow database files, which meant that you, as the database administrator, were responsible for monitoring the size of a database file and its contents. If a database needed more room, you had to manually increase the size of the database file. Likewise, the advantage to the automatic shrink option is that SQL Server can decrease the amount of disk space a database uses if your users delete thousands of rows.

So what does this have to do with designing a database? Well, one big reason is that you must specify an initial size for your database's data and transaction log files when you create the database. Although sizing your database and transaction log files exactly correct when you create them isn't as critical (because of the automatic grow and shrink options), you do still need to set an initial size. Based on this initial size, SQL Server can then grow and shrink your database as needed.

In addition, estimating the size of a database is one of the topics you need to know for the exam. Microsoft does want you to understand how SQL Server uses disk space — and to be able to calculate a rough estimate of how much disk space a particular table or database needs. So even though it isn't as dire a question in SQL Server 2000, you still need to understand how to estimate the space requirements for a database.

Database objects

In SQL Server, you create a database's data file — and then you create an object within that file. For example, you might create a database's data file and set its initial size to 1MB. Then within that database, you create a table — and that table uses space within the database's data file. We tend to talk about a table as using disk space, but that isn't entirely correct — it's the database that uses disk space, and the table uses space within the database. Indirectly, though, a table does use disk space because if your table becomes so large that it needs more space in the database, you must increase the size of your database's data file in order to accommodate that table.

Pages, extents, and bears — oh, my!

SQL Server 2000 uses two units of disk space to store a database: pages and extents. (We're just kidding about the bears.) First of all, SQL Server stores data in 8KB chunks called pages. This is the smallest unit of disk space SQL Server can use, so at a minimum, a database object such as a table uses at least 8KB of space within your database file.

When you design a table, you specify the width of each of its columns. For example, consider Figure 8-1. This figure shows you the columns that make up the authors table in the pubs sample database installed with SQL Server 2000. You can find the maximum width for a row in this table by adding up the values you see in the Size column in this dialog box. A row can't span more than one 8KB data page, so the maximum row size for any table can't exceed 8KB. (To be precise, the maximum row size is 8,060 bytes because each row has 132 bytes of overhead.)

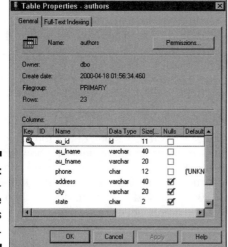

Figure 8-1:
The structure of the authors table.

You can expect to see a few questions on estimating the size of a table (and thus a database) based on a table's row size. For example, if we tell you that each row in a table within a database is 5,492 bytes, and we expect that the table will have a total of 10,000 rows, how much space will you need to store this table? Because a row can't span multiple pages, SQL Server will use one page to store each row. The total size of this table then is 8KB multiplied by 10,000 pages, or 80,000 KB (which is roughly 80MB).

SQL Server organizes pages into *extents*. An extent consists of eight contiguous 8KB pages for a total of 64KB of space. If a database object such as a table uses less than an extent's worth of space (64KB), SQL Server allocates space for that object within an existing extent; such an extent is considered mixed because it contains pages for different objects. But if an object's size exceeds 64KB, SQL Server allocates extents solely for use by that object; these extents are considered uniform because they contain only that object's pages. Microsoft designed SQL Server to store its database objects this way in order to prevent small objects from using an entire extent's worth of space. In addition, larger objects can expand more efficiently by expanding within a uniform extent than they can if SQL Server must continually allocate new pages to the object from mixed extents.

Estimating the size of a database

So how do you estimate the size of a database? Well, first of all, you need to estimate how much space each of the database's tables will use. You can estimate the amount of space a table will use by first determining the total width of a row. For example, you might create a table in which you have the following columns:

- ✔ Last Name
- ✔ First Name
- ✔ Telephone number

For the sake of keeping things simple, assume that the widths of these three columns add up to 100 bytes. You can calculate how many rows you can store per page by using the following formula:

```
8,060 bytes / size of one row = # of rows per page
```

Given this formula, if the size of one row for your table is 100 bytes, SQL Server can store 80.6 rows per page. Actually, you can't have a row span multiple pages, so you should round down if this formula results in decimal places. So for this table, SQL Server can store only 80 rows per page. Now assume that you estimate that your table will have a total of 100,000 rows. You can calculate how many pages your table will use by using this formula:

```
Total # of rows in table / # of rows per page = # of pages to
                   store table
```

Continuing with our example, if we estimate that our table will have 100,000 rows, and we can store 80 rows per page, it will take SQL Server 1,250 pages to store this table. So the total amount of disk space we need in our database for this table alone is 1,250 pages multiplied by 8KB per page, or 10,000KB (roughly 10MB).

So if you want to estimate the size of a database, you need to repeat these calculations for each of the tables you expect to have in the database. Also keep in mind that SQL Server automatically copies system tables from the model database to the master database (and these use disk space). All of your other database objects also use disk space. For example, any indexes you create will use disk space as well. The amount of disk space an index uses depends on the size of its key (the columns on which you're indexing).

In addition to all of your user-defined objects in a database, keep in mind that SQL Server also creates system objects in each database. For example, SQL Server creates a system table called sysusers in every database for storing information about that database's users. SQL Server creates these objects by copying them from the model database. These objects use approximately 1MB of your database's space.

For the exam, make sure you understand how to estimate the amount of disk space a database will require.

Estimating the size of a transaction log

As a general rule, Microsoft recommends that you set a transaction log's initial size equal to from 10 to 25 percent of its database. For example, if you estimate that your database will be 50MB in size, create its transaction log with an initial size of 5 to 12.5MB. You can use the lower figure (10 percent) if you expect that your data won't change very often (and thus you won't have as many transactions). Use the higher figure (25 percent) if you expect your data to change often.

While we're talking about the transaction log, now is a good time to talk about the two broad categories of database systems. You can generally define a database system as either an online transaction processing (OLTP) system or a decision support system (DSS).

OLTP database systems

With OLTP systems, users are continually adding, modifying, and deleting data. For example, a database system such as the one Amazon.com uses to record customer orders is considered an OLTP system. These systems are characterized as having lots of transactions. As a result, if you are designing a database for this type of system, make sure that you define its transaction log as being at least 25 percent of the database's size — if not larger.

DSS database systems

On the other hand, as compared to an OLTP system, a DSS doesn't usually experience constant changes. For example, a company typically uses a DSS to analyze sales trends over a unit of time (such as daily, weekly, monthly, or yearly). Most companies populate the database for a DSS by importing the data from one or more databases for OLTP systems. For example, a company with retail stores all over the country would create the data in its DSS database by importing the sales databases from all of its stores. It can then use this database to analyze sales all over the country.

You typically find that the database for a DSS is updated only periodically. (It could be as often as nightly, or on a weekly or monthly basis.) Because its data doesn't change very often, you won't need nearly as large a transaction log for a DSS database. So you should create a transaction log that is only around 10 percent of the database's size.

You may see a question on sizing the transaction log for a database based on the type of database system that you're implementing (OLTP or DSS).

Optimizing Performance

One of the concepts you must grasp when we talk about databases and their transaction logs is that these types of files work your server's hard disks very hard (especially in an OLTP environment). On a very active system, your server continually reads from and writes to your database's files, which means that anything you do to improve your server's hard disk subsystem's performance will have a dramatic effect on SQL Server's overall performance!

Buy the best hardware you can afford

One of the better techniques you can use to improve your server's overall performance, and the performance of a database, is to get the fastest hard disk subsystem you can. In addition, think about how SQL Server uses a database versus its transaction log. SQL Server reads and writes to a database randomly. That is, your users won't typically retrieve data that's in one spot in the database — that data could be anywhere. On the other hand, SQL Server writes to and reads from a transaction log sequentially.

Because SQL Server uses the data and transaction log files differently, you see a big improvement if you place your database's transaction log on its own little hard disk — with nothing else on it. You may see a question or two on your exam checking to see that you know that this strategy improves performance.

Implement filegroups

Now here's where designing a database gets complicated. You can create multiple files for a database, and you can group these files into filegroups. (You can't include transaction logs in filegroups. SQL Server manages the disk space used by transaction logs separately from databases.)

You use filegroups as a technique to group database files together to make it easier to administer your database, and to improve its performance. As we've already discussed, SQL Server calls the first data file you create for a database the primary data file, and its filegroup the primary filegroup. Any additional files you create for a database are called secondary data files. You can create secondary data files within the primary filegroup, or you can create them in a user-defined filegroup.

But why would you use filegroups? Well, filegroups make managing groups of files together instead of individually possible. In addition, when you create an object and assign it to a filegroup, SQL Server distributes that object across all the files within the filegroup. Because SQL Server uses all the files within the filegroup simultaneously for reading and writing, using an object that's spread across multiple files is faster than using an object within a single file. So if you have a very large table, you can see better performance with it spread across multiple files.

The primary filegroup

SQL Server uses the primary filegroup to store the primary data file. When you create a database, SQL Server copies all the system tables from the model database and places them in this primary data file. These system tables contain information such as who can access the database (in the sysusers table), users' permissions (in sysobjects and syspermissions), and what objects you've created (in sysobjects).

One of the things you don't want to have happen to you is for this primary filegroup to run out of disk space. That's because if it runs out of space, you won't be able to add any information to your database's system tables — which pretty much means you won't be able to use your database. Either configure this filegroup to automatically grow, or make sure you place it on a hard disk on which you have plenty of available space.

The default filegroup

By default (no pun intended), SQL Server makes your primary filegroup also your default filegroup. If you create a new object and don't specify its file-group, SQL Server puts it in the default filegroup — by default (pun intended). Because the primary filegroup is so important (mostly because it contains all of your database's system tables), either designate one of your other filegroups as the default, or make sure that your primary filegroup has plenty of available disk space.

You can designate a different filegroup as the default filegroup when you create a database. You can also change the default filegroup later by using either SQL Server Enterprise Manager or the ALTER DATABASE Transact-SQL statement. Know how to change the default filegroup for the exam!

User-defined filegroups

When you create user-defined filegroups, you get better performance if you can place them on separate hard disks. Also use your user-defined filegroups to isolate the files containing tables that your users query frequently from those that your users modify frequently.

For example, assume that you're designing a database for a client with a retail Web site. You expect that your client will have approximately 2,500 sales transactions per day. Because of this volume, you want to have the client's program automatically archive the previous month's transactions to history tables. So, you plan to have two types of tables: the tables for storing the current month's sales, and tables for storing all previous months' sales. The tables in which your client stores the current month's sales will be modified frequently; in contrast, the tables in which your client stores the sales history will be queried frequently (but not modified). In this scenario, you should design your database with a minimum of two filegroups. You could use the primary filegroup for the current sales tables, and a second filegroup on a separate hard drive for storing the sales history tables.

Other advantages to filegroups

In addition to the performance advantages, you also find that filegroups make managing your databases easier. For example, if you have very large databases, you may want to back up only specific files or filegroups instead of the complete database in order to minimize backup time. You can also use filegroups to group tables together so that you can perform maintenance tasks on them at the same time.

Use RAID

Another strategy you may use to improve the performance of your databases is to implement a redundant array of independent disks (RAID) for your server's hard disk subsystem. RAID comes in levels 0, 1, 5, and 10. You can implement RAID by using either Windows 2000 Server (which is called a software RAID) or by using RAID hardware. Windows 2000 supports software RAID levels 0, 1, and 5 only. Because implementing a software RAID adds to the workload of your server, you see better performance when you implement a hardware RAID. For this reason, and because hardware RAID supports level 10, you should implement a hardware RAID instead of a software RAID.

RAID 0

RAID level 0, also called disk striping, enables your server to write (stripe) data across multiple hard disks. RAID level 0 gives you the best performance when reading from and writing to multiple disks of any of the RAID levels. But, it doesn't offer you any fault tolerance. If any of the hard disks in the array fails, you won't be able to access any of the data.

RAID 1

RAID level 1 (disk mirroring) enables your server to make a complete copy of one hard disk's data onto a second disk. RAID level 1 doesn't offer your server enhanced performance, but it does improve reliability. In this scenario, if either hard disk fails, you can still access your data. This reliability comes at a price, though, because RAID 1 requires that you duplicate your disk space. In other words, if you want to have a total of 40GB of available disk space and you plan to implement RAID 1, you must buy a total of 80GB in disk space.

RAID 5

RAID level 5, disk striping with parity, enables your server to stripe data along with parity information across multiple hard disks. This parity information makes it possible for your server to reconstruct a single disk's information in the event of a failure. In fact, even if a single disk fails, your server can continue to function. After you replace the failed disk, your server can easily reconstruct its information.

Keep in mind that you can implement RAID 5 within Windows 2000 Server, or you can use a hardware implementation. With a hardware implementation, the hard disk controller is responsible for striping the data and parity information across multiple drives. In contrast, with a software implementation, Windows 2000 Server is responsible for striping data and parity information.

RAID 5 offers you enhanced performance when reading data from your server's hard disks. However, RAID 5 is slower when it comes to writing to the server's hard disks because it must calculate and write the parity information in addition to the actual data. But the real reason most people implement RAID 5 is that it provides you not only with enhanced read performance, but also very good reliability, because your server can reconstruct a single disk in the event of a failure.

RAID 5 also minimizes the cost of reliability because you don't have to duplicate 100 percent of your disk space (as you do with mirroring). RAID 5 distributes parity information across all the disks in the array so that you can reconstruct a single disk. This reliability means that you lose only the equivalent of one disk's space when you implement RAID 5. For example, if you create a RAID 5 array consisting of four 10GB disks, your available disk space is 30GB.

RAID 10

If your budget permits, one of the more reliable and high performance strategies you can implement is RAID 10. RAID 10 is a combination of RAID 0 and RAID 1, which means that you mirror (RAID 1) a stripe set (RAID 0). The advantage to RAID 10 is that you have the high performance of striping without parity (so both reads and writes are very fast), and the reliability of mirroring. Of course, if you implement RAID 10, you're completely duplicating your disk space — so if you have eight 10GB hard disks, your available disk space is only 40GB.

RAID and filegroups

You can use RAID with or without multiple filegroups. Simply by implementing a RAID system, you make it possible for your server to stripe data across multiple disks (in much the same way that SQL Server can take advantages of files in different filegroups). Using RAID with a single filegroup instead of multiple filegroups also simplifies administration.

Recommendations

We spend a lot of time in this chapter talking about filegroups in great detail as a strategy for distributing your server's database workload across multiple disks. We must tell you, though, that in many cases you see just as big of a performance enhancement simply by implementing a RAID system — and you don't have to worry about manually distributing the filegroups across multiple disks.

So what do we recommend? You should first and foremost implement a RAID system. If you want to make backing up a very large database easier, consider implementing multiple files within a single filegroup. This strategy makes possible backing up each file separately while still keeping things simple. In addition, using multiple files enables SQL Server to take advantage of the performance enhancement of using a separate thread to read or write to each file.

We also recommend that you put your transaction log on a separate physical disk from the array containing your database. Further, if your database is critical, consider mirroring the disk on which you've placed the transaction log. As we discuss in Chapters 14 and 15, you can reconstruct a database's data by restoring your last backup and then applying the transactions in the transaction log. And if you mirror the disk containing the transaction log, reapplying the information in the transaction log is much easier!

One last thing: Keep in mind that SQL Server uses the tempdb database as its scratchpad for performing tasks such as sorting data. You can improve SQL Server's performance by putting tempdb on a separate disk subsystem from your user databases. If possible, put tempdb on a separate RAID array so that SQL Server can take advantage of data striping.

Prep Test

1 You created a database with a logical name of "sales" in SQL Server Enterprise Manager. You didn't specify a physical filename for its data file. What name did SQL Server assign to this file?

A ○ sales_db

B ○ sales_log

C ○ sales

D ○ sales_data

2 You've been asked to administer a SQL server you didn't configure. After looking at the database files in the data folder, you see that the sales database has three files: sales_data.mdf, sales_data.ndf, and sales_log.ldf. What is the sales_data.ndf file?

A ○ An archive file

B ○ A secondary data file

C ○ A backup file

D ○ A replication file

3 Your client has asked you to design a database for their sales data. After analyzing the client's needs, you've determined that you must create two tables. The width of a row in the first table is 100 bytes. The width of a row in the second table is 250 bytes. You estimate that both tables will have 100,000 rows. Based on these two tables, what is the minimum size you should assign to the database?

A ○ 4.375MB

B ○ 43MB

C ○ 3.5MB

D ○ 35MB

4 You plan to create a 20GB database for your client's point-of-sale system. How big should you make the transaction log?

A ○ 2GB

B ○ 20GB

C ○ 5GB

D ○ 3.5GB

5 You have estimated the width of a row for a table as 1,250 bytes. What should you do next in order to estimate how much disk space you will need for this table?

A ○ Calculate the number of pages the table will need.

B ○ Calculate the number of rows you can store per page.

C ○ Determine whether or not your server is configured to use mixed extents.

D ○ Multiply the total number of rows in the table by 8KB.

6 You want to optimize your server's performance for a large database. In addition, you want to minimize the amount of time it requires to back up the database. Your server contains two hard disks. Which of the following is the best solution for designing this database?

A ○ Implement disk mirroring.

B ○ Create a single data file and filegroup on one disk, and use the other disk for the transaction log.

C ○ Create two data files within a single filegroup on one disk; implement disk mirroring.

D ○ Create two data files and place each in a separate filegroup. Place the filegroups on separate hard disks.

7 You get better performance with a software disk array as compared to a hardware disk array.

A ○ True

B ○ False

8 Which RAID level offers you the best fault tolerance at the lowest price?

A ○ RAID 0

B ○ RAID 1

C ○ RAID 5

D ○ RAID 10

9 You would like to make managing your database easy while still optimizing performance. Which strategy is best?

A ○ Implement multiple files within a single filegroup.

B ○ Implement multiple files within multiple filegroups.

C ○ Use a single file and filegroup on a RAID system.

D ○ Use multiple files within a filegroup on a RAID system.

Answers

1 **D.** SQL Server Enterprise Manager automatically appends _data to a data-base's logical name when you create a database. *See "Choosing Filenames and Locations."*

2 **B.** SQL Server uses the extension .ndf for all of a database's secondary data files. *See "Choosing Filenames and Locations."*

3 **B.** You need 1,250 pages (roughly 10MB) to store the first table, and 3,125 pages (roughly 25MB) to store the second table. You must make the database at least 35MB in size. *See "Estimating the size of a database."*

4 **C.** Microsoft recommends that you make the transaction log's size equal to 25 percent of the database's size for OLTP systems. *See "Estimating the size of a transaction log."*

5 **B.** After you know the width of a table's row, your next step is to calculate how many rows SQL Server can store per page. You can then determine how many pages SQL Server needs to store the table. *See "Estimating the size of a data-base."*

6 **D.** Creating two data files in two separate filegroups enables you to optimize your server's performance (by distributing the workload across multiple files) and minimize the amount of time it takes to back up the database. *See "Implement filegroups."*

7 **B.** Software disk arrays increase the workload on your server. *See "Use RAID."*

8 **C.** RAID 5 enables you to implement fault tolerance without having to com-pletely duplicate your server's hard disk space (as in mirroring). *See "Use RAID."*

9 **D.** Using a RAID system optimizes performance, and using a single filegroup minimizes your administrative overhead. *See "Use RAID."*

Chapter 9

Creating Databases

• •

Exam Objectives

▶ Creating databases

▶ Setting database options by using the CREATE DATABASE statement

▶ Adding filegroups

▶ Configuring filegroup usage

• •

*I*n this chapter, we (at long last) show you how to create databases! We explore all the techniques you can use to create a database and filegroups within it, including the ins and outs of the CREATE DATABASE statement, using SQL Server Enterprise Manager, and working with the Create Database wizard. Along the way, we point out all the types of questions you can expect on the exam.

Quick Assessment

Creating databases

1 You create a database by using _____, _____, or _____.

2 You restrict the size of a database by using the _____ parameter when creating a database with a SQL statement.

3 You must define both _____ and _____ names for a database's data file.

4 If you don't specify megabytes or kilobytes when using the size parameter, SQL Server assumes that the number you specify is in _____.

5 You can use up to _____ characters in a database's name.

Setting database options by using the CREATE DATABASE statement

6 You can configure a database's collation settings when you create it by using the _____ keyword in the `CREATE DATABASE` statement.

Adding filegroups

7 You create a user-defined filegroup with a SQL statement by using the _____ keyword.

8 You add files to a user-defined filegroup by _____ in the SQL statement.

Configuring filegroup usage

9 True or False: You can change the default filegroup when you create a database.

Answers

1 *SQL Server Enterprise Manager, the Create Database Wizard, or the* CREATE DATABASE *statement.* Check out "Implementing a Database."

2 *Maxsize.* See "Using the CREATE DATABASE statement."

3 *Logical and physical.* Review "Using the CREATE DATABASE statement."

4 *Megabytes.* See "Using the CREATE DATABASE statement."

5 *128.* Study "Using the CREATE DATABASE statement."

6 COLLATE. Look at "Configuring a database's collation method."

7 FILEGROUP. Check out "Creating user-defined filegroups."

8 *Listing the files after the* FILEGROUP *keyword.* See "Creating user-defined filegroups."

9 *False.* Study "Creating user-defined filegroups."

Implementing a Database

SQL Server offers you three choices for creating a database: SQL Server Enterprise Manager, the Create Database Wizard, and the CREATE DATABASE Transact-SQL statement. Before you start creating a database, though, we want you to have a good understanding of the parameters you must specify during database creation. Looking at these parameters as part of the CREATE DATABASE statement is easiest, but keep in mind that you must also configure these parameters when you create a database in SQL Server Enterprise Manager or with the Create Database Wizard.

You can create up to 32,767 databases in SQL Server 2000.

Using the CREATE DATABASE *statement*

Here's the basic syntax for the CREATE DATABASE statement:

```
CREATE DATABASE database_name
ON
        PRIMARY (NAME = logical_file_name,
        FILENAME = 'physical_file_name',
        SIZE = size,
        MAXSIZE = maxsize,
        FILEGROWTH = filegrowth_increment)
LOG ON
        (NAME = logical_file_name,
        FILENAME = 'physical_file_name',
        SIZE = size,
        MAXSIZE = maxsize,
        FILEGROWTH = filegrowth_increment)
```

We capitalize the SQL keywords so that you can easily identify them; and we use lowercase, italicized letters to indicate the parameters you must specify in this statement. We also separate the various parts of the CREATE DATABASE statement to make it easier to read. As far as SQL Server goes, however, you can use upper- or lowercase letters, and you don't have to put the various pieces of the statement on separate lines. (But it's easier to read the statement if you do.)

Table 9-1 explains the basic parameters we use in the CREATE DATABASE statement.

Table 9-1	Parameters for Creating Databases
Parameter	**Use to Specify**
Database_name	The logical name of the database. You use this name to manage the database in SQL Server Enterprise Manager, and to query it in SQL Server Query Analyzer.
Logical_file_name	The logical name you want to assign to one of the database's files. If you create only one file, this file is the database's primary data file.
Physical_file_name	The actual name and location of the operating system file on the hard disk.
Size	The initial size of the database or transaction log file. You can specify this size in KB or MB.
Maxsize	The maximum size to which you want to permit the database to grow. If you don't specify a maximum size, SQL Server enables the unrestricted file growth option. Be aware that if you don't specify a maximum size, SQL Server will automatically grow the file until your server runs out of disk space.
Filegrowth_increment	The increment (either in KB, MB, or percentages) with which you want SQL Server to grow the file. By default, SQL Server sets the file growth increment to ten percent. Make sure that you configure this increment large enough so that SQL Server won't have to continually grow the file. (Growing a file increases your server's workload.)

If you don't specify megabytes or kilobytes for the size and maxsize parameters, SQL Server assumes megabytes for the number you specify. Likewise, if you don't specify megabytes, kilobytes, or percent for the file growth increment, SQL Server assumes that the number you specify is in megabytes.

In Lab 9-1, you create a database named Sales with the following parameters:

- A logical database name of Sales.
- One data file in the primary filegroup, with a logical name of sales_data and a physical filename and location of C:\Program Files\Microsoft SQL Server\MSSQL\DATA\sales_data.mdf.
- A data file with an initial size of 1MB, no maximum size, and the file growth increment of 10 percent.

✔ A transaction log with a logical name of sales_log and a physical file-name and location of C:\Program Files\Microsoft SQL Server\MSSQL\DATA\sales_log.ldf.

✔ A transaction log with an initial size of 1MB, a maximum size of 50MB, and the file growth increment of 10 percent.

Lab 9-1   Using the CREATE DATABASE Statement

1. **If necessary, log on to your server as Administrator.**

2. **From the Microsoft SQL Server menu, choose SQL Server Query Analyzer.**

3. **Log in to your SQL Server using Windows Authentication.**

   As shown in Figure 9-1, you can log in by using either your Windows 2000 user account or a SQL Server login ID.

Figure 9-1:
You must log in before you can execute a query in SQL Server Query Analyzer.

4. **In the Query pane, type the following query:**

```
CREATE DATABASE Sales
ON
    PRIMARY (NAME = sales_data,
    FILENAME = 'C:\Program Files\Microsoft SQL
        Server\MSSQL\DATA\sales_data.mdf',
    SIZE = 1MB,
    FILEGROWTH = 10%)
LOG ON
    (NAME = sales_log,
    FILENAME = 'C:\Program Files\Microsoft SQL
        Server\MSSQL\DATA\sales_log.ldf',
    SIZE = 1MB,
    MAXSIZE = 50MB,
    FILEGROWTH = 10%)
```

Separate each of the parameters for the data file and transaction log with commas. In the filename portion of the statement, make sure you put your comma on the outside of the single quote.

5. **Choose Query⇨Execute.**

   You can also press Ctrl+E or F5 to have SQL Server Query Analyzer execute the query.

6. **When SQL Server has processed your query, take a look at the Messages pane.**

   Messages appear stating that the CREATE DATABASE process allocated 1MB for both the sales_data and sales_log files.

7. **Open SQL Server Enterprise Manager.**

8. **In the contents pane, expand your server's Databases folder.**

   You should see the Sales database listed.

9. **Right-click the Sales database and choose Properties.**

   As shown in Figure 9-2, you can use the General page of the Sales database's Properties dialog box to see a lot of information about the database. For example, you can see the total size of the database (notice that the size is for both the data file and the transaction log), the amount of space still available, the number of current users, the date of the last database and transaction log backups, whether or not you defined a maintenance plan, and the collation setting for the database.

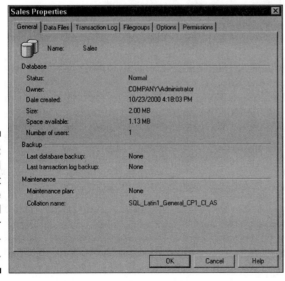

Figure 9-2:
You can find out a lot from the General page for your database.

10. **Select the Data Files tab.**

   As shown in Figure 9-3, here's where you can see a list of the files that make up the database. You can also see to what filegroup they belong, as well as each file's settings for automatic growth, file growth increment, and maximum size. Notice that because we didn't specify a maximum size for the database, your data file is configured for unrestricted file growth.

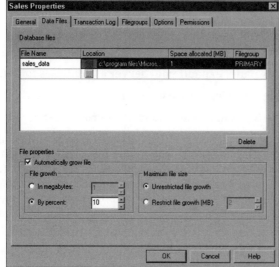

Figure 9-3:
Use the Data Files page to view and configure the data files for a database.

11. **Select the Transaction Log tab.**

   The Transaction Log page enables you to configure the settings for your database's transaction log. As you can see, this page is almost identical to the Data Files page. You can use this page to define additional transaction log files for the database and configure all the files' size properties.

12. **Select the Filegroups tab.**

   As shown in Figure 9-4, you use this page to configure a filegroup as read-only, change the default filegroup, or delete a filegroup.

13. **Click Cancel to close the Sales Properties dialog box without saving any changes.**

If you're in a hurry, you can actually create a database simply by executing the following statement:

```
CREATE DATABASE database_name
```

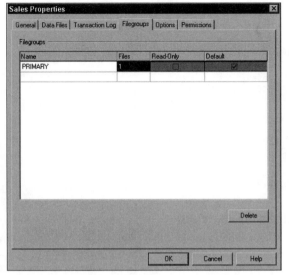

Figure 9-4:
You can
change the
default file-
group after
you create a
database.

SQL Server creates the database with the following parameters:

✔ Assigns a logical database name and data filename that's the same as the database_name you specify. The data filename is *database_name*.mdf.

✔ Configures one data file and a transaction log file. Both can automatically grow, no maximum size, and a file growth increment of ten percent.

✔ The transaction log's logical name is *database_name*_log, and its filename is *database_name*_log.ldf.

Because SQL Server automatically generates the logical name for the transaction log file by appending "_log" to the database name, you can't use a database name with more than 124 characters. If you do, the CREATE DATABASE statement fails.

Creating multiple data files

We show you the basics of the CREATE DATABASE statement in the preceding section, and now we want to show you how you can get fancy with it. First of all, what if you want to create multiple files for your database? With the CREATE DATABASE statement, you create multiple files by specifying each file's information in parentheses, and separating them by a comma. For example, to create a database with multiple files in the primary filegroup, your CREATE DATABASE statement looks like this:

```
CREATE DATABASE database_name
ON
        PRIMARY (NAME = logical_file_name#1,
        FILENAME = 'physical_file_name#1',
        SIZE = size,
        MAXSIZE = maxsize,
        FILEGROWTH = filegrowth_increment),
        (NAME = logical_file_name#2,
        FILENAME = 'physical_file_name#2',
        SIZE = size,
        MAXSIZE = maxsize,
        FILEGROWTH = filegrowth_increment)
LOG ON
        (transaction log file info)
```

Creating user-defined filegroups

What if you want to get fancy with creating databases by defining multiple filegroups? You can do so by using the FILEGROUP keyword to specify a new filegroup name within the CREATE DATABASE statement. In the following example, we use the term *file* to refer to all the information you define for a file (such as the logical and physical filenames, size, maximum size, and file growth increment). Here's how to define multiple filegroups:

```
CREATE DATABASE database_name
ON
        PRIMARY (file #1),
        (file #2)
        [,...n]
        FILEGROUP filegroup_name
                (file #3)
                [,...n]
LOG ON
        (transaction log file info)
        [,...n]
```

We use the [, . . . n] to indicate that you can specify any number of files for both the database's data files and its transaction log files. You can define up to 256 filegroups for each database. The file information you specify after the PRIMARY parameter adds files to the primary filegroup; likewise, the file information you specify after the FILEGROUP *filegroup_name* parameter adds files to a user-defined filegroup.

SQL Server automatically configures the primary filegroup as the default filegroup for the database. You can't change the default filegroup when you create the database, but you can change it later by using the ALTER DATABASE statement or by modifying the database's properties in SQL Server Enterprise Manager.

Configuring database options

You can configure a few database options as part of the CREATE DATABASE statement. For example, you can configure a database to use a different collation method from the setting you chose when you installed SQL Server. You specify the collation setting in the CREATE DATABASE statement as follows:

```
CREATE DATABASE database_name
ON
        PRIMARY (file #1)
LOG ON
        (transaction log file info)
COLLATE collation_name
```

You replace collation_name with the name of the collation settings you want to use for this database. The collation method controls how SQL Server sorts character data. For example, you might use the SQL collation name of SQL_Latin1_General_CP1_CI_AS to configure your database to use a SQL collation method (SQL), the dictionary order sorting method (Latin1_General), code page 1252 (CP1), case-insensitive (CI), and accent-sensitive (AS) settings.

The ability to configure a database's collation method separately from your server's collation settings is new in SQL Server 2000. Because it's a new feature, you may see a question about this database option on the exam.

Using SQL Server Enterprise Manager

Ahh, the good life! As we're sure you already know, the graphical Windows interface makes just about everything easier — and creating a database is no exception. Although you must specify all the same parameters that you see with the CREATE DATABASE statement when you create a database in SQL Server Enterprise Manager, you won't have to do as much typing. Lab 9-2 walks you through creating a database in SQL Server Enterprise Manager with the following properties:

- ✔ A logical database name of Accounting.

- ✔ One data file in the primary filegroup, with a logical name of accounting_data and a physical filename and location of C:\Program Files\Microsoft SQL Server\MSSQL\DATA\Accounting_data.mdf.

- ✔ The data file with an initial size of 1MB, a maximum size of 100MB, and a file growth increment of 10 percent.

- ✔ A user-defined filegroup named Filegroup1, and a secondary data file with a logical name of Acctg_history, and a physical filename and location of C:\Program Files\Microsoft SQL Server\MSSQL\DATA\ Acctg_history.ndf.

✔ The Acctg_history data file with an initial size of 1MB, a file growth increment of 10 percent, and unrestricted filegrowth (no maximum size).

✔ A transaction log with a logical name of accounting_log and a physical filename and location of C:\Program Files\Microsoft SQL Server\MSSQL\DATA\Accounting_log.ldf.

✔ The transaction log with an initial size of 1MB, a maximum size of 50MB, and the file growth increment of 10MB.

Lab 9-2   Creating a Database in SQL Server Enterprise Manager

1. **In SQL Server Enterprise Manager, right-click your server's Databases folder and choose New Database.**

2. **In the Name text box, type** Accounting.

   This assigns the logical name of Accounting to the database.

3. **Select the Data Files tab.**

   Notice that SQL Server Enterprise Manager automatically assigned the logical name of Accounting_Data and filename of *x*:\Program Files\Microsoft SQL Server\MSSQL\DATA\Accounting_Data.mdf to the primary data file for the database (*x*: represents the drive letter on which you installed SQL Server). SQL Server Enterprise Manager also set its default size to 1MB and file growth increment to 10 percent.

4. **Below File Properties, select the Restrict File Growth (MB) option and enter** 100 **in the text box.**

   This limits the Accounting_Data data file to 100MB in size.

5. **Click in the empty cell below Accounting_Data in the File Name column.**

   You use this cell to define the name of a secondary data file for the database.

6. **Type** Acctg_history.

   As shown in Figure 9-5, you see that SQL Server Enterprise Manager automatically defines the physical name and location of this file for you. If you plan to use filegroups as a strategy for distributing the database across multiple disks, you should change the default location of this file to another disk. SQL Server Enterprise Manager also configures the new file with a default size of 1MB and puts it in the primary filegroup. (You can override any of these settings.)

7. **Click in the Filegroup cell for the Accounting_history data file.**

   By typing a new name in this column, you create a new filegroup for the Accounting database.

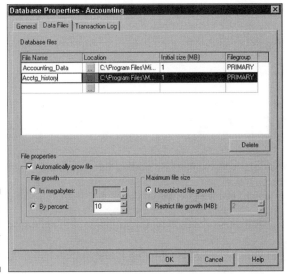

8. **Type** Filegroup1.

   You've created a user-defined filegroup and added the file Acctg_history to it. By default, SQL Server Enterprise Manager configured this file with an initial size of 1MB, a file growth increment of 10 percent, and no maximum size.

9. **Select the Transaction Log tab.**

   SQL Server Enterprise Manager automatically defined the transaction log with a name of Accounting_log.ldf, put it in the Data directory, an initial size of 1MB, and a file growth increment of 10 percent.

10. **Below File Properties, set the maximum size of the transaction log to 50MB.**

11. **Click OK to create the database.**

    You now have a database named Accounting that consists of two data files in two different filegroups, plus a transaction log file. Because each file has the default size of 1MB, your Accounting database is 3MB in size.

Using the Create Database Wizard

Now here's where creating a database gets even easier. If you find completing the information in a dialog box overwhelming, the Create Database Wizard is for you! The Create Database Wizard walks you through creating a database step-by-step. You launch the wizard within SQL Server Enterprise Manager by choosing Tools➪Wizards. This opens the Select Wizard dialog box, and you can choose wizards from the Database, Data Transformation Services, Management, and Replication categories. To launch the wizard, expand the Database category, select the Create Database Wizard, and click OK. This wizard then walks you through specifying the database name, its file locations, sizes, and file growth properties.

Configuring a database's collation method

By default, SQL Server assigns your server's collation setting to any new databases you create unless you specify otherwise. You can assign a different collation setting from that of your server to any new database regardless of which method you use to create the database.

Keeping Track of Your Databases

The system tables you see both in your user-defined databases as well as the master database contain information called metadata. If you'll excuse the redundancy, metadata is data about data. What we mean is that metadata is all the information that keeps track of the data on your server.

For example, each time you create a database, SQL Server updates the master database with information about your new database. SQL Server uses tables such as sysdatabases and sysaltfiles to track the name and location of the database's files, as well as each file's size. Microsoft refers to the information SQL Server stores in the master database as the *system catalog*. Table 9-2 describes the tables SQL Server uses most often in the master database.

Table 9-2	System Catalog Tables
Table Name	*Enables SQL Server to Track*
Syslogins	The login IDs on your server
Sysmessages	Both system error and warning messages
Sysdatabases	All of your databases

Because creating a database modifies the master database, always back up the master database after you create, modify, or delete a database.

Microsoft refers to the system tables within each of your user databases as the database catalog. These tables track database-specific information, as described in Table 9-3.

Table 9-3	Database Catalog Tables
Table Name	*Enables SQL Server to Track*
Sysusers	Which of your server's login IDs can access the database.
Sysobjects	The objects you have defined within the database.

Never modify the system tables in either the master database or any user database directly. If you do, SQL Server may not be able to recover properly if you have a server failure.

Using stored procedures

So how do you go about viewing metadata? One way is to use stored procedures. SQL Server includes a few stored procedures you can use in SQL Server Query Analyzer to view information about your databases, their files, and filegroups. (Of course, you can see the same information just by going into SQL Server Enterprise Manager as well.) Table 9-4 describes these stored procedures.

Table 9-4	Stored Procedures for Viewing Database Information
Stored Procedure	*Enables You to View*
sp_helpfile	Information about the files that make up your current database.
sp_helpfile *file_name*	Information about a specific database file.
sp_helpfilegroup	The names of the filegroups in your current database, and the number of files each filegroup contains.
sp_helpfilegroup *filegroup*	Information about a specific filegroup.
sp_helpdb	Information about all the databases on your server. This information includes the database name, size, owner, database ID, creation date, and the status of the database.
sp_helpdb *database_name*	Information about a specific database.
sp_spaceused	The amount of disk space a database is using.
sp_spaceused *object_name*	The amount of space in a database a particular object (such as a table) is using.

These stored procedures are ones that Microsoft considers essential for viewing information about databases, their files, and filegroups. Make sure that you know the names and functions of all of these stored procedures for the exam.

Using information schema views

SQL Server includes several views that you can use to retrieve metadata from your server. We describe some of the information schema views in Table 9-5.

Table 9-5	Information Schema Views
View Name	*Enables You to View*
INFORMATION_SCHEMA.COLUMNS	A list of all the columns defined in the tables within your current database
INFORMATION_SCHEMA.TABLES	A list of all the tables within your current database
INFORMATION_SCHEMA.TABLES_PRIVELEGES	Information about the security configured on the tables in your current database

Prep Test

1 **How many databases can you create in SQL Server 2000?**

A ○ 512

B ○ 1,024

C ○ Unlimited

D ○ 32,767

2 **You want to create a database named Test with all the default parameters for a database. What's the easiest way to create this database by using the** CREATE DATABASE **statement?**

A ○ CREATE DATABASE test

B ○ CREATE DATABASE test
```
   ON
       PRIMARY (NAME = test)
```

C ○ CREATE DATABASE test WITH DEFAULTS

D ○ CREATE DATABASE test
```
   ON
       PRIMARY (NAME = test_data,
       FILENAME = 'test.mdf')
   LOG ON
       (NAME = test_log,
       FILENAME = 'test.ldf')
```

3 **You can configure SQL Server to automatically grow a database file in which of the following increments? (Choose all that apply.)**

A ❑ Percent

B ❑ Kilobytes

C ❑ Megabytes

D ❑ Gigabytes

4 **What happens if you execute this statement:** CREATE DATABASE Inventory**?**

A ○ You receive an error message.

B ○ Your database has a logical name of Inventory_Data.

C ○ SQL Server names the transaction log Inventory_log.ldf.

D ○ SQL Server configures both the data and transaction log files with a maximum size of 50MB.

5 Which of the following methods enable you to specify a different collation method for a database when you create the database?

A ○ SQL Server Enterprise Manager

B ○ CREATE DATABASE

C ○ SQL Server Profiler

D ○ The Create Database Wizard

6 You are currently using the Sales database in SQL Server Query Analyzer. You want to view information about the files in the Accounting database. Which stored procedure should you use?

A ○ sp_helpdb

B ○ sp_helpfile

C ○ sp_helpfile Accounting

D ○ sp_helpdb Accounting

7 Which of the system databases does SQL Server modify when you create a new database? (Choose all that apply.)

A ❑ Model

B ❑ Master

C ❑ Tempdb

D ❑ None

8 If you don't specify otherwise, SQL Server sets your database files' file growth increment to what value?

A ○ 10MB

B ○ 10 percent

C ○ 25MB

D ○ 25 percent

Answers

1 **D.** You can create a maximum of 32,767 databases in SQL Server 2000 (but we hope you don't need that many!). *See "Implementing a Database."*

2 **A.** The quickest and easiest way for you to create a database is to execute the statement `CREATE DATABASE database_name`. SQL Server then creates both the data and transaction log files for your database, and uses the default database options. Study "Using the `CREATE DATABASE` *statement*."

3 **A, B,** and **C.** You can configure the automatic growth increment for a database's files in kilobyte, megabyte, or percent values. *See "Using the* `CREATE DATABASE` *statement."*

4 **C.** SQL Server assumes that you want to use all the default settings with this statement, so it automatically defines the name for the database's transaction log as *database_name*_log.ldf. *See "Using the* `CREATE DATABASE` *statement."*

5 **A, B,** and **D.** One of the new changes in SQL Server 2000 is that you can define different collation settings for databases than that of your server. *See "Configuring a database's collation method."*

6 **D.** Because the Accounting database isn't your current database, you must explicitly specify that you want to view its files. This means that you must use the `sp_helpdb` Accounting command. (You can use `sp_helpfile` to view information only about your current database's files.) *See "Keeping Track of Your Databases."*

7 **B.** SQL Server records all the information about your databases in the master database. *See "Keeping Track of Your Databases."*

8 **B.** SQL Server automatically sets your data and transaction log files' file growth increment to ten percent. *Study "Using the* `CREATE DATABASE` *statement."*

Chapter 10

Managing Databases

• •

Exam Objectives

▶ Setting database options by using the ALTER DATABASE statement

▶ Configuring database options for performance

▶ Expanding and shrinking a database

▶ Adding filegroups

▶ Attaching and detaching databases

• •

*A*fter you create a database (see Chapter 9), you can make changes to its configuration by using either the ALTER DATABASE statement or SQL Server Enterprise Manager. You can change just about anything about your database, including:

✔ Modifying database options. For example, you can configure a database as read-only or single user.

✔ Changing the current size, file growth increment, and maximum file size of any data file or transaction log.

✔ Adding a new file or deleting any file except the primary data file and the first transaction log file.

✔ Creating a new filegroup and adding files to it. (You can't add any of the existing files to the new filegroup; you must create new files to add them to the filegroup.)

✔ Deleting a filegroup.

✔ Changing the default filegroup.

In this chapter, we explore many of the settings you can use to configure a database. And because we know your database needs can change, we show you how to both increase and decrease the size of a database. We also review how you can easily move a database from one server to another or one disk to another by detaching and attaching the database.

Quick Assessment

Setting database options by using the ALTER DATABASE statement

1 The _____ option enables only the members of the db_owner database role, dbcreator server role, and sysadmin server role to access the database.

2 You use the _____ option to reconfigure a database for access by any user.

Configuring database options for performance

3 Use the _____ option to minimize the amount of disk space used by a database's transaction log.

Expanding and shrinking a database

4 You can configure SQL Server to automatically grow a file by using the _____ clause with the ALTER DATABASE statement.

5 If you haven't enabled a database to automatically grow, you can increase its size by adding _____ data files.

6 You can configure SQL Server to automatically decrease the size of a database by enabling the _____ database option.

7 You have deleted several thousand rows from a table in one of your database's files. You haven't configured SQL Server to automatically decrease the size of this database. Use the _____ command to reclaim the free space in this one file.

8 True or False: You can delete a database even if it's open as long as it isn't participating in replication.

Adding filegroups

9 You can add a new filegroup to a database with the ALTER DATABASE statement by using the _____ clause.

Attaching and detaching databases

10 You can attach a database by using either the _____ utility or _____ stored procedure.

Answers

1 `RESTRICTED_USER`. **Review "State options."**

2 `MULTI_USER`. **See "State options."**

3 `RECOVERY SIMPLE`. **See "Recovery options."**

4 `MAXSIZE = UNLIMITED`. **Review "Increasing the size of a database."**

5 *Secondary.* **See "Increasing the size of a database."**

6 `AUTO_SHRINK`. **See "Auto options."**

7 `DBCC SHRINKFILE`. **See "Decreasing the size of a database."**

8 *False.* **Review "Deleting a Database."**

9 `ADD FILEGROUP` *filegroup_name*. **See "Increasing the size of a database."**

10 *SQL Server Enterprise Manager or* `sp_attach_db`. **Study "Detaching and Attaching Databases."**

Changing Database Options

You can use either SQL Server Enterprise Manager or the ALTER DATABASE statement to change the options on a database. SQL Server 2000 divides these options into five categories: Auto, Cursor, Recovery, SQL, and State. We explain these categories and their most common options first, and then we move on to how to modify them.

You can expect to see a question or two on the Auto, Recovery, SQL, and State database options, but not Cursor options. For this reason, we don't review the Cursor options you can configure.

Auto options

You use the Auto options to control actions SQL Server performs automatically. Table 10-1 describes the most common Auto options you might configure.

We use the SQL keywords for the option names in this table. You must use these keywords when configuring database options by using the ALTER DATABASE statement.

Table 10-1	Auto Database Options
Option	**Enables You To**
AUTO_CLOSE	Specify whether or not you want SQL Server to automatically shut down a database when it's no longer in use. This option is disabled by default.
AUTO_SHRINK	Configure SQL Server to automatically and periodically decrease the size of the database.

Recovery options

You use the Recovery options to control how much data SQL Server records in a database's transaction log. In addition, these options control whether or not SQL Server deletes committed transactions from the transaction log. We describe the Recovery options in Table 10-2.

Table 10-2	Recovery Database Options
Option	*Enables You To*
RECOVERY FULL	Configure SQL Server to record all database actions in the transaction log, including bulk imports of data. This is the default option for all versions of SQL Server 2000 except the Desktop Edition.
RECOVERY BULK_LOGGED	Enable SQL Server to record all normal database transactions (such as INSERT, UPDATE, or DELETE) in the transaction log, but only minimal information about bulk imports.
RECOVERY SIMPLE	Configure SQL Server to clear the transaction log after it commits transactions to the database. This is the default Recovery option for the SQL Server 2000 Desktop Edition.

For the exam, make sure you know how each of these Recovery options affects backing up and restoring a database. The Full Recovery option enables you to recover a database by restoring your last full backup of the database, restoring any subsequent transaction log backups, and then applying any changes in the transaction log that have occurred since your last backup. The Bulk Logged Recovery option also enables you to recover a database by restoring your last full backup of the database, any subsequent transaction log backups, and any changes since your last backup. However, because bulk operations are only minimally logged, you run the risk of losing the changes made during bulk data operations. With the Simple Recovery option, you can recover a database only by restoring your last full backup of the database.

SQL options

Although SQL Server is based on the ANSI standard for the structured query language that was updated in 1992 (and thus called SQL-92), it isn't compliant with all the standard's requirements. For example, SQL Server handles null values in comparison statements differently than the SQL-92 standard specifies. You can use database options to configure SQL Server 2000 to comply with the ANSI SQL-92 standards.

Although many options exist that you can turn on for strict ANSI SQL-92 compliance, Table 10-3 describes the two options you need to make sure you know for the exam.

Table 10-3	SQL Database Options
Option	*Enables You To*
ANSI_NULL_DEFAULT	Specify whether or not any new columns you define for existing or new tables support nulls by default. Default value is off.
ANSI_NULLS	Control how SQL Server evaluates comparisons to a null value. If you turn on this option, any comparisons to a null value are null; if you turn off the ANSI_NULLS option, any comparisons to a null value are true. Default value is off.

State options

Last but not least, the State database options make it possible for you to control who can access your database — and what they can do. For example, you may configure your database as read-only if you want to prevent users from changing the data. We describe the State options in Table 10-4.

Table 10-4	State Database Options
Option	*Enables You To*
OFFLINE	Configure SQL Server to perform a complete shutdown of the database.
ONLINE	Configure SQL Server to open the database and make it available for use.
READ_ONLY	Restrict users' access to only reading the database. Users can't make any changes.
READ_WRITE	Enable users to both read and make changes to a database.
SINGLE_USER	Permit only one user to access the database at a time.
RESTRICTED_USER	Permit only the members of the db_owner database role or the dbcreator and sysadmin server roles to access the database.
MULTI_USER	Permit all users to access the database (provided they have the necessary permissions).

The ALTER DATABASE *statement*

One of the techniques you can use to change a database's options is to use the ALTER DATABASE statement. Use the following syntax:

```
ALTER DATABASE database_name
SET option
```

Depending on the option you're configuring, you may or may not have to include the keywords ON or OFF. For example, here's how you configure the pubs database as read-only:

```
ALTER DATABASE pubs
SET READ_ONLY
```

The sp_dboption stored procedure

You can also use the sp_dboption stored procedure to change a database's options. Use the following syntax:

```
sp_dboption 'database_name', 'option_name', 'option_value'
```

Notice that you must specify a value for an option (such as ON or OFF). For example, to configure the Accounting database as read-only, use the following statement:

```
sp_dboption 'Accounting', 'READ_ONLY', 'ON'
```

Using sp_dboption with just the database name and option name enables you to only view the current setting for that option, not change it. For example, if you execute the following statement, SQL Server displays the current setting for the read-only parameter:

```
sp_dboption 'Accounting', 'READ_ONLY'
```

SQL Server Enterprise Manager

You can also modify a database's options by using SQL Server Enterprise Manager. Simply right-click the database, choose Properties, and then click the Options tab. As shown in Figure 10-1, you can configure many of the database options by using the database's Properties dialog box. However, you can't configure all of them. For those that you can't configure in SQL Server Enterprise Manager, use the ALTER DATABASE statement instead.

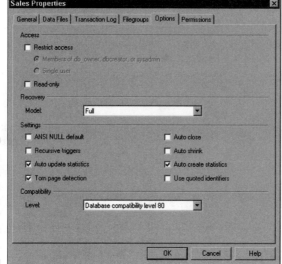

Figure 10-1:
Configuring
a database's
options in
SQL Server
Enterprise
Manager.

Managing Database Size

As a database administrator, you need to carefully monitor the amount of space available in your databases and their transaction logs. If you run out of free space within a database, and you haven't configured it for automatic growth, your users won't be able to add any data to the database. Conversely, if you delete a lot of information from a database, you won't need as much space in the database's files as before. So you need to also make sure that you delete unused space in a database.

Increasing the size of a database

You can increase the size of your databases and their transaction logs by using any of the following methods:

✔ Automatically, by enabling the automatic growth option for the database, transaction log, or both.

✔ Manually, by increasing the size of the database's data file(s) and transaction log.

✔ Manually, by adding secondary data files or additional transaction log files.

Implementing automatic file growth

If you don't configure a data file or transaction log for automatic file growth when you create a database, you can always come back later and enable this option by using either SQL Server Enterprise Manager or the ALTER DATABASE SQL statement. You enable automatic file growth in SQL Server Enterprise Manager by using the following steps:

1. **Right-click the database and choose Properties.**

2. **Click either the Data Files or Transaction Log tab.**

3. **Select a file, and then choose Unrestricted File Growth.**

4. **Click OK to save your changes.**

To enable automatic file growth on a database's file by using the ALTER DATABASE statement, use the following syntax:

```
ALTER DATABASE database_name
        MODIFY FILE
        (NAME = logical_file_name,
        MAXSIZE = UNLIMITED)
```

Notice that you can use this same syntax for either a data file or a transaction log file by replacing the *logical_file_name* with the name of the appropriate file. Lab 10-1 steps you through changing the Accounting_Data file for the Accounting database to support unlimited file growth.

Lab 10-1   Enabling Automatic File Growth

1. **Open SQL Server Query Analyzer and log in to your server with Windows authentication.**

2. **In SQL Server Query Analyzer, execute the following query:**

   ```
   sp_helpdb accounting
   ```

   As shown in Figure 10-2, the maxsize for the Accounting_Data file is 102,400KB (which is 100MB).

3. **Now execute this query to change the maximum size for the Accounting_Data file:**

   ```
   ALTER DATABASE Accounting
   MODIFY FILE
   (NAME = Accounting_Data,
   MAXSIZE = UNLIMITED)
   ```

   This statement changes the maximum size for the Accounting_Data file to unlimited.

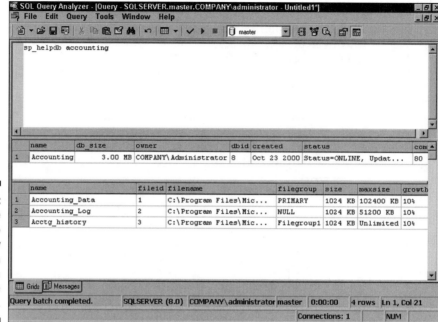

Figure 10-2:
Use
sp_helpdb
to view
information
about a
database
and its files.

4. **Use the** sp_helpdb **stored procedure again to view information about the files in the Accounting database.**

You have configured the Accounting_Data file for unlimited file growth.

If you decide to enable unlimited file growth, make sure that you have enough available disk space. Also monitor their sizes so that you know if your server is about to run out of disk space (before it happens). Consider setting a maximum size on your database's files if you don't have a lot of free disk space.

Manually increasing file sizes

You can increase the current sizes of any of the data and transaction log files that make up a database by using either ALTER DATABASE or by modifying the database's properties in SQL Server Enterprise Manager. Use the following syntax to increase a file's size with ALTER DATABASE:

```
ALTER DATABASE database_name
    MODIFY FILE
    (NAME = logical_file_name,
    SIZE = new_size)
```

Adding secondary data and transaction log files

The last technique you can use to increase a database's size is to add files to it. You do so by adding secondary data files, transaction log files, or both.

You can add these files in SQL Server Enterprise Manager, or by using ALTER DATABASE. Use the following syntax to add a new data file:

```
ALTER DATABASE database_name
       ADD FILE
       (NAME = logical_file_name,
       FILENAME = 'physical_file_name',
       SIZE = size,
       MAXSIZE = maxsize,
       FILEGROWTH = filegrowth_increment)
       [TO FILEGROUP filegroup_name]
```

The square brackets in SQL syntax indicate that a clause is optional.

You don't have to specify a filegroup as part of this statement. If you don't specify a filegroup, and the database has multiple filegroups, SQL Server creates the new file in the default filegroup. You can create a new filegroup with the ALTER DATABASE statement by adding the following clause:

```
ADD FILEGROUP filegroup_name
```

If you want to add another transaction log file, use this syntax:

```
ALTER DATABASE database_name
       ADD LOG FILE
       (NAME = logical_file_name,
       FILENAME = 'physical_file_name',
       SIZE = size,
       MAXSIZE = maxsize,
       FILEGROWTH = filegrowth_increment)
```

Decreasing the size of a database

You've deleted a bunch of rows from your database's tables, and now its files are too big. So now what do you do? You have a couple of alternatives:

- Configure SQL Server to automatically shrink the database.
- Manually shrink the database or individual files.

Automatically shrinking a database

SQL Server can automatically shrink a database if you enable the auto-shrink option. You can enable this option by using either SQL Server Enterprise Manager, ALTER DATABASE, or the sp_dboption stored procedure.

After you enable this option, SQL Server automatically shrinks the database's data and transaction log files whenever they have more than 25 percent free space. SQL Server shrinks the database in the background so that it doesn't have any effect on your users.

You can't change the percentage of free space required to trigger SQL Server to shrink the database. You may see a question or two about how auto-shrink works and this percentage on the exam.

Manually shrinking a database

You manually shrink a database by using either database consistency checker (DBCC) commands or SQL Server Enterprise Manager. SQL Server shrinks a database by removing free space. On the other hand, SQL Server shrinks a transaction log by first removing the inactive portion of the log. If that doesn't reduce the transaction log enough, SQL Server will tell you it can't shrink the log any further — and then provide you with a message stating what steps you should take to reduce the log's size.

You can use the DBCC SHRINKDATABASE command to shrink all the database's data and transaction log files; use DBCC SHRINKFILE to shrink individual data or transaction log files. With the DBCC SHRINKDATABASE command, you can optionally specify the target percentage of free space you want to remain in the database after you shrink it. If you don't specify a target percentage, SQL Server removes all the free space from the database. In the following example, SQL Server attempts to shrink all the files in the Accounting database so that it has 25 percent free space:

```
DBCC SHRINKDATABASE (Accounting, 25)
```

You can use the DBCC SHRINKFILE command to shrink specific files, either by removing all the available free space or shrinking them to a specific target size. The target size you specify shouldn't be smaller than the amount of space in use in the file, and you must specify it in megabytes. If you specify a size that's smaller than the database's actual data, SQL Server shrinks the database as much as it can.

Use the DBCC SHRINKFILE command along with the EMPTYFILE option to force SQL Server to move all the objects in a secondary data file to other files in the same filegroup. You use this option when you want to delete a data file from a database.

SQL Server Enterprise Manager provides you with the easiest way to shrink a database. You can do so simply by right-clicking the database, and then choosing All Tasks➪Shrink Database. This opens the Shrink Database dialog box shown in Figure 10-3. Notice that you can use this dialog box to shrink the database based on a percentage, schedule the shrinking process to occur at off-peak hours, or shrink specific files instead of the whole database.

With all the methods we talk about in this chapter for shrinking a database, SQL Server shrinks the database or specific files by removing only the unused pages at the end of these files. Notice that the Shrink Database dialog box enables you to specify that you want SQL Server to move pages to the beginning of the file before shrinking the database. This option enables SQL Server to fill up pages that aren't completely full with data so that it can further shrink the database. Just be aware that moving these pages is a resource-intensive operation, so it can have a big impact on your server's performance!

Figure 10-3:
Use the
Shrink
Database
dialog box
to shrink a
database or
specific
files.

Deleting a Database

You can delete a database by using either SQL Server Enterprise Manager or the DROP DATABASE SQL statement. Deleting a database removes it from your server's list of active databases, and deletes all of its files from your server's hard disk. You can't delete a database if any of the following conditions are valid:

- ✔ It's in the process of being restored.
- ✔ The database is open and in use by a user.
- ✔ You've published one of its tables for replication purposes.

In addition, you can't delete any of the system databases (such as master). Keep in mind that when you delete the database, any login IDs you configured to use this database for their default database will no longer have a default database.

Using the DROP DATABASE statement

Use the following syntax to delete a database in SQL Server Query Analyzer:

```
DROP DATABASE database_name
```

SQL Server assumes you know what you're doing when you execute this statement. It doesn't ask you to confirm that you want to delete the database — it just deletes it. So always make sure that you really want to delete the database before executing the DROP DATABASE statement!

Using SQL Server Enterprise Manager

You delete a database in SQL Server Enterprise Manager by right-clicking it and choosing Delete from the shortcut menu. In contrast to its equivalent SQL statement, this action does ask you to confirm that you want to delete the database. As shown in Figure 10-4, it also prompts you to confirm that you want to delete the entire backup and restore history for this database from your server. This doesn't delete the actual backups; instead, it deletes the information in the system tables that tracks your backups of the database.

Figure 10-4:
Deleting a
database in
SQL Server
Enterprise
Manager.

Detaching and Attaching Databases

SQL Server enables you to detach and attach a database as a technique for moving a database. This technique enables you to easily move a database from one disk to another, or even from one SQL server to another. And using detach/attach rather than backing up and restoring a database is a lot faster. Perform the following steps to move a database by detaching and attaching it:

1. **Detach the database from the source server.**

2. **Move the database's files to their new location.**

3. **Attach the database.**

Detaching a database

One of the new features in SQL Server 2000 is that you can now detach a database by using SQL Server Enterprise Manager. (In SQL Server 7.0, you detached a database by using the sp_detach_db stored procedure.) By the way, when you detach a database from a server, SQL Server doesn't delete any of the database's files — it just removes the information about the database from its system tables. Lab 10-2 shows you how to detach a database within SQL Server Enterprise Manager.

1. **Open SQL Server Enterprise Manager.**

2. **In your server's Databases folder, right-click the database you want to detach and choose All Tasks➪Detach Database.**

   As shown in Figure 10-5, SQL Server Enterprise Manager displays a Detach Database dialog box that you can use to verify that no users are currently using the database. (You shouldn't detach a database if anyone is using it!) You can also have SQL Server update the database's statistics before it detaches the database. SQL Server uses these statistics to determine whether processing a query by using a table's indexes or by performing a table scan is faster.

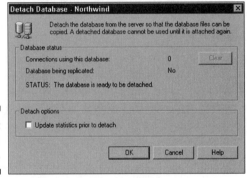

Figure 10-5:
Detaching a
database.

3. **Click OK to detach the database.**

4. **Click OK again to confirm the message stating that SQL Server successfully detached the database.**

5. **Open Windows Explorer.**

   Double-check that the database's files are still on your server.

6. **Access the C:\Program Files\Microsoft SQL Server\MSSQL\Data folder.**

7. **Take a look at the contents of the Data folder.**

   You should see both the database's primary data file and its transaction log file.

8. **Close Windows Explorer.**

After you detach a database, your next step is to move its files to their new location. Make sure you move all files, including the primary data file, any secondary data files, and the transaction log files.

Attaching a database

Like its detach counterpart, you can attach a new database within SQL Server Enterprise Manager as well. You need the name and physical location of the database's primary data file in order to attach it. You can also attach a database by using the sp_attach_db stored procedure. We walk you through attaching a database in Lab 10-3. (For this lab, we assume that you completed Lab 10-2 and have detached a database.)

Lab 10-3	Attaching a Database in SQL Server Enterprise Manager

1. **In SQL Server Enterprise Manager, right-click your server's Databases folder and choose All Tasks⇨Attach Database.**

   The Attach Databases dialog box appears. You must specify the name of the primary database file in order to attach the database.

2. **Click the Browse button (...).**

   SQL Server Enterprise Manager opens the Browse for Existing File dialog box. You can use this dialog box to locate the primary data file for the database you want to attach.

3. **Browse to the C:\Program Files\Microsoft SQL Server\MSSQL\Data and select the database's primary data file (an .mdf file).**

4. **Click OK.**

   As shown in Figure 10-6, you now see a list of the files in the database, as well as the name of the database and its owner. By default, SQL Server assumes you want to attach the database with its original name. You can change this name by modifying it in the Attach As text box.

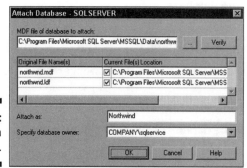

Figure 10-6:
Attaching a
database.

5. **Click OK to attach the database.**

6. **When the attach process is complete, click OK again to close the message box that states it completed successfully.**

    The database is again in your server's Databases folder.

You can attach a database to SQL Server 2000 even if the collation setting used by that database differs from that of the server.

Prep Test

1 Which of the following utilities can you use to change a database's options? (Choose all that apply.)

A ❑ SQL Server Enterprise Manager

B ❑ SQL Server Profiler

C ❑ SQL Server Setup

D ❑ ALTER DATABASE

2 Which database option enables SQL Server to shut down the database when it's no longer in use?

A ○ AUTO_SHUTDOWN

B ○ OFFLINE

C ○ AUTO_CLOSE

D ○ None. SQL Server automatically shuts down a database when it isn't in use.

3 Which database recovery option conserves the most disk space?

A ○ RECOVERY FULL

B ○ RECOVERY BULK_LOGGED

C ○ RECOVERY SIMPLE

D ○ RECOVERY MINIMAL

4 You configured your database with the RECOVERY FULL database option. You just discovered that one of your database files is corrupt. What information should you restore to recover this database? (Choose all that apply.)

A ❑ Your last full backup of the database

B ❑ All backups of the transaction log since your last full database backup

C ❑ Any new changes in the transaction log that occurred since your last backup

D ❑ Your last full backup of your entire server

5 You configured your database with the RECOVERY SIMPLE database option. One of your users deleted all the rows in a table by mistake. You now want to restore the database. What information should you restore to recover this database?

A ○ Your last full backup of the database

B ○ Your last backup of the transaction log

C ○ Any new changes in the transaction log that occurred since your last backup

D ○ Your last full backup of your entire server

6 You have turned on the `ANSI_NULLS` database option. What happens when you execute the following statement?

```
SELECT *
FROM titles
WHERE price = NULL
```

A ○ You receive an error message.

B ○ SQL Server processes the query successfully and displays all rows in the titles table that have `NULL` in the price column.

C ○ SQL Server processes the query successfully and displays no rows in the result set.

D ○ SQL Server processes the query successfully and displays all the rows in the titles table in the result set, regardless of whether or not they have `NULL` in the price column.

7 You plan to perform maintenance on a database. You want to restrict access to the database to only the system administrator. What option should you enable?

A ○ `OFFLINE`

B ○ `READ_ONLY`

C ○ `SINGLE_USER`

D ○ `RESTRICTED_USER`

8 Which of the following techniques enables SQL Server to automatically increase the size of a database?

A ○ Enabling the `AUTO_GROW` database option

B ○ Setting the database files' maximum size to Unlimited

C ○ Increasing the file growth increment to 100%

D ○ Executing the `sp_setmaxsize` stored procedure

9 When you enable the `AUTO_SHRINK` database option, at what point does SQL Server shrink the database?

A ○ Whenever the server's CPU is idle

B ○ When any of the database's files has more than 25% free space

C ○ When the free space in a file reaches the percentage you specified when you enabled the `AUTO_SHRINK` option

D ○ When you execute the `DBCC SHRINKDATABASE` command

10 You are attempting to delete a database but are receiving an error message. What might be the problem? (Choose all that apply.)

A ❏ The database is currently in use.

B ❏ The database is configured with the read-only option.

C ❏ One of its tables is currently participating in replication.

D ❏ You are currently restoring the database.

11 **You currently have two databases on your SQL server: Accounting and Sales. Because of their workload, you have decided to install a second server and move one of the databases to this server. What is the easiest way to move the database?**

A ○ Back up the database on the source server and restore it to the new server.

B ○ Detach the database from the source server, move its files, and attach it on the new server.

C ○ Use the bulk copy program to extract the data from the source server and import it on the new server.

D ○ Use SQL Server Setup to transfer the database.

Answers

1 **A** and **D.** You can use both SQL Server Enterprise Manager and the ALTER DATABASE statement to change a database's options. You can also use the sp_dboption stored procedure to change a database's options. *See "Changing Database Options."*

2 **C.** You enable the AUTO_CLOSE option when you want SQL Server to shut down the database after the last user disconnects from that database. *Review "Auto options."*

3 **C.** When you enable the RECOVERY SIMPLE database option, SQL Server automatically clears committed transactions from the transaction log. *See "Recovery options."*

4 **A, B,** and **C.** When you enable the RECOVERY FULL database option, SQL Server keeps all the transactions in the transaction log, even after it has committed them. This means that you can recover a database by first restoring your last full backup, then restoring your last transaction log backup, and then restoring any of the subsequent transactions in the transaction log. *Study "Recovery options."*

5 **A.** Because you enabled the RECOVERY SIMPLE option, your only choice is to restore your last full backup of the database. *See "Recovery options."*

6 **C.** When you turn on the ANSI_NULLS option, your server evaluates any equivalencies to NULL as null. As a result, you won't see any rows in the result set. You also don't see any error messages. *Study "SQL options."*

7 **D.** Use the RESTRICTED_USER option to configure a database for use only by the system administrator. *See "State options."*

8 **B.** You enable automatic file growth for a database by setting its files' maximum size to unlimited. *See "Increasing the size of a database."*

9 **B.** SQL Server shrinks the database only when any of its files has 25 percent or more free space. *See "Decreasing the size of a database."*

10 **A, C,** and **D.** You can't delete a database if it's in use or currently being restored, or if one of its tables is published for replication. *Study "Deleting a Database."*

11 **B.** Use detach to remove the database from the source server, and then attach to add the database to the new server. *See "Detaching and Attaching Databases."*

Chapter 11

Creating and Managing Database Objects

• •

Exam Objectives

▶ Creating database objects
▶ Managing database objects

• •

*T*he heart and soul of any SQL Server installation is the database objects. You use these objects to store data and ensure the accuracy of that data. You use indexes to optimize your server's performance when processing queries. And you use objects such as stored procedures to reduce the development time for custom applications.

In this chapter, we explore the fundamental objects you can create in a database. Study this chapter carefully, because you can expect to see several questions on your exam about both creating and managing these objects.

Quick Assessment

Creating
database
objects

1 You use _____ to speed up SQL Server's searches of tables.

2 An object's fully qualified name consists of these four components: _____, _____, _____, and _____.

3 You are defining the columns for a table. You want a column to store numbers from 1 to 9,999. You should use the _____ data type.

4 You can use a(n) _____ constraint to make sure that a column always contains data, even if users don't enter data into that column when they add a row.

5 You can create up to _____ indexes for a table.

Managing
database
objects

6 You must delete all _____ and _____ that refer to a column before you can delete a column from a table.

7 You can re-establish an index's fill factor by using the DBCC _____ statement.

8 You can force SQL Server to recompile a stored procedure by using the _____ stored procedure.

Answers

1 *Indexes.* See "Reviewing Database Object Types."

2 *The server, database, owner, and object names.* Check out "Referring to Database Objects."

3 *Integer.* See "Implementing Tables."

4 *Default.* See "Implementing constraints."

5 *250.* See "Implementing Indexes."

6 *Indexes and constraints.* See "Managing tables."

7 `DBREINDEX`. Study "Managing indexes."

8 `sp_recompile`. See "Managing stored procedures."

Reviewing Database Object Types

Before we look at creating and configuring database objects, we want to take a moment to review the types of objects you can create. Table 11-1 describes these objects for you.

Table 11-1	Types of Database Objects
Object	*Enables You To*
Constraint	Specify rules for validating data entry. You can use constraints to make sure that your users enter accurate data into a column.
Index	Speed up searches of tables. SQL Server can retrieve the results of a query by searching an index instead of scanning a table row-by-row.
Stored procedure	Save a series of SQL statements. You might think of a user-defined stored procedure as a small program that's stored on your SQL server.
Table	Define the columns of information you want to store for a specific entity such as customers, inventory, or sales information. You store a table's information in rows.
Trigger	Configure SQL Server to perform a series of SQL statements when a user adds, deletes, or modifies the contents of a table.
View	Define the specific columns within a table (or tables) you want users to see. For example, you may use a view on an employee table to enable users to see only an employee's address information and not her salary.

Referring to Database Objects

When you access database objects (such as in stored procedures, programs and queries), you must refer to those objects by using either a fully qualified name or a partial name. An object's fully qualified name consists of four components:

- ✔ The name of your SQL server
- ✔ The name of the object's database

✔ The name of the database's owner

✔ The object's name

You separate each component in an object's name with a period. For example, the fully qualified object name for the table named authors, in the pubs database, owned by the special database owner user (dbo), and on a server named Sales, is

```
Sales.pubs.dbo.authors
```

You don't always have to use an object's fully qualified name to access it. Instead, you can use a partial name. You use a partial name when you omit some of the components of a fully qualified name. You can do so if you want SQL Server to use the current values for your connection. For example, if you're already connected to your server and working in SQL Server Query Analyzer, and you're already using the pubs database as the dbo user, you can refer to the authors table as just plain old authors.

Here are some examples of partial names:

✔ server.database..object

Notice that because we're omitting the name of the owner but still specifying the server and database names, we must indicate where the owner name goes by inserting a period.

✔ server..owner.object

✔ database..object

✔ object

Keep in mind that when you use a partial name, SQL Server assumes that:

✔ If you don't specify a server name, you want to use your current server's name.

✔ If you don't specify a database name, you want to use your current database.

✔ If you don't specify an owner name, SQL Server assumes that the owner is the database user associated with your login ID.

Implementing Tables

You create a table within a database by defining the columns of information you want it to contain. For example, think about what types of information you may store in a table for tracking your customers. For this type of table, you want to have columns to store information such as the customer's name, telephone, address, and so on.

As part of each column's definition, you specify the type of data you plan to store in the column. You might define a column's data type as character, which means that you can store both character and numeric data in the column. On the other hand, you might define a column's data type as numeric if you plan to store only numbers in the column. We define some of the basic data types you use for columns in Table 11-2.

Table 11-2		Column Data Types
Data Type	*SQL Keyword*	*Use to Store*
Character	`char(#)`	Alphanumeric data. Character columns have fixed widths, which means that whether or not a character column contains any data, it uses the space in your database.
Unicode character	`nchar(#)`	Alphanumeric Unicode data. Like the char data type, the nchar data type uses a fixed amount of space in your database.
Variable character	`varchar(#)`	Alphanumeric data. Unlike character columns, variable character columns use space in your database only if they contain data.
Unicode variable character	`nvarchar(#)`	Alphanumeric Unicode data. Like varchar, nvarchar columns use space in your database only if they contain data.
Datetime	`datetime`	Both date and time information. The datetime data type enables you to store dates from 1/1/1753 to 12/31/9999 and time in milliseconds past midnight.
Integer	`int`	Whole numbers from –2,147,483,648 to 2,147,483,648.
Numeric	`numeric(p,s)`	Numbers with decimal places. Replace p with the number of digits of precision — or how many total digits, including the decimal places, you expect to store in the column. Replace s with the scale — or how many decimal places you want the column to have.

Creating a table

You can create a table in SQL Server Query Analyzer (or a program) by using the CREATE TABLE statement. Here's the syntax:

```
CREATE TABLE table_name
(column_name column_properties,
next_column_name column_properties,
[..n] )
```

For example, here's a CREATE TABLE statement to create a table for storing last and first names:

```
CREATE TABLE mytable
(lastname char(15), firstname char(15))
```

Instead of using a SQL statement, you can create a table by using SQL Server Enterprise Manager. Lab 11-1 walks you through creating a table for storing names and phone numbers.

Lab 11-1   Creating a Table in SQL Server Enterprise Manager

1. **Open SQL Server Enterprise Manager.**

2. **In your server's Databases folder, expand the database in which you want to create a table.**

   For this lab, you can use the Accounting database, which we show you how to create in Chapter 9. If you don't have this database, you can use either the Northwind or Pubs sample databases instead.

3. **Right-click the Tables object and choose New Table.**

   The New Table window appears. (For those of you who have used Microsoft Access, this window should look pretty familiar!)

4. **In the Column Name cell, type a name for the first column.**

   Use whatever name you like; we use LastName in our example.

5. **Press Tab to move to the Data Type column.**

   Notice that SQL Server assigns the character data type to the column by default. We use character for this column's data type.

6. **Press Tab to move to the Length column.**

7. **Type a value for the length of the column.**

   If you want to follow along with our example, use 25 for the length to assign the length of 25 characters to your new column.

8. **Take a look at the Allow Nulls column.**

   You use this column to specify whether or not you want SQL Server to permit your users to leave the column blank during data entry. By default, SQL Server configures your columns to permit nulls.

9. **Define two more columns for your table.**

   As shown in Figure 11-1, we use the following column names, data types, and lengths for our example table:

   FirstName: `Character(25)`

   Telephone: `Character(14)`

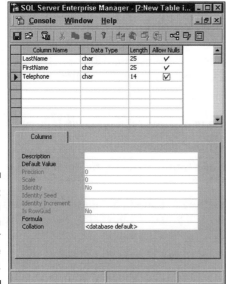

Figure 11-1:
Creating a
table in
SQL Server
Enterprise
Manager.

10. **On the toolbar, click Save.**

11. **Enter a name for your table, then click OK.**

    You can use any name you like for your table; we use the name mytable for our example.

12. **Close the New Table window.**

    Your new table appears in the list of tables for your database.

13. **Right-click your new table and choose Open Table⊅Return All Rows.**

    Because you don't have any data in your table, you don't see any rows in the Data window. But you can also use this window to add new rows to your table. (By the way, although this is a quick way to add a row to your table, you typically should use the INSERT SQL statement to add rows to your table.)

14. **Enter data into the first row of your table.**

As shown in Figure 11-2, we added a last name, first name, and telephone number into our table. SQL Server saves your new row when you move your cursor to the next blank row. (You can also tell that SQL Server saved your row if you no longer see a pencil to the left of the first column.)

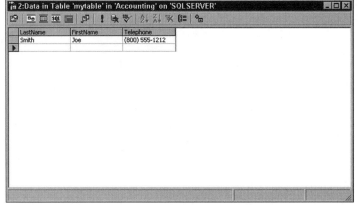

Figure 11-2: Adding data to a table in SQL Server Enterprise Manager.

15. **Close the Data window.**

Implementing constraints

When you create a table, you can add constraints to it in order to make sure that your users enter valid data. For example, you're responsible for designing the tables for a point-of-sale system. You want to link the invoice table to your customer table so that the sales clerks can't enter a customer account number on an invoice unless that customer's account exists. You can link these two tables together by defining the account column in the customer table as a primary key, and then defining that same column in the invoice table — but as a foreign key. After you link two tables together in a foreign key to primary key relationship, SQL Server won't let you enter a customer account in the invoice table that doesn't exist in the customer table. Likewise, you can't delete a customer if that customer has invoices in the invoice table.

We describe the types of constraints you can define in Table 11-3.

You can define a table's constraints when you create it, or you can add constraints later using the ALTER TABLE statement or SQL Server Enterprise Manager.

Table 11-3	Constraints
Constraint	*Enables You To*
Check	Define a range of valid values for a column.
Default	Set a default value for a column. SQL Server uses this value if a user doesn't enter any data into the column.
Foreign key	Specify that this column must match the primary key of either the same table or another table in the database.
Primary key	Require that users enter a unique value in this column for each row in the table; prevents users from storing null values in this column. SQL Server automatically creates an index based on a table's primary key.
Unique	Define that a column's values must be unique. Use this constraint if you want to enforce a column's uniqueness but you don't want it to be the table's primary key.

If you have several tables with columns for which you want to define the same default constraint, you can create a default constraint object. You can then bind the constraint object to specific columns in the tables by using the `sp_bindefault` stored procedure.

For the exam, you can expect to see questions that include database diagrams. These diagrams enable you to view the tables in a database and the relationships (or lack of relationships) between those tables. You create a database diagram within SQL Server Enterprise Manager. For the exam, review the layout of these diagrams and the meaning of each symbol in the diagram.

Managing tables

As a database administrator, you may have to perform a few tasks when managing tables. These include

- ✔ Adding a new column
- ✔ Modifying a column's properties
- ✔ Deleting a column
- ✔ Deleting the table itself

You can use both the ALTER TABLE SQL statement and SQL Server Enterprise Manager to modify the structure of a table. Use the DROP TABLE statement or SQL Server Enterprise Manager to delete a table.

Implementing Views

You use a view to make it possible for your users to see only certain columns (or even rows) in a table. You might think of a view as a saved SELECT statement, and anything you can SELECT in SQL Server Query Analyzer, you can put into a view.

One of the biggest advantages to a view (and we talk more about this in Chapter 21) is that you can give users permissions to use a view but not the underlying table, which means that the only way your users can see the data is by using the view.

Creating a view

You create a view by using either SQL Server Enterprise Manager or the CREATE VIEW SQL statement. To create a view in SQL Server Enterprise Manager, right-click on the database's view object and choose New View. Here's the basic syntax for the CREATE VIEW statement:

```
CREATE VIEW view_name
AS
SELECT column_list
FROM table_name
```

Lab 11-2 walks you through creating a view named UtahAuthors that's based on the authors table in the pubs database.

Lab 11-2   Creating a View

1. **If necessary, open SQL Server Query Analyzer and connect to your server with Windows authentication.**

2. **Type the following query:**

```
USE pubs
GO
CREATE VIEW UtahAuthors
AS
SELECT au_lname, au_fname, phone
FROM authors
WHERE state = 'UT'
```

3. **Choose Query⇨Execute to create your view.**

4. **Choose Edit⇨Clear Window to clear your previous query.**

5. **Execute the following query:**

```
SELECT *
FROM UtahAuthors
```

The view shows you that the authors table in the pubs database contains two authors who live in Utah.

6. **Close SQL Server Query Analyzer.**

Managing views

Management tasks for views include modifying the view's definition and deleting the view. To modify a view, use the ALTER VIEW statement (or, of course, SQL Server Enterprise Manager). Likewise, you can delete a view by using either the DROP VIEW statement or SQL Server Enterprise Manager.

Implementing Indexes

When you query a table, SQL Server retrieves the results by using one of two methods: by scanning all the pages within the table (this method is called a table scan), or by using indexes. With a table scan, SQL Server scans the entire table, row by row, to retrieve the results of your query. In contrast, if SQL Server uses the index, it searches the index itself to find the rows that match your query — and then it retrieves the results from your table.

You define a table's index based on one or more columns; these columns then become the index's key. SQL Server supports two types of indexes for each table: clustered and nonclustered. With a clustered index, SQL Server physically stores the table's rows in order by its key. You can define only one clustered index per table. For example, you might define a clustered index on a customer table based on the zip code column. SQL Server then stores the rows in the table sorted by the zip code column.

Unlike a clustered index, a nonclustered index is a separate database object. You define a nonclustered index by specifying its keys (the columns on which you want to index the table). SQL Server stores the index's keys, along with an identifier value that points to each row's location in the table, in the nonclustered index.

You can define a total of 250 indexes for a table. Of those indexes, only one can be clustered — and the rest must be nonclustered.

Specifying a fill factor

One of the optional parameters you can specify when you create an index is its fill factor. SQL Server uses the fill factor to determine how full it should fill an index's pages when you create the index. Keep in mind that as you add data to a table, SQL Server must update your index's information. If your index's pages are 100 percent full, SQL Server must split pages to make room for the new information. Because splitting pages is resource-intensive, you typically use a lower fill factor than 100 percent to reduce the impact on your server of updating your indexes. Be aware, though, that using a lower fill factor increases the number of pages SQL Server must use to store an index.

Make sure you understand the role of the fill factor for the exam. Consider decreasing an index's fill factor if you expect a lot of changes to your data (such as with an online transaction processing system). On the other hand, if you define the index's fill factor as too low, you can end up increasing your server's workload because it must scan so many additional pages.

SQL Server only creates the index with the fill factor percentage you specify — it doesn't maintain this fill factor as you add data to or delete data from the table. You can force SQL Server to rebuild an index in order to reset the index's fill factor by using the DBCC DBREINDEX statement. You can also rebuild an index to reset its fill factor by using the CREATE INDEX statement with the DROP_EXISTING option.

Creating an index

You create an index by using either the CREATE INDEX statement or SQL Server Enterprise Manager. Here's the syntax for creating an index in SQL:

```
CREATE index_type INDEX index_name
ON table_name (column_name [,...n])
```

For example, to create a nonclustered index on the authors' last and first names based on the authors table, use this query:

```
CREATE NONCLUSTERED INDEX AuthorName
ON authors (au_lname, au_fname)
```

You create an index in SQL Server Enterprise Manager by right-clicking the table for which you want to define an index and choosing All Tasks⇨Manage Indexes. In Lab 11-3, we walk you through creating a nonclustered index in SQL Server Enterprise Manager.

Lab 11-3	Creating an Index in SQL Server Enterprise Manager

1. **If necessary, switch to SQL Server Enterprise Manager.**

2. **In the console tree, select a database's Tables object.**

   Select a database that contains a table for which you want to define a nonclustered index, or use the pubs sample database.

3. **In the details pane, right-click the table for which you want to define an index and choose All Tasks⇨Manage Indexes.**

If you're using the pubs database, you can create the index on the authors table. The Manage Indexes dialog box you see in Figure 11-3 appears. You can use this dialog box to manage your existing indexes, or create a new index.

Figure 11-3:
Managing indexes in SQL Server Enterprise Manager.

4. **Click New to open the Create New Index dialog box.**

5. **In the Index Name text box, type a name for the index.**

   For example, if you're using the authors table, you can use AuthorNames for your index name.

6. **Check the columns you want to include in your index.**

   If you're using the authors table, check the au_lname and au_fname columns.

7. **Take a look at the Clustered Index option at the bottom of the dialog box.**

   As shown in Figure 11-4, you can't configure this index as a clustered index if your table already has one. If you're creating an index on the authors table, this option tells you that you already have a clustered index.

8. **Check Fill Factor to enable the fill factor option on your index.**

   Notice that SQL Server Enterprise Manager automatically configures your index with a fill factor of 80 percent.

9. **Click OK to create your index.**

10. **Click Close.**

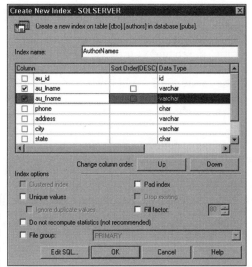

Figure 11-4:
Creating a
new index.

Managing indexes

One of the more common tasks you must perform to manage indexes is to rebuild them. For example, you might rebuild an index in order to re-establish its fill factor. Another reason why you might rebuild an index is to force SQL Server to reorganize the index's rows on its pages. SQL Server can search an index more efficiently if an index's rows are close together on fewer pages than it can if the index's rows are spread across many pages.

You use one of the database consistency checker commands, DBCC SHOWCONTIG, to determine how fragmented an index's pages are. (An index is considered fragmented if few rows are spread across many pages. Fragmentation occurs when you add, change, or delete data from the table on which the index is based.) Make sure you review the type of information DBCC SHOWCONTIG displays when you're studying for the exam. We explain the information displayed by DBCC SHOWCONTIG in more detail in Chapter 13.

You can rebuild an index either by deleting it and recreating it, or by using the DBCC DBREINDEX command. Here's the syntax:

```
DBCC DBREINDEX ('database.owner.table_name', index_name,
          fill_factor)
```

Implementing Stored Procedures

A stored procedure is actually nothing more than a series of SQL statements, just like any other query you execute in SQL Server Query Analyzer. But, stored procedures offer you a few advantages. First, when your server parses and compiles a stored procedure, it caches that stored procedure's execution plan — so the next time you run that same stored procedure, it executes faster. (In contrast, SQL Server must parse and compile a query each time you run it.) Second, you can call stored procedures from other applications (such as those written in Visual Basic) instead of explicitly writing the query into your application. If you have to later change the query within the stored procedure, doing so by editing the stored procedure is much easier than changing your application's code.

One of the stronger arguments for using stored procedures is that you can grant your users the necessary permissions to run the stored procedures without having to grant them permissions to the database's tables. In other words, you can use stored procedures as an extra measure of security for protecting your server. You can expect to see a question or two on your exam about using stored procedures to help secure your server.

Creating a stored procedure

You probably know the drill by now, but you can create a stored procedure by using either — you guessed it — the CREATE PROCEDURE SQL statement or SQL Server Enterprise Manager. Here's the basic syntax for the SQL method:

```
CREATE PROCEDURE procedure_name
AS
          SQL statement [...n]
GO
```

For example, the following statement creates a stored procedure that lists the titles of books from the pubs database, and their authors:

```
USE pubs
GO
CREATE PROCEDURE AuthorTitles
AS
  SELECT a.au_fname+' '+a.au_lname AS 'Author Name', t.title
  FROM authors AS a JOIN titleauthor as ta
  ON a.au_id = ta.au_id
  JOIN titles AS t
  ON ta.title_id = t.title_id
  ORDER BY a.au_lname, a.au_fname
GO
```

You create a stored procedure within SQL Server Enterprise Manager by first expanding the database in which you want to create the stored procedure. Then, right-click the database's Stored Procedures object and choose New

Stored Procedure. As shown in Figure 11-5, SQL Server Enterprise Manager opens a dialog box in which you can type your SQL statements. (SQL Server Enterprise Manager automatically types in the basic structure of the CREATE PROCEDURE statement for you.)

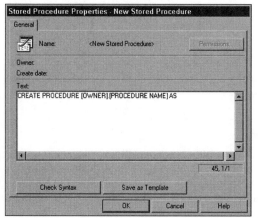

Figure 11-5:
Creating a
procedure
in SQL
Server
Enterprise
Manager.

Running a stored procedure

SQL Server requires that you run a stored procedure either as the first line of a query, or that you precede it with the EXEC keyword. For example, if you execute the following query, you receive an error message:

```
SELECT *
FROM authors
sp_helpdb pubs
```

Because you aren't executing the stored procedure as the first line of the query, SQL Server can't process this query. Instead, use the following syntax:

```
SELECT *
FROM authors
EXEC sp_helpdb pubs
```

Managing stored procedures

SQL Server includes several stored procedures that you can use to view information about your stored procedures. (In fact, you can even use these stored procedures to view the contents of the system stored procedures.) We describe these procedures in Table 11-4.

Table 11-4	Viewing Stored Procedures
Stored Procedure	*Enables You to View*
`sp_helptext procedure_name`	The SQL statements contained in the stored procedure.
`sp_help procedure_name`	Who owns the stored procedure, and the date and time it was created.
`sp_depends procedure_name`	The names of the tables the stored procedure references.
`sp_stored_procedures`	A list of the stored procedures in your current database.

The first time you run a stored procedure after your server boots up, SQL Server compiles it and caches its execution plan in RAM. From this point on, SQL Server runs the stored procedure by using this cached version. If you make significant changes to the data on which the stored procedure is based, you might find it necessary to recompile the stored procedure. You can do so by using either of the following statements:

```
EXEC procedure_name WITH RECOMPILE
```

Or

```
EXEC sp_recompile procedure_name
```

Implementing Triggers

You define triggers on tables within a database to enable your SQL server to automatically perform specific tasks based on users' actions. These tasks can be as simple as keeping an audit trail of changes made to a sensitive table, or as complex as enforcing data integrity through a series of checks. You create a trigger by using either the CREATE TRIGGER statement or SQL Server Enterprise Manager.

You base triggers on the INSERT, UPDATE, and DELETE SQL statements. For example, you might want to keep a record of who deleted rows from a table. In this scenario, you should base your trigger on the DELETE statement. (The trigger will fire regardless of whether you use the actual DELETE statement in a query or you delete a row within an application.)

Prep Test

1 Which of the following database objects can you use to ensure the integrity of your data? (Choose all that apply.)

A ❑ Constraint

B ❑ Index

C ❑ Trigger

D ❑ Stored procedure

2 You are currently using the Northwind database as the dbo user. You want to view a list of authors from the authors table in the pubs database. By default, Setup configures the pubs database with dbo as its owner. What is the shortest name you can use to query the authors table without changing your current database?

A ○ authors

B ○ pubs.authors

C ○ pubs..authors

D ○ server.pubs.dbo.authors

3 If you don't specify a database name as part of an object's name, what database does SQL Server assume the object is stored in?

A ○ Your login ID's default database

B ○ The Master database

C ○ Your current database

D ○ The Model database

4 You would like to minimize the amount of space text data uses in your database. Which of the following data types enables you to conserve space in a database?

A ○ Integer

B ○ Character

C ○ Varchar

D ○ Numeric

5 You want to define a relationship between the inventory and invoice tables so that your sales clerks can't enter an item number into an invoice unless that item is in the inventory table. Which constraints enable you to establish this relationship? (Choose all that apply.)

A ❑ Default

B ❑ Primary key

C ❑ Check

D ❑ Foreign key

6 To which of the following objects must your users have permissions in order to access a view?

A ○ All tables on which the view is based, along with the view itself

B ○ Only the view

C ○ Only the tables and indexes on which the view is based

D ○ All tables and indexes on which the view is based, and the view itself

7 What does the fill factor parameter do?

A ○ It controls how SQL Server writes to each of a database's secondary data files.

B ○ It specifies how full SQL Server fills a table's pages as you add rows to the table.

C ○ It controls how full SQL Server fills an index's pages when you add rows to the table.

D ○ It specifies how full SQL Server fills an index's pages when you create the index.

8 How many clustered indexes can you create per table?

A ○ 249

B ○ 250

C ○ 1

D ○ None. You define clustered indexes only on the database, not each table.

9 What command should you use to analyze how fragmented an index's pages are?

A ○ DBCC DBREINDEX

B ○ DBCC SHOWFRAG

C ○ DBCC CHECKFRAG

D ○ DBCC SHOWCONTIG

10 Which stored procedure should you use to view the SQL statements that make up a stored procedure?

A ○ `sp_help procedure_name`

B ○ `sp_stored_procedure`

C ○ `sp_helptext procedure_name`

D ○ `sp_edit procedure_name`

Answers

1 **A, C,** and **D.** You can use constraints to have SQL Server check all data before it's added to a table. But you can also use triggers and stored procedures to enforce data integrity. *See "Reviewing Database Object Types."*

2 **C.** At a minimum, you must specify the name of the database because the authors table isn't in your current database. *Study "Referring to Database Objects."*

3 **C.** If you don't specify a database name as part of the object's name, SQL Server looks for the object in your current database. *Study "Referring to Database Objects."*

4 **C.** Only the varchar and nvarchar data types enable you to conserve the space used by text data in a database. That's because columns that use this data type only use space if they actually have data in them. *Study "Implementing Tables."*

5 **B** and **D.** You use a primary key to foreign key relationship to make sure that the data entered into the foreign key column exists in the primary key column. *Review "Implementing constraints."*

6 **B.** One of the big advantages to a view is that users can access a view without your having to assign them permissions for the underlying table. *See "Implementing Views."*

7 **D.** The fill factor controls how full SQL Server fills an index's pages only when you create the index. *Study "Specifying a fill factor."*

8 **C.** You can define only one clustered index for a table. *Study "Implementing Indexes."*

9 **D.** You use the DBCC SHOWCONTIG command to determine the amount of fragmentation on an index's pages. *Study "Managing indexes."*

10 **C.** Use the sp_helptext stored procedure whenever you want to view the contents of that stored procedure. *Review "Managing stored procedures."*

Part IV
Managing, Monitoring, and Troubleshooting Databases

The 5th Wave   By Rich Tennant

"Our automated response policy to a large company wide data crash is to notify management, back up existing data and sell 90% of my shares in the company."

In this part . . .

SQL Server 2000 provides a wealth of tools and information that you can use to manage, monitor, and troubleshoot your databases. In this part, we explore many of these utilities, and provide you with tips and tricks on how to optimize your databases. In addition, we show you how to troubleshoot problems — and how to back up and restore databases.

In Chapter 12, we explore the techniques you can use to optimize databases, queries, indexing, recompiling, and locking. In Chapter 13, we review optimizing data storage through the use of files and filegroups and by managing database fragmentation. In Chapters 14 and 15, we show you how to back up and restore your databases. And in Chapter 16, we explore the utilities you can use to troubleshoot your server and its databases.

Chapter 12

Managing and Optimizing Database Performance

Exam Objectives

▶ Optimizing database performance

▶ Optimizing indexing, recompiling, and locking

▶ Modifying the database schema

*W*hen it comes to optimizing databases, and your SQL Server environment in general, you need to consider many things. First of all, have you chosen the most efficient indexes for your tables? Have you taken the necessary steps to minimize locking in your applications so that your users aren't sitting around twiddling their thumbs? Do you know if you've done everything you can to minimize recompiles of stored procedures? And have you optimized your queries? And finally, is the structure of your database adequate for your users' needs?

In this chapter, we show you the techniques and tools for optimizing indexing, queries, stored procedure recompiling, and locking. Although we could give you an abundance of tips and tricks, we focus in this chapter on only the techniques and tools you can expect to see on the exam.

Quick Assessment

Optimizing
database
performance

1   You can limit long-running queries by configuring the _____.

2   You can determine which queries are using your server's resources the most by using _____.

Optimizing
indexing

3   You should use clustered indexes to optimize queries that retrieve a(n) _____.

4   You should create nonclustered indexes only if they eliminate more than _____ of the rows in your table for a specific query.

5   A nonclustered index optimizes _____ queries.

6   You can determine whether or not SQL Server uses an index to retrieve a result set by executing the _____ command in SQL Server Query Analyzer.

7   You can use the _____ to have SQL Server suggest indexes for your database.

Optimizing
recompiling

8   SQL Server does not automatically recompile a stored procedure when you create a new _____.

9   You can force SQL Server to recompile a stored procedure by executing the stored procedure with the _____ clause.

Optimizing
locking

10   SQL Server uses a(n) _____ lock when you execute an INSERT, UPDATE, or DELETE statement.

11   A(n) _____ occurs when two processes have locked resources and each process needs the other process's resources.

12   A(n) _____ occurs when a process holds an exclusive lock on a resource for a long period of time.

Modifying
the data-
base
schema

13   You can expand a database by adding a(n) _____ data file.

Answers

1 *Query Governor.* Check out "Limit long-running queries."

2 *SQL Server Profiler.* Study "Analyze query performance."

3 *Range of rows.* See "Optimizing clustered indexes."

4 *90 percent.* Study "Optimizing nonclustered indexes."

5 *Highly selective.* See "Optimizing nonclustered indexes."

6 *SET SHOWPLAN_ALL ON.* Take a look at "Managing index statistics."

7 *Index Tuning Wizard.* See "Using the Index Tuning Wizard."

8 *Index.* See "Optimizing Recompiling."

9 `WITH RECOMPILE`. Study "Optimizing Recompiling."

10 *Exclusive.* See "Types of locks."

11 *Deadlock.* Study "Deadlocks and blocking locks."

12 *Blocking lock.* Study "Deadlocks and blocking locks."

13 *Secondary.* Review "Modifying the Database Schema."

Optimizing Indexing

Before we take a look at how you can optimize your server's indexes, you must understand the architecture SQL Server uses for its indexes. As you know, SQL Server enables you to define two types of indexes for a table: clustered and nonclustered. For both types of indexes, SQL Server uses the Balanced-tree (B-tree) architecture for storing the pages of the index. Although you might be tempted to think of the B-tree architecture as looking like one of the trees in your backyard, don't. Instead, think of the B-tree architecture as an upside-down tree, as shown in Figure 12-1.

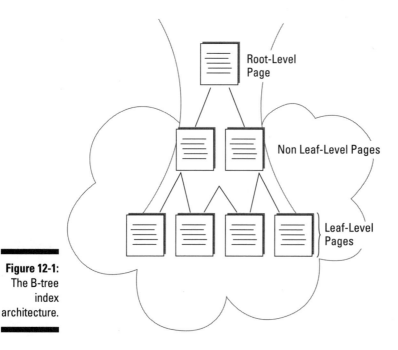

Figure 12-1:
The B-tree
index
architecture.

With the B-tree architecture, SQL Server establishes levels within an index. The top level of the index is called the root-level page. Branching off of the root-level page, SQL Server creates at least one level of what are called non–leaf-level pages (these are also called intermediate pages). At the lowest level of the index, are leaf-level pages. When SQL Server uses the index, it navigates it by beginning at the root-level page, through the non–leaf-level pages, and then to your leaf-level pages.

Defining the B-tree architecture

We like to use a phone book analogy for how SQL Server uses this B-tree architecture. Think about how you find your friend Mary Q. Contrary's phone number in a phone book. You probably begin your search by looking in the Table of Contents to find where the last names that begin with "C" are in the phone book. This process is similar to how SQL Server starts its search of an index by looking at the root-level page. (So you can think of the root-level page as the Table of Contents for your index.)

Next, you use the range of names listed at the top of each page in the phone book to narrow your search to a specific page. For example, the top of one page might say "Cannoli – Constantinople," and the next "Constanza – Daigle." This type of search is what SQL Server does when it scans your index's non–leaf-level pages.

Finally, after you find the page that contains the last name of Contrary, you can find your friend Mary's phone number. Likewise, the same thing happens when SQL Server reaches the leaf-level pages of your index: It can retrieve the data.

The most important fact you need to realize about the B-tree architecture is that it is *balanced*, which means that any search of the index requires that SQL Server navigate the same number of levels and pages in the index to retrieve the data. Because the index must be balanced, SQL Server must merge or split pages as you delete or add data from the table on which the index is based.

So right about now you're probably brewing a second pot of coffee and wondering why we're telling you all of this. Here's why: You can take steps to minimize the impact of searching the levels of an index that dramatically improve the performance of your server. To understand how you can optimize indexes, we need to look at clustered and nonclustered indexes separately.

Optimizing clustered indexes

With a clustered index, your index is the actual table itself and not a separate database object. (Remember, you use a clustered index to configure the order in which SQL Server stores the rows in a table.) This means that the leaf-level pages of the index are the data pages of your table. And because your clustered index is your table itself, it is far and away the fastest-performing index for your table.

So how can you optimize a clustered index? Your best strategy is to make sure you design it properly. If you think about it, a clustered index gives you the best performance for queries that retrieve a range of rows instead of a single row. That's because your data is already stored in order by a specific value.

Here's the bottom line: You get only one clustered index per table, so make it a good one. And a clustered index is optimized for queries that retrieve ranges of rows instead of those that retrieve only one row. So design your clustered index so that its keys can be used to retrieve ranges of rows.

Optimizing nonclustered indexes

Before we talk about optimizing nonclustered indexes, we want to detour just a little bit to talk about the nonclustered index architecture. That's because when you build a nonclustered index, you can base it on a table for which either you have or have not defined a clustered index. (By the way, a table for which you have not defined a clustered index is called a heap.)

Okay, so what's the big deal? Well, if you build a nonclustered index based on a table that's a heap, the index consists of the index's key values plus a row identifier (RID). SQL Server uses the RID to locate specific rows in a table whenever it uses the index. On the other hand, if you build a nonclustered index based on a table for which you have defined a clustered index, SQL Server must first navigate the nonclustered index — and then it must navigate the clustered index to retrieve the data.

Because a nonclustered index is a separate database object, retrieving data based on this type of index is just plain old slower than retrieving it from a clustered index. So, you need to make sure that using your nonclustered index is worth SQL Server's effort. If your nonclustered index isn't highly selective (meaning you use it to retrieve only a few rows), using the nonclustered index can actually be much slower than simply performing a table scan. That's because to resolve a query based on a nonclustered index, SQL Server must first navigate the nonclustered index to find where the data is in your table, and then it must retrieve the data.

Generally, you should create a nonclustered index only if it's highly selective — which means it can eliminate more than 90 percent of your table's rows. For example, assume that you have a table with rows for your company's 25,000 employees. If you defined a nonclustered index based on the gender of those employees, such an index would not be highly selective, mostly because only two possible values exist for the gender column (male or female). So this index could eliminate roughly only 50 percent of the rows when responding to queries that use this index.

So here's what you need to know: Create a nonclustered index only if the index can eliminate 90 percent of a table's rows when processing a query. Otherwise, SQL Server can retrieve your query's results much faster simply by performing a table scan. The columns that are your best candidates for nonclustered index keys are those containing highly unique information such as account numbers, social security numbers, and so on.

Managing index statistics

When it comes to processing a query, SQL Server has to determine whether or not using an index or scanning the table is faster. To help determine which method is most efficient, SQL Server automatically creates and maintains statistics about a table's indexes and their data. SQL Server's query optimizer then uses these statistics whenever it processes a query.

Updating statistics

One technique you can use to manage index statistics is to force SQL Server to update the statistics. You might do this if you created an index on an empty table and then loaded the table with data. You can use the following SQL statement to force SQL Server to update the statistics for all of a table's indexes:

```
UPDATE STATISTICS table_name
```

Analyzing index usage

You can configure SQL Server Query Analyzer to display the query execution plan it uses when it processes a query, which enables you to determine whether or not SQL Server's query optimizer uses an index to process a query. You configure SQL Server Query Analyzer to display its query execution plan by either using its menus or by executing this SQL statement:

```
SET SHOWPLAN_ALL ON
```

Likewise, you can turn off the display of the query execution plan by executing this statement:

```
SET SHOWPLAN_ALL OFF
```

Table 12-1 describes the different messages you can see when you review a query execution plan.

Table 12-1	Query Optimizer Messages
Message	*Means that the Query Optimizer*
Index Seek	Uses a nonclustered index to retrieve the result set when processing your query.
Clustered Index Seek	Uses the clustered index to retrieve the result set when processing your query.
Clustered Index Scan	Scans the clustered index to process your query. This message means that the query optimizer essentially performs a table scan on a table with a clustered index. In this scenario, the clustered index does not improve the performance of the query.
Table Scan	Scans the table to process your query. This message means that your table doesn't have a clustered index, and the query optimizer can't use any of the table's nonclustered indexes to improve the query's performance.

We use Lab 12-1 to walk you through displaying the query execution plan and analyzing its information.

Lab 12-1   Analyzing Index Usage

1. **Open SQL Server Query Analyzer and log on to your server with Windows authentication.**

2. **Execute the following query:**

```
SET SHOWPLAN_ALL ON
```

   This statement turns on the display of a query's execution plan — and turns off the display of your query's result set.

3. **Clear the Query window.**

4. **Execute the following query based on the employees table:**

```
USE Northwind
SELECT *
FROM employees
```

5. **Take a look at the query execution plan, as shown in Figure 12-2.**

   You can see that SQL Server's query optimizer performs a clustered index scan. This means that even though the employees table has a clustered index, SQL Server must perform a table scan to retrieve your query's result set.

6. **Clear the Query window.**

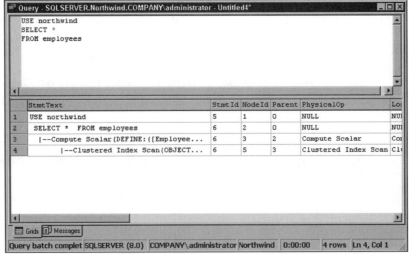

Figure 12-2:
Analyzing
index usage.

7. **Execute the following query:**

```
SELECT *
FROM employees
WHERE lastname = 'fallahan'
```

8. **Examine the query execution plan, as shown in Figure 12-3.**

In contrast to your first query, SQL Server uses an index seek to retrieve the results for this query. In other words, SQL Server is using a nonclustered index to retrieve your query's results.

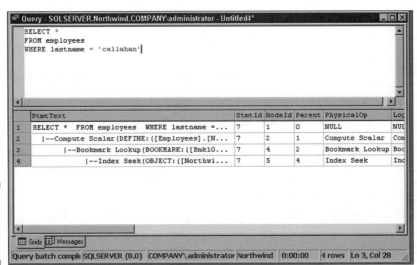

Figure 12-3:
Using a non-
clustered
index.

9. **Now execute the following query:**

```
SELECT *
FROM employees
WHERE employeeid = 1
```

10. **Look at the query execution plan, as shown in Figure 12-4.**

    This plan tells you that SQL Server is using the clustered index to resolve your query.

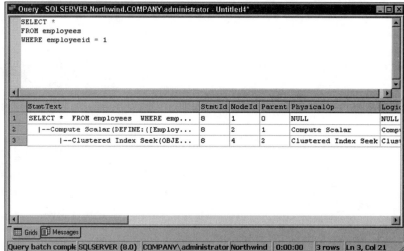

Figure 12-4:
Using the clustered index.

11. **Clear the Query window.**

12. **Turn off the display of the execution plan by executing**

```
SET SHOWPLAN_ALL OFF
```

You can also see how SQL Server retrieves a query's result set by using the following command:

```
SET STATISTICS IO ON | OFF
```

If you turn on statistics, SQL Server Query Analyzer displays a message indicating the types of operations it used to retrieve the results, including

- The number of scans
- The number of pages read from the data cache in RAM (logical reads)

✔ The number of pages read from your server's hard disk (physical reads)

✔ The number of pages SQL Server read into your server's cache to process the query (read-ahead reads)

Using the Index Tuning Wizard

If you find all of these choices for defining your tables' indexes overwhelming, you aren't alone! To help guide you through creating the best indexes for your database, you can use the Index Tuning Wizard in SQL Server Enterprise Manager. This wizard works by analyzing your server's workload, which is essentially all the queries you execute against the tables in a database.

You provide the Index Tuning Wizard with information about your typical queries by using SQL Server Profiler to capture the typical workload on your server. In essence, SQL Server Profiler records the queries you execute against the data to a workload file. When you have a workload file, you can use the Index Tuning Wizard to analyze the workload, make suggestions for new indexes, and even create the indexes for you.

You use SQL Server Profiler to monitor events on your server. You can capture these events to a file or a table for further analysis. The information SQL Server Profiler captures is referred to as a trace.

Optimizing Queries

You optimize queries by first making sure that your hardware is optimized, and second, identifying and eliminating poorly designed queries. Poorly designed queries can have a huge impact on your server's performance, so we want to give you a few tips on how you can help protect your server.

Use the appropriate hardware

Keep in mind that all the following hardware components can have an impact on a query's performance:

✔ Slow network components (such as network cards, hubs, and routers)

✔ Insufficient RAM in your server

✔ Slow hard disk subsystem

If you haven't realized it by now, Microsoft's tag line shouldn't be "Where do you want to go today?" It should be "More is better." In other words, the more RAM and hard disks you install in your server, and the faster CPU, network, and hard disks you use, the better an application will run — and SQL Server 2000 is no exception. So your first technique when optimizing queries is actually to optimize your hardware.

Limit long-running queries

Think about what happens if a user connects to a 150,000-row table that's 500MB in size from a client computer and executes the following query:

```
SELECT *
FROM table_name
```

This query circumvents all the advantages to SQL Server because it requires that your server send all the table's rows to the client's computer. One technique you can use to help reduce the impact of poorly designed queries is to configure the Query Governor. This setting enables you to prevent long-running queries from eating up your server's resources.

You can configure the query governor with a setting from 0 to 2,147,483,647. This setting is measured in seconds. If SQL Server examines the query execution plan and estimates that a query will take longer than the number of seconds you specify, it will not process the query. By default, SQL Server Setup doesn't enable the Query Governor.

You can expect to see a question or two about the function of the Query Governor on your exam.

We show you where you can set the Query Governor in Lab 12-2.

Lab 12-2	Configuring the Query Governor

1. **Open SQL Server Enterprise Manager.**

2. **In the console tree, right-click your server and choose Properties.**

3. **Select the Server Settings tab.**

   You configure the Query Governor by using this page of your server's Properties dialog box.

4. **Check Use Query Governor to Prevent Queries Exceeding Specified Cost, as shown in Figure 12-5.**

   Use the up or down arrows or type a limit (in seconds) for the Query Governor.

5. **Click OK to close your server's Properties dialog box and save your changes.**

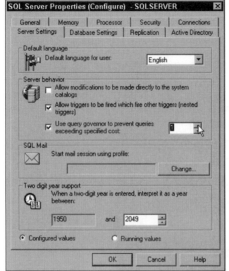

Figure 12-5:
Configuring
the Query
Governor.

Analyze query performance

The best defense against poorly designed queries is a good offense, and the best offense is knowledge. Because many of the queries executed against your server may actually be part of a custom application designed by programmers (and not you), figuring out which query is the culprit can be hard. One of the better tools you can use to analyze queries is SQL Server Profiler.

When you use SQL Server Profiler to analyze queries, you specifically want to capture the events that relate to the TSQL (Transact-SQL) and Stored Procedure event classes. In particular, pay close attention to the `RPC:Completed` and `SQL:BatchCompleted` events because they give you a good idea of which queries took the longest to complete.

Make sure that you know the usage of SQL Server Profiler for your exam. You can expect to see questions prompting you to resolve a performance problem based on the information you see in a trace.

In Lab 12-3, we examine how to use SQL Server Profiler to analyze queries.

Lab 12-3	Using SQL Server Profiler

1. **From the Microsoft SQL Server menu, choose SQL Server Profiler.**

2. **Choose File⇨New⇨Trace.**

3. **Connect to your server with Windows authentication.**

   SQL Server Profiler now opens the Trace Properties dialog box so that you can define what you want to monitor on your server.

4. **In the Trace Name text box, type a name for the trace.**

   In our example, we use Testing Queries.

5. **From the Template Name drop-down list, select SQLProfilerTSQL_Duration.**

   This predefined template in SQL Server Profiler is designed to track the duration of SQL queries.

6. **Check Save to File, and accept the default filename for the trace.**

   Your dialog box now looks like Figure 12-6.

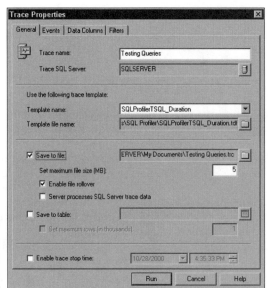

Figure 12-6:
Configuring
a trace file.

7. **Select the Events tab.**

   Notice that the SQLProfilerTSQL_Duration template automatically configured SQL Server Profiler to trace the RPC:Completed and SQL:Batch Completed events.

8. **Select the Data Columns tab.**

   You use the Data Columns page to specify the information you want to record to your trace file about each event.

9. Use the Up and Down buttons to configure SQL Server Profiler to group the data columns by Duration first, and then TextData.

10. Configure the Columns to contain the following data columns (in order): NTUserName, CPU, EventClass, and SPID, as shown in Figure 12-7.

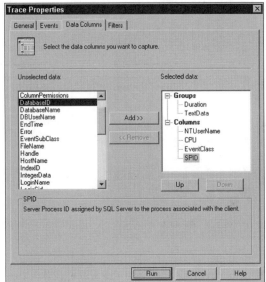

Figure 12-7:
Defining the data columns for a trace.

11. **Select the Filters tab.**

    You can use filters to enable SQL Server Profiler to record only specific events, or to prevent SQL Server Profiler from recording specific events. We want to configure SQL Server Profiler not to record the events generated by the SQL Server services account.

12. **In the Trace Event Criteria list, expand DBUserName\Not like.**

13. **In the text box, type your server's services account name, as shown in Figure 12-8.**

14. **Click Run to start the trace.**

15. **In SQL Server Query Analyzer, execute the following queries:**

```
USE northwind
SELECT * FROM employees
GO
SELECT * FROM customers
GO
SELECT * FROM employees CROSS JOIN customers
GO
```

TIP

> We use the GO keyword in between each statement so that SQL Server treats each SELECT statement as a separate batch.

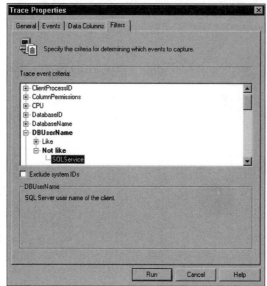

Figure 12-8:
Excluding the services account from the trace.

16. **Switch to SQL Server Profiler and stop the trace. (Click the Stop button on the toolbar.)**

17. **Take a look at the Duration column.**

    As shown in Figure 12-9, you can use this column to determine which query took the longest to run. In our example, the CROSS JOIN query took the longest to run because it joins every row in the employees table with every row in the customers table. (In real life, you wouldn't run such a query — we use it here just to show you how you can determine which query is using the most resources on your server.)

18. **If you haven't done so already, select the row in the trace file that contains the CROSS JOIN statement.**

    Notice that SQL Server Profiler displays the query in the bottom half of your screen. When you're trying to figure out which query is hogging all of your server's CPU time, this information is what you need. You can see the exact SQL statement here — and you can even copy and paste it into SQL Server Query Analyzer if you want. Notice, too, that we included the Windows NT user name as part of our trace file. So your trace file not only shows you the problem query, but also "whodunit."

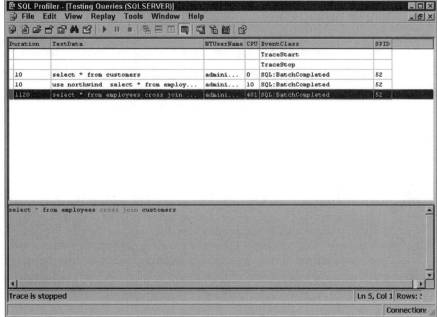

Figure 12-9:
Identifying
a long-
running
query.

Optimizing Recompiling

Another consideration when optimizing your database's performance is how
SQL Server goes about recompiling its stored procedures. By default, SQL
Server compiles a stored procedure the first time you run it. If you restart
your server, your server's procedure cache is cleared — which means that
SQL Server must recompile the stored procedure again the next time you run
it. It also recompiles a stored procedure whenever any of the tables it uses
are changed. But, SQL Server does not recompile a stored procedure when
you create a new index. So if you create a new index that improves the performance of your stored procedure, make sure that you force SQL Server to
recompile the stored procedure.

You can force SQL Server to recompile a stored procedure by using a variety
of techniques. First, you can explicitly recompile the stored procedure by
executing the following statement in SQL Server Query Analyzer:

```
EXEC sp_recompile stored_procedure_name | table_name
```

You can use either a specific stored procedure name or a table name. If you
use a table name, SQL Server recompiles all stored procedures and triggers
that reference that table.

You can also force SQL Server to recompile a stored procedure when you run it by adding an option to it, as follows:

```
EXEC stored_procedure_name WITH RECOMPILE
```

Finally, you can configure SQL Server to always recompile a stored procedure whenever you execute it. To do so, use the WITH RECOMPILE clause as part of your CREATE PROCEDURE statement, as follows:

```
CREATE PROCEDURE procedure_name
WITH RECOMPILE
AS
        SQL statements
```

Use the WITH RECOMPILE clause only if you expect the data that's accessed by the stored procedure to change frequently or if your stored procedure uses parameters or temporary variables with wide variations in their values. Be aware that forcing SQL Server to recompile the stored procedure each time you run it slows down the performance of the stored procedure.

Optimizing Locking

Because SQL Server is a multiuser system, it uses locking to protect the integrity of your data. These locks prevent two users from making conflicting changes to the same row at the same time. The advantage to locks is that they protect your data. But this protection can come at a price: slower performance. That's because if one user has a row locked that another needs access to, that user must wait to access the row.

Locks don't necessarily have to be just on a single row of a table. SQL Server can also place locks on the following resources:

- ✔ An index row
- ✔ A table row
- ✔ A single 8KB page
- ✔ An extent (eight 8KB pages)
- ✔ An entire table, including its indexes
- ✔ An entire database

We cover how to monitor and troubleshoot locks in more detail in Chapter 16.

Types of locks

SQL Server uses two types of basic locks: shared and exclusive. SQL Server uses shared locks for read transactions; in contrast, it uses exclusive locks with write transactions. A shared lock doesn't prevent other users from accessing the data; instead, a shared lock does prevent other users from locking the data exclusively. You might think of a shared lock as a red flag that SQL Server uses to indicate to other users that another user has the resource open. And a shared lock is shareable — which means that other transactions and thus users can place a shared lock on the same resource at the same time. (For example, you could have three users reading the same row in a table at the same time.)

SQL Server uses an exclusive lock whenever you execute a query that changes data. In other words, SQL Server uses an exclusive lock whenever you use the INSERT, UPDATE, or DELETE SQL statements. And like its name implies, an exclusive lock is just that: As long as you have the resource locked, no other users can access that resource. In fact, an exclusive lock can't coexist with a shared lock.

Deadlocks and blocking locks

One of the problems you can encounter with locking is deadlocks. A deadlock occurs when two users or processes each have a resource locked, and each user or process needs to use the other user or process's resource. The good news is that SQL Server automatically resolves deadlocks for you. It does so by choosing a "deadlock victim." (We could make all kinds of jokes about that phrase, but we'll spare you.) SQL Server chooses its victim based on which user's transaction is the least expensive to undo. SQL Server then aborts the deadlock victim's process so that the other process can get access to the resources it needs.

A blocking lock occurs when a process holds an exclusive lock on a resource for a long period of time. As a result, the blocking lock prevents other processes from using that resource. For this reason, blocking locks can adversely affect your server's performance, because if a user has an exclusive lock on a resource, no other users can access the resource until the user has released the lock. The bad news is that SQL Server doesn't automatically resolve blocking locks. As the database administrator, one of your tasks is to monitor for blocking locks — and then take steps to resolve them.

Monitoring and resolving blocking locks

You can view the locks on your server by using either SQL Server Enterprise Manager or the sp_who and sp_lock stored procedures. SQL Server uses abbreviations to indicate the type of lock a user has placed on a resource: S for shared, X for exclusive. (A few other special use locks also exist; see Books Online for more information on the special use locks.)

Table 12-2 describes the utilities you can use to monitor and resolve locking on your server.

Table 12-2	Utilities for Monitoring Locks
Utility	*Enables You To*
SQL Server Enterprise Manager	View and resolve blocking locks on your server. SQL Server Enterprise Manager displays any processes that are blocked, as well as the processes that are blocking them.
sp_who	Identify who is currently logged on to your server, the process (or processes) they are currently running, and the server process ID number (SPID) SQL Server has assigned to each process.
sp_lock	View the current locks on your server by server process ID number (SPID). This stored procedure indicates that a process is blocked by a lock by displaying "WAIT" in the status column.

In Lab 12-4, we have you create a blocked lock so that you can see what it looks like in both SQL Server Enterprise Manager and SQL Server Query Analyzer.

Lab 12-4   Monitoring Locks

1. **In the console tree of SQL Server Enterprise Manager, expand your server's Management folder.**

2. **Expand the Current Activity object.**

   Within the Current Activity object, you see objects that you can use to view process information, locks per process ID, and locks per object.

3. **Select the Locks/Process ID object, and take a look at the details pane.**

   As shown in Figure 12-10, seeing a few locks on your server is normal.

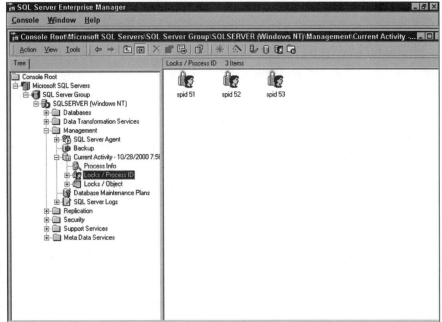

Figure 12-10:
Viewing
locks in SQL
Server
Enterprise
Manager.

4. Switch to SQL Server Query Analyzer.

5. Execute the following query:

```
EXEC sp_lock
```

This query enables you to view the current locks on your server. You
should see a few shared locks on your server, and possibly some special
use locks. (Look at the Mode column to determine the type of lock.)

6. On the toolbar, click the New Query button.

A second Query window opens in SQL Server Query Analyzer.

7. In your new Query window, execute the following query:

```
USE Northwind
BEGIN TRANSACTION
    UPDATE employees
    SET firstname = 'Mary'
    WHERE employeeid = 1
```

You have locked a row in the employees table with an exclusive lock
because you're using the UPDATE statement. And because you don't
have a COMMIT TRANSACTION (or ROLLBACK TRANSACTION) statement at

the end of these statements, you create a blocked lock. SQL Server won't release this lock unless you either kill the process in SQL Server Enterprise Manager, commit the transaction, or roll it back.

8. **Switch back to your first Query window, and run the** sp_lock **stored procedure again.**

You have several new locks, one of which is exclusive. Your UPDATE query placed an exclusive lock on the row with an employeeid of "1" in the employees table.

9. **Open a third Query window and execute the following query:**

```
USE Northwind
SELECT firstname
FROM employees
WHERE employeeid = 1
```

When you execute this query, SQL Server can't retrieve the result set because your UPDATE query has an exclusive lock on the same row. So you should see that SQL Server is processing the query (indicated by the revolving globe), but no result set.

10. **Switch back to your first Query window, and run the** sp_lock **stored procedure again.**

Because your SELECT query must place a shared lock on the row in the employees table, and your UPDATE query has that row locked, your SELECT query is blocked. You can tell that it's blocked when you look at the results of the sp_lock stored procedure by examining the Status column. A WAIT message, as shown in Figure 12-11, indicates that the process is blocked.

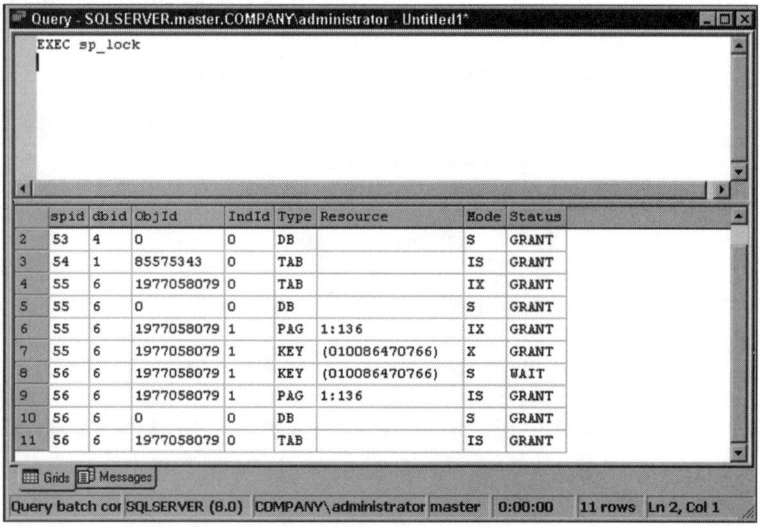

Figure 12-11:
The WAIT message indicates a blocked lock.

	spid	dbid	ObjId	IndId	Type	Resource	Mode	Status
2	53	4	0	0	DB		S	GRANT
3	54	1	85575343	0	TAB		IS	GRANT
4	55	6	1977058079	0	TAB		IX	GRANT
5	55	6	0	0	DB		S	GRANT
6	55	6	1977058079	1	PAG	1:136	IX	GRANT
7	55	6	1977058079	1	KEY	(010086470766)	X	GRANT
8	56	6	1977058079	1	KEY	(010086470766)	S	WAIT
9	56	6	1977058079	1	PAG	1:136	IS	GRANT
10	56	6	0	0	DB		S	GRANT
11	56	6	1977058079	0	TAB		IS	GRANT

Query - SQLSERVER.master.COMPANY\administrator - Untitled1*

```
EXEC sp_lock
```

Grids | Messages

Query batch cor | SQLSERVER (8.0) | COMPANY\administrator | master | 0:00:00 | 11 rows | Ln 2, Col 1

11. **Switch to SQL Server Enterprise Manager.**

12. **In the console tree, right-click the Current Activity object and choose Refresh.**

    SQL Server Enterprise Manager doesn't dynamically refresh the Current Activity information. You must manually refresh it instead.

13. **Select the Locks/Process ID object.**

    As shown in Figure 12-12, you now have both a blocking and a blocked process. The blocking process is your uncommitted UPDATE transaction, and the blocked process is your SELECT query.

14. **In the details pane, right-click the blocking process and choose Properties.**

    As you can see in Figure 12-13, the Process Details dialog box enables you to view the SQL statement causing the block. In addition, you can send a message to the connection causing the block — and you can kill the process.

15. **Click Kill Process to abort the UPDATE transaction; click Yes to confirm that you want to kill this process.**

    This action kills the UPDATE transaction, which is the equivalent of executing a ROLLBACK TRANSACTION statement.

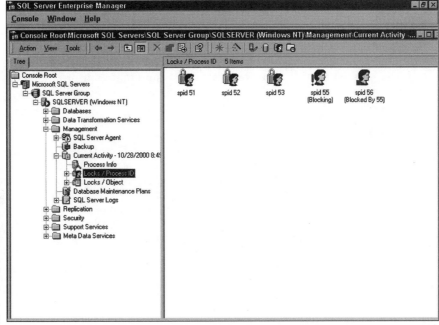

Figure 12-12:
Viewing blocking and blocked locks in SQL Server Enterprise Manager.

Figure 12-13:
The process
details for a
blocking
lock.

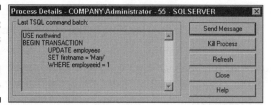

16. **Right-click the Current Activity object and choose Refresh.**

17. **In the console tree, select the Locks/Process ID object again.**

    You no longer have a blocked or blocking process on your server.

18. **Switch back to SQL Server Query Analyzer and run the** `sp_lock` **stored procedure again.**

    You no longer have any processes marked with a status of "WAIT."

19. **In SQL Server Query Analyzer, choose File⇨Disconnect All to close all of your Query windows.**

20. **When prompted, click No to All to close the Query windows without saving their changes.**

What can you do?

At this point, you're probably wondering what you can do to optimize locks. On the one hand, you have to have locks in order to protect your server's data. On the other hand, locks can degrade your server's performance. If you're using a custom program, make sure that your programmers have taken whatever steps they can to minimize the effect of locking on your server.

What it boils down to is that as the database administrator, you might not have any control over your server's applications, so the only thing you can do to optimize locking is just to respond to and resolve blocking locks. You can monitor for blocking locks by using SQL Server Enterprise Manager or the `sp_lock` stored procedure. You can then kill any blocking locks within SQL Server Enterprise Manager. If the process causing the blocking lock is critical, then you can at least use the information in SQL Server Enterprise Manager to identify the query that's causing the problem. You can then take this information to your programmers — and yell at them. (Just kidding.) Actually, your programmers can use this information to help them identify the source of the problem, and (hopefully) rewrite the program to avoid causing blocking locks.

Modifying the Database Schema

While you're in the midst of optimizing indexing, queries, recompiling, and locking, you may discover that you also need to modify your database's schema in order to optimize performance. Because we cover earlier how you modify a database in great detail, we just want to remind you of the database components you can modify. You can modify the database schema by

- ✔ Increasing the size of the database's data files, transaction log files, or both
- ✔ Decreasing the size of the database's data files, transaction log files, or both
- ✔ Adding or removing data files or transaction log files
- ✔ Creating new filegroups
- ✔ Specifying a user-defined filegroup as the default filegroup
- ✔ Modifying the database options for your database
- ✔ Changing the name of a database and any of its objects
- ✔ Creating, modifying, or deleting any database objects

For more information on how to modify anything about the database itself, see Chapter 10. And for more information on how to create, modify, or delete database objects, see Chapter 11.

Prep Test

1 An index is made up of what types of pages? (Choose all that apply.)

A ❑ Root-level

B ❑ Leaf-level

C ❑ Intermediate-level

D ❑ Heaps

Scenario 1: Managing Indexes

Use the following scenario to answer questions 2 through 4: You are designing the indexing for a table containing employee information. The table contains columns for storing each employee's name, social security number, address, phone number, department, manager, and salary.

2 You plan to query the employee table frequently by employees' social security numbers. What type of index should you create to optimize this query?

A ○ A clustered index on the social security number column

B ○ A nonclustered index on the social security number column

C ○ None

3 You plan to query this table to generate lists of employees by department. What type of index should you create to optimize this query?

A ○ A clustered index on the department column

B ○ A nonclustered index on the department column

C ○ None

4 You plan to query the employee table by employee name. What type of index should you create?

A ○ A clustered index on the employee last and first name columns

B ○ A nonclustered index on the employee last and first name columns

C ○ None

5 **You have configured SQL Server Query Analyzer to display the query execution plan for a query. When you execute a query, it displays "clustered index scan." What does this message mean?**

A ○ The table has a clustered index that does not improve the performance of the query.

B ○ The query optimizer used the table's clustered index to process the query.

C ○ Nothing. The query optimizer always displays this message regardless of how it resolves the query.

D ○ The query optimizer used your table's clustered index to scan the non-clustered index to process the query.

6 **Which of the following techniques can you use to optimize queries? (Choose all that apply.)**

A ❑ Upgrade the RAM in your server.

B ❑ Configure the Query Governor.

C ❑ Use SQL Server Profiler to analyze queries.

D ❑ Recompile all the queried table's stored procedures.

7 **True or False: SQL Server automatically recompiles a stored procedure whenever you modify the table on which it's based.**

A ○ True

B ○ False

8 **Which of the following resources can be locked in SQL Server 2000? (Choose all that apply.)**

A ❑ A table row

B ❑ An index row

C ❑ A page

D ❑ A database

9 **True or False: SQL Server automatically resolves blocking locks for you.**

A ○ True

B ○ False

10 **You can monitor blocking locks by using which utilities? (Choose all that apply.)**

A ❑ SQL Server Enterprise Manager

B ❑ The `sp_who` stored procedure

C ❑ The `sp_lock` stored procedure

D ❑ The `sp_blockinglock` stored procedure

Answers

1 **A, B,** and **C.** An index consists of a root-level page, intermediate-level pages, and leaf-level pages. *See "Defining the B-tree architecture."*

2 **B.** Because an index on the social security number column is highly selective, create a nonclustered index on this column. *See "Optimizing nonclustered indexes."*

3 **A.** Create a clustered index for this column because any queries against the department column typically return a range of rows. *See "Optimizing clustered indexes."*

4 **B.** Create a nonclustered index on the employee last and first name columns. *See "Optimizing nonclustered indexes."*

5 **A.** The "clustered index scan" message indicates that the table has a clustered index, but that this index doesn't improve the performance of the query. *Study "Managing index statistics."*

6 **A, B,** and **C.** All of these techniques improve the performance of queries. *See "Optimizing Queries."*

7 **A.** SQL Server recompiles a stored procedure whenever you change the table on which it's based. *Study "Optimizing Recompiling."*

8 **A, B, C,** and **D.** Depending on what types of actions you're performing, SQL Server can lock all of these resources. *Study "Optimizing Locking."*

9 **B.** SQL Server automatically resolves deadlocks, not blocking locks. *See "Deadlocks and blocking locks."*

10 **A** and **C.** The sp_who stored procedure enables you to view only information about who's connected to your server, not locks. *Study "Monitoring and resolving blocking locks."*

Chapter 13

Optimizing Data Storage

- -

Exam Objectives

▶ Optimizing files and filegroups

▶ Managing database fragmentation

- -

*O*ne of your tasks as a database administrator is to fine-tune your server's configuration over time. And one of the more important configuration parameters you need to keep your eye on is your server's files and filegroups. You can use System Monitor to determine whether your server's hard disk subsystem can keep up with the workload. If you find that your server's hard disk subsystem can't keep up, use strategies such as implementing new files and filegroups, and distributing them across multiple hard disks to distribute the workload. Also monitor tables and indexes for fragmentation in order to optimize how your server uses its database files.

In this chapter, you review procedures for monitoring both your server's hard disk subsystem and database fragmentation, and the steps you can take to resolve any problems you detect.

Quick Assessment

Optimizing files and filegroups

1 You have a hard disk performance problem if your SQL server's PhysicalDisk: %DiskTime counter exceeds _____.

2 You should be concerned if your server's PhysicalDisk: Avg. Disk Queue Length exceeds _____.

3 To determine how often SQL Server is reading from your hard disk, use the _____ counter.

4 You should monitor both hard disk and _____counters when analyzing your server's hard disk subsystem's performance.

5 By creating _____, you can improve hard disk performance without upgrading your server's hardware.

Managing database fragmentation

6 You use the _____ command to determine the fragmentation for a specific index.

7 The statistic for _____enables you to determine how full a table or index's pages are.

8 If you rebuild a(n) _____SQL Server automatically rebuilds all the table's nonclustered indexes.

9 To minimize lock contention, use the _____command to defragment an index.

10 Use the _____ command to rebuild an index with a new fill factor percentage.

Answers

1 *90 percent.* Read "Using System Monitor."

2 *Two times the number of hard disks in your server.* See "Using System Monitor."

3 *PhysicalDisk: Disk Reads/sec.* Study "Using System Monitor."

4 *Memory.* See "Using System Monitor."

5 *Multiple files and filegroups.* See "Resolving performance problems."

6 `DBCC SHOWCONTIG (table_name, index_name).` See "Monitoring fragmentation."

7 *Average Page Density (Full).* See "Monitoring fragmentation."

8 *Clustered index.* See "Resolving fragmentation."

9 `DBCC INDEXDEFRAG.` Study "Resolving fragmentation."

10 `DBCC DBREINDEX.` See "Resolving fragmentation."

Optimizing Files and Filegroups

As you know, SQL Server works your server's hard disks fairly hard. Optimizing your server's hard disks makes a big difference in your SQL environment's overall performance. So you may be wondering whether your strategy for implementing files and filegroups, and how you've distributed them across your server's hard disks, is giving you the best performance. One of the better tools you can use to determine how your server's hard disks are performing is the Windows 2000 System Monitor.

Using System Monitor

Although SQL Server itself manages when information is read from or written to your server's hard disks, Windows 2000 actually performs those tasks. So you can use all the same techniques for monitoring hard disk performance on any Windows 2000 computer to determine how well your server's hard disks are performing with SQL Server.

Table 13-1 reviews the counters that Microsoft considers most important when monitoring a SQL server's hard disk performance. Make sure you know these counters and their functions for the exam.

Table 13-1	System Monitor Counters for Analyzing Hard Disks
Object and Counter	*Enables You to Analyze*
PhysicalDisk: %Disk Time	The amount of time your server spends reading and writing to the hard disk. You have a hard disk performance problem if you see a consistent value of 90 percent or greater for this counter.
PhysicalDisk: Avg. Disk Queue Length	The average number of disk read and write requests pending for your server to process. This number should be less than two times the number of hard disks in your server.
PhysicalDisk: Disk Reads/sec	The number of read operations executed per second on your server's hard disk(s). This value is hardware dependent, so it varies depending on the type of hard disks and controllers you're using. In general, you want your server's disk reads per second to be high — but you don't want this value to be very close to the capacity of your hard disks.

Object and Counter	Enables You to Analyze
PhysicalDisk: Disk Writes/sec	The number of write operations executed per second on your server's hard disk(s). Like the Disk Reads/sec counter, this value is hardware dependent. And like Disk Read/sec, you want this counter to be high but not at your hard disks' capacity.

Always monitor memory counters in addition to hard disk counters. For example, always monitor the Memory: Pages/sec counter in addition to your hard disk counters. By monitoring both types of counters, you can determine whether your server's hard disks really are slow — or if your server simply doesn't have enough RAM.

Not having enough memory in your server can make your server's hard disk subsystem seem as if it is overloaded. That's because Windows 2000 must continually page information between RAM and your server's page file. On your exam, make sure that you look at all the performance values Microsoft gives you in the questions before you select an answer.

Resolving performance problems

So what should you do if you monitor these counters and you determine that your server's hard disk subsystem is overloaded? Here are some suggestions:

- ✔ Make sure that your server has enough RAM.

- ✔ Upgrade your hard disk subsystem by installing faster hard disks and a better hard disk controller.

- ✔ If you haven't already done so, install a disk array.

- ✔ Create multiple filegroups, and multiple files within each filegroup. Wherever possible, distribute the filegroups across multiple hard disks.

- ✔ If your server has more than one user database, consider installing a second SQL server and splitting the databases between your servers.

Managing Database Fragmentation

One of the facts of life in a database environment is that your databases change: Rows get added and deleted from tables (and also the indexes), SQL Server can auto-grow and shrink your database, and objects can be added and deleted as well. As SQL Server makes these changes, your tables and indexes can become fragmented over time.

Fragmentation in this context can mean two things. First, it means that a table or index might be using 100 pages, but each page isn't completely full. This type of fragmentation is called *page fragmentation*, and the amount of information on a particular page is called its *row density*. The lower the row density per page for a table, the greater the page fragmentation — and the more pages SQL Server must process when retrieving a result set for a query. Second, fragmentation can occur when you add a large amount of information to a table, and SQL Server must spread the pages containing that information over different extents in the database. This type of fragmentation is called *extent fragmentation*.

Both types of fragmentation can degrade your server's performance because SQL Server must work harder to retrieve data. On the other hand, in an OLTP system in which your users are continually inserting and deleting data, fragmentation can work to your advantage: SQL Server can insert new rows without having to split a table's pages. If fragmentation isn't desirable for your database environment, as a database administrator, you should monitor for fragmentation — and if you find it, take steps to resolve it.

Monitoring fragmentation

So how do you determine whether your tables or indexes are fragmented? The best way is to use the DBCC SHOWCONTIG command. As shown in Figure 13-1, this command enables you to view both page and extent fragmentation for a table or index.

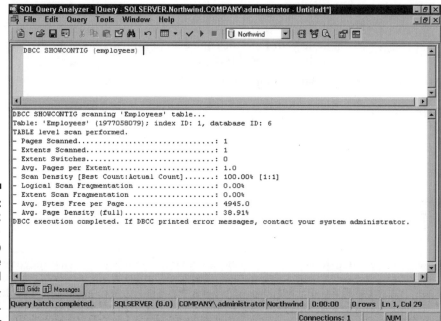

Figure 13-1: Use DBCC SHOWCONTIG to analyze table and index fragmentation.

Here's the basic syntax for viewing a table's fragmentation information:

```
DBCC SHOWCONTIG (table_name)
```

When you use the DBCC SHOWCONTIG command, you see a bunch of statistics about your table or index (or both). These statistics help you determine whether or not the object is fragmented, and whether the fragmentation is extent or page fragmentation. We describe the key statistics in Table 13-2.

Table 13-2   Interpreting the Statistics in DBCC SHOWCONTIG

Statistic	*Enables You to Identify*
Extent Switches	How many times DBCC had to change extents while scanning the table or index's pages. The greater the number of extent switches, the greater the extent fragmentation of the object.
Average Pages per Extent	The average number of pages in each of the table or index's extent(s).
Scan Density [Best Count: Actual Count]	How contiguous the pages of the table or index are within its extents. The Best Count value indicates the ideal value; the Actual Count is the actual number of extent switches DBCC had to make. A value of 100 percent means that the Best Count and Actual Count values are the same, and that table or index is contiguous. A value of less than 100 percent indicates that some extent fragmentation has occurred.
Average Bytes Free per Page	The number of free bytes per page in the table or index. One problem with this statistic is that it doesn't take into account the size of your table or index's rows. In general, you want the number of bytes free per page to be low because it indicates that your table or index's pages have a greater number of rows per page. But keep in mind that you might see a higher number just because your table's row size is large.
Average Page Density (Full)	How full a table or index's pages are. This statistic does take into account the size of a row, so it's the more accurate statistic for analyzing page density. A higher percentage indicates fuller pages and less fragmentation; a lower percentage indicates greater fragmentation and less full pages. The higher this number, the better performance you see for this object.

You can expect to see a question or two on your exam displaying the output for the DBCC SHOWCONTIG command and prompting you to choose a solution based on this information.

Resolving fragmentation

You've analyzed your tables and indexes, and now you know you have fragmentation. Your next step is to resolve the fragmentation. How you go about resolving it depends on where the fragmentation is and what types of indexes you've defined. For example, if your table is fragmented and you've configured it with a clustered index, the table and the index are the same object. As a result, you can defragment a table and its clustered index simply by rebuilding the index. Likewise, you can defragment a nonclustered index by rebuilding it as well.

If you rebuild a clustered index, SQL Server automatically rebuilds all the table's nonclustered indexes as well, because a nonclustered index consists of the values in the index's key (such as last names) plus a row identifier. The row identifier tells the nonclustered index where it can find a row in the table. So if you rebuild a clustered index, all of its row identifiers change — so SQL Server automatically rebuilds the nonclustered indexes as well.

But what if your table is fragmented, and you haven't configured it with a clustered index? The easiest way to defragment the table is to go ahead and create a clustered index (which defragments the table), and then drop the index. The only drawback to this solution is that you will incur the cost of having SQL Server rebuild the table's nonclustered indexes twice: once when you create the clustered index, and then again when you delete it.

SQL Server 2000 includes two commands that you can use to rebuild an index: DBCC DBREINDEX and DBCC INDEXDEFRAG. You can also rebuild an index by using the CREATE INDEX statement with the WITH DROP_EXISTING clause.

Using DBCC DBREINDEX

You use the DBCC DBREINDEX command to rebuild an index without dropping and recreating it. Here's the syntax:

```
DBCC DBREINDEX ('database.owner.table'[, index_name [,
          fill_factor] )
```

We use the square brackets to indicate that both the index_name and fill_factor parameters are optional. If you don't specify an index name (or fill factor for that matter), SQL Server rebuilds all the indexes for the table.

Using DBCC INDEXDEFRAG

The DBCC DBREINDEX command places exclusive locks on your table, indexes, or both as it reindexes them. As a result, using DBCC DBREINDEX to rebuild large clustered or nonclustered indexes can cause blocking locks and end up delaying the processing of other users' queries. To counteract this problem, Microsoft added the DBCC INDEXDEFRAG statement to SQL Server 2000. The big advantage to this command is that it enables you to defragment indexes online, which means that it doesn't hold locks for very long periods of time.

Use the following syntax to defragment your indexes:

```
DBCC INDEXDEFRAG (database_name, table_name, index_name)
```

When this command defragments an index, it also reestablishes the fill factor percentage you specified when you created the index.

Prep Test

1 You think that your SQL server's hard disk can't keep up with its workload. Which of the following counters should you monitor? (Choose all that apply.)

A ❑ Memory: Pages/sec

B ❑ PhysicalDisk: %DiskTime

C ❑ PhysicalDisk: Split IO/sec

D ❑ Processor: % ProcessorTime

2 Which of the following are valid techniques for resolving performance problems with your server's hard disk subsystem? (Choose all that apply.)

A ❑ Reinstall SQL Server 2000 to eliminate fragmentation.

B ❑ Install a disk array.

C ❑ Create multiple filegroups and assign each filegroup to a separate hard disk.

D ❑ Increase the RAM in your server.

3 What causes page fragmentation in a table? (Choose all that apply.)

A ❑ Reindexing a table

B ❑ Inserting rows

C ❑ Modifying rows

D ❑ Deleting large numbers of rows

4 After analyzing the results of DBCC SHOWCONTIG, you've determined that your table is fragmented. You have defined a clustered index for this table, and two nonclustered indexes. What should you do?

A ○ Rebuild the table only.

B ○ Rebuild the clustered index.

C ○ Rebuild the nonclustered indexes.

D ○ Use the SELECT INTO statement to create a new table and copy the data from the old table into the new table.

5 You have a table for which you haven't defined a clustered index. After analyzing the results of the DBCC SHOWCONTIG command, you want to defragment the table. What should you do?

A ○ Use the DBCC TABLEDEFRAG command to defragment the table.

B ○ Use the DBCC DBREINDEX command to reindex the table's nonclustered indexes.

C ○ Create a clustered index on the table and then drop the index.

D ○ Create a nonclustered index on the table and then drop the index.

6 Which of the following commands enables you to check fragmentation on a table and all of its indexes?

A ○ `DBCC SHOWCONTIG (table_name)`

B ○ `DBCC SHOWCONTIG (table_name, ALL_INDEXES)`

C ○ `DBCC SHOWCONTIG (table_name, *)`

D ○ `DBCC SHOWCONTIG (table_name) WITH ALL_INDEXES`

7 What advantages does the `DBCC INDEXDEFRAG` command offer you over `DBCC DBREINDEX`? **(Choose all that apply.)**

A ❑ Supports online defragmentation

B ❑ Reduces server workload during defragmentation

C ❑ Minimizes locks placed on tables and indexes during defragmentation

D ❑ Re-establishes index fill factors

Answers

1 **A** and **B.** Always monitor both memory and physical disk counters to determine whether your hard disks can't keep up with the workload due to insufficient RAM. In addition, we use the PhysicalDisk: %Disk Time counter to determine how busy the server is in servicing disk I/O requests. *Study "Using System Monitor."*

2 **B, C,** and **D.** You can improve your server's hard disk subsystem's performance by installing a disk array, assigning filegroups to a separate hard disk, or by upgrading the RAM in your server. *See "Resolving performance problems."*

3 **B** and **D.** Tables become fragmented over time due to the insertion and deletion of rows. *Study "Managing Database Fragmentation."*

4 **B.** You should rebuild the clustered index to defragment the table. SQL Server will then automatically rebuild the table's nonclustered indexes for you. *See "Resolving fragmentation."*

5 **C.** You can defragment a table for which you haven't defined a clustered index by creating a clustered index and then dropping that index. *See "Resolving fragmentation."*

6 **D.** You use the `WITH ALL_INDEXES` clause to have the `DBCC SHOWCONTIG` command check fragmentation on all of a table's indexes. *Study "Monitoring fragmentation."*

7 **A** and **C.** The `DBCC INDEXDEFRAG` statement enables you to perform online defragmenation, which minimizes the locks placed on resources during the defragmentation process. *See "Resolving fragmentation."*

Chapter 14

Backing Up Databases

· ·

Exam Objectives

▶ Performing backups

▶ Performing disaster recovery operations

· ·

*Y*ou use database backups to protect yourself from a variety of problems. These include everything from restoring a database in the event of a server hardware failure, to restoring a database when a user accidentally (or even maliciously) changes or deletes your data, to restoring a database after a virus or catastrophic event (such as fires or floods).

We don't mean to get on our soapboxes here, but there's no excuse for not having good backups of your data — especially with the tools provided with SQL Server 2000. In this chapter, we examine how you go about backing up your databases. We also look at how you design your backup strategy. (In Chapter 15, we show you how to restore your databases from these backups.)

Don't let the fact that we list only two exam objectives for this chapter mislead you! You can expect to see quite a few questions on your exam on backing up databases.

Quick Assessment

Performing backups

1 A(n) _____ backup makes a full copy of your database.

2 Only a(n) _____ backup truncates a database's transaction log.

3 You can perform a transaction log backup only if you've configured a database to use the _____ or _____ recovery models.

4 The _____ recovery model enables you to recover a database to a specific point in time.

5 You must back up the following system databases: _____, _____, and _____.

6 You should create a(n) _____ backup device if you plan to schedule backups.

Performing disaster recovery operations

7 In the event of a database failure, you should first back up the transaction log with the _____ option before you do anything else.

8 Your only choice for recovering a database that's using the simple recovery model is to restore _____.

Answers

1 *Complete.* Review "Preparing to Back Up SQL Databases."

2 *Transaction Log.* Study "Preparing to Back Up SQL Databases."

3 *Full or Bulk_Logged.* See "Choosing a database recovery model."

4 *Full.* Study "Choosing a database recovery model."

5 *Master, model, and msdb.* Review "Managing the backup process."

6 *Permanent.* Study "Performing Backups."

7 `NO_TRUNCATE`. Study "Designing a Backup Strategy."

8 *Your last complete backup of the database.* See "Complete backup strategy."

Preparing to Back Up SQL Databases

SQL Server's Backup enables you to back up a database even as users access it. SQL Server backs up the following:

✔ The database schema and file structure for both system and user databases

✔ The data

✔ The transactions in the transaction log that have occurred since your last backup

Table 14-1 describes the types of backups you can perform in SQL Server. Make sure you know these for the exam!

Table 14-1	Backup Types
Backup Type	*Enables You to Back Up*
Complete (Full)	All the pages that make up your database. In addition, SQL Server also backs up any transactions that occur during the backup itself.
Differential	Only the extents of the database that have been changed since your last complete backup. You can create a differential backup only if you've created a complete backup first.
Transaction log	All the transactions that have been recorded to the transaction log since your last full or differential backups.
File/Filegroup	Only a specific data file or filegroup. You use this backup type for backing up very large databases.

When you back up a transaction log, SQL Server backs up the transactions that have been added to the log since you last backed it up — and then it clears (truncates) the log. The amount of data that's stored in the transaction log varies depending on the database recovery model you choose.

Choosing a database recovery model

One of your first steps in designing your recovery strategy for SQL Server 2000 is to choose the database recovery model you want to implement for your database. SQL Server supports three different models, each impacting the methods you must use to recover a database in the event of a failure.

The key question to keep in mind here is that if you have a failure (whether due to server hardware, corrupted data, or a disaster), how much of the data do you want to recover? For example, do you want to recover all the data, including what's stored in your last backup plus anything that's changed since your last backup? Or will it be enough if you just restore your last backup?

The reason these questions are important is because they determine the recovery model you need to use for your database. In order to recover all the data, including those changes after your last backup, you must be able to back up and then restore the transaction log. And, the transaction log must contain the necessary information. Each of these recovery models has a different spin on what it keeps in the transaction log, so depending on which model you implement, you may or may not be able to recover all the changes since your last backup.

Make sure you understand the differences between the three recovery models, and the impact each has on what you can back up and restore, for the exam.

The full recovery model

When you configure a database to use the full recovery model, SQL Server 2000 logs all of your changes to the database in its transaction log. These changes include all data transactions (such as adding, modifying, and deleting rows), as well as all bulk operations (for importing data) and any indexes you create. With bulk operations, SQL Server records every row you insert by using the bulk copy program (bcp) or the BULK INSERT SQL statement. By using the full recovery model, recovering a database up to the point of the failure is possible.

Given that this model enables you to recover a database completely, you may be wondering why you wouldn't always use it. Well, the answer is that this level of logging costs you both in server disk space (because the transaction log will be quite big) and performance (because your server must record everything in the transaction log). Use this model only if every change to your database is critical.

The full recovery model is the only model that enables you to recover your database to any point in time.

The bulk_logged recovery model

With the bulk_logged recovery model, SQL Server doesn't use as much space in the transaction log for the following activities:

- ✔ Any new indexes you create
- ✔ All bulk load operations

> ✔ The SELECT INTO statement
>
> ✔ Any changes to text fields by using the WRITETEXT and UPDATETEXT statements

SQL Server records the fact that these changes took place, but it doesn't record each and every row modification in the transaction log.

The advantage to using the bulk_logged recovery model is that it reduces the amount of disk space you need for your database's transaction log. In addition, SQL Server can perform bulk load operations significantly faster because it won't have to log each and every change to a row in a table. A couple of disadvantages exist to using this model, however. First, although you can restore all of your data in the event of a failure, you won't be able to restore the data to a specific point in time. Second, your backups of the transaction log can (and typically will) be much larger than the log itself because SQL Server copies the modified extents to the log backup.

If you configure a database to use the bulk_logged recovery model, but you don't perform any bulk load operations, you can still recover your database to a specific point in time. The main difference between the full and bulk_logged recovery models is the level of logging for bulk load operations.

The simple recovery model

If you use the simple recovery model, SQL Server doesn't keep any of the changes you make to the database after it has committed those changes. (SQL Server truncates the transaction log at regular intervals to clear out committed transactions.) Because SQL Server truncates the log, you lose any of the changes you make to the database after your last backup in the event of a failure. The advantage to the simple recovery model is that it minimizes the amount of disk space used by a database's transaction log. In addition, bulk load operations will be faster because SQL Server doesn't have the added overhead of recording them in the log files. Use this model if you have a small database or the data in your database doesn't change very often.

You can't back up a database's transaction log if you've configured the database to use the simple recovery model. In fact, you can't choose the transaction log when you back up in SQL Server Enterprise Manager — and if you execute the BACKUP LOG SQL statement, you receive an error message.

In all versions prior to SQL Server 2000, you controlled whether or not SQL Server automatically truncated the transaction log by setting a database option. This option is called *truncate log on checkpoint*, and is equivalent to configuring a database to use the simple recovery model. Microsoft included the truncate log on checkpoint option in SQL Server 2000 for compatibility with older versions of SQL Server.

Configuring a database's recovery model

You configure your database's recovery model by using either the ALTER DATABASE SQL statement or SQL Server Enterprise Manager. Here's the syntax for the ALTER DATABASE statement:

```
ALTER DATABASE database_name
SET RECOVERY {FULL | BULK_LOGGED | SIMPLE}
```

Lab 14-1 walks you through the steps for configuring a database to use the full recovery model in SQL Server Enterprise Manager.

Lab 14-1   Configuring a Database Recovery Model

1. **If necessary, log on to your server as Administrator and open SQL Server Enterprise Manager.**

2. **In the console tree, right-click the desired database and choose Properties.**

3. **Select the Options tab.**

   You configure the database's recovery model on this page.

4. **Look at the recovery model.**

   By default, SQL Server configures the selected database to use the simple recovery model.

5. **From the Model drop-down list, select Full, as shown in Figure 14-1.**

6. **Click OK to save your changes.**

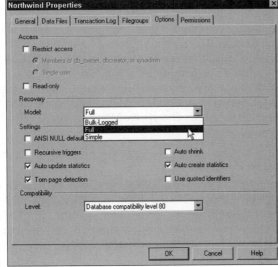

Figure 14-1:
You can configure a database to use either the full, bulk_logged, or simple recovery models.

Managing the backup process

Before we look at how you back up in SQL Server 2000, we want to look at the who, what, and where of backups. First, SQL Server doesn't let just anyone back up a database. You must either be a member of the sysadmin server role, or a member of the db_owner or db_backupoperator database roles, to back up a database. (You can also create your own database roles and assign the necessary permissions to those roles for backing up a database.)

You can back up to a file, tape, or a named pipe. Use a disk file to back up either to your server's local hard disk or a network drive. After you back up to a file, you can then back up this file to tape outside of SQL Server. You can back up to tape only if the tape drive is directly attached to your SQL server. Use a named pipe if you want to back up by using third-party backup software.

After you have the necessary permissions, the final consideration is what you should back up. You should back up both system and user databases. Of the system databases, backing up the master, model, and msdb databases is essential.

Backing up the master database

The master database is SQL Server's heart and soul, mostly because it tracks all of your databases and their associated files. For this reason, backing up the master database is critical. In addition, always back up the master database whenever you perform activities such as creating, modifying, or dropping a user database.

If you lose the master database due to a server failure or corruption, SQL Server won't be able to access any of your user databases until you restore the master database.

You can rebuild the master database if you don't have a current backup. You do so by running the Rebuild Master (rebuildm.exe) utility in a Command Prompt window. Keep in mind that rebuilding the master database returns it to its original state (as if you've just installed SQL Server). As a result, the master database won't have any information about your user databases. You can update the master database with information about your user databases by reattaching them in SQL Server Enterprise Manager or by using the sp_attach_db stored procedure.

Backing up the msdb database

In addition to backing up the master database, you should also back up the msdb database. SQL Server uses this database to store all of your automation information. For example, SQL Server stores your jobs for automating tasks such as backing up the server in the msdb database. It also uses the msdb database to store operator and alerts information.

The Rebuild Master utility rebuilds not only the master database, but also all of your server's system databases. Be aware that when SQL Server rebuilds the msdb database, you lose all of your jobs, alerts, and operators. You can recover your jobs, alerts, and operators only if you have a backup of the msdb database. And if you don't have a backup, you must recreate all of these objects.

Backing up the model database

As you know, SQL Server uses the model database as a template for any new databases you create. Any objects you create in the model database are copied to new databases. Back up the model database only if you've added any new objects to it.

Backing up user databases

In addition to backing up the system databases, you need to also back up your user databases (for obvious reasons!). Back up a user database whenever you perform any of the following tasks:

- You add or modify the database's data.

- You create a new index. Backing up the database after you create a new index enables SQL Server to restore the index if you have to restore the database. If you back up only the transaction log after creating an index, you won't be able to restore the index because SQL Server records only the fact that you created the index in the transaction log.

- You have SQL Server perform a non-logged operation (such as a bulk load of data).

- You truncate the transaction log. After you truncate the transaction log, you can recover a database only by restoring a backup of that database. You won't be able to restore the database by using its transaction log.

Performing Backups

Before you back up your database, you must first choose whether you want to back up to a temporary or permanent backup device. A device is the file in which SQL Server stores your backup. You use permanent backup devices whenever you want to reuse these files — such as when you define a scheduled backup. Use temporary backup devices as a quick way to create a backup device as part of the backup itself.

Creating permanent backup devices

You can create your backup devices on a hard disk, tape drive, or named pipe. One enhancement in SQL Server's backup is that it enables you to execute a parallel striped backup, which means that you can back up to multiple devices simultaneously — which makes for a significantly faster backup. So, for example, you may want to create three or four backup devices to back up a large user database instead of only a single backup device.

You can create a total of 64 backup devices for a database. SQL Server keeps track of your backup devices in the sysdevices table within the master database.

You create a permanent backup device by using either the `sp_addumpdevice` stored procedure or SQL Server Enterprise Manager. (You create temporary devices as part of the backup itself.)

You create a permanent backup device in SQL Server Enterprise Manager by first expanding your server's Management folder. Next, right-click the Backup object and choose New Backup Device. You can then create a permanent backup file on disk or tape. We walk you through creating a backup device in Lab 14-2.

Lab 14-2	Creating a Permanent Backup Device in SQL Server Enterprise Manager

1. **In SQL Server Enterprise Manager, expand your server's Management folder.**

2. **In the console tree, right-click the Backup object and choose New Backup Device.**

   As shown in Figure 14-2, SQL Server Enterprise Manager opens the Backup Device Properties – New Device dialog box. You can use this dialog box to create a new device either on disk or tape. If you don't have a locally attached tape drive on your server, you can't choose the Tape Drive Name option.

   SQL Server defaults to creating the new device in the C:\Program Files\Microsoft SQL Server\MSSQL\Backup folder on your server. You can create this file anywhere on your server's hard disk. You can also create the device on a mapped network drive.

   Notice the View Contents button. If you specify the name of an existing device, you can click View Contents to see what backups you're currently storing in the device.

3. **In the Name text box, type a name for your backup device — for example,** Northwindbkup.

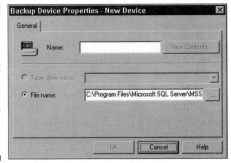

Figure 14-2:
You can
create per-
manent
backup
devices in
SQL Server
Enterprise
Manager.

4. **Look at the File Name text box.**

By default, SQL Server Enterprise Manager automatically assigns the filename of *name*.bak (for example, Northwindbkup.bak) to the device for
you. You can accept this name, or click in the File Name box and change it.

5. **Click OK to create the disk backup device.**

6. **Look at the details pane in SQL Server Enterprise Manager.**

As shown in Figure 14-3, your new device is listed, along with its physical filename and device type.

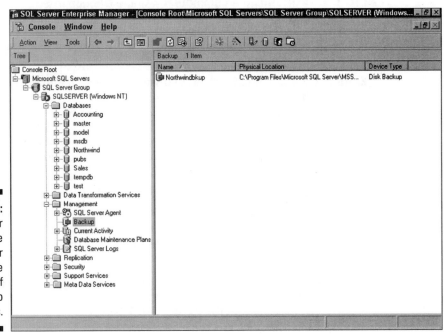

Figure 14-3:
SQL Server
Enterprise
Manager
lists the
details of
your backup
devices.

Now that you've created a backup device, your next step is to perform the backup itself. You can perform complete, differential, transaction log, or file/filegroup backups.

Performing a complete database backup

A complete database backup enables you to back up the entire database along with any transactions that occurred during the backup. In addition, SQL Server backs up any transactions that are in your transaction log but not yet committed to the database. You can perform a complete backup of a database by using either the BACKUP SQL statement or SQL Server Enterprise Manager, and you can back up to a permanent or a temporary backup device.

You can back up a database in SQL Server Enterprise Manager by using a variety of techniques. For example, you can right-click any database and choose All Tasks⇨Backup Database to back it up. You can also right-click the Backup object and choose Backup A Database. And here's a third option: Choose Tools⇨Wizards; then run the Backup Wizard to back up any database.

Lab 14-3 shows you how to back up a database by using SQL Server Enterprise Manager.

Lab 14-3	Performing a Complete Database Backup in SQL Server Enterprise Manager

1. **In SQL Server Enterprise Manager, expand your server's Databases folder if necessary.**

2. **Right-click the database that you want to back up and choose All Tasks⇨Backup Database.**

3. **Look at the default options.**

   SQL Server Enterprise Manager assumes that you want to perform a complete backup of the database. In addition, it configures your backup to append to the backup device.

4. **Click Add to display the Select Backup Destination dialog box.**

   You use this dialog box to choose the backup device to which you want to back up. Choose the File Name option to back up to a temporary device. Alternatively, choose the Backup Device option to back up to a permanent backup device you've already created.

   You can perform a parallel striped backup in SQL Server Enterprise Manager by choosing multiple backup devices. SQL Server then stripes your backup across all the devices you specify.

5. **Choose Backup Device, and verify that you're using the correct device, as shown in Figure 14-4.**

   Lab 14-2 describes the procedure for creating a permanent backup device.

Figure 14-4:
You can
back up to a
temporary
or perma-
nent device
in SQL
Server
Enterprise
Manager.

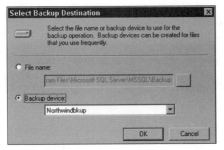

6. **Click OK to close the Select Backup Destination dialog box.**

   As shown in Figure 14-5, you're now ready to start the backup.

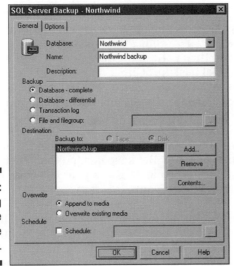

Figure 14-5:
Performing
a complete
database
backup.

7. **Click OK to begin.**

8. **Click OK to close the message box stating that the backup completed successfully.**

After you complete the backup, you can view the contents of any permanent backup device by right-clicking the device in SQL Server Enterprise Manager and choosing Properties. Next, click View Contents to see what's stored in the device. As shown in Figure 14-6, you can see the name of the database, the type of backup the device contains (complete, differential, and so on), and the date the backup was performed.

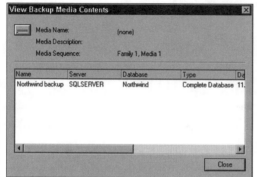

Figure 14-6:
Viewing the
contents of
a backup
device.

Performing a differential database backup

If your database is large, you may find that performing complete backups of it on a nightly basis is impossible. You can minimize the amount of time you need to back up the database by performing a complete backup at a regular interval (such as weekly), and then performing only a differential backup on a nightly basis. With a differential backup, SQL Server backs up any extents containing changes your users have made since your last complete backup. In addition, SQL Server backs up any changes that occur while you're performing the differential backup.

The advantage to a differential backup is that you can reduce the amount of time you need to back up the database. But keep in mind that when you want (or need) to restore the database, you must restore your last complete backup — plus your last differential backup.

One thing you need to consider is that if you modify a row several times, a differential backup contains only the most recent modifications of that row. Differential backups can't keep track of the history of changes to a row. In contrast, transaction log backups enable you to keep track of all the changes made to a row.

Try to use names for your backup devices in which you plan to store differential backups that identify them as such. For example, you might use a name like Northwind_diff to identify a backup device for storing a differential backup of the Northwind database.

Like complete database backups, you perform differential backups by using either the BACKUP DATABASE statement along with the WITH DIFFERENTIAL clause, or by using SQL Server Enterprise Manager.

You receive an error message if you attempt a differential backup of a database for which you haven't yet performed a complete backup. As we describe in Lab 14-4, you perform a differential backup in SQL Server Enterprise Manager simply by choosing the Differential backup option.

Lab 14-4   Performing a Differential Database Backup in SQL Server Enterprise Manager

1. **In SQL Server Enterprise Manager, create a new backup device to store the differential backup.**

2. **Right-click the database you want to back up and choose All Tasks⇨Backup Database.**

   You must choose a database for which you already have a complete backup. For example, you could use the database you backed up in Lab 14-3.

3. **On the General page of the SQL Server Backup dialog box, below Backup, select Database – Differential, as shown in Figure 14-7.**

   This setting configures SQL Server Enterprise Manager to perform a differential backup of the database.

4. **Specify the backup device to which you want to back up. You can use a permanent or a temporary device.**

5. **Click OK to begin the backup.**

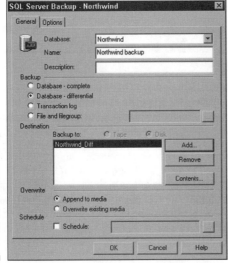

Figure 14-7:
Performing a differential backup in SQL Server Enterprise Manager.

Performing a transaction log backup

In addition to performing complete and differential database backups, you can also back up your database's transaction log — provided you have configured your database to use either the full or bulk_logged recovery models. (If you've configured your database to use the simple recovery model, SQL Server periodically removes the committed transactions from the transaction log.)

Backing up the transaction log enables you to capture the history of what's been changed in a database since your last complete or differential backup. The advantage to a transaction log backup is that it typically is much smaller (and thus faster to perform) than differential and complete database backups. In addition, after SQL Server backs up the transaction log, it truncates it. If you configure a database to use either the full or bulk_logged recovery models, until you back up the transaction log (and thus truncate it), the transaction log continues to grow in size until it either reaches its maximum size or your server runs out of disk space.

You can back up a transaction log by using either the BACKUP LOG SQL statement or SQL Server Enterprise Manager.

Using the BACKUP LOG statement

When you're ready to back up the transaction log, here's the basic syntax:

```
BACKUP LOG database_name
TO backup_device
[WITH OPTIONS]
```

Table 14-2 lists the BACKUP LOG statement options that you need to know for the exam.

Table 14-2	BACKUP LOG **Options**
Option	*What It Does*
NO_TRUNCATE	Configures SQL Server to back up the transaction log without truncating (deleting) its committed transactions. Most importantly, this option enables you to back up a database's transaction log in the event of a failure so that you can attempt to recover the transactions in the log.
TRUNCATE_ONLY	Truncates the transaction log without actually backing it up. You typically use this option with the BACKUP LOG statement to clear a full transaction log. But be aware that the TRUNCATE_ONLY option does just that. Your next step after performing this statement should be to perform a complete backup of your database.

Option	What It Does
NO_LOG	This option is essentially the same as TRUNCATE_ONLY. By using this option with the BACKUP LOG statement, you force SQL Server to truncate the log. The only difference between the two options is that SQL Server does not log the BACKUP LOG statement in the transaction log if you use the NO_LOG option. In contrast, SQL Server does log the BACKUP LOG statement if you use the TRUNCATE_ONLY option.

As you may have already gathered from some of these options, one of the reasons why you use the BACKUP LOG statement is not really to back up the transaction log. Instead, you use this statement to truncate a full transaction log. Know how to truncate the transaction log, because once the log is full, your users can't make any changes to the database until you clear the log.

Using SQL Server Enterprise Manager

You perform a transaction log backup in SQL Server Enterprise Manager by using almost the same steps as backing up a database. The only difference is that you must make sure you choose the appropriate options for a transaction log backup. For example, if you want to be able to recover a database after a failure, make sure you perform the transaction log backup using the WITH NO_TRUNCATE option.

By default, SQL Server Enterprise Manager automatically truncates a transaction log after it backs it up. If you don't want SQL Server Enterprise Manager to truncate the log, you must configure the backup options to prevent it from doing so.

Lab 14-5 walks you through the steps for performing a backup of a database's transaction log.

Lab 14-5	Performing a Transaction Log Backup in SQL Server Enterprise Manager

1. **In SQL Server Enterprise Manager, create a new backup device to store the transaction log backup.**

2. **Right-click the database with the transaction log you want to back up and choose All Tasks⇨Backup Database.**

   Make sure that you choose a database that's using either the full or bulk_logged recovery model. (You can't back up the transaction log for a database that's using the simple recovery model.) If necessary, use the Northwind sample database.

3. On the General page of the SQL Server Backup dialog box, below Backup, select Transaction Log, as shown in Figure 14-8.

This setting configures SQL Server Enterprise Manager to perform a backup of the database's transaction log.

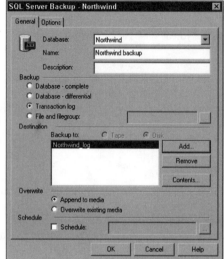

Figure 14-8:
Performing a transaction log backup in SQL Server Enterprise Manager.

4. Specify the backup device to which you want to back up. You can use a permanent or a temporary device.

5. Select the Options tab.

As shown in Figure 14-9, SQL Server Enterprise Manager will remove inactive entries from the log (truncate) after it completes the backup. If you don't want SQL Server Enterprise Manager to truncate the log, uncheck this option.

6. Click OK to begin the backup.

Performing a file or filegroup backup

One of the solutions SQL Server offers you for managing the backup of very large databases is that you can back up individual files or filegroups instead of the whole database. If you plan to perform file or filegroup backups, make sure that you back up all the files that make up the database on a rotating basis. In addition, also back up the transaction log in order to make sure that you can restore the complete database in the event of a failure.

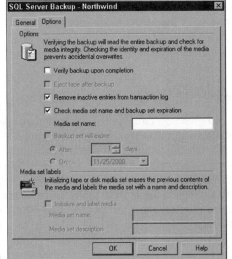

Figure 14-9:
SQL Server
automati-
cally
truncates
the transac-
tion log after
it completes
the backup.

You must pay special attention to your file/filegroup backups after creating an index. If you create an index, and you've configured the database to the simple recovery model, SQL Server logs only that the index was created in the transaction log (and not the contents of the index). If you subsequently restore your database backup, SQL Server immediately executes the CREATE INDEX statement to recreate the index. For the CREATE INDEX statement to be successful, all of the files affected by the index must contain the same information they contained when you originally created the index. Because of this limitation, if the index and its associated table are in different filegroups, you must back up both filegroups after you create an index.

Make sure that you understand the impact on the backup process if you store a table and its indexes in separate filegroups for the exam.

Designing a Backup Strategy

In previous sections of this chapter, you review all the different types of back-ups from which you can choose. In this section, we want to talk about how you go about selecting a backup strategy. Do you want to perform only com-plete backups? Or do you want to use complete backups along with differen-tial and transaction log backups?

Make sure that you understand the different backup strategies, along with the reasons why you might choose one over the other, for your exam. Because how you back up has a huge impact on how you restore a database, you also want to make sure you know the steps you must take to restore a database with each strategy.

You can expect to see quite a few questions on your exam that have you select a backup strategy or specify the steps to restore the database based on your backup strategy.

Recovering transactions

Before we talk about the strategies you can use for backing up a database, we want to make sure you understand that in the event of a database failure, you should always attempt to recover the transactions in a database's transaction log. The reason this is important is that if you can recover these transactions, you have a chance of restoring your database up to the point just before the failure. If you don't recover the transactions in the transaction log, you can restore your database only to the point of your last complete, differential, or transaction log backup.

In other words, if you have a database failure, your first step should always be to attempt to back up the transaction log for the database. Make sure you back it up with the NO_TRUNCATE option. You can then restore your database backups, followed by the transaction log backup, to recover the database.

Complete backup strategy

With a complete backup strategy, you perform only a full backup of the database on a regular basis. For example, you might back up the database on a nightly basis. Choose this strategy only if your database is small (so performing a complete backup doesn't take too long). One thing to keep in mind is that if you perform only nightly backups of the database, you lose any transactions posted to the database during the day if you have to restore the database. For this reason, use this strategy only if you don't make a lot of changes to the database.

If you plan to perform only complete backups of the database and no transaction log backups, you must make sure that the transaction log doesn't fill up. One technique you can use to ensure that SQL Server truncates the transaction log is to configure the database to use the simple recovery model. Alternatively, you can create an alert to monitor the size of the transaction log, and if the log becomes full, the alert can then call a job to truncate the log.

How you restore when you use the complete backup depends on whether or not you have configured your database with the simple recovery model. If you're using the simple recovery model, your only choice is to restore your last complete backup, which means that you lose all the transactions that have occurred since your last backup.

On the other hand, if you're using either the full or bulk_logged recovery model along with a complete backup strategy, use the following steps to recover a failed database:

1. **Back up the transaction log with the** NO_TRUNCATE **option.**
2. **Restore your last complete backup of the database.**
3. **Restore the backup of the transaction log you performed in Step 1.**

Complete database and transaction log backup strategy

The next strategy you can use to back up a database is to perform a complete database backup (such as nightly), followed by transaction log backups (such as at four-hour intervals). This strategy enables you to minimize the amount of data you lose in the event of a database failure.

You must use either the full or bulk_logged recovery models with this strategy.

Here's how you recover a database when you use this strategy:

1. **Back up the transaction log with the** NO_TRUNCATE **option.**

   Notice that this is always your first step. By backing up the transaction log with the NO_TRUNCATE option, you can recover any transactions that have occurred since your last backup.

2. **Restore your last complete database backup.**
3. **Restore any transaction log backups you have made since your last full backup.**
4. **Restore the transaction log backup you performed in Step 1.**

Differential backup strategy

With a differential backup strategy, you use a combination of all three types of backups: complete, differential, and transaction log. You typically perform a complete backup of the database on a weekly basis, a differential backup nightly, and then a transaction log backup at regular time intervals (such as hourly).

You recover a database when you use the differential backup strategy by performing the following steps:

1. **Back up the transaction log with the** NO_TRUNCATE **option.**

2. **Restore your last complete database backup.**

3. **Restore your last differential backup.**

4. **Restore any transaction log backups you have made since your last differential backup.**

5. **Restore the transaction log backup you performed in Step 1.**

Consider the following scenario: You perform a complete backup of your Sales database on Sunday mornings at 2:00 a.m. In addition, you perform a differential backup of the database every night except Sunday at 11:00 p.m. You also have scheduled a backup of the Sales database's transaction log to take place at 9:00 a.m., 12:00 p.m., 3:00 p.m., and 6:00 p.m. If your database fails at 2:30 p.m. on Wednesday, what steps should you take to restore the database? You should use the following steps:

1. **Back up the transaction log with the** NO_TRUNCATE **option.**

2. **Restore the complete database backup from 2:00 a.m. on Sunday.**

3. **Restore your differential backup from Tuesday night at 11:00 p.m.**

4. **Restore the transaction log backups from 9:00 a.m. and 12:00 p.m. on Wednesday.**

5. **Restore the transaction log backup you performed in Step 1.**

You can expect to see scenario-based questions for restoring backups like the preceding example on your exam.

File or filegroup backup strategy

With a file or filegroup backup strategy, you typically perform a complete backup of the database on a weekly (or monthly) basis, back up individual files or filegroups nightly, and then back up the transaction log throughout the day. For example, if you have a database consisting of three files, you could perform a complete backup of the database on Sunday night and then back up each of the three files on a rotating basis throughout the week. You might back up File1 on Monday and Thursday nights, File 2 on Tuesday and Friday nights, and File3 on Wednesday and Saturday nights. You can then back up the transaction log periodically throughout the day.

With the file or filegroup backup strategy, you can recover one or more files, or the entire database. You recover a single file with the file or filegroup backup strategy by using the following steps:

1. **As usual, back up the transaction log with the** NO_TRUNCATE **option.**

2. **Restore your last backup of the corrupted file.**

3. **Restore all transaction log backups since your last backup of the corrupted file.**

4. **Restore the transaction log backup you created in Step 1.**

Remember, if you have an index in one file or filegroup, and its associated table in another file or filegroup, you must restore both files in order to recover the index.

Prep Test

1 **When should you back up a user database? (Choose all that apply.)**

- **A** ❑ After adding a new login ID
- **B** ❑ After adding data to one of its tables
- **C** ❑ Whenever you add a linked server
- **D** ❑ After truncating the transaction log

2 **Which strategy do you typically use for backing up a very large database?**

- **A** ○ Complete
- **B** ○ Transaction Log
- **C** ○ Differential
- **D** ○ File or Filegroup

3 **To what point can you recover a database if you've configured it to use the simple recovery model?**

- **A** ○ To a specific point in time by restoring a complete backup plus any subsequent transaction log backups
- **B** ○ Up to the most recent changes by restoring a complete backup plus any subsequent transaction log backups
- **C** ○ Up to your last complete backup of the database
- **D** ○ Up to your last transaction log backup of the database

4 **Which of the following actions are not logged if you configure a database to use the bulk_logged recovery model? (Choose all that apply.)**

- **A** ❑ SELECT INTO
- **B** ❑ Bulk imports of data
- **C** ❑ Changes to text fields with the WRITETEXT and UPDATETEXT statements
- **D** ❑ Any new indexes you create

5 **Why are backups of the transaction log smaller if you configure a database to use the bulk_logged recovery model instead of the full recovery model?**

- **A** ○ Because SQL Server doesn't record any of the changes made by bulk operations in the transaction log.
- **B** ○ Because SQL Server records only the end result of bulk operations in the transaction log.
- **C** ○ Because SQL Server records only bulk operations in the transaction log and automatically truncates all other committed transactions.
- **D** ○ Because SQL Server automatically truncates all committed transactions from the transaction log with the bulk_logged recovery model.

6 **What database(s) does SQL Server rebuild when you use the Rebuild Master utility? (Choose all that apply.)**

A ❑ Master

B ❑ Model

C ❑ Msdb

D ❑ Tempdb

7 **What types of backup devices does SQL Server support? (Choose all that apply.)**

A ❑ Tape

B ❑ Disk file

C ❑ Named pipe

D ❑ TCP/IP socket

8 **How do you create a temporary backup device?**

A ○ With the `sp_addumpdevice` stored procedure

B ○ With the `sp_addtempdevice` stored procedure

C ○ As part of the `BACKUP DATABASE` or `BACKUP LOG` statements

D ○ By using the Temporary Backup Device object in SQL Server Enterprise Manager

Answers

1 **B** and **D.** You don't need to back up a user database after adding a new login ID or linked server definition because SQL Server stores this information in the master database. *See "Managing the backup process."*

2 **D.** Although any of these strategies enables you to back up any database, you typically use a file or filegroup backup strategy to back up very large databases. *See "Designing a Backup Strategy."*

3 **C.** You can't back up a database's transaction log if you've configured it to use the simple recovery model because SQL Server truncates the database's transaction log. You can recover the database only by restoring your last complete backup of the database. *See "Choosing a database recovery model."*

4 **A, B, C,** and **D.** The bulk_logged recovery model prevents SQL Server from logging any of these activities on your server. *Study "Choosing a database recovery model."*

5 **B.** With the bulk_logged recovery model, SQL Server tracks the extents in the database that are changed as a result of any bulk load operations. It then backs up these extents the next time you back up the database. *See "Choosing a database recovery model."*

6 **A, B,** and **C.** SQL Server rebuilds these databases whenever you rebuild the master database. *See "Managing the backup process."*

7 **A, B,** and **C.** SQL Server can back up to a tape, disk file, or named pipe. *Study "Creating permanent backup devices."*

8 **C.** You create a temporary backup device as part of the BACKUP statement itself. *See "Performing Backups."*

Chapter 15

Restoring Databases

• •

Exam Objectives

▶ Restoring data

▶ Recovering the system state

▶ Configuring, maintaining, and troubleshooting log shipping

• •

*S*QL Server enables you to restore backups of your databases by using either SQL Server Enterprise Manager or the RESTORE Transact-SQL command. The steps you use to restore databases vary depending on the type of backup you're restoring (complete, differential, transaction log, or file/ filegroup). In this chapter, we explore all the details for restoring the different types of backups. In addition, we show you how to set up a standby server so that your users can still access a critical database in the event your production server fails.

Quick Assessment

1 SQL Server _____ uncommitted transactions during the automatic recovery process.

2 Use the _____ SQL command to view the name of the database contained in a backup device.

3 You must use the _____ option with the RESTORE statement if you want to be able to restore additional transaction log backups.

4 You can force SQL Server to overwrite an existing database with the backup of a different database by using the _____ option.

5 When you restore a database, it isn't accessible by your users unless you specify the _____ option.

6 You must have a(n) _____ in order to restore a database to a specific point in time.

7 If you don't have a current backup of the master database, you can recover it by using the _____.

8 In order for log shipping to be successful, you must configure the database on your production server to use the _____ recovery model.

9 You can configure log shipping for up to _____ database(s).

10 Use the _____ stored procedure to make your standby server your production server.

Answers

1 *Rolls back.* Read "Performing Database Recovery."

2 RESTORE FILELISTONLY. Study "Restoring User Databases."

3 WITH NORECOVERY. See "Using the RESTORE SQL statement."

4 WITH REPLACE. Study "Using the RESTORE SQL statement."

5 WITH RECOVERY. See "Using the RESTORE SQL statement."

6 *Transaction log backup.* See "Restoring from the different backup types."

7 *Rebuild Master utility.* Study "Restoring System Databases."

8 *Full.* See "Implementing a Standby Server."

9 *One.* Study "Implementing a Standby Server."

10 sp_change_secondary_role. Study "Modifying the log shipping configuration."

Performing Database Recovery

One of the safety mechanisms Microsoft built into SQL Server is that it automatically performs database recovery steps whenever you boot up your server. SQL Server begins the recovery process by scanning the transaction log. If SQL Server finds any transactions that are marked as committed in the transaction log, but haven't been written to the database, it then writes the transactions to the database. (This process is called "rolling forward" transactions.) If SQL Server finds any transactions marked uncommitted in the log, it verifies that these transactions have not been written to the database. In the event SQL Server determines that these uncommitted transactions have been written to the database, it removes them. (This process is called "rolling back" transactions.)

The advantage to the automatic recovery process is that it can fix many of the problems caused by an improper shutdown of your server. The other advantage is that it's done automatically for you. You can view the results of the automatic recovery process by examining the messages posted by the MSSQLServer service in the Application log, as shown in Figure 15-1.

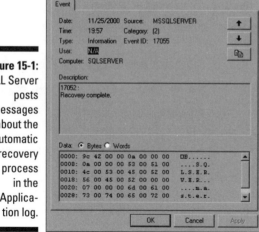

Figure 15-1:
SQL Server posts messages about the automatic recovery process in the Application log.

In addition to the automatic recovery process, SQL Server enables you to manually recover a database by restoring it from backup. But before SQL Server permits you to restore a database, it does try to prevent you from making a mistake. For example, SQL Server won't let you restore a database if the database you specify in the RESTORE statement already exists on your server, and the name of the database in the backup device is different from this name. In other words, SQL Server won't let you restore a backup of the

Sales database to the database name of Accounting if you already have an Accounting database on your server. It also won't let you restore the database if you don't have all the files necessary to restore the database.

When you restore a database, SQL Server automatically recreates all the database's files and schema. You don't have to create the database files and schema before restoring it.

Restoring User Databases

When you're ready to restore a database, SQL Server includes a few commands that you can use to verify the contents of your backup devices. You can use these commands, or you can check the contents of backup devices in SQL Server Enterprise Manager. Table 15-1 describes these commands.

Table 15-1	Commands for Verifying the Contents of a Backup Device
Command	*Enables You to*
RESTORE HEADERONLY	View information about the backup contained in the backup device. This information includes the backup name and description, the backup type performed (complete, differential, transaction log, or file/filegroup), and the date, time, and size of the backup.
RESTORE FILELISTONLY	Determine the logical and physical names of the database or transaction log files contained in the backup device, the type of file (database or transaction log), filegroup, size, and the maximum file size.
RESTORE LABELONLY	View information about the backup media containing the backup file.
RESTORE VERIFYONLY	Check that all the files that make up a backup set are present and that you are able to read them.

Preparing to restore a database

After you verify that you have a good backup (and that you have the right backup device), you're ready to begin restoring the database. But before you start, you need to take a few safety precautions. First of all, restrict access to the database so that users can't access it during the restore process. Restrict access to the database to only the members of the db_owner, dbcreator, or sysadmin roles. You can do so by modifying the properties of the database in SQL Server Enterprise Manager, as shown in Figure 15-2.

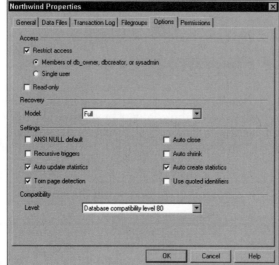

Figure 15-2:
Restrict access to a database before attempting to restore it.

Next, always attempt to back up the transaction log. Use the BACKUP LOG SQL statement or SQL Server Enterprise Manager, and make sure that you don't have SQL Server truncate the log. This backup enables you to attempt to recover any transactions that have occurred since your last backup of the database or its transaction log.

Now that you're ready, you restore a database by using either the RESTORE Transact-SQL statement or SQL Server Enterprise Manager.

You don't have to drop the database before you restore it. SQL Server can overwrite a damaged user database during the restore process.

Using the RESTORE SQL statement

Here's the syntax you should use to restore a database:

```
RESTORE DATABASE database_name
FROM device_name
WITH OPTIONS
```

Table 15-2 describes the options you can use with the RESTORE DATABASE statement. Make sure you understand the function of each of these options for your exam.

Table 15-2	RESTORE DATABASE **Options**
Option	*What It Does*
FILE	Restores a specific backup within a backup device. Use this option if you've appended multiple backups to the same backup device.
MOVE...TO	Enables you to restore a backup of a database to a different location (such as a different hard disk, server, or a standby server). As an alternative, you can use the sp_attach_db and sp_detach_db stored procedures to move a database from one server to another.
NORECOVERY	Prevents SQL Server from performing automatic recovery of the database by rolling forward or back transactions. You should use this option whenever you have multiple database backups to restore. If you don't specify the NORECOVERY option, SQL Server performs automatic recovery — and you can't restore any subsequent backups of the database. Note: Your users can't access the database until you restore your last backup and specify the RECOVERY option.
RECOVERY	Restores the last backup of a database or its transaction log. When you specify this option, SQL Server restores the backup and then performs automatic recovery of the database to roll back or roll forward transactions from the transaction log. After you complete the restore with the RECOVERY option, users can access the database.
REPLACE	Enables you to force SQL Server to overwrite an existing database on your server even if the backup contains a different database with the same name.
RESTART	Enables you to pick up an interrupted database restore from the point at which the restore process failed.

Conversely, you use the following syntax to restore a transaction log backup:

```
RESTORE LOG database_name
FROM device_name
WITH options
```

In addition to supporting the same options listed in Table 15-2, the RESTORE LOG statement also enables you to use the STOPAT option. This option lets you restore the transaction log backup to a specific point in time. In other words, you want SQL Server to "stop at" a specific time when restoring the log.

Using SQL Server Enterprise Manager

You can restore a database in SQL Server Enterprise Manager by using either of two methods. One method is to right-click a database and choose All Tasks⇨Restore Database. You can also restore a database by using the Restore Database Wizard. In Lab 15-1, we walk you through restoring a database and two transaction log backups.

Lab 15-1	Restoring a Database in SQL Server Enterprise Manager

1. **If necessary, log on as Administrator and open SQL Server Enterprise Manager.**

2. **Create a new database named Marketing. Accept the default file-names, locations, and sizes for the database.**

3. **Create three disk backup devices named Mktg_complete, Mktg_trx1, and Mktg_trx2. Accept the default filenames and locations for these files.**

   You're going to back up the Marketing database and its transaction log to these devices.

4. **Perform a complete backup of the Marketing database to the Mktg_complete backup device.**

5. **Perform two transaction log backups, one to each of the transaction log backup devices (Mktg_trx1 and Mktg_trx2).**

6. **In the console tree, right-click the Marketing database and choose All Tasks⇨Restore Database.**

   As shown in Figure 15-3, SQL Server Enterprise Manager opens the Restore Database dialog box. Notice that it automatically lists your backups of the Marketing database and its transaction log.

7. **Uncheck your transaction log backups. You're going to begin by restoring only your complete backup of the database.**

8. **Select the Options tab, and take a look at the Recovery Completion State options.**

   As shown in Figure 15-4, you can restore the database with recovery, or restore the database with no recovery so that you can restore your transaction log backups. By default, SQL Server Enterprise Manager restores your backup with recovery. Make sure that you don't leave this option enabled if you want to restore transaction log backups.

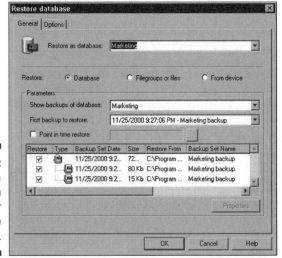

Figure 15-3:
Restoring a
database in
SQL Server
Enterprise
Manager.

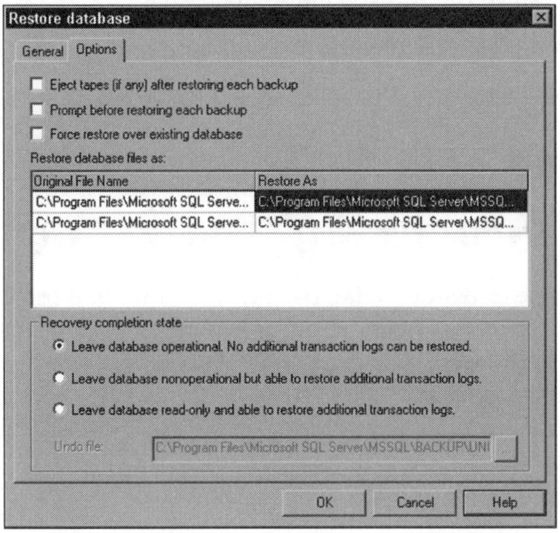

Figure 15-4:
Configuring
recovery
options for
restoring a
database.

Use the Leave Database Nonoperational option if you want to further
restore transaction log backups, and you don't want users to access the
database. Use the Leave Database Read-Only option if you plan to
restore additional transaction log backups but do want your users to
have read-only access to the database. (You typically use this option
when you're setting up a standby server. We talk more about standby
servers in the section "Implementing a Standby Server," later in this
chapter.)

9. Select the Leave Database Nonoperational option.

10. **Click OK to begin the database restore.**

11. **When the restore is complete, click OK to close the message box.**

12. **Look at the Marketing database in SQL Server Enterprise Manager.**

    Because you chose the Leave Database Nonoperational option, SQL Server Enterprise Manager indicates that the database is Nonoperational by displaying the database as unavailable (grayed out), and with a "Loading" message next to the database name.

13. **Right-click the Marketing database again and choose All Tasks⇨Restore Database.**

    Notice that SQL Server Enterprise Manager automatically assumes you want to restore your two transaction log backups of the Marketing database. You can restore each backup individually, or you can restore them both at the same time. If you restore both at the same time, you should use the default recovery option of Leave Database Operational. This option enables SQL Server to roll forward or back transactions as needed.

14. **Click OK to restore the transaction log backups.**

15. **Click OK again when the restore is complete.**

    The Marketing database is no longer unavailable and marked as "Loading."

Restoring from the different backup types

The methods you use to restore a database depend on the types of backups you have.

Complete database backup

Restore a complete database backup if any of the following conditions occur:

- A database file becomes damaged or is deleted.
- Your server's hard disk fails.
- You want to restore a database to a different server.

Make sure that you restore the database with the NORECOVERY option if you want to also restore any differential or transaction log backups. On the other hand, if you want to restore the database and don't have any additional backups, restore it with the RECOVERY option. You can expect to see a few questions verifying that you know the purpose of both the NORECOVERY and the RECOVERY options for restoring a backup.

Differential backup

You restore a differential backup to recover the parts of the database that have changed since your last complete backup. For this reason, you must restore your complete database backup before you restore the differential backup. As always, make sure that you restore the differential backup with the NORECOVERY option if you want to restore any additional transaction log backups.

Transaction log backup

Restoring a transaction log backup enables you to restore the changes to the database that have occurred since your last complete or differential database backup. One of the advantages to restoring a transaction log backup is that it enables you to restore the database to a specific point in time, as shown in Figure 15-5.

Figure 15-5:
Transaction log backups enable you to restore a database to a specific point in time.

You can't restore a database to a specific point in time unless you have configured it to use either the full or Bulk_Logged recovery model, and you have backed up its transaction log. For more information on these recovery models and their effect on backups, review Chapter 14.

You restore a database to a specific point in time in SQL Server Enterprise Manager by checking Point In Time Restore, and then specifying the point to which you want to restore. Use the WITH STOPAT option as part of your RESTORE LOG statement to restore to a specific point in time by using Transact-SQL.

When you restore a database to a specific point in time by restoring a transaction log backup, SQL Server automatically recovers the database. Keep in mind that this means you can't restore any subsequent backups of the transaction log after the recovery process is complete.

File or filegroup backup

As we've already mentioned, you use the file or filegroup backup strategy to help reduce the amount of time you need to back up very large databases. Likewise, you can restore individual files or filegroups from these backups. But in order to restore a specific file or filegroup backup, you must also restore all the transaction log backups you made after backing up the file/filegroup. (SQL Server applies only those transactions that affect the restored file when you restore the transaction log backup.)

Restoring System Databases

You face one of two possibilities when you must recover your system databases: Either you have backups of the system databases, or you don't. (In our opinion, there's no excuse for you not having backups of the system databases!)

From backups

If you lose any of your system databases (such as master, msdb, or model) due to corruption or a server disk failure, your best bet is to restore the database from backup. One problem you may run into, though, is that if it's the master database that's damaged, you may not be able to even start SQL Server. And if you can't start SQL Server, you won't be able to restore your backup. If you run into this problem, here's what you need to do:

1. **Rebuild the system databases by using the Rebuild Master utility (rebuildm.exe).**

2. **Start SQL Server in single-user mode by entering the following command in a Command Prompt window:**

```
sqlserver -c -m
```

3. **Restore your backup of the master database.**

4. **Restart your server and then restore the model and msdb databases.**

   You must restore the model and msdb databases in addition to master because the Rebuild Master utility rebuilds all three databases.

Without backups

So your worst nightmare has come true: Your server's master database is corrupt and you don't have a backup. Although you won't be able to recover everything, you can at least recover most of what you lost. Here's how:

1. **Rebuild the system databases by using the Rebuild Master utility (rebuildm.exe).**

2. **Start SQL Server.**

3. **Attach or restore your user databases. If your user databases and their associated files are intact, you can simply reattach them to your server by running the** sp_attach_db **stored procedure. On the other hand, if you also lost your user databases when you lost the master database, you must restore the user databases from their backups.**

Reattaching the databases to your server by using the sp_attach_db stored procedure instead of restoring them from backup is significantly faster.

Implementing a Standby Server

If your SQL server and its data are critical, one of the techniques you can use to ensure that your users can always access the data is to set up one or more standby SQL servers. You use a standby server in essence to mirror your production server. Prior to SQL Server 2000, you configured a standby server by manually backing up the database on the production server, and then restoring it to the standby server. You then kept the database current by backing up its transaction log on the production server and restoring it to the standby server.

One of the enhancements in SQL Server 2000 is that you no longer have to manually back up and restore a database and its transaction log between your production and standby server. Instead, you can use the new *log shipping* feature. This feature enables SQL Server to automatically apply changes in the transaction log to your standby server at specific time intervals.

You must configure the database on your production SQL server to use the full recovery model for log shipping to work. You can configure log shipping for only one database on your server.

Defining log shipping

Log shipping works by creating jobs on both your production and standby servers. The SQLServerAgent service on both servers is then responsible for performing these jobs. The log shipping jobs include:

✓ **A job to back up the transaction log on the production server.** This job is performed by the SQLServerAgent service on the production server.

✓ **A job to copy the transaction log backup from the production server to the standby server.** This job is performed by the SQLServerAgent service on the standby server.

✔ **A job to restore the transaction log backup on the standby server.**
The SQLServerAgent service performs the restore without recovering
the database so that it can apply additional transaction log backups
to the database. This job is performed by the SQLServerAgent service
on the standby server.

In order for these jobs to work, you must make sure that the SQLServerAgent
service on the standby server is configured to log on with a domain user
account. This account must have administrator permissions on both the production and standby servers.

Configuring log shipping

The easiest method you can use for configuring log shipping is to use the
Database Maintenance Plan Wizard, as shown in Figure 15-6. This wizard
walks you through the following tasks for log shipping:

✔ Creating an initial copy of the database on your standby server(s).

✔ Establishing a shared folder in which it will place the backups of the
transaction logs. (Your standby servers connect to this share to copy
the transaction log backups.)

✔ Defining which of the standby servers should take over the role of the
production server in the event of a failure.

✔ Configuring the transaction log backups and the schedule for shipping
them to the standby servers.

✔ Implementing a server monitor so that you can determine the status of
the log shipping process. You can implement the server monitor on your
production or standby servers, or on a completely separate server.

Figure 15-6:
Use the
Database
Mainte-
nance Plan
Wizard to
configure
log shipping.

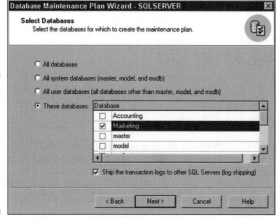

You can configure your standby server to use either the No Recovery or Standby mode. With the No Recovery mode, the SQLServerAgent service restores the backups of the production server database's transaction log without recovering the database, which means that users can't connect to the standby server to access the database. For performance reasons, you may want to make the standby server accessible for read-only database access. If so, configure the standby server to use Standby mode. This option enables the SQLServerAgent service to restore the transaction log backups and make the database read-only.

The Database Maintenance Plan Wizard doesn't copy your login IDs from the production server to your standby servers. In order for a standby server to be able to take over as your production server in the event of a failure, you must copy the logins to the standby server. Otherwise, your users won't be able to log in to the standby server. The easiest way to copy your login IDs from the production server to a standby server is to use the Data Transformation Services (DTS) Export Wizard to export copies of the login IDs.

Expect to see a few questions on your exam about configuring standby servers.

Modifying the log shipping configuration

Because you implement a standby server so that it can become your production server if your original server fails, you must know how to make a standby server your production server. First, make sure that you've copied the login IDs from the production server to your standby server. Next, use the stored procedures described in Table 15-3 to switch the production and standby servers' roles.

Table 15-3	Stored Procedures for Switching Server Roles	
Stored Procedure	**Execute on**	**What It Does**
sp_change_ primary_role	Production server	Disables the job for backing up the transaction log on the production server. This stored procedure also does a final backup of the transaction log. At this point, the production server becomes a standby server.
sp_change_ secondary_role	Standby server	Disables the job for copying the transaction log from the production server, restores the final transaction log backup, and recovers the database so that your users can connect to it. At this point, the standby server is now your production server.

(continued)

Table 15-3 *(continued)*

Stored Procedure	Execute on	What It Does
sp_change_ monitor_role	Monitor server	Reconfigures the server monitor to make it aware which server is now the production server, and which server is now a standby server.
sp_resolve_ logins	New production server	Updates the login IDs on what is now your production server (formerly the standby server) by examining the backup from the original production server.

After you execute these stored procedures to make your standby server your production server, your last step is to make this server accessible to your clients. Depending on your client applications, you may find that renaming your new production server or changing its IP address is necessary.

You rename a SQL server by running SQL Server Setup again.

Prep Test

1 Which option should you use when restoring a database to restore a specific backup from a backup device that contains multiple backups?

A ○ BACKUP

B ○ FILE

C ○ REPLACE

D ○ RESTART

2 Which of the following does SQL Server perform during the automatic recovery process? (Choose all that apply.)

A ❑ It rolls forward any committed transactions.

B ❑ It rolls back any uncommitted transactions.

C ❑ It truncates the transaction log.

D ❑ It writes a message to the application log about the automatic recovery process.

3 Which of the following steps should you perform before restoring a database backup? (Choose all that apply.)

A ❑ Configure the database as read-only.

B ❑ Restrict access to the database to members of the db_owner, dbcreator, and sysadmin roles.

C ❑ Back up the transaction log with the RECOVERY option.

D ❑ Back up the transaction log with the NO_TRUNCATE option.

4 You want to move a database from one server to another. Which of the following techniques can you use? (Choose all that apply.)

A ❑ Use the sp_detach_db and sp_attach_db stored procedures to move the database.

B ❑ Use SQL Server Setup to move the database.

C ❑ Back up the database on the source server and restore it to another server with the MOVE TO option.

D ❑ Use the sp_database_move stored procedure to move the database.

5 After restoring a transaction log backup, you notice that SQL Server Enterprise Manager displays a database's status as "Loading." What should you do?

A ○ Modify the database options to remove the read-only option.

B ○ Use sp_load_db to complete the restore to the database.

C ○ Restore a transaction log backup using the WITH RECOVERY option.

D ○ Stop and restart the MSSQLServer service.

6 Which of the following steps must you perform to restore the master database if you don't have a backup? (Choose all that apply.)

A ❑ Rebuild the system databases.

B ❑ Recreate all of your user databases.

C ❑ Reattach the user databases by using `sp_attach_db`.

D ❑ Run SQL Setup again to configure the master database.

7 Log shipping fails unless you configure which of the following? (Choose all that apply.)

A ❑ You configure the SQLServerAgent service on the production server to log on with a domain user account.

B ❑ You configure the SQLServerAgent service on the standby server to log on with a domain user account.

C ❑ You make the SQLServerAgent service user account a member of Administrators.

D ❑ You execute the `sp_start_logshipping` stored procedure on the production server.

8 Which stored procedure should you use to update the login IDs on a standby server by examining the backup of the production server?

A ○ `sp_update_logins`

B ○ `sp_resolve_logins`

C ○ `sp_restore_logins`

D ○ `sp_check_logins`

Answers

1 **B.** You use the FILE option to restore only a specific backup within a backup device. *See "Restoring User Databases"*

2 **A, B,** and **D.** SQL Server scans the transaction log during automatic recovery. If it finds any uncommitted transactions in the database, it rolls them back; likewise, if it finds committed transactions in the log that aren't in the database, it rolls these transactions forward. It then writes a message to the application log about the status of the automatic recovery process. *See "Performing Database Recovery."*

3 **B** and **D.** Always restrict access to the database before restoring it. In addition, you should back up the transaction log without truncating it before beginning the restore. *Study "Preparing to restore a database."*

4 **A** and **C.** You can move a database by using either the sp_attach_db and sp_detach_db stored procedures, or by backing up and restoring the database with the MOVE TO option. *Study "Using the RESTORE SQL statement."*

5 **C.** SQL Server marks a database's status as Loading if you restore a backup using the NORECOVERY option. *See "Using the RESTORE SQL statement."*

6 **A** and **C.** You can recover the master database by first rebuilding it, and then reattaching all of your user databases. *Study "Restoring System Databases."*

7 **B** and **C.** You must configure the SQLServerAgent service on the standby server to log on with a domain user account. Otherwise, the standby server won't be able to connect to the production server to download a copy of the transaction log backup. In addition, this user account must be a member of Administrators or have the necessary permissions to connect to the production server. *Study "Defining log shipping."*

8 **B.** You can use the sp_resolve_logins stored procedure to update the login IDs on a standby server by examining the backup of the production server. *Study "Modifying the log shipping configuration."*

Chapter 16

Using Database Monitoring and Troubleshooting Tools

⬤ ⬤

Exam Objectives

▶ Performing integrity checks with the Database Maintenance Plan Wizard and the Database Consistency Checker (DBCC)

▶ Troubleshooting transactions and locking with Transact-SQL, SQL Server Enterprise Manager, and SQL Server Profiler

⬤ ⬤

SQL Server includes several utilities that you can use to both monitor and troubleshoot your server. In this chapter, we explore how you can verify your database's integrity by using the Database Maintenance Plan Wizard and the Database Consistency Checker (DBCC) commands. We also show you how to troubleshoot transactions and locking by using Transact-SQL, SQL Server Enterprise Manager, and SQL Server Profiler.

Quick Assessment

1 The _____ is responsible for carrying out the tasks you configure with the Database Maintenance Plan Wizard.

2 The Database Maintenance Plan Wizard runs the _____ command when it checks a database's integrity.

3 You suspect that one of your tables within a database is corrupt. You should run the _____ DBCC command.

4 SQL Server reports errors when you run the `DBCC CHECKDB` command against a database. To fix these errors, you should first use the _____ option.

5 SQL Server supports both the _____ and _____ categories of locks.

6 SQL Server uses the _____ lock when you update a row in a table.

7 You can view lock information in SQL Server Query Analyzer by executing _____.

8 A(n) _____ enables a user to read uncommitted data.

9 The _____ transaction isolation level is the most restrictive level you can configure.

Answers

1 *SQLServerAgent service.* See "Preparing for a maintenance plan."

2 DBCC CHECKDB. Read "Checking database integrity."

3 DBCC CHECKTABLE. Check out "Using the Database Consistency Checker (DBCC) Commands."

4 REPAIR FAST. Study "Using the Database Consistency Checker (DBCC) Commands."

5 *Basic and special use.* Study "Troubleshooting Transactions and Locks."

6 *Exclusive.* Study "Troubleshooting Transactions and Locks."

7 sp_lock. See "Using Transact-SQL."

8 *Dirty read.* Review "Using Transact-SQL."

9 *Serializable.* Review "Using Transact-SQL."

Implementing a Maintenance Plan

As a SQL Server administrator, making sure that you maintain the databases on your server is important. Maintenance tasks include

✔ Optimizing data and index page usage

✔ Removing unused space from a database

✔ Checking and repairing your databases and indexes

✔ Scheduling backups

To make taking care of all of these tasks easy on you, SQL Server includes a Database Maintenance Plan Wizard that walks you through configuring and scheduling all of these jobs. You run this wizard within SQL Server Enterprise Manager. Because the jobs and options you can configure within the Database Maintenance Plan Wizard are so important, we want to take a few minutes to walk you through each of its pages.

Pay close attention to each of the jobs you can configure within the Database Maintenance Plan Wizard. You can expect to see quite a few questions on your exam about the role each of these jobs plays in maintaining your server and its databases.

Preparing for a maintenance plan

The Database Maintenance Plan Wizard essentially walks you through scheduling a series of jobs on your server. The service responsible for managing and executing these jobs is the SQLServerAgent service. So, before you run the Database Maintenance Plan Wizard, make sure that you've configured the SQLServerAgent service properly — or your maintenance jobs won't run.

You can start the SQLServerAgent service by using SQL Server Enterprise Manager, SQL Service Manager, or the Services object within the Computer Management MMC.

If you have any problems starting the service, here are a few things you need to check:

✔ Make sure you've configured the service to log on with a valid user account and password.

✔ Verify that the service account isn't disabled or required to change passwords.

✔ Double-check that you've given the service account the necessary permissions for your server. Microsoft recommends that you make the service account a member of your SQL server's local Administrators group.

In Lab 16-1, we take you through the steps for using the Database Maintenance Plan Wizard, giving you an overview of the types of jobs you can create with the wizard.

Lab 16-1	Creating a Maintenance Plan with the Database Maintenance Plan Wizard

1. **If necessary, log on to your server as Administrator and open SQL Server Enterprise Manager.**

2. **In the console tree, select your server.**

3. **Choose Tools⇨Database Maintenance Planner to start the Database Maintenance Plan Wizard.**

4. **Click Next on the Welcome page.**

5. **On the Select Databases page, select a database for which you want to define a maintenance plan.**

   Use one of your user databases, or select the Northwind sample database. As shown in Figure 16-1, you can define one plan for all your databases, regardless of type. You can also define two plans, one for system databases and one for user databases. Or, you can define a completely separate plan for each database on your server. By default, SQL Server assumes that you want to define a plan for each database.

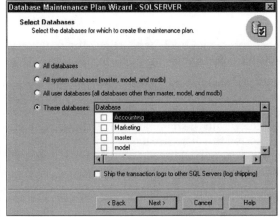

Figure 16-1:
Selecting a
database.

6. **Click Next.**

7. **On the Update Data Optimization Information page, check the tasks you want to perform.**

   As shown in Figure 16-2, SQL Server uses the Update Data Optimization Information page to enable you to automate reorganizing your data and index pages within the data files. Notice that the Update Data Optimization Information page also includes an option that you can use to schedule when SQL Server will run these jobs. By default, SQL Server schedules the data optimization jobs to run once a week. (We describe each of these tasks in detail in the section "Updating data optimization information," later in this chapter.)

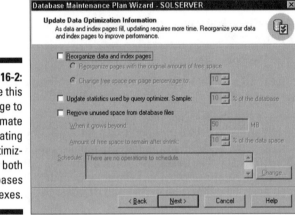

Figure 16-2:
Use this page to automate updating and optimizing both databases and indexes.

8. **Click Next.**

9. **On the Database Integrity Check page, check the database integrity tasks you want to perform.**

   These tasks execute the `DBCC CHECKDB` statement with different parameters. By default, the Database Maintenance Plan Wizard schedules a job to check your database's integrity, as shown in Figure 16-3. It checks the allocation of space within the database file, along with its structural integrity. We describe the database integrity checks that the Database Maintenance Plan Wizard performs in more detail in the section "Checking database integrity," later in this chapter.

10. **Click Next.**

11. **Look at the options on the Specify the Database Backup Plan page.**

   By default, the Database Maintenance Plan Wizard assumes that you want to perform a complete database backup to a disk device, and that you want to schedule the backup to run once a week on Sundays at 2:00 a.m., as shown in Figure 16-4.

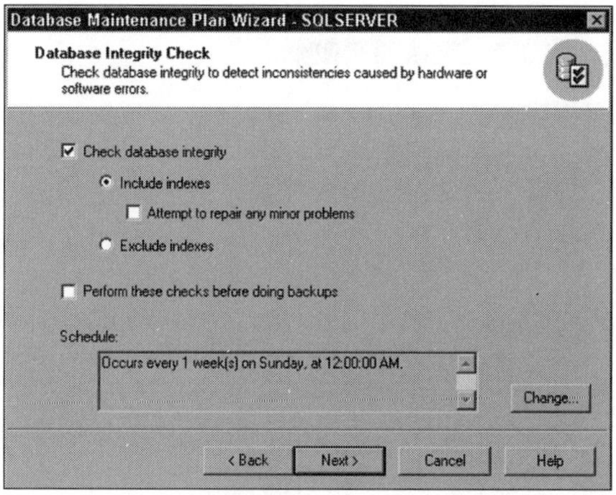

Figure 16-3:
Use this page to automate checking the structural integrity of your database and its indexes.

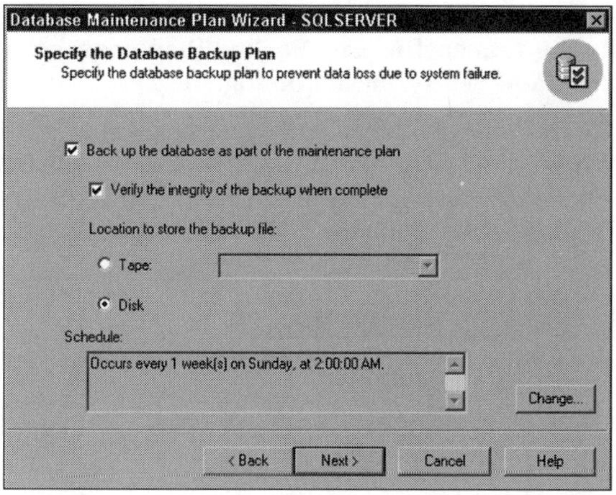

Figure 16-4:
Use this page to schedule a job for backing up the database.

12. **Make sure you schedule a job to back up to disk and then click Next.**

    When you choose to back up your database to a disk device, the Database Maintenance Plan Wizard displays a page for you to define information about the disk devices, as shown in Figure 16-5. This information includes the directory to which you want to back up, whether or not you want to create subdirectories for each database, and the file extension you want to use for the backup device. You can also specify how long you want to keep old backup files in this directory. The default value is four weeks.

13. **Click Next to accept the default settings.**

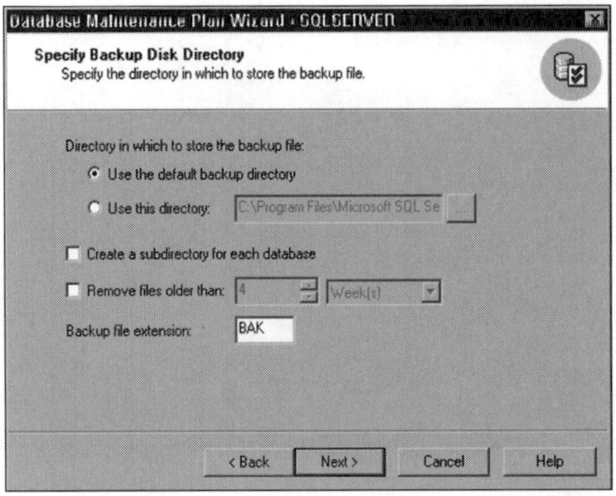

Figure 16-5:
If you choose to back up to a disk device, you must also specify the direc-tory in which you want to store the backup devices.

14. **On the Specify the Transaction Log Backup Plan page, schedule a job to back up your database's transaction log.**

    As shown in Figure 16-6, you can specify whether you want the job to back up the transaction log to disk or tape. By default, the Database Maintenance Plan Wizard schedules the transaction log backup to run on Monday through Saturday nights at 12:00 a.m.

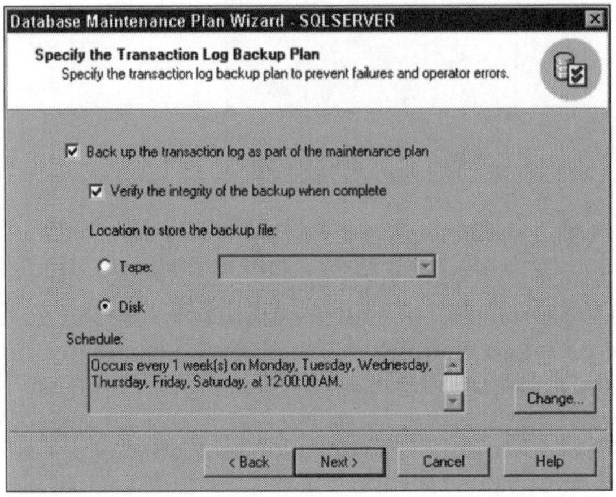

Figure 16-6:
Use this page to schedule transaction log backups.

15. **Click Next.**

    As with backing up the database, if you choose to back up the transac-tion log to a disk device, the Database Maintenance Plan Wizard next prompts you to define where and for how long you want to store the backup devices, as shown in Figure 16-7.

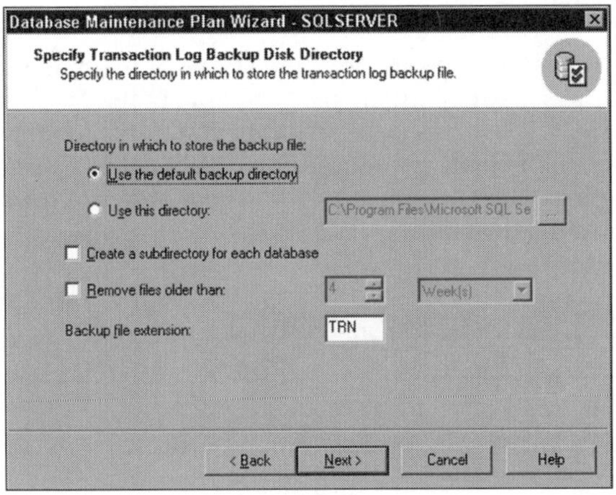

Figure 16-7:
Use this page to specify where and for how long you want to store the transaction log backups.

16. **Click Next.**

17. **Configure the Database Maintenance Plan Wizard to create a text file maintenance report.**

This report enables you to view the status of each maintenance job. As shown in Figure 16-8, you can specify that you want SQL Server to delete any reports that are more than four weeks old. In addition, you can define an operator and then configure SQL Server to notify this operator by e-mail.

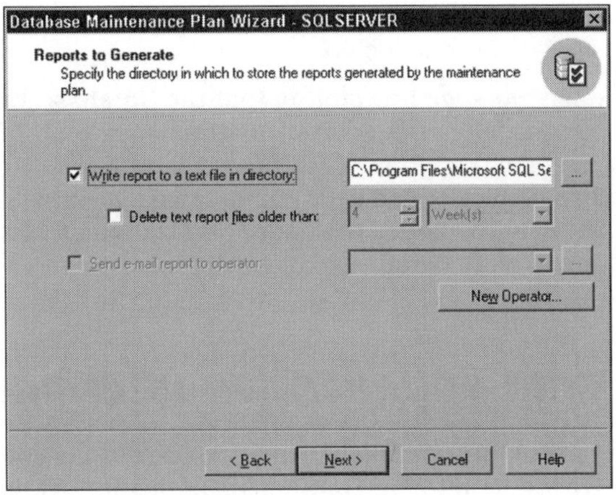

Figure 16-8:
Use the Reports page to configure how SQL Server reports the status of the maintenance jobs.

18. **Click Next.**

19. Take a look at the Maintenance Plan History page.

SQL Server stores information about the status of the maintenance jobs you define in the sysdbmaintplan_history table in the Msdb database. As shown in Figure 16-9, this page prompts you to configure whether you want to store the history information on a local or a remote server. In addition, you can use this page to limit the number of rows in the sysdbmaintplan_history table.

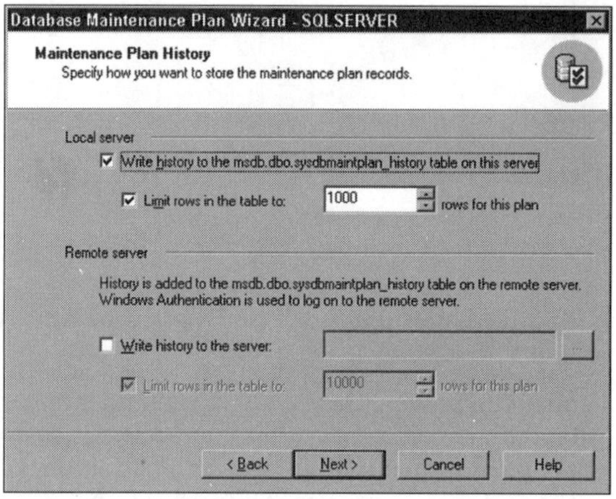

Figure 16-9: Use this page to limit the size of the history table that tracks the results of the maintenance jobs.

20. Click Next and then click Finish.

The Database Maintenance Plan Wizard creates the jobs for performing the maintenance tasks you selected.

21. When you see the message box stating that the Database Maintenance Plan Wizard successfully created your maintenance plan, click OK.

Now that you've had a chance to see what the Database Maintenance Plan Wizard looks like, we want to explain the data optimization and integrity checks it can perform in more detail.

Updating data optimization information

You use the Update Data Optimization Information page in the Database Maintenance Plan Wizard to automate optimizing both your database and its associated indexes. Jobs you can perform include:

✔ **Reorganize Data and Index Pages.** This job enables you to reestablish the fill factor for all the indexes in the database. If you choose the Reorganize Pages With The Original Amount Of Free Space option, SQL

Server recreates all the indexes with the fill factor you specified when you originally created them. If you choose the Change Free Space Per Page Percentage To option, SQL Server creates the indexes with the percentage of free space you specify on each of the pages that make up your indexes.

✔ **Update Statistics Used by Query Optimizer.** When you choose this option, SQL Server updates the statistics it uses to determine the best method for processing a query. It does so by sampling a number of rows in the table. By default, SQL Server samples 10 percent of the rows.

✔ **Remove Unused Space From Database Files.** This option enables you to automate removing any unused space from your database files. You can configure how you want SQL Server to shrink your database by specifying a size limit beyond which you want SQL Server to shrink the database (the default value is 50MB), and the amount of free space you want to keep in the database file after SQL Server shrinks it (the default value here is 10 percent).

Checking database integrity

The Database Maintenance Plan Wizard prompts you to schedule jobs for checking the integrity of your database and its indexes with the DBCC CHECKDB statement. As part of the database integrity check, you can specify whether you want to include or exclude your database's indexes. The database integrity check runs faster if you exclude the indexes. On the other hand, if you exclude the indexes, DBCC CHECKDB can't repair any problems it detects. Instead, you must repair these problems manually.

If you choose to include indexes, you can also have DBCC CHECKDB attempt to repair any minor problems it detects. Although Microsoft recommends that you choose this option, be aware that if you do choose it, SQL Server must put the database in single-user mode while it performs the integrity check. As a result, your users won't be able to access the database until the integrity check completes.

Using the Database Consistency Checker (DBCC) Commands

In addition to the maintenance jobs you configure with the Database Maintenance Plan Wizard, you can also manually check the integrity of your databases and tables by using some of the DBCC commands. We describe these DBCC commands in Table 16-1.

Table 16-1	The Database Consistency Checker Commands
Command	**What It Does**
DBCC CHECKALLOC	Enables you to check the consistency of the pages that make up a database. Example: DBCC CHECKALLOC 'database_name'
DBCC CHECKDB	Checks for corruption in a database. This command checks all the objects in your database, including tables, indexes, and stored procedures. For example, DBCC CHECKDB verifies that the pages that make up a data file or an index are linked together correctly. In addition, this command checks your indexes to determine whether they're sorted properly. DBCC CHECKDB incorporates the DBCC CHECKALLOC and DBCC CHECKTABLE commands; for this reason, if you run DBCC CHECKDB, you don't need to run the other commands. Example: DBCC CHECKDB 'database_name'
DBCC CHECKTABLE	Checks the integrity of a specific table. When you run this command for a table, SQL Server checks both the table and its indexes. Example: DBCC CHECKTABLE 'table_name'

With all of these commands, you can turn off the checking of nonclustered indexes by adding the NOINDEX parameter. (You can't turn off the checking of each table's clustered index because the clustered index is the table itself.)

By default, none of these DBCC commands repairs anything — they simply tell you if they find errors or not. The DBCC CHECKALLOC, CHECKTABLE, and CHECKDB commands all support the same options for repairing the problems they detect. We describe the options you can use to repair problems in Table 16-2.

Table 16-2	Repair Options for DBCC Commands
Option	**What It Does**
REPAIR_FAST	Performs minor repairs that it can complete quickly and without any data loss. For example, the REPAIR_FAST option can fix problems such as extra keys in a nonclustered index.
REPAIR_REBUILD	Performs all the repairs that REPAIR_FAST does, plus it also performs time-consuming repairs such as rebuilding indexes. Like the REPAIR_FAST option, REPAIR_REBUILD performs only those repairs that won't result in data loss.

Option	What It Does
`REPAIR_ALLOW_DATA_LOSS`	Performs both minor and time-consuming repairs, including those that can result in data loss. For example, this option enables SQL Server to deallocate rows and pages as needed to fix page allocation errors. You can execute the DBCC command with the `REPAIR_ALLOW_DATA_LOSS` option within a transaction so that you can easily undo its repairs. Always back up a database after performing a `DBCC` statement against it with the `REPAIR_ALLOW_DATA_LOSS` option.

You must place a database in single-user mode before you can repair it with one of these options. You can configure the single-user option by modifying the properties of a database in SQL Server Enterprise Manager.

When you're attempting to repair a database, always begin with the `REPAIR_FAST` option first. If this option doesn't correct the problem, use the `REPAIR_REBUILD` option next. Resort to the `REPAIR_ALLOW_DATA_LOSS` option only if the first two options don't fix your problem.

Be prepared for questions prompting you to choose between repair options (such as `REPAIR_FAST` and `REPAIR_REBUILD`) on your exam.

Troubleshooting Transactions and Locks

Because transactions and locks can have a big impact on the performance of your server, SQL Server 2000 includes a variety of tools you can use to troubleshoot them. For example, you can use SQL Server Enterprise Manager, SQL Server Profiler, and Transact-SQL commands to analyze transactions and locks.

We focus primarily on troubleshooting locks, because where transactions cause problems for you is with locking, not the transactions themselves.

SQL Server supports two types of locks: basic and special use. We describe each of the types of locks in Table 16-3. Although the basic locks are fairly self-explanatory, we want to talk a minute about the special use locks. The special use locks are primarily intent locks. With an intent lock, SQL Server implements a locking hierarchy. For example, if you're in the process of reading a row in a table, SQL Server places an intent shared (IS) lock on that page in the table, and the table itself. By placing the IS lock on those resources, SQL Server prevents other users from placing an exclusive lock on the page or table while you're reading that row.

Table 16-3	Types of Locks
Lock	Description
Shared (S)	Used whenever a process is reading a resource (such as with the SELECT statement). This lock is called shared because other transactions can put shared locks on the same resource at the same time.
Exclusive (X)	Used whenever a process is changing data (such as with the INSERT, UPDATE, or DELETE statements). With an exclusive lock, only the process locking the resource can use the resource. In other words, if you execute a transaction that places an exclusive lock on a resource, no other users can access that resource until you release the lock.
Intent Shared (IS)	Placed whenever a transaction is reading a resource. This lock prevents another process from placing an exclusive lock at a higher level. For example, if you're reading a row in a table, SQL Server places an IS lock on the page containing the row and the table itself.
Intent Exclusive (IX)	Used whenever a transaction is modifying a resource. Like the IS lock, this lock prevents another process from placing a lock at a higher level.
Shared with Intent Exclusive (SIX)	Placed whenever a transaction reads and changes some of the data within a resource.
Update (U)	Used whenever SQL Server plans to modify one of a table's pages. This lock prevents processes from placing exclusive locks on the same page, but it doesn't prevent processes from placing shared locks on the page.

SQL Server 2000 supports locks on the following resources: a single row in a table, a single row in an index, an 8KB page of a table or index, an extent (eight 8KB pages), an entire table and its indexes, and an entire database.

As you've probably already figured out, some of these locks can't coexist with the others. For example, you can't have both a shared and an exclusive lock on the exact same resource at the same time. In Table 16-4, we define which locks can coexist with each other.

Table 16-4	Coexistence of Locks					
Requested Lock	*S*	*X*	*IS*	*IX*	*SIX*	*U*
Shared (S)	Yes	No	Yes	No	No	Yes
Exclusive (X)	No	No	No	No	No	No
Intent Shared (IS)	Yes	No	Yes	Yes	Yes	Yes
Intent Exclusive (IX)	No	No	Yes	Yes	No	No
Shared with Intent Exclusive (SIX)	No	No	Yes	No	No	No
Update	Yes	No	Yes	No	No	No

So right about now you're probably wondering why we're telling you all of this. Well, the answer is that if one user's transaction puts an exclusive lock on a resource, no other user can use that resource until the first user's transaction completes. And in a large database environment with lots of users, exclusive locks can seriously degrade your system's performance.

Using Transact-SQL

When it comes to troubleshooting locks (and thus transactions) with Transact-SQL, you primarily use two stored procedures: sp_lock and sp_who. The sp_lock stored procedure enables you to view a list of the active locks on your server by SQL Server Process ID (SPID). You can then obtain a list of the processes running on your server and their associated SPID by running the sp_who stored procedure.

Identifying exclusive locks

The first thing you want to do when troubleshooting locks is to find out whether or not your users are placing any exclusive locks. One way you can do so is with the sp_lock stored procedure. In Figure 16-10, we show you the output of the sp_lock command. Most importantly, you want to examine the Mode column, because it indicates whether or not a process has an exclusive lock on a resource. (Refer to Table 16-3 for the abbreviations for the different types of locks.) As you can see in Figure 16-10, the process with the SPID of 54 has placed an exclusive lock on a resource. If your users are unable to access a row, table, or the database itself, this process is your problem.

For the exam, make sure you can identify which processes are blocking other processes based on the information you see when you run sp_lock.

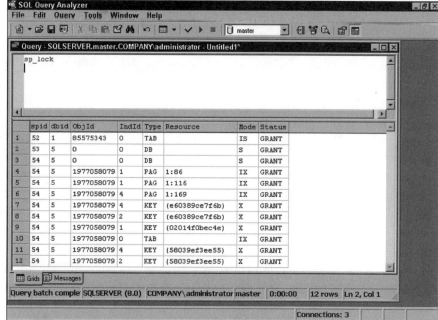

Figure 16-10:
Use
sp_lock to
troubleshoot
locking on
your server.

Configuring transaction isolation levels

One technique you can use to manage locking and its impact on your server's performance is to configure the transaction isolation level. You can configure the isolation level at either the session- or table-level. With session-level locking, you control the locking for a user's session with the server. Each of the isolation levels you can set varies as to how it manages shared and exclusive locks.

Keep in mind that although eliminating locking on your server improves performance (because users don't have to wait for a lock to release to access data), you can encounter problems with data inconsistencies. You evaluate each of the transaction isolation levels by determining whether or not they prevent the following data inconsistencies:

- ✔ **Dirty reads,** in which SQL Server permits a user to read uncommitted data. For example, a dirty read occurs when one user executes a transaction to modify a row and even though that modification hasn't been committed, another user reads that row with the modification.

- ✔ **Nonrepeatable read,** in which a transaction accesses a row multiple times and obtains different data each time.

✔ **Phantom read,** in which an insert or a delete is executed against a row that is currently being read by another transaction. For example, if you eliminate locking, it's possible for one user to select a range of rows while another user is deleting a row within that range. If the transaction isolation level permits phantom reads, then in this scenario, a user might see a row in the result set that another user has already deleted.

In Table 16-5, we describe the levels of isolation you can configure on your server — starting with the least restrictive and working our way up to the most restrictive.

Table 16-5	**Isolation Levels**
Isolation Level	*What It Does*
READ UNCOMMITTED	Enables SQL Server to read any of the data on a page whether or not SQL Server has committed the data. With this isolation level, SQL Server doesn't use any locks and ignores other sessions' locks on the data. As a result, this level permits dirty reads, nonrepeatable reads, and phantom reads.
READ COMMITTED	Prevents dirty reads but not repeatable reads and phantom reads. With this transaction isolation level, SQL Server considers a transaction's shared lock only until it reads the data, but enforces a transaction's exclusive lock until it commits the transaction. READ COMMITTED is the default transaction isolation level in SQL Server 2000.
REPEATABLE READ	This level of isolation prevents both dirty reads (the reading of uncommitted data) and non-repeatable reads, but doesn't prevent phantom reads. In other words, SQL Server respects both shared and exclusive locks until their associated transactions complete.
SERIALIZABLE	Prevents dirty reads, non-repeatable reads, and phantom reads. This is the most restrictive of the transaction isolation levels. With the SERIALIZABLE isolation level, SQL Server holds a transaction's lock (whether it's a shared or an exclusive lock) until the transaction completes. Although this level guarantees that all users see the same exact data, it also has the greatest impact on your server's performance.

You configure the session isolation level by using the following syntax:

```
SET TRANSACTION ISOLATION LEVEL
(READ COMMITTED | READ UNCOMMITTED | REPEATABLE READ |
        SERIALIZABLE)
```

On the other hand, you configure table-level locking as part of a transaction itself. For example, the following query updates the authors table in the pubs database using the SERIALIZABLE isolation level:

```
BEGIN TRANSACTION
UPDATE authors(SERIALIZABLE)
SET state = 'UT'
COMMIT TRANSACTION
```

Microsoft generally recommends that you use the default session and table isolation levels. Doing so enables SQL Server to determine the best method of implementing locks on your resources. For the purpose of the exam, remember that using the READ UNCOMMITTED isolation level provides you with the best performance.

Using SQL Server Enterprise Manager

You can use SQL Server Enterprise Manager to determine whether any of the current transactions on your server are blocking other transactions. SQL Server Enterprise Manager displays this information within the Current Activity object for your server. You can view the locks per process ID (SPID) as well as the locks per object. Lab 16-2 shows you how to view the locks on your server in SQL Server Enterprise Manager:

Lab 16-2   Viewing Locks in SQL Server Enterprise Manager

1. **In SQL Server Enterprise Manager, expand the Management folder for your server.**

2. **Expand the Current Activity object.**

3. **In the console tree, select either the Locks/Process ID or Locks/Object to view the associated lock information.**

    As shown in Figure 16-11, you can determine whether any process (and thus transaction) has an exclusive lock that's preventing another process from executing.

SQL Server Enterprise Manager doesn't dynamically refresh the locking information. To refresh the information you see for both Locks/Process ID and Locks/Object, you must select the Current Activity object and choose Action⇨Refresh.

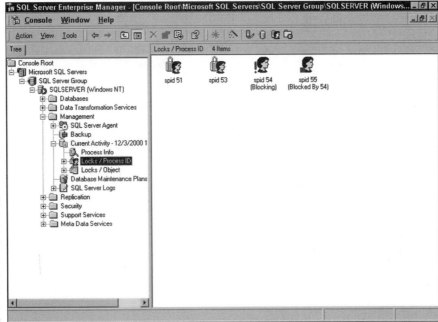

Figure 16-11:
Use the
Current
Activity
object in
SQL Server
Enterprise
Manager to
troubleshoot
locking.

Using SQL Server Profiler

SQL Server Profiler also enables you to troubleshoot locking on your server.
You can create a trace file that enables you to determine the cause of deadlocks (where two users each have a resource locked and are trying to use the
other user's resource) as well as monitor information about locks. Lab 16-3
shows you how to analyze locking in SQL Server Profiler.

Lab 16-3   Viewing Locks in SQL Server Profiler

1. **From the Microsoft SQL Server menu, choose Profiler to launch SQL
   Server Profiler.**

2. **Choose File⇨New⇨Trace.**

3. **In the Connect To SQL Server dialog box, log on to the server for
   which you want to analyze locking.**

4. **In the Trace Properties dialog box, specify whether you want to capture the trace to a file or a table.**

5. **Select the Events tab.**

   As shown in Figure 16-12, you trace locking by adding the appropriate
   lock event classes to your trace file. For example, choose Lock: Deadlock
   to trace the deadlocks on your server.

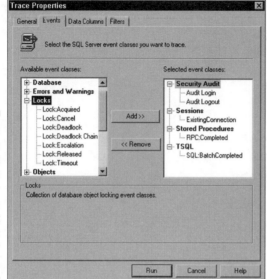

Figure 16-12:
Add the
lock event
classes
to your
trace file to
troubleshoot
locking in
SQL Server
Profiler.

6. **Select the Data Columns tab.**

   Use this page to add or remove columns of information from your trace
   file.

7. **Select the Filters tab.**

   You can use this page to configure SQL Server Profiler to include or
   exclude specific transactions from the trace file.

8. **Click Run to begin capturing the trace file.**

Prep Test

1 Which of the following tasks does SQL Server include in a database's maintenance plan? (Choose all that apply.)

A ❑ Checking database integrity

B ❑ Optimizing database space usage

C ❑ Configuring alerts to monitor transaction log space usage

D ❑ Backing up a database and its transaction log

2 Which of the following objects can you include in the same database maintenance plan? (Choose all that apply.)

A ❑ System and user databases

B ❑ User databases only

C ❑ System databases only

D ❑ All files on your server

3 Which of the following tasks can you configure for optimizing data space in the Database Maintenance Plan Wizard?

A ○ Reorganize data and index pages

B ○ Drop and recreate indexes

C ○ Update statistics used by Query Optimizer

D ○ Modifying the Query Governor

4 Which option should you use with the `DBCC CHECKDB` command if you want to repair a database as much as possible but without the possibility of losing any data?

A ○ REPAIR_FAST

B ○ REPAIR_REBUILD

C ○ REPAIR_ALLOW_DATA_LOSS

D ○ REPAIR

5 What happens if the Database Maintenance Plan Wizard Server detects any database consistency problems?

A ○ It automatically repairs any consistency problems.

B ○ It terminates the job and reports an error.

C ○ It notifies any operators you define so that they can repair the problem.

D ○ It records an error in the Application log and then continues with checking the database's consistency.

6 You want to speed up consistency checking when you run the DBCC CHECKDB command. What should you do?

A ○ Run DBCC CHECKDB with the NO-NONCLUSTERED option.

B ○ Nothing — the DBCC CHECKDB command doesn't check nonclustered indexes unless you explicitly configure it to do so.

C ○ Use SQL Server Profiler to determine the results of the DBCC statement.

D ○ Run DBCC CHECKDB with the NOINDEX option.

7 A shared lock can coexist with which of the following locks? (Choose all that apply.)

A ❑ Update

B ❑ Shared

C ❑ Exclusive

D ❑ Intent Shared

Answers

1 **A, B,** and **D.** You can define jobs within the Database Maintenance Plan Wizard to check database integrity, optimize the database's use of disk space, and back up a database and its transaction log. *See "Implementing a Maintenance Plan."*

2 **A.** Although it isn't advisable, you can include both your system and user databases in a single database maintenance plan. *See "Implementing a Maintenance Plan."*

3 **A.** You can configure SQL Server to reorganize data and index pages to optimize data space usage by using the Database Maintenance Plan Wizard. *Refer to "Implementing a Maintenance Plan."*

4 **B.** You use the `REPAIR_REBUILD` option when you want the `DBCC CHECKDB` command to repair as much of the database as it can, including performing time-consuming repairs, without losing any of your data. *Study "Using the Database Consistency Checker (DBCC) Commands."*

5 **A.** The Database Maintenance Plan Wizard can run the `DBCC CHECKDB` command to both check a database and to perform minor repairs. Keep in mind that if you choose to have Database Maintenance Plan Wizard fix any errors, SQL Server must put your database in single-user mode while it performs the maintenance jobs. *See "Checking database integrity."*

6 **D.** By using the `NOINDEX` option, you restrict the `DBCC CHECKDB` command to checking only the data itself and not the nonclustered indexes. *See "Checking database integrity."*

7 **A, B,** and **D.** A shared lock can't coexist with an exclusive lock. *Study "Troubleshooting Transactions and Locks."*

Part V
Transferring Data

The 5th Wave   By Rich Tennant

BEAL & WASP
DATABASE
CONSULTANTS

"Your database is beyond repair, but before I tell you
our backup recommendation, let me ask you a
question. How many index cards do you think will fit
on the walls of your computer room?"

In this part . . .

*B*ecause Microsoft realizes that most of the networks you support today don't just have SQL servers, SQL Server 2000 includes components that enable you to connect and transfer data between SQL Server and just about anything. In this part, we examine many of these components, including how to implement connectivity with IIS, transfer data with Data Transformation Services, and design and configure replication.

In Chapter 17, we examine how you create a virtual directory within an IIS server so that your users can access the SQL server through a Web browser. We show you how to use Data Transformation Services in Chapter 18. And in Chapter 19, we walk you through what you need to know both for designing and implementing replication of a database.

Chapter 17

Integrating SQL Server with Internet Information Services

*O*ne of the new features included in SQL Server 2000 is support for the Extended Markup Language (XML). In case you're thinking "So what?", the advantage to supporting this language is that it enables your users to query the SQL Server from within a Web browser. And the BIG advantage to supporting queries from a Web browser is that your users can access SQL data without requiring any special client software on their computers (such as SQL Server Query Analyzer). This advantage also means that you can easily develop Web applications to query SQL Server. In this chapter, we show you how to configure a virtual directory to connect your SQL server to your Internet Information Services (IIS) server, and how to query your server through a Web browser.

Because XML support is one of the new features in SQL Server 2000, Microsoft is really proud of it. You can expect to see a few questions on how you configure virtual directories and access them through a URL query on your exam.

Quick Assessment

Setting up IIS virtual directories to support XML

1 You integrate SQL Server with an IIS server by configuring a(n) _____.

2 You use _____ queries to query your SQL server through a Web browser.

3 Use the _____ utility to integrate SQL Server with IIS.

Extracting data with SQL Server 2000

4 You can access a SQL Server through HTTP by executing _____, _____, or _____ queries.

Answers

1 *Virtual directory.* Review "Configuring a Virtual Directory for SQL Server."

2 *XML.* Study "Accessing SQL Server with HTTP."

3 *IIS Virtual Directory Management for SQL Server.* See "Configuring a Virtual Directory for SQL Server."

4 *URL query, XML template file, or XPath query.* Study "Accessing SQL Server with HTTP."

Configuring a Virtual Directory for SQL Server

In order to set up support for XML queries, you must first link your SQL Server to an Internet Information Services (IIS) server. In IIS, you use a virtual directory to enable users to access a new folder with its own set of Web pages (separate from your home pages) within your IIS server. Your users connect to this virtual directory by specifying the name you've associated with the virtual directory itself. For example, you use the URL of `www.microsoft.com/sql` to access the sql virtual directory within Microsoft's Web site. One of the advantages to a virtual directory is that it can be on the same server or on a different server, and the actual folder containing the Web pages can be anywhere on the server.

If you want to establish a connection between an IIS virtual directory and SQL Server 2000, you must use the IIS Virtual Directory Management for SQL Server utility to do so. After you establish the connection, users can connect to your SQL Server by using the Hypertext Transport Protocol (HTTP).

To set up a virtual directory, you first need an IIS server available to you. You can install IIS on your SQL server, or you can install it on a separate server. After you have an IIS server, your next step is to configure the virtual directory for SQL Server. We walk you through configuring a virtual directory for SQL Server within your default Web site in IIS in Lab 17-1.

For the purposes of this book, we installed IIS on our SQL server. Keep in mind that in a production environment, you typically install IIS on its own server for performance and security reasons.

Lab 17-1   Configuring a Virtual Directory for SQL Server

1. **In Windows Explorer, create a new folder. (If you want to follow along with our example, name this new folder C:\Northwind.)**

   You're going to configure this folder as your virtual directory for SQL Server.

2. **From the Microsoft SQL Server program group, choose Configure SQL XML Support in IIS.**

   The IIS Virtual Directory Management for SQL Server utility appears. You use this utility to configure a virtual directory for SQL Server within a Web site. (For those of you already familiar with administering an IIS server, you may notice that this utility looks very similar to the Internet Services Manager utility.)

3. **In the console tree, right-click the Default Web Site and choose New⇨ Virtual Directory to open the New Virtual Directory Properties dialog box.**

You use this dialog box to configure the properties for linking IIS to SQL Server.

4. **As shown in Figure 17-1, enter a name for the virtual directory — for example, Northwind.**

The name you specify here is what your users will type when they connect to your server through a Web browser. For example, if you name this virtual directory Northwind and your IIS server is named www.company.com, your users access the virtual directory by typing **www.company.com/Northwind**.

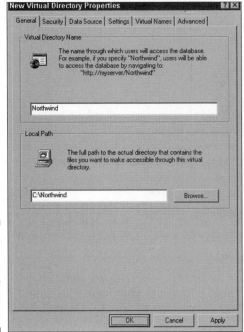

Figure 17-1:
Defining a
virtual
directory
name
and path.

5. **In the Local Path text box, type the full path to the folder you created in Step 1 (in our example, C:\Northwind, as shown in Figure 17-1).**

You must specify a folder to contain the files that make up the virtual directory for SQL Server.

6. **Select the Security tab and take a look at your options.**

You use this page to specify how you want users to log on to your SQL server when they connect through the virtual directory. You can have users log on with a specific SQL login ID, a Windows login ID, or you can use Windows Integrated Authentication.

7. **Select the Use Windows Integrated Authentication option, as shown in Figure 17 2.**

8. **Select the Data Source tab.**

   By default, the IIS Virtual Directory Management for SQL Server utility assumes that you want to connect to your local SQL server. You can use the Browse button (...) on this page to select a different SQL server if necessary.

9. **As shown in Figure 17-3, from the Database drop-down list, select the database to which you want to connect the virtual directory.**

10. **Select the Settings tab.**

    Use this page to configure the types of queries you want to support in this virtual directory. By default, your virtual directory supports queries only in the form of templates. We talk more about the types of queries supported through a Web browser in the section "Accessing SQL Server with HTTP," later in this chapter.

11. **Check Allow URL Queries.**

    As shown in Figure 17-4, this option enables you to type your query directly into the Address text box of a Web browser.

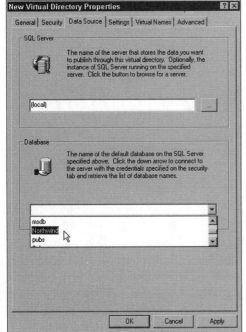

Figure 17-3:
Connecting
a virtual
directory to
a specific
database.

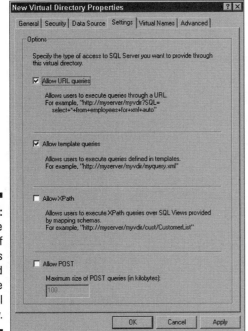

Figure 17-4:
Defining the
types of
queries
supported
by the
virtual
directory.

12. **Click OK to create the virtual directory.**

    You can go ahead and close the IIS Virtual Directory Management for SQL Server utility.

Accessing SQL Server with HTTP

After you configure a virtual directory for SQL Server, your next step is to access it through a Web browser such as Internet Explorer. You can use any of the following techniques to query your server (provided you have configured your SQL server's virtual directory to support that technique):

- ✓ **Specifying a query directly against database objects in the address line of the browser.** This type of query is called a URL query.

- ✓ **Using an XML template file to query the database.** With a template file, you create a document that contains both your Transact-SQL query along with XML formatting.

- ✓ **Executing an XML Path Language (XPath) query.** You use XPath to create an XML view of a database (this view is also called a mapping schema file); you use XPath queries to query this view.

Prep Test

1 **Which utility should you use to configure a SQL Server virtual directory?**

A ○ Internet Services Manager

B ○ IIS Virtual Directory Management for SQL Server

C ○ SQL Server Enterprise Manager

D ○ Active Directory Users and Computers

2 **Which of the following properties must you define for a SQL Server virtual directory? (Choose all that apply.)**

A ❑ The virtual directory's name

B ❑ The folder for the virtual directory

C ❑ The data source information

D ❑ The types of queries you want the virtual directory to support

3 **What types of login IDs can you use when configuring the login security for a virtual directory? (Choose all that apply.)**

A ❑ SQL login ID

B ❑ Windows login ID

C ❑ Windows Integrated Authentication

D ❑ The guest login ID

4 **Which of the following query types does a SQL Server virtual directory support by default? (Choose all that apply.)**

A ❑ URL queries

B ❑ XML templates

C ❑ XPath queries

D ❑ Transact-SQL scripts

Answers

1 **B.** You can configure a virtual directory for SQL Server only within the IIS Virtual Directory Management for SQL Server utility. *See "Configuring a Virtual Directory for SQL Server."*

2 **A, B, C,** and **D.** You must configure all of these properties for a virtual directory. *Study "Configuring a Virtual Directory for SQL Server."*

3 **A, B,** and **C.** You can configure a virtual directory to support SQL login IDs or a specific Windows login ID, or enable support for Windows Integrated Authentication. *Review "Configuring a Virtual Directory for SQL Server."*

4 **A, B,** and **C.** You can query a SQL Server through a Web browser by using URL queries, XML templates, or XPath queries. *Study "Accessing SQL Server with HTTP."*

Chapter 18

Importing and Exporting Data

Exam Objectives

▶ Importing and exporting data

▶ Developing and managing Data Transformation Services (DTS) packages

▶ Creating and managing linked servers

▶ Converting data types

*B*ecause the odds are that you won't be running only SQL Server 2000 on your network, Microsoft includes a variety of utilities that you can use to import and export data from your SQL server. In this chapter, we show you how to import and export data by using a variety of utilities and methods, including the Data Transformation Services, bulk copy program, and heterogeneous queries.

Quick Assessment

Importing and export-ing data

1 You should use the _____ utility to create complex DTS packages.

2 The _____ utility is best suited for transferring data between SQL Server 2000 and a mainframe database.

3 The fastest method for moving a database from one server running SQL Server 2000 to another uses the _____ and _____ stored procedures.

Developing and manag-ing DTS packages

4 SQL Server stores a DTS package in the _____ database when you save it to your server.

5 You should save a DTS package to a(n) _____ if you want to distribute it to other SQL servers.

6 You can secure a DTS package by assigning _____ and _____ passwords.

7 You control the workflow of a DTS package by defining _____.

8 A(n) _____ precedence constraint enables a DTS package step to execute only if the preceding step succeeds.

Creating and manag-ing linked servers

9 You create a linked server by defining at least a(n) _____ and a(n) _____.

10 You query a linked server in SQL Server Query Analyzer by using the linked server's _____.

Converting data types

11 You specify which columns you want to import or export by defining _____.

12 You combine data into a single column by using a(n) _____.

Answers

1   *DTS Designer.* Review "Importing and Exporting Data."

2   `bcp`. Study "Importing and Exporting Data."

3   `sp_detach_db` *and* `sp_attach_db`. Review "Importing and Exporting Data."

4   *Msdb.* Review "The DTS Import/Export Wizard."

5   *COM-Structured Storage File.* See "The DTS Import/Export Wizard."

6   *Owner and User.* Study "The DTS Import/Export Wizard."

7   *Precedence constraints.* See "The DTS Designer."

8   *On Success.* Study "The DTS Designer."

9   *OLE DB Provider and an OLE DB data source.* See "Defining a linked server."

10 *Fully qualified name.* Study "Executing a heterogeneous query."

11 *Column mappings.* Review "The DTS Import/Export Wizard."

12 *Script.* Study "The DTS Import/Export Wizard."

Importing and Exporting Data

When it comes to importing and exporting data between SQL Server 2000 and just about anything, SQL Server offers you a whole host of tools. One of the things you need to make sure you understand for your exam is which tool to use for a given scenario. We describe these tools and when to use them in Table 18-1.

Table 18-1	Import and Export Utilities
Utility	*Use To*
DTS Import/Export Wizard	Create simple DTS packages for importing, exporting, and transforming data between heterogeneous data sources.
DTS Designer	Create complex data transfer packages between heterogeneous data sources. Most importantly, you can use DTS Designer to set specific workflows for DTS packages.
DTS Bulk Insert task	Create packages for transferring large amounts of data; based on the BULK INSERT SQL statement. *Note:* You can't transform data when you use a DTS Bulk Insert package.
SELECT...INTO	Select data from one or more tables and create a new table based on that data. The source of the data can be another SQL server, or any OLE DB or ODBC data source.
Bulk copy program (bcp)	Import and export data in either the SQL Server or ASCII text format.
Replication	Maintain replicas of both a table's structure and its data on multiple databases (usually stored on different servers).
sp_attach_db/sp_detach_db	Detach (remove) a database from one SQL server and attach (copy) it to another server.
BACKUP/RESTORE	Back up a database on one server and restore it to a different SQL server.

Because we cover Backup/Restore in Chapters 14 and 15, replication in Chapter 19, and the sp_attach_db and sp_detach_db stored procedures in Chapter 10, we do not cover them again in this chapter.

Many of the utilities we talk about in this chapter are part of what Microsoft calls its Data Transformation Services (or DTS for short). You use DTS to create packages (jobs) for importing or exporting data, or both. You can also use DTS to transform data — which means that SQL Server will make changes to the data during the import or export process.

Using Data Transformation Services (DTS)

Microsoft is (rightfully) very proud of its Data Transformation Services. DTS consists of a grand wizard (the DTS Import/Export Wizard), along with a Designer program that together enable you to perform anything from straightforward data transfers up to complex transformations of data between heterogeneous data sources. In case you're wondering what we mean when we say "heterogeneous," we describe the types of data sources and destinations DTS supports in Table 18-2.

Table 18-2	Supported Data Sources
Data Source	*Examples*
ODBC	Oracle, Microsoft Access, IBM DB2 databases
OLE DB	SQL Server, Microsoft Access, Microsoft Excel, Microsoft Internet Publishing
Text Files	ASCII-delimited or fixed-length text files
Custom	Any third-party OLE DB provider

The DTS Import/Export Wizard

You use the DTS Import/Export Wizard to either import or export data from a SQL server. To be precise, you don't actually have to involve a SQL server in the transfer — you can use this wizard to transfer data between any of the supported data sources. Here's what the Import/Export Wizard enables you to do:

✔ Copy a table or view between heterogeneous data sources.

✔ Use a query to import or export data between heterogeneous data sources. This query can be based on a single table, multiple tables through the use of table joins, or even tables on different servers (provided you've defined these servers as linked servers).

✔ Transfer the database schema (including user-defined data types, constraints, defaults, indexes, rules, stored procedures, and triggers) and data between SQL Server databases.

✔ Transform the data.

✔ Run the DTS package as soon as you create it, or schedule it to run at a later time or on a regular basis.

Transforming data

One of the more important features of Data Transformation Services is that it can not only import and export data, but it can also make changes to the data during that process. Types of transformations DTS can perform include:

✔ Changing any of the column properties, including data type, name, whether or not the column permits nulls, its size — and if numeric, the scale and precision.

✔ Skipping the importing or exporting of some of the columns in a table.

✔ Combining data from multiple sources into a single table.

✔ Dividing data from a single source into multiple tables.

✔ Combining data from multiple columns into a single column.

✔ Dividing data from a single column into multiple columns.

If you want to import numeric data from several different sources, each with different settings for precision (the number of total digits in the column) and scale (the number of decimal places), into a single column, make sure you configure the destination column with precision and scale settings that can accommodate the largest possible values from any of the source tables.

When you use the DTS Import/Export Wizard, you control which columns are imported or exported and change a column's properties by using the Column Mappings page of the Column Mappings and Transformations dialog box. If you want to make changes such as combining or dividing data, you can write your own custom script for performing such transformations during the import or export process. DTS supports scripts written in Microsoft Jscript, PerlScript, or the Microsoft Visual Basic Scripting (VBScript) languages.

You can run into trouble if you attempt to import or export international data between servers or databases configured to use different code pages and collations. In order to avoid losing data, store any international data in Unicode. By storing the data in Unicode, you avoid losing the data when it's transferred between servers.

Saving a package

When you create a package, the DTS Import/Export Wizard enables you to save the package to one of several different locations. These locations include:

- ✔ In the sysdtspackages table within the msdb database on your server.
- ✔ In SQL Server Meta Data Services. This service stores the package within a database so that other applications can reuse and access it.
- ✔ In a COM-Structured Storage File. This saves the package as a .dts file so that it can be accessed outside of SQL Server. You can then easily distribute and schedule this package on other servers.
- ✔ In a Visual Basic File for use in Visual Basic programs.

Scheduling a package

One of your options when you save a package is to schedule it to run at a later time — or to schedule it to occur on a recurring basis. The SQLServerAgent service is responsible for executing all scheduled jobs, including any DTS packages. As a result, making sure the SQLServerAgent service is configured to log in as a domain user account with administrative privileges on your SQL server is critical. In addition, make sure that you've configured the SQLServerAgent service to start whenever your server starts.

You configure the SQLServerAgent service's properties in SQL Server Enterprise Manager. In the console tree, expand the Management folder below your server. Right-click the SQL Server Agent object and choose Properties. You configure the service account on the General page of the Properties dialog box, and you configure the service to restart automatically on the Advanced page.

Securing a package

When you create and save a package, the DTS Import/Export Wizard gives you two options for securing that package. First, you can specify an Owner Password. A user must know this password in order to see or change the properties of the package. Second, you can specify a User Password. Users must enter this password before they can run the package.

In Lab 18-1, we walk you through creating and saving a DTS package to export data from one database into a new database on your SQL server.

 1. **If necessary, log on to your server as Administrator and start SQL
    Server Enterprise Manager.**

 2. **In the console tree, expand your server and select the Databases
    folder.**

    You must establish a connection to your server before you can start the
    DTS Import/Export Wizard.

 3. **Choose Tools⇨Data Transformation Services⇨Export Data to start the
    DTS Import/Export Wizard.**

 4. **On the introductory page, click Next.**

 5. **Select the Data Source drop-down list.**

    As you can see in Figure 18-1, the DTS Import/Export Wizard includes
    support for many different data sources.

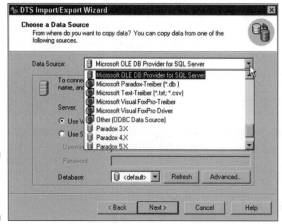

Figure 18-1:
Selecting a
data source.

 6. **From the Data Source drop-down list, select the Microsoft OLE DB
    Provider for SQL Server.**

    You choose this provider as a data source whenever you want to export
    data from SQL Server; likewise, choose this provider as the destination
    whenever you want to import data into SQL Server.

 7. **Make sure that you're connecting to your server — and that you're
    using Windows Authentication to log in.**

    When SQL Server runs your DTS package, it must log in to the data
    source and destination you specify. You can configure your package to
    use either Windows Authentication or SQL Server Authentication.

8. **From the Database drop-down list, select the database from which you want to export data.**

   If you want to follow along with the example that we use throughout this lab, choose to export data from the Northwind database to a new database on your server.

9. **Click Next.**

10. **On the Choose a Destination page, verify that the Microsoft OLE DB Provider for SQL Server is selected as the destination.**

    Because you're going to export data between databases on your own server, you must use the Microsoft OLE DB Provider for SQL Server for both the data source and destination.

11. **Accept the default setting of (local) for your server name and Windows Authentication.**

12. **From the Database drop-down list, select New, as shown in Figure 18-2.**

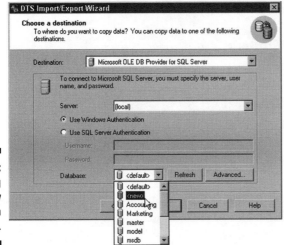

Figure 18-2:
Creating
a new
destination
database.

13. **Enter a name for the destination database, and specify a size for its data and log files.**

    If you want to follow along with our example, name the new database Practice and assign a data and log file size of 2MB each, as shown in Figure 18-3.

14. **Click OK to close the Create Database dialog box, and then click Next to continue with the DTS Import/Export Wizard.**

Figure 18-3:
Naming
the new
database.

15. **As shown in Figure 18-4, you can now choose whether you want to copy a table, design a query to select data, or copy database objects to the new database.**

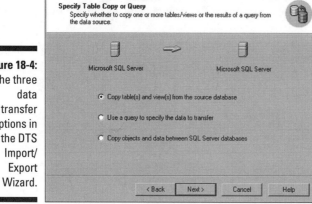

Figure 18-4:
The three
data
transfer
options in
the DTS
Import/
Export
Wizard.

16. **We're going to use the default option, Copy Table(s) and View(s) From the Source Database, so click Next.**

You now see a list of the tables and views defined in the database from which you're exporting data. You can use this list to choose what you want to export to the destination database.

17. **In the Source column, check the tables that you want to export.**

In our example, we select the [Northwind].[dbo].[Customers] table, as shown in Figure 18-5.

You may want to widen the Source column if you can't see the table names. Click and drag the divider line between the Source and Destination columns to widen the Source column. Notice that the DTS Import/Export Wizard automatically assumes that you want to name the destination table the same as the source table (Customers).

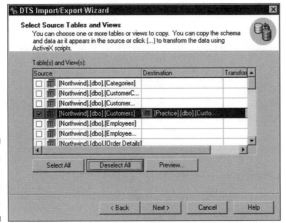

Figure 18-5:
Selecting a
table to
export.

18. **In the Transform column for the selected table, click on the Browse (...) button to open the Column Mappings and Transformations dialog box shown in Figure 18-6.**

You use this dialog box to configure any data transformations you want to take place during the export process.

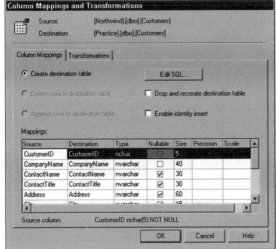

Figure 18-6:
You can
transform
data when
you use
the DTS
Import/
Export
Wizard.

19. **Click Cancel to close the Column Mappings and Transformations dialog box.**

20. **Click Next.**

21. **On the Save, Schedule, and Replicate Package page, check Save DTS Package.**

    When you select the Save DTS Package option, the DTS Import/Export Wizard defaults to saving it to your server, as shown in Figure 18-7. Notice that the DTS Import/Export Wizard automatically configured your package to run immediately. You can also use this page to schedule your package to run later by checking Schedule DTS Package, and then specifying a date and time.

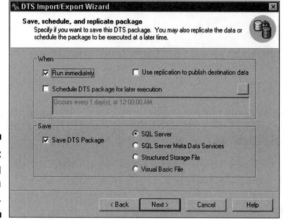

Figure 18-7:
Scheduling and saving a package.

22. **Click Next.**

23. **In the Name text box, enter a name for your package — for example,** Northwind Customers.

    You can also use this page to define Owner and User Passwords for this DTS package.

24. **Click Next, and then click Finish to run the package.**

25. **Click OK to close the message box stating that your package ran successfully.**

26. **Take a look at the Executing Package dialog box, as shown in Figure 18-8.**

    This dialog box enables you to see the steps SQL Server performed as part of your package — and the success or failure of each step.

27. **Click Done.**

    If you've followed along with our example, a new database named Practice is now in your server's Databases folder — and it contains the table named Customers. This table is an exact copy of the Customers table in the Northwind database.

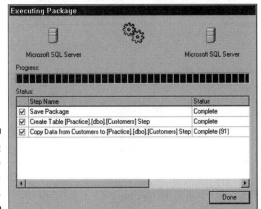

Figure 18-8:
Viewing the
results of a
package.

You can also create a DTS package by using the dtswiz command-line utility. This utility includes parameters that you can specify to bypass the various pages of the wizard.

The DTS Designer

The DTS Designer includes all the functionality of the DTS Import/Export Wizard, plus it enables you to

- ✔ Design complex data transformations.
- ✔ Define the workflow of a package so that you can control the exact sequence of steps it performs.
- ✔ Use the Bulk Insert task for importing or exporting large amounts of data.

If you find that you want to make complicated changes to your data, or you want to define different steps based on whether or not a prior step succeeds or fails, then use the DTS Designer instead of the DTS Import/Export Wizard.

You can use the DTS Designer not only to create new packages, but also to modify a package you created with the DTS Import/Export Wizard.

You control the workflow of a package by defining precedence constraints between each of the package's steps. In other words, you use precedence constraints to manage which step in the package DTS executes when — and what DTS should do if a step succeeds or fails. We describe the three types of precedence constraints you can define in Table 18-3.

Table 18-3	Types of Precedence Constraints
Type	**Enables a Step to Execute**
On Completion	Immediately after the preceding step completes. DTS Designer displays this type of as a blue and white arrow.
On Failure	Only if the preceding step fails. DTS Designer displays this type of as a red and white arrow.
On Success	Only if the preceding step succeeds. DTS Designer displays this type of as a green and white arrow.

Think of these constraints as modifying the step that follows them. In other words, they precede the next step in the workflow of the package.

In addition to defining precedence constraints, you can also specify a step priority. You use this priority to have SQL Server execute a step at idle (meaning only when the server isn't busy), normal, or high priority.

In Lab 18-2, we take a look at the steps that make up the DTS package you created in Lab 18-1. In addition, we examine this package's precedence constraints.

Lab 18-2   Editing a DTS Package in DTS Designer

1. **In SQL Server Enterprise Manager, in the console tree, expand the Data Transformation Services folder.**

2. **Select the Local Packages object, and take a look at the details pane.**

   You see the package you created in Lab 18-1.

3. **Right-click the package you want to edit and choose Design Package to open the package in the DTS Designer, as shown in Figure 18-9.**

4. **Point to the arrow connecting the Connection 1 and Create Table steps.**

   After a moment, a pop-up message indicates that this is an On Completion precedence constraint.

5. **Right-click the On Completion precedence constraint and choose Properties.**

   As shown in Figure 18-10, in our example, the source step creates the Customers table within the Practice database. After this step completes, the destination step takes place — which copies the data from the Northwind database's Customers table to the Practice database.

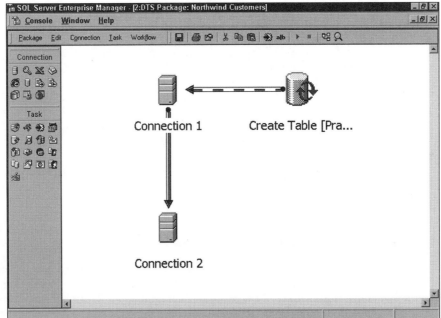

Figure 18-9:
Editing a package in the DTS Designer.

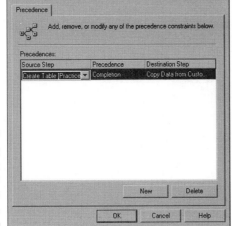

Figure 18-10:
An On Completion precedence constraint.

6. **Click Cancel to close the Workflow Properties dialog box.**

7. **Close DTS Designer without saving your changes.**

Using Heterogeneous Queries

A heterogeneous query enables you to query data not only on other SQL servers, but also on any data source that supports the OLE DB interface (such as Microsoft Access or Oracle databases). You can use such queries to view information from other data sources — or to import and export data between those sources by using the SELECT...INTO SQL statement. Before you can execute a heterogeneous query, though, you must first define the server you want to query (the OLE DB data source) as a linked server.

Microsoft uses the terms *heterogeneous queries* and *distributed queries* interchangeably.

Defining a linked server

You define a linked server by specifying how you want to connect to that server. At a minimum, you must specify an OLE DB provider and an OLE DB data source. An OLE DB provider is a dynamic link library that manages the communications between SQL Server 2000 and the linked server. SQL Server 2000 includes OLE DB providers for connecting to data sources such as Microsoft Access, Oracle, SQL Server, and Exchange Server, as shown in Figure 18-11. The OLE DB data source is the actual data on the linked server you plan to access — typically a database.

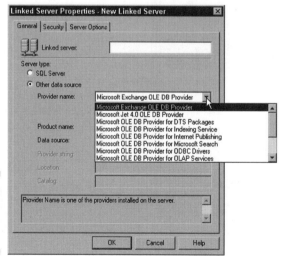

Figure 18-11: Choosing an OLE DB provider.

You define a linked server by using either SQL Server Enterprise Manager or the `sp_addlinkedserver` stored procedure. To define a linked server in SQL Server Enterprise Manager, begin by expanding your server's Security folder. Next, right-click the Linked Servers object and choose New Linked Server. Figure 18-12 shows you the General page of the Linked Server Properties dialog box in SQL Server Enterprise Manager. In this example, we're defining a Microsoft Access database on a computer named AccessServer as the OLE DB data source.

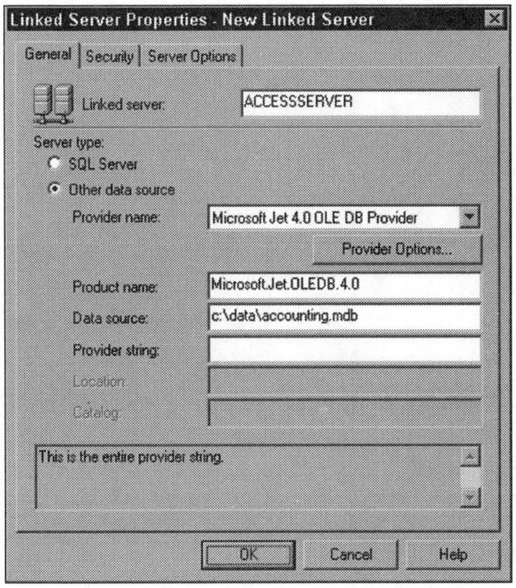

Figure 18-12:
Specifying
the OLE DB
data source.

The purpose of defining a linked server is to make it easy for your users or applications to query another data source. Because this data source is separate from your own SQL server, you must specify security information as part of the linked server definition. Your SQL server uses this security information to determine how it should log on to the linked server. You can configure your SQL server to log on by using either of the following two methods:

✔ **SQL Server can log in to the linked server by using the login ID and password of the user who executed the heterogeneous query.** In other words, the user's login ID and password must exist on both the SQL server and the linked server. You configure this option by checking Impersonate on the Security page of the Linked Server Properties dialog box, as shown in Figure 18-13.

✔ **You can map each user on the SQL server to a single login ID on the linked server.** SQL Server then uses the appropriate login ID to log in to the linked server whenever a user executes a heterogeneous query. In this scenario, the SQL Server user logs in as this user on the linked server. Configure this type of security by specifying a remote user name and password that are valid on the linked server, as shown in Figure 18-14.

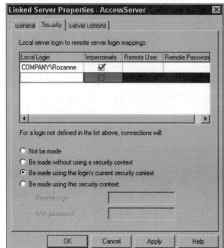

Figure 18-13:
Imperso-
nating a
user on the
linked
server.

Figure 18-14:
Mapping a
local user to
a login ID on
the linked
server.

No matter how your users connect to the linked server, they must have the necessary permissions to execute the query on that server. Make sure that you assign the appropriate permissions to the login ID you specify when you define the linked server, or your users will not be able to query the database on that server.

Executing a heterogeneous query

After you define a linked server, you can query the data on that server either by using the linked server's fully qualified name within a SQL statement, or by using the OPENQUERY function. Keep in mind that you can access the data on the linked server simply to view it, or you can combine it with data on your own SQL server through the use of table joins, or you can even import it into a table on your server by using the SELECT...INTO statement.

Using a linked server's fully qualified name

One of the ways you can execute a heterogeneous query against a linked server is simply by specifying the linked server name and database. For example, take a look at the following query:

```
SELECT * FROM
linked_server_name.database_name.owner_name.table_name
```

In this example, you specify the linked server name as you defined it either in SQL Server Enterprise Manager or with the sp_addlinkedserver stored procedure.

When you execute a heterogeneous query using the linked server's fully qualified name, be aware that the processing of that query is done on your local SQL server and not the linked server. If you want the processing of the query to take place on the linked server instead, you must use the OPENQUERY function.

Using the OPENQUERY function

As an alternative to querying a linked server by using the four-part object name, you can use the OPENQUERY function instead. This function enables you to not only query the linked server, but also forces the query to be processed on the linked server. Here's the syntax:

```
OPENQUERY(linked_server_name, 'SQL query')
```

You then reference this function as part of a SELECT statement.

Importing and Exporting Data with bcp

SQL Server 2000 includes a command-line utility, the bulk copy program (bcp), which enables you to import and export data in either the standard SQL Server format or the ASCII text format. Although DTS provides you with many more options and is easier to configure, many database administrators use bcp to transfer data because it provides them with the fastest performance and the least amount of overhead.

You use `bcp` to perform the following tasks:

- ✔ Import data from a text file into a SQL Server table or view.
- ✔ Export data from a SQL Server table or view into a text file.

You'll find that `bcp` is most commonly used when you want to transfer large amounts of data between SQL Server and another database management system (such as one on a mainframe).

Here's the basic syntax for `bcp`:

```
bcp database.owner.table [in | out] filename /parameters
```

Instead of importing or exporting data from a table, you can alternatively specify a view or query. You use "in" when you want to import data — and use "out" to export data.

The `BULK INSERT` SQL statement enables you to perform the exact same functions as `bcp`, but within SQL Server Query Analyzer instead of at the command line.

Prep Test

1 You would like to import a table from an Oracle database into SQL Server 2000. During the import process, you want to combine two of the columns in the Oracle table into a single column in the SQL Server table. Which import tool should you use?

A ○ The DTS Import/Export Wizard; use column mappings to combine the two columns.

B ○ The bulk copy program (bcp).

C ○ The DTS Bulk Insert task.

D ○ The DTS Import/Export Wizard; use a script to combine the two columns.

2 You would like to import a database from one SQL server to another. The database does not yet exist on the destination server. Which of the following import utilities enables you to import the database and its schema to another SQL server? (Choose all that apply.)

A ❏ The bulk copy program (bcp).

B ❏ The DTS Import/Export Wizard.

C ❏ The sp_attach_db stored procedure.

D ❏ BACKUP and RESTORE.

3 Which of the following data sources can you use in DTS? (Choose all that apply.)

A ❏ Oracle

B ❏ Microsoft Access

C ❏ ASCII text file

D ❏ DB2

4 Which of the following can you import or export when you use the bulk copy program?

A ○ Table schema

B ○ Data

C ○ Indexes

D ○ Login IDs

5 **How should you save a DTS package if you want to make it available for use by other applications?**

A ○ In the msdb database

B ○ In SQL Server Meta Data Services

C ○ In a COM-structured storage file

D ○ In a Visual Basic file

6 **You have scheduled a DTS package to import data from an Oracle database to a SQL Server database on a nightly basis. On Wednesday morning, you notice that the Tuesday's Oracle data isn't in your SQL Server database. What should you check? (Choose all that apply.)**

A ❑ Verify that the Data Transformation Services are started.

B ❑ Make sure that the SQLServerAgent service is started.

C ❑ Verify that you've specified the right user password.

D ❑ Verify that you've specified the right owner password.

7 **You would like SQL Server to notify you in the event that a DTS package step doesn't succeed. You've added a Send Mail step to your package. What type of precedence constraint should you put on the Send Mail step?**

A ○ On Completion

B ○ On Success

C ○ On Failure

D ○ On Error

8 **Your SQL Server environment consists of two servers, Sales and Accounting. Users of the Accounting server would like to be able to execute distributed queries so that they can query the Sales server. You have configured login IDs for the users in the Accounting department on both servers. You plan to add the Sales server as a linked server on the Accounting server. How should you configure the login security for the linked server?**

A ○ Map the Accounting users' login IDs on the Accounting server to login IDs on the Sales server.

B ○ Configure the Accounting users' login IDs to impersonate their login IDs on the Sales server.

C ○ Configure both servers to use the same service account and password.

D ○ Create a login ID for the Accounting server on the Sales server. Configure the linked server object to use this login ID.

Answers

1 **D.** You must use a script if you want to combine multiple columns into a single column. *See "The DTS Import/Export Wizard."*

2 **B, C,** and **D.** All of these utilities except for bcp enable you to import both the database's schema and its data to a SQL server. With `bcp`, you can import or export only data — not the schema. *Review "Importing and Exporting Data."*

3 **A, B, C,** and **D.** You can use all of these data sources in DTS. *Study "Using Data Transformation Services (DTS)."*

4 **B.** You can use `bcp` only to transfer data, not the schema. *See "Importing and Exporting Data."*

5 **B.** You should save the DTS package to SQL Server Meta Data Services to make it available to other applications. *Review "The DTS Import/Export Wizard."*

6 **B** and **C.** The SQLServerAgent service is responsible for executing the DTS package, so if it isn't started, the package won't run. In addition, make sure that you've specified the correct user password. *See "The DTS Import/Export Wizard."*

7 **C.** You use an On Failure precedence constraint to configure a step to execute only if the preceding step doesn't succeed. *Study "The DTS Designer."*

8 **B.** Because the users' login IDs exist on both servers, configure the Accounting users to impersonate themselves on the linked server. *Review "Defining a linked server."*

Chapter 19

Installing, Configuring, and Troubleshooting Replication

Exam Objectives

▶ Configuring replication services

▶ Maintaining replication services

▶ Troubleshooting replication services

*S*QL Server uses replication to make having copies of the same data on multiple servers possible (and even easy) for you. As you know, networks tend to grow — and so do databases. Most companies eventually reach a point where one SQL server can't handle the workload. And if a company installs a second SQL server, they typically want the same data on both servers.

You can easily make the same data available on multiple servers by configuring replication. And the good news is that with replication, SQL Server is responsible for making sure that the data is the same on both servers — not you. In this chapter, we explain everything you need to know about designing and configuring replication for the exam.

Quick Assessment

Configuring replication services

1 The three types of servers that participate in replication are: _____, _____, and _____.

2 In _____ replication, SQL Server periodically copies a complete copy of the publication to its subscribers.

3 When you configure a publication to support updating subscribers, SQL Server uses the _____ protocol to coordinate changes between the publisher and subscriber.

4 Conflicts can arise with _____ replication.

5 SQL Server uses the _____ agent to send snapshots from the distributor to a subscriber.

6 _____ subscriptions increase the workload on the publisher.

7 You can transform the data in a publication by creating a(n) _____.

8 You can help resolve conflicts in merge replication by assigning a(n) _____ to each subscription.

Maintaining replication services

9 You can use the _____ utility on the distributor to view the status of replication.

Troubleshooting replication services

10 If a replication agent is unable to communicate with a subscriber, check the configuration of the _____ service.

Answers

1 *Distributor, publisher, and subscriber.* See "Breaking Into the Publishing Business."

2 *Snapshot.* Study "Snapshot replication."

3 *Two-phase commit (2PC).* See "Updating subscribers."

4 *Merge.* Study "Merge replication."

5 *Distribution.* See "Distribution Agent."

6 *Push.* Study "Selling Subscriptions."

7 *DTS package.* See "Configuring publications."

8 *Priority.* Review "Subscribing to a publication."

9 *Replication Monitor.* See "Using the Replication Monitor."

10 *SQL Server Agent.* Study "Hiring a Replication Agent."

Breaking Into the Publishing Business

SQL Server uses a publishing analogy both to assign roles to the servers that participate in replication, as well as to the data itself. Before we go into how you configure replication, we want to start by defining some of the replication terminology as it applies to both servers and the replicated data.

Publisher

When you configure replication in SQL Server, the first server you configure is the publisher. The publisher stores the master copy of each of the databases from which you want to replicate data. In addition, it's responsible for making the published data within those databases available for replication. Finally, the publisher identifies and forwards any changes to the published data to the distributor server.

Distributor

In replication, the server you configure as the distributor is responsible for keeping track of all the changes to the published data — and making it available to all the published data's subscribers (we talk about the subscribers next). The distributor keeps track of these changes in the distribution database. How much work the distributor performs depends on the type of replication you implement. For example, if you implement transactional replication (which requires that all servers have identical copies of the data at the same time), the distributor performs much more work than it does with snapshot replication (which requires that the distributor periodically copy a snapshot of the data to the subscribers).

You can install a single server to act as both the publisher and the distributor. If the workload is too great for one server, consider splitting up the workload over two separate servers. You can also configure a single distributor to distribute data from more than one publisher.

Subscriber

Like a subscriber to a magazine, a subscriber SQL server receives copies of publications (the replicated data). As part of your replication strategy, you choose whether or not you want to permit a subscriber to make changes to the publication. If you do, the subscriber sends any changes it makes to the data back to the publisher so that those changes can then be replicated to other subscribers. Such a subscriber is called an *updating* subscriber.

Publication

Sticking with our publishing analogy, you specify what you want to replicate to other servers by defining publications. A publication consists of one or more articles. When a server subscribes to a publication, it receives all the articles within that publication — just as you receive all the articles in a magazine (whether you want all of them or not). You can create one or more publications based on a database; however, a publication can't contain data from multiple databases.

A subscriber receives copies of all the articles within a publication, which means that you shouldn't include articles within a publication unless you want the publication's subscribers to receive all of its articles. Use publications to organize the articles that you want to make available to subscribers.

Article

Your articles contain the actual data you want to replicate across the servers. An article can consist of any of the following:

- ✔ An entire table
- ✔ Only specific columns from a table (you configure this type of article by defining a vertical filter)
- ✔ Only specific rows from a table (configure by defining a horizontal filter)
- ✔ Only specific columns and rows from a table (configure by defining both horizontal and vertical filters)
- ✔ Other database objects, such as views, user-defined functions, and stored procedures

Choosing a Replication Type

In the preceding section, we talk about the basic components of replication. Here, we describe the types of replication you can configure. SQL Server supports three basic flavors of replication: snapshot, transactional, and merge. With the exception of merge replication, you typically configure replication such that the data can be modified only on the publisher and not the subscribers. However, you can configure subscribers in both snapshot and transactional replication to update the data — but we talk more about that in the section "Updating subscribers" later in this chapter.

Snapshot replication

With snapshot replication, the publisher periodically takes a snapshot of the publication and replaces the data on the subscribers. SQL Server doesn't monitor the data for changes — it simply copies a new snapshot out to the subscribers periodically. Although this strategy makes sure that the subscribers have a complete copy of the data, it does increase your network traffic, because SQL Server doesn't simply copy the changes to the data during replication. Instead, it creates a new snapshot of all the data in the publication — and replicates it to the publication's subscribers.

Use snapshot replication if

- ✔ Your subscribers need read-only access to the data.

- ✔ Your application can support inconsistencies between the copy of the database on the subscriber versus that on the publisher. (Keep in mind that SQL Server updates the subscriber's copy only at intervals and not when the data is changed.)

- ✔ The publication's data doesn't change very often, or you have only a small amount of data.

Regardless of which replication type you choose, SQL Server always uses snapshot replication to make the initial copy of the data on the subscriber.

Transactional replication

You use transactional replication when you want SQL Server to replicate transactions to a publisher's subscribers. Because SQL Server replicates only committed transactions instead of an entire snapshot of the database, this type of replication doesn't have as big of an impact on your network's traffic. SQL Server begins transactional replication by first taking a snapshot of the publication so that it can be replicated to its subscribers. Next, SQL Server monitors the publisher's transaction log for new transactions. (Specifically, SQL Server checks for transactions using the INSERT, UPDATE, and DELETE statements that affect the columns included in your publication.) When it detects a new transaction, it copies the transaction to the distribution database on the distributor. From there, the distributor replicates the transaction to the publication's subscribers.

Use transactional replication if

- ✔ You want changes to be quickly replicated to subscribers (replication typically occurs within seconds).

- ✔ Your subscribers have reliable connections to the publisher.

- ✔ You're using an application that requires that the data be as consistent as possible between the SQL servers.

Updating subscribers

Before we talk about merge replication, we want to take a moment to talk about support for updating subscribers. In previous sections of this chapter, we talk about both snapshot and transactional replication as if subscribers can't make changes. In this scenario, the data is changed only on the publisher and then replicated to the subscribers. This strategy is nice because it's simple and straightforward. However, you may want to implement a strategy where your subscribers can make changes. If that's the case, you have the following choices: You can configure your subscribers as immediate updating, queued updating, or both.

With immediate updating subscribers, the subscriber immediately sends any changes made to the publication's data to the publisher. The publisher then replicates those changes out to other subscribers. In order for the updates to take place immediately, the subscriber and the publisher must have a permanent connection between them, which means that the subscriber and publisher must be on the same LAN or connected via a reliable WAN.

You use queued updating subscribers if the connection between the publisher and subscriber isn't permanent. With queued updating subscribers, the subscriber queues changes to the publication's data — and then periodically sends those changes to the publisher. When the publisher receives the changes, it then replicates them out to other subscribers.

 If you configure a publication to support both immediate updating and queued updating subscribers, the subscriber uses the queued update method only in the event it can't communicate with the publisher. By configuring a publication to support both types of updates, you add fault tolerance to the replication process.

When you configure a publication to support updating subscribers, SQL Server uses the two-phase commit (2PC) protocol along with the Microsoft Distributed Transaction Coordinator (MS DTC) service to coordinate changes between the subscriber and the publisher. If a user changes the data on a subscriber, SQL Server uses the 2PC protocol to establish a connection between the subscriber and the publisher and commit the transaction to both servers. When the publisher receives the change, what it does next depends on whether you're using snapshot or transactional replication. If you're using snapshot replication, the publisher updates all other subscribers the next time it sends a snapshot of the data. If you're using transactional replication, the publisher replicates the transaction either immediately or based on the time interval you specified when you configured replication.

 Because conflicts may arise, configure snapshot or transactional replication to support updating subscribers only if the subscribers typically don't make a lot of changes to the data or the types of changes they make don't overlap very often. For example, although you may have a publication that contains all the customers for your company, each store usually makes changes only to their customers' information.

Merge replication

When you use merge replication, the publisher and all subscribers can make changes to the publication's data. The publisher accumulates these changes and then updates all subscribers. Because conflicts can frequently arise when the publisher merges the data, SQL Server includes options within SQL Server Enterprise Manager you can use to resolve those conflicts. If you're using a custom application, you can also develop your own custom resolvers into the application.

In order to facilitate conflict resolution, SQL Server must make changes to the publication's database. These changes include

- ✔ Identifying a column it can use to uniquely identify each row in the table during replication. If such a column doesn't exist, SQL server adds a unique identifier column to the table.

- ✔ Creating triggers on both the publisher and the subscribers' copies of a table in order to facilitate tracking changes. SQL Server uses these triggers to determine when a table's data has been changed.

- ✔ Adding system tables to the publication database for tracking conflicts and their resolution.

Use merge replication if

- ✔ You want the publisher and all subscribers to be able to make changes to the publication.

- ✔ You don't have permanent connections between the publisher and the subscribers.

- ✔ Your application includes the necessary programming for resolving conflicts.

You can't implement vertical filtering with merge replication.

Hiring a Replication Agent

SQL Server uses a series of agents to perform all of its replication tasks. When you configure replication, SQL Server configures these agents to run as jobs. You manage all of these agents by using the Replication Monitor within SQL Server Enterprise Manager.

The SQLServerAgent service is responsible for monitoring and executing jobs on your server — so it's also responsible for performing the jobs created by replication.

Snapshot Agent

SQL Server uses the Snapshot Agent to make an initial copy of the publication you want to replicate to subscribers. The Snapshot Agent is responsible for duplicating the database schema and its data for each article in a publication. After the Snapshot Agent finishes this task, it updates the distribution database with information about the publication's status.

Distribution Agent

Your server uses the Distribution Agent with both snapshot and transactional replication. Its job is to distribute snapshots and transactions from the distributor to all subscribers. Depending on how you configure subscriptions, the Distribution Agent runs on different servers. For example, if you configure a subscriber to pull its subscription, the Distribution Agent runs on the subscriber. On the other hand, if you configure the publisher to push a subscription to the subscriber, the Distribution Agent runs on the distributor.

Log Reader Agent

SQL Server uses the Log Reader Agent in transactional replication to keep track of the changes made to the publication. The Log Reader Agent finds these changes by monitoring the transaction log of the database from which you've defined a publication. When the Log Reader Agent finds new transactions that must be replicated, it sends these changes to the distribution database on the distributor. (After the Log Reader Agent puts these transactions in the distribution database, the Distribution Agent takes over and sends them out to the subscribers.)

Merge Agent

As you've probably already guessed, SQL Server uses the Merge Agent in merge replication. Its job is to send the initial snapshot of the publication to all subscribers. In addition, the Merge Agent is responsible for monitoring for any new changes to the data. When merge replication takes place, the Merge Agent uploads the subscriber's changes to the publisher and downloads the publisher's changes to the subscriber.

SQL Server creates a Merge Agent for each subscription. If you've configured the publisher to push the subscription to a subscriber, the Merge Agent runs on the distributor. Likewise, if you've configured the subscriber to pull the subscription, the Merge Agent runs on the subscriber.

Queue Reader Agent

SQL Server uses the Queue Reader Agent if you configure snapshot or transactional replication to support queued updating subscribers. The Queue Reader Agent runs on the distributor. Its main job is to receive all queued updates from subscribers and to apply those updates to the publication. SQL Server uses only one Queue Reader Agent to manage all publishers and publications for a distributor.

Selling Subscriptions

SQL Server enables you to configure two types of subscriptions: push and pull. With a push subscription, the publisher is responsible for monitoring and updating subscribers. With a pull subscription, each subscriber is responsible for connecting to the publisher for updates.

For the exam, keep the following facts in mind:

- ✔ Push subscriptions increase the workload on the publisher; pull subscriptions reduce the publisher's workload.
- ✔ Use push subscriptions if you want to centralize administration of all replication tasks.
- ✔ Use push subscriptions if you want greater control and stricter security for publications.
- ✔ Use pull subscriptions if you don't need strict security for publications or you have a high number of subscribers.

Designing Replication

SQL Server supports three physical replication models: Central Publisher/Distributor, Central Subscriber/Multiple Publisher, and Multiple Publisher/Multiple Subscriber. You implement replication by choosing a replication type (snapshot, transactional, or merge) and a physical replication model. You can use any of the replication types with any of the models.

Make sure you're familiar with the three physical replication models for the exam. You can expect to see a few scenario-based questions prompting you to choose a replication model.

Central Publisher/Distributor

With the Central Publisher/Distributor model, you use one server to act as both the publisher and the distributor, as shown in Figure 19-1. All of your remaining servers subscribe to the publications on that server. If the replication workload on the publisher/distributor is too heavy, you can implement a separate server to act as the distributor, as shown in Figure 19-2.

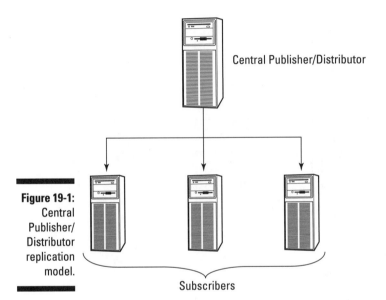

Central Publisher/Distributor

Figure 19-1:
Central
Publisher/
Distributor
replication
model.

Subscribers

Although you can use the Central Publisher/Distributor model with any of the replication types, it's best suited for snapshot or transactional replication without updating subscribers. Make sure that you configure the replicated data on the subscribers as read-only by restricting users' permissions.

Central Subscriber/Multiple Publishers

You use the Central Subscriber/Multiple Publishers replication model when you want multiple servers to update the data on a single subscriber server, as shown in Figure 19-3. You use this replication model when you want to consolidate information from multiple servers. You typically use transactional replication with this model.

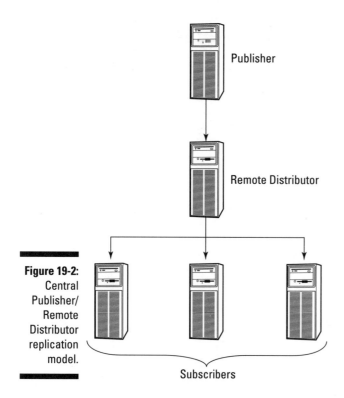

Figure 19-2: Central Publisher/ Remote Distributor replication model.

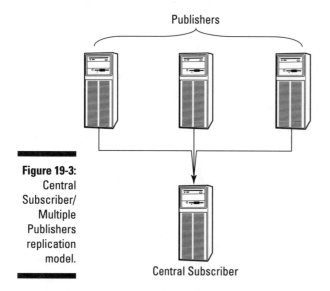

Figure 19-3: Central Subscriber/ Multiple Publishers replication model.

Because each publisher can update the data, make sure that all the tables you include in the publication have unique primary keys so that each row can be uniquely identified, regardless of the publisher. One technique you can use to avoid conflicts is to implement horizontal filtering so that each publisher has access only to its own data (instead of all the data).

Multiple Publishers/Multiple Subscribers

With the Multiple Publishers/Multiple Subscribers model, all servers are both publishers and subscribers, as shown in Figure 19-4. This model works best with either merge or transactional replication. Like the Central Subscriber/ Multiple Publisher model, this model works best if each publisher/subscriber changes only its own data — yet all publisher/subscribers can view other participants' data.

Figure 19-4:
Multiple
Publishers/
Multiple
Subscribers
replication
model.

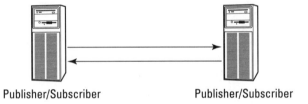

Publisher/Subscriber   Publisher/Subscriber

Configuring Replication

Here's an overview of the steps you need to complete when you're ready to implement replication:

1. **Install publishing on the distributor. (You can configure a single computer to act as both the distributor and the publisher, or you can install a separate distributor and publisher.)**

2. **If you've decided to install a separate publisher, install publishing on the publisher.**

3. **Configure your publications and their articles.**

4. **Configure subscriptions. You can configure the publisher to push subscriptions to subscribers, or you can configure each subscriber to pull a subscription.**

Installing the publisher/distributor

If you plan to use the same server as both your publisher and your distributor, you can install publishing by using any of the following methods in SQL Server Enterprise Manager:

- ✔ Choose Tools➪Replication➪Configure Publishing, Subscribers, and Distribution. This option starts the Configure Publishing and Distribution Wizard.

- ✔ Choose Tools➪Replication➪Create and Manage Publications. If you choose this option and you haven't yet configured your server as a publisher, SQL Server Enterprise Manager automatically starts the Configure Publishing and Distribution Wizard for you.

- ✔ Choose Tools➪Wizards. Expand the Replication category and then select the Configure Publishing and Distribution Wizard, as shown in Figure 19-5.

- ✔ In the console tree of SQL Server Enterprise Manager, right-click a database and choose New➪Publication.

In Lab 19-1, we show you the steps for installing your server as a publisher/distributor. (Because we're assuming you have only one server to practice with, we're going to have your server act not only as the publisher/distributor, but also the subscriber.) Keep in mind that you can use the Configure Publishing and Distribution Wizard to install your server as a distributor, publisher, and configure publications all in one swoop. But for the sake of keeping things simple, we save having you configure a publication for Lab 19-2.

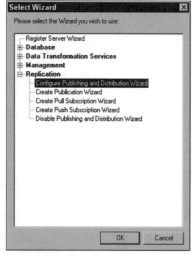

Figure 19-5: SQL Server Enterprise Manager includes wizards for configuring all the replication components.

Lab 19-1   Configuring a Publisher/Distributor

1. **If necessary, log on as Administrator and start SQL Server Enterprise Manager.**

2. **In the console tree, expand the SQL Server Group and select your server to establish a connection.**

3. **Choose Tools⇨Replication⇨Configure Publishing, Subscribers, and Distribution to start the Configure Publishing and Distribution Wizard.**

4. **On the Welcome page, click Next.**

   As shown in Figure 19-6, the wizard first wants to configure your server as the distributor. Notice that you have to configure the distributor first if you want to install separate distributor and publisher servers.

5. **Click Next to configure your server as the distributor.**

   The wizard now prompts you to define the folder in which it will place the snapshots publications. By default, it creates this folder as C:\Program Files\Microsoft SQL Server\MSSQL\ReplData.

6. **Click Next to accept the default snapshot folder name.**

   As shown in Figure 19-7, a message prompts you to confirm that you want to use this folder. This message is important because it's telling you that subscribers with pull subscriptions to your publication may not be able to access this data. You must make sure that you configure the subscriber servers with a service account that has administrative permissions to this folder.

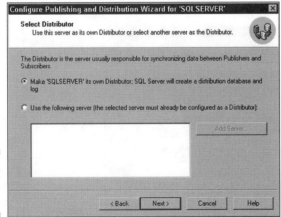

Figure 19-6:
Configuring
a distributor.

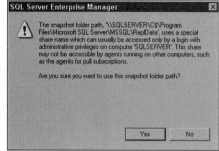

Figure 19-7:
Double-
checking
permissions.

7. Click Yes to continue.

The wizard displays its Customize the Configuration page. This page enables you to either accept the default configuration settings (which includes enabling all the SQL servers you've registered in SQL Server Enterprise Manager as subscribers), or change these settings. For the most part, you typically can accept the default settings. We're going to have you customize the settings so that you can see what they are.

8. Choose Yes, Let me set the distribution database properties, and then click Next.

9. As shown in Figure 19-8, you can use the Provide Distribution Database Information page to configure the database that the distributor uses to store transactions and replication history information. We want to use the defaults, so click Next.

As shown in Figure 19-9, you can use the next page to enable publisher servers to use your server as their distributor.

Figure 19-8:
Configuring
the
distribution
database.

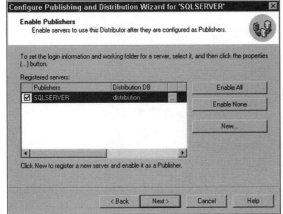

Figure 19-9:
Enabling
publishers.

By default, the Configure Publishing and Distribution Wizard automatically enables your server as a publisher. By adding a server, you essentially give that server the necessary permissions to use your server as a distributor — but you don't configure it as a publisher. You still have to install publishing on that server.

10. **Click Next.**

11. **You use the Enable Publication Databases page to specify whether or not you want to permit publications to be created for each of your server's user databases. Click Next (we show you how to configure publications in the next lab.)**

    By default, SQL Server Enterprise Manager doesn't enable any of the databases for publication.

12. **Take a look at the Enable Subscribers page, shown in Figure 19-10.**

    You use this page to permit a subscriber to subscribe to a server's publications. A subscriber can't subscribe to any of your server's publications unless you enable them as a subscriber first. By default, the Configure Publishing and Distribution Wizard assumes you want to enable all the servers you've registered in SQL Server Enterprise Manager as subscribers.

13. **Click Next.**

14. **At long last, you're done! Click Finish.**

    The Configure Publishing and Distribution Wizard now creates the distribution database, configures your server as both the distributor and publisher, and enables your server as a subscriber.

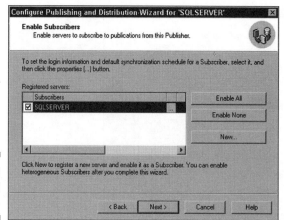

15. **Click OK to close the message stating your server was successfully configured.**

16. **Click Close to close the message informing you that the Configure Publishing and Distribution Wizard added a new object, the Replication Monitor, to SQL Server Enterprise Manager's console tree.**

    SQL Server installs the Replication Monitor on all distributors. You use this utility to monitor the status of replication, and to view the schedules of replication tasks.

Configuring publications

Your next step when implementing replication is to configure your publications. You can configure a publication by using any of the following methods in SQL Server Enterprise Manager:

- Choose Tools⇨Replication⇨Create and Manage Publications.

- In the console tree, right-click a database and choose New⇨Publication.

- Choose Tools⇨Wizards. Expand the Replication category and select the Create Publication Wizard.

In Lab 19-2, we walk you through creating a publication.

Lab 19-2   Creating a Publication

1. **In SQL Server Enterprise Manager, choose Tools⇨Replication⇨Create and Manage Publications.**

   Notice that you can't create a publication based on any of the system databases.

2. **Click Create Publication to start the Create Publication Wizard.**

3. **On the Welcome page, check Show Advanced Options In This Wizard, and then click Next.**

4. **From the Databases list, select the database you want to use and then click Next.**

   We configure a publication based on the Northwind database.

5. **Take a look at the Select Publication Type page, as shown in Figure 19-11.**

   You use this page to choose between the snapshot, transactional, and merge publication types.

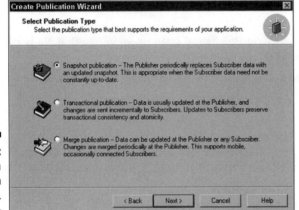

Figure 19-11:
Selecting a
publication
type.

6. **Select Transactional publication and then click Next.**

7. **Look at the Updatable Subscriptions page, shown in Figure 19-12.**

   You can configure a publication to support subscribers that are Immediate Updating, Queued Updating, or both. If you want to permit subscribers to immediately update their copies of the data, you may also want to configure them to support queued updates. This strategy enables the subscriber to queue changes in the event the primary connection to the publisher fails.

8. **Click Next.**

   We want to configure the publication to not permit updating subscribers.

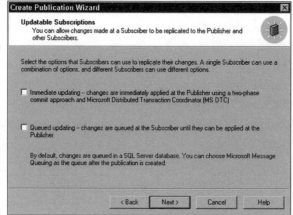

9. **On the Transform Published Data page, verify that No is selected, and then click Next.**

   We want to publish the data without any transformations.

10. **Take a look at the Specify Subscriber Types page, shown in Figure 19-13.**

    You can configure a server running SQL Server 2000 to replicate with those servers running SQL Server 2000, SQL Server 7.0, and hetero-geneous data sources such as Oracle or Microsoft Access.

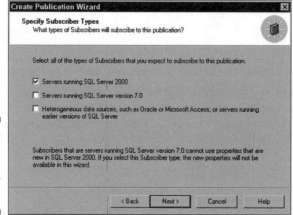

11. **Because you're configuring your server to replicate with itself, click Next to accept the default subscriber type setting of SQL Server 2000.**

12. **On the Specify Articles page, check the objects you want to publish as articles (the Customers table, in our example), and then click Next.**

    As shown in Figure 19-14, you use the Specify Articles page to define which tables, stored procedures, and views you want to publish in your publication. Notice that you can't choose objects from other databases. A publication can't span multiple databases.

Figure 19-14:
Choosing a
publication's
articles.

13. **On the Select Publication Name and Description page, enter a name for your publication. Click Next.**

    We used Northwind Customers as the name of our publication.

14. **Look at the Customize the Properties of the Publication page, shown in Figure 19-15.**

    If you want to define horizontal or vertical filters on any of the articles in a publication, you must choose the Yes, I will define filters, enable anonymous subscriptions, or customize other properties option. We want to leave the Customers table as is.

15. **Click Next.**

16. **Click Finish to create the publication.**

17. **Click Close to close the message stating SQL Server Enterprise Manager successfully created your publication.**

18. **Click Close to close the Create and Manage Publications dialog box.**

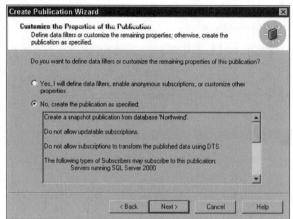

Figure 19-15:
Use this
page to
specify
whether or
not you
want to
define filters
on the arti-
cles in a
publication.

19. **In the console tree of SQL Server Enterprise Manager, expand the
Databases folder.**

Because you've published the Customers table within the Northwind
database, SQL Server Enterprise Manager displays the Northwind database with the shared icon (the hand), as shown in Figure 19-16.

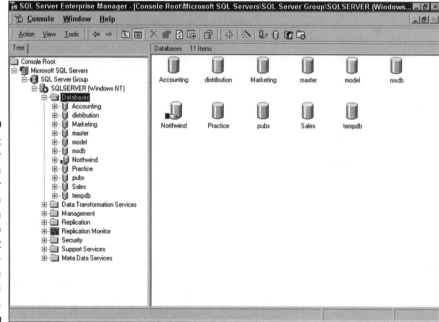

Figure 19-16:
SQL Server
Enterprise
Manager
uses the
shared icon
(hand) to
indicate that
you've pub-
lished data
within a
database.

Subscribing to a publication

Where you go to configure a subscription depends on whether you've chosen to implement push or pull subscriptions. If you want to use push subscriptions, begin by connecting to the publisher in SQL Server Enterprise Manager. Next, use either of the following techniques to define a push subscription:

- ✓ Choose Tools⇨Replication⇨Push Subscriptions to Others.
- ✓ Choose Tools⇨Wizards. Expand the Replication category, and then select the Create Push Subscription Wizard.

You create a pull subscription by connecting to the subscriber in SQL Server Enterprise Manager. You can then use any of the following methods to create a pull subscription:

- ✓ Choose Tools⇨Replication⇨Pull Subscriptions to *server_name*. (SQL Server Enterprise Manager replaces *server_name* with your server's computer name.)
- ✓ Right-click a database and choose New⇨Pull Subscription.
- ✓ Choose Tools⇨Wizards. Expand the Replication category, and then select the Create Pull Subscription Wizard.

When you configure subscriptions to publications that use merge replication, you can set priorities for each subscriber so SQL Server can determine how to resolve conflicts. By default, SQL Server configures all subscribers to use the same priority setting as the publisher (which means that SQL Server doesn't consider priorities when resolving conflicts by default). If you want to prioritize subscribers, you do so by assigning a priority value from 0 to 99.99, with a higher number giving a subscriber higher priority.

In Lab 19-3, we walk you through creating a push subscription to the Northwind Customers publication you created in Lab 19-2. We're going to have you create the subscription in a new database named Subscription.

Lab 19-3	Configuring a Push Subscription

1. **In SQL Server Enterprise Manager, choose Tools⇨Replication⇨Push Subscriptions to Others.**

2. **As shown in Figure 19-17, expand the database and select the publication from which you want to push a subscription, and then click Push New Subscription.**

3. **On the Welcome page, click Next.**

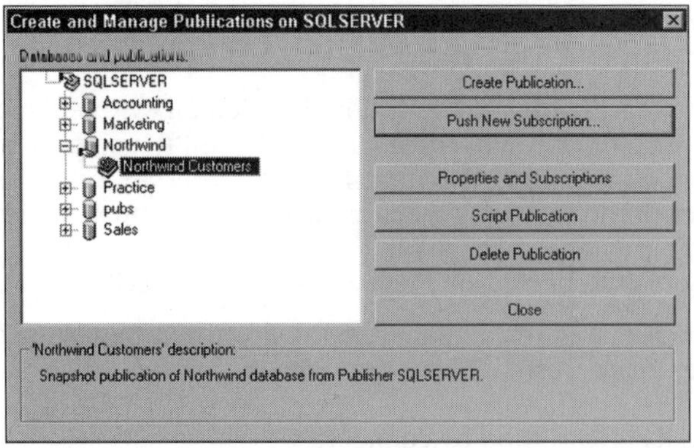

Figure 19-17:
Select the
publication
from which
you want to
push a
subscription.

4. **On the Choose Subscribers page, select your server and then click Next.**

   Keep in mind that you can select only the servers you've enabled as subscribers on the publisher.

5. **On the Choose Destination Database page, click Browse or Create.**

   The Browse Databases dialog box appears. You use this dialog box to either select an existing database in which to place the subscription or to create a new database.

6. **Click Create New.**

7. **In the Name text box, type a name for the new database (in our example, it's Subscription), and then click OK.**

   You can accept the default sizes and filenames for the database's data file and transaction log.

8. **Verify that the new database is selected, click OK, and then click Next.**

9. **Take a look at your options for configuring the Distribution Agent, as shown in Figure 19-18.**

   You can configure your server (as the publisher) to push changes to the subscriber continuously or at specific time intervals. By default, the Push Subscription Wizard configures your server to push the subscription every hour.

10. **Select Continuously to configure your server to push changes continuously to the subscriber. Click Next.**

11. **On the Initialize Subscription page, check Start the Snapshot Agent to begin the initialization process immediately option, as shown in Figure 19-19.**

    Before SQL Server can begin replicating the changes between the publisher and the subscriber, it must first make an initial copy of the publication on the subscriber. This page enables you to specify when you want SQL server to initialize the subscription. If you don't have SQL Server run the initialization process immediately, SQL Server waits until the next time the Snapshot Agent is scheduled to run to initialize the subscription. (By default, SQL Server configures the Snapshot Agent to run once per day.)

12. **Click Next.**

13. **If necessary, check the option to have the Push Subscription Wizard start the SQLServerAgent service for you, and then click Next.**

    The SQLServerAgent service must be running in order for replication to occur.

14. **Click Finish to create the subscription.**

15. **Click Close to close the message stating that your subscription was created successfully.**

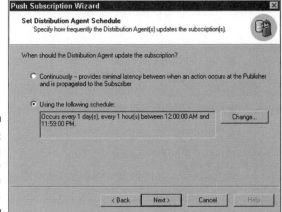

Figure 19-18:
Configuring the Distribution Agent.

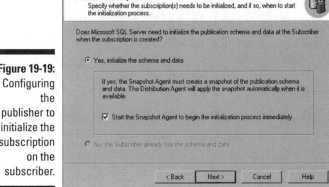

Figure 19-19:
Configuring the publisher to initialize the subscription on the subscriber.

16. **Close the Create and Manage Publications dialog box.**
17. **Take a look at the tables in the database you created (Subscriptions, in our example).**

    You now have a copy of the Customers table in addition to all the normal system tables. You received this copy of the Customers table through replication.

In this next lab, we have you modify a row in the Customers table in the Northwind database to verify that SQL Server replicates your change.

Lab 19-4	Testing Replication

1. **In the Northwind database, right-click the Customers table and choose Open Table⇨Return All Rows.**
2. **In the first row, change the value of the ContactName column to your name.**
3. **Click in the next row to force SQL Server Enterprise Manager to save your changes.**
4. **Close the Customers table.**
5. **In the Subscription database, display all rows in the Customers table.**

    SQL Server has automatically replicated your change to the same row in this table.

Managing Replication

After you configure a server as a distributor, publisher, or subscriber, you can make changes to its configuration by using the appropriate properties dialog box within SQL Server Enterprise Manager.

Managing a publisher/distributor

To modify the properties of a publisher/distributor, in SQL Server Enterprise Manager, choose Tools⇨Replication⇨Configure Publishing, Subscribers, and Distribution. Opening the Publisher and Distributor Properties dialog box enables you to configure the following options

- ✔ Using multiple distribution database files to allocate the workload across more than one file
- ✔ Setting a minimum length of time SQL Server will store replication history in the distribution database

✔ Setting a maximum time limit for storing transactions in the distribution database

✔ If your server's a distributor, defining other publishers that can use your server as their distributor

✔ Enabling or disabling transactional and merge replication for any of your user databases

✔ Enabling subscribers to use your server as a publisher

Notice that some of these options apply to distributors only (such as the distribution database settings) and other options apply to publishers only (such as which subscribers can use your server). If you've configured a separate publisher and distributor, you can use this dialog box to configure only those settings that apply to the server's role in replication.

After you've added publications to the distribution database, you can't remove them without first disabling all publishers. If you disable a publisher, SQL Server automatically deletes all publications on the publisher — and all subscriptions to those publications.

Managing a publication and its subscriptions

You manage a publication and its subscriptions by choosing Tools➪Replication➪Create and Manage Publications. When SQL Server Enterprise Manager opens the Create and Manage Publications dialog box, select the publication you want to manage and click Properties and Subscriptions. (You can also use the Create and Manage Publications dialog box to delete a publication.) If the publication has subscriptions, you can't modify many of the publication's properties.

If you're unable to modify the properties of a publication because it has subscriptions, you must first drop all subscriptions to the publication. Then, modify the publication's properties — and redefine all subscriptions to the publication.

The tasks you can perform in the Publication Properties dialog box include

✔ Specifying how long SQL Server will wait for a subscription to be updated before dropping it automatically. (The default is 336 hours, or two weeks.)

✔ Indicating whether or not any of the articles have vertical or horizontal filters.

✔ Creating a new push subscription or modifying the properties of an existing subscription.

✔ Viewing the status of replication for this publication.

✔ Defining alternate locations for a publication's snapshot files. You might modify this option in order to make it possible for SQL Server to load a publication's snapshots from other media such as CD-ROM.

Using the Replication Monitor

SQL Server automatically adds a handy utility, the Replication Monitor, to SQL Server Enterprise Manager when you configure a server as a distributor. You use the Replication Monitor to perform the following tasks:

✔ View a list of the distributor's publishers

✔ Display a publisher's publications, and all subscriptions to those publications

✔ Monitor the replication history for a publication or subscription

✔ View the replication agents associated with a specific publication

✔ View or modify the schedule of any of the replication agents

✔ Configure alerts to notify you of the status of replication

Prep Test

1 A client has asked you to configure replication for his company's SQL servers. The client would like the table containing the current pricing information to be replicated to all branch offices, but doesn't want the users at the branch offices to be able to modify the data. Your client typically changes prices once a quarter. What type of replication should you use?

A ○ Snapshot

B ○ Transactional

C ○ Merge

D ○ Queued-updating

2 You are responsible for designing replication for a SQL Server environment. Given the nature of the data and the application, you've determined that users must be able to make changes at the subscribers. You expect that each subscriber will make frequent changes. What type of replication should you use?

A ○ Snapshot with immediate updating subscribers

B ○ Transactional replication with Immediate updating subscribers

C ○ Transactional replication

D ○ Merge replication

3 Regardless of which type of replication you configure, SQL Server always uses which of the replication agents?

A ○ Snapshot Agent

B ○ Distribution Agent

C ○ Log Reader Agent

D ○ Merge Agent

4 When you configure a pull subscription to a snapshot publication, on what server does the Distribution Agent run?

A ○ Publisher

B ○ Distributor

C ○ Subscriber

D ○ None

5 Which of the following strategies reduce the workload on a publisher? (Choose all that apply.)

A ❑ Implementing only push subscriptions

B ❑ Implementing only pull subscriptions

C ❑ Installing a separate distributor

D ❑ Reducing the size of the distribution database

6 You would like to restrict the columns from a table that are included in an article. What should you do?

A ○ Transform the data.

B ○ Define a vertical filter.

C ○ Use the `SELECT...INTO` statement to create a new table with only the columns you want to replicate.

D ○ Define a horizontal filter.

7 You have configured a publication to support both immediate updating and queued updating subscribers. When will the subscribers use queued updates?

A ○ Whenever replication takes place.

B ○ Only when you enable the Queue Reader Agent.

C ○ When the subscriber can't communicate with the publisher.

D ○ You can't configure a publication to support both immediate updating and queued updating subscribers.

8 Which of the following can an article contain? (Choose all that apply.)

A ❑ Table

B ❑ Multiple tables

C ❑ View

D ❑ Stored procedure

Answers

Replication

1 **A.** Given that the subscribers don't need to make changes to the data, and that the data won't change very often, snapshot replication is the best choice for the client. *See "Snapshot replication."*

2 **D.** Use merge replication because each subscriber needs to make frequent changes to the data. *Review "Merge replication."*

3 **A.** SQL Server uses the Snapshot Agent to create an initial copy of all publications, regardless of which replication type you choose. *Study "Snapshot Agent."*

4 **C.** The Distribution Agent runs on the subscriber when you configure a pull subscription. *See "Distribution Agent."*

5 **B** and **C.** You can reduce the workload on the publisher by installing a separate distributor (so that the publisher doesn't have to manage distributing changes) and by implementing pull subscriptions. *Study "Selling Subscriptions" and "Distributor."*

6 **B.** You can use a vertical filter (or vertical partition) to restrict the columns that are replicated from a table. *See "Configuring publications."*

7 **C.** The subscriber uses queued updating only if it can't communicate with the publisher. *Review "Updating subscribers."*

8 **A, B, C,** and **D.** An article can contain a table, multiple tables, view, stored procedures, and user-defined functions. *Study "Article."*

Part VI
Securing SQL Server

The 5th Wave   By Rich Tennant

"A centralized security management system sounds fine, but then what would we do with the dogs?"

In this part . . .

Because SQL Server is what its name implies — a server, you must take whatever steps you can to protect it. You use security to control who can log in to your SQL server — and then when they're in, what those users can do on the server.

You can begin your review of the steps for securing a SQL server in Chapter 20, which explains how to configure users' login IDs. SQL Server uses login IDs to control who can log in to your server. In Chapter 21, we show you how to implement permissions. You use permissions to control what your users can do in each database. You can wrap up your tour of security by reviewing how to configure your server to comply with the government's C2 security requirements, which we describe in Chapter 22.

Chapter 20

Configuring Login Security

- -

Exam Objectives

▶ Configuring mixed security modes or Windows authentication

▶ Creating and managing logins

- -

*Y*ou use login security on a SQL Server to control who can gain access to your server. In this chapter, we show you how to choose who authenticates users' login attempts (Windows NT/2000 or SQL Server itself) and how to add login IDs to your server.

For the exam, make sure you understand the differences between authentication modes and the types of login IDs you can create.

Quick Assessment

Configuring
mixed secu-
rity modes
or Windows
authentica-
tion

1 Configure SQL Server to use _____ if you want it to permit UNIX users to log in.

2 Users log in with _____ connections when they use Windows login IDs.

3 You configure your server's authentication mode by modifying the properties of the _____ in SQL Server Enterprise Manager.

Creating
and manag-
ing logins

4 Setup automatically creates the _____ SQL login ID.

5 You can use the _____ stored procedure to create a Windows login ID.

6 Use the _____ stored procedure to create a SQL login ID.

7 You can change a SQL login ID's password by using the _____ stored procedure.

Answers

1 *Mixed authentication mode.* Review "Mixed authentication mode."

2 *Trusted.* See "Configuring an Authentication Mode."

3 *Server object.* Study "Configuring an Authentication Mode."

4 s*a.* Review "Default login IDs."

5 `sp_grantlogin.` See "Windows login IDs."

6 `sp_addlogin.` See "SQL login IDs."

7 `sp_password.` Review "SQL login IDs."

Configuring an Authentication Mode

SQL Server can authenticate login requests by using either Windows authentication or SQL authentication. With Windows authentication, your SQL Server trusts a Windows 2000 domain controller to authenticate a user's login request. This type of login connection is called a *trusted connection*. With SQL authentication, SQL Server itself authenticates a user's login request. You can configure your SQL Server to support only Windows authentication, or you can configure it to support both Windows and SQL authentication (what's called mixed mode).

You can expect to see a few questions on the exam on selecting a server's authentication mode based on the types of clients your SQL server must support.

Windows authentication mode

With Windows authentication, you can take advantage of SQL Server's integration with Windows 2000 (and Windows NT) by having users log in with their Windows user accounts. (This login occurs in the background — users don't have to enter their user names and passwords again when they connect to the SQL server.) Some of the advantages to using only Windows authentication include

- ✔ You can define login IDs based on Windows 2000 groups instead of having to create a login ID for each individual user.
- ✔ You can implement features such as auditing, enforcing a minimum password length, password expiration date, and account lockout.
- ✔ You can take advantage of the fact that Windows 2000 automatically encrypts passwords before it sends them across the network.
- ✔ You don't have to worry about users having to remember different user accounts and passwords for accessing SQL Server. In fact, the login process occurs in the background when users connect to SQL Server.

In order to support Windows authentication, your users must be able to log in to either a Windows 2000 or Windows NT domain, which means your clients must be running a Windows-based operating system such as Windows 9x, Windows Me, Windows NT, or Windows 2000.

Mixed authentication mode

If you have non-Windows clients such as those running UNIX or Linux, or Internet-based clients, you should use the mixed authentication mode instead. This mode enables users to log in with either a Windows or SQL login ID.

TIP

You must stop and restart the MSSQLServer service if you change your server's authentication mode.

In Lab 20-1, we show you how to configure your server's authentication mode.

Lab 20-1   Configuring the Authentication Mode

1. **If necessary, log in as Administrator and start SQL Server Enterprise Manager.**

2. **In the console tree, right-click your server and choose Properties.**

3. **Select the Security tab.**

   As shown in Figure 20-1, you use the Security page to configure your server to support either Windows authentication (by choosing the Windows only option) or mixed authentication (by choosing the SQL Server and Windows option).

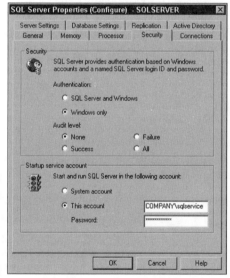

Figure 20-1:
Configuring
the authen-
tication
mode.

4. **Select SQL Server and Windows to configure your server to support both Windows and SQL login IDs, and then click OK.**

5. **Click Yes to have SQL Server Enterprise Manager restart the MSSQLServer service.**

6. **If necessary, click Yes again to confirm that you want to stop the SQLServerAgent service.**

   Stopping the MSSQLServer service also stops the SQLServerAgent service because it needs the MSSQLServer service to run.

7. **Click Yes to reconnect to your server.**

Creating Login IDs

You create both SQL and Windows login IDs by using either SQL Server Enterprise Manager or Transact-SQL. SQL Server stores the login IDs you define in the sysxlogins table within the master database. You must be a member of either the system administrators or security administrators server roles to create login IDs. (By default, members of the built-in Administrators Windows 2000 group are members of the system administrators server role.)

One of the parameters you configure for each login ID is a default database. SQL Server automatically connects you to your default database when you log in to the server. Be aware that configuring a user with a default database doesn't automatically give the user permissions to access that database. You still have to assign permissions to the user. We talk about permissions in detail in Chapter 21.

If you forget to assign a default database to a login ID, the user receives an `Invalid object` error message whenever she attempts to log in to SQL Server. You can assign a default database to a login ID by modifying its properties within SQL Server Enterprise Manager or by using the `sp_defaultdb` stored procedure.

Default login IDs

The first time you look in your server's Logins folder, you may be surprised to find that you already have login IDs defined on your server. By default, Setup creates the following login IDs during installation:

- ✔ A Windows login ID for the BUILTIN\Administrators local group on your server.

- ✔ A SQL login ID named sa (for system administrator). This account has all rights and permissions on your SQL server. You can use this login ID only if you configure your server to use mixed mode authentication.

- ✔ If you configured the SQL Server services to log in with a domain user account, Setup creates a Windows login ID for the service account you specify.

Windows login IDs

By creating Windows login IDs, you enable users to log in to SQL Server with their Windows 2000 domain user accounts. Essentially, you create a Windows login ID by specifying the name of a user or group you want to permit to log in to SQL Server. (To be precise, you aren't really creating a Windows login ID — you're permitting a Windows login ID created in Active Directory Users and Computers to log in to your SQL server. However, Microsoft refers to this process as "creating a login ID," so we stick with that terminology here.) If you specify a Windows 2000 group, SQL Server permits all the members of that group to log in to your server.

Always try to create login IDs based on Windows 2000 groups. Using groups reduces administrative overhead because you won't have to create and manage a login ID for each user. However, when you add a login ID for a group, all the group's members can log in to SQL Server — you can't prevent one of the group's members from logging in. For this reason, add a login ID for a group only if you want all of its members to have access to SQL Server.

You specify the login ID in the form of *domain_name\user_name.* Replace *domain_name* with the name of the domain in which you've installed your SQL server; replace *user_name* with the user's or group's name. (You can't specify the name of the login ID by using User Principal Names. For example, you can't define a login ID by using the name *user@company.com.*)

When you delete a Windows 2000 user or group, SQL Server doesn't delete that user or group's login ID in order to prevent orphaned objects (objects without any owner). After you verify that the user or group does not own any objects, you can delete the user or group's login ID from SQL Server.

Granting access

You can create a Windows login ID by using either the `sp_grantlogin` stored procedures or SQL Server Enterprise Manager. Here's the syntax for `sp_grantlogin`:

```
sp_grantlogin 'domain_name\user_name'
```

In Lab 20-2, we show you how to create Windows login ID based on a user and a group account.

Lab 20-2   Creating Windows Login IDs

1. **In Active Directory Users and Computers, create a user with your first and last names, and use your first name for the logon name. Use a password of your choice.**

2. **Create two more users named UserA and UserB, each with a password of password. Create a new domain local group named SQLUsers and add UserA and UserB as members of this group.**

3. **Close Active Directory Users and Computers.**

4. **In SQL Server Enterprise Manager, expand the Security folder below your server and select the Logins object.**

   In the details pane, you see a list of the login IDs defined on your server. At a minimum, you should see login IDs for the BUILTIN\Administrators Windows group, your service account, and the sa user.

5. In the console tree, right-click Logins and choose New Login.

6. In the Name text box, type your first name. From the Domain drop-down list, select your SQL server's Windows 2000 domain.

As shown in Figure 20-2, SQL Server Enterprise Manager assumes that you want to grant access to this login ID, and that you want master as the default database.

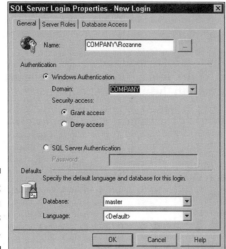

Figure 20-2:
Creating a
Windows
login ID.

7. From the Database drop-down list, select Northwind to change your default database.

8. Click OK to create your login ID.

9. Right-click Logins again and choose New Login.

This time you create a login ID for a Windows group.

10. In the Name text box, type SQLUsers. From the Domain drop-down list, select your domain.

11. Configure the login ID with a default database. (In our example, we used the Northwind database as the login ID's default database.) Click OK to create the login ID for your group.

12. Verify that you can connect to SQL Server as UserA. Begin by logging on to Windows 2000 as UserA with a password of password. Open SQL Server Query Analyzer and log in with Windows Authentication.

13. Log back on to Windows 2000 as Administrator.

Denying access

You can make sure that a Windows 2000 user or group can't log in to your SQL server by denying access. You do so by using either SQL Server Enterprise Manager or the sp_denylogin stored procedure. If you deny access to a user's login ID, or any group of which the user is a member, that user can't log in to SQL server.

Revoking access

You remove a Windows login ID from SQL Server by using either SQL Server Enterprise Manager or the sp_revokelogin stored procedure. Keep in mind that if you've added a login ID for a user and for a group of which the user is a member, revoking only one of the login IDs won't prevent the user from logging in. You must either revoke both login IDs, or deny the login ID access.

SQL login IDs

You add SQL login IDs by specifying not only the login name, but also the password. SQL Server encrypts this password and stores it as part of the login IDs row in the master..sysxlogins table. You can use letters, numbers, and symbols as part of the login ID's name, but you can't use a backslash, reserved login ID (such as sa), or null.

Adding a SQL login ID

You can use either SQL Server Enterprise Manager or the sp_addlogin stored procedure to create a SQL login ID. Here's the syntax:

```
sp_addlogin 'login', 'password', 'database_name'
```

Make sure you know the difference between the sp_grantlogin and sp_addlogin stored procedures for the exam. You use sp_grantlogin to create a Windows login ID; use sp_addlogin to create a SQL login ID.

In Lab 20-3, we walk you through creating a SQL login ID.

Lab 20-3   Creating a SQL Login ID

1. **If necessary, open SQL Server Enterprise Manager.**

2. **In the console tree, right-click the Logins object and choose New Login.**

3. **In the Name text box, type** UserC.

4. **Select SQL Server Authentication, as shown in Figure 20-3.**

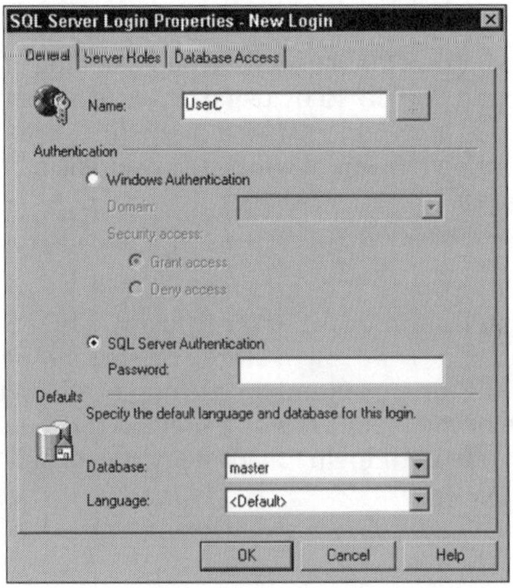

Figure 20-3:
Creating
a SQL
login ID.

5. **In the Password text box, type** password.

6. **Make the Northwind database UserC's default database.**

7. **Click OK to save your changes.**

8. **In the Confirm New Password text box, type** password, **and then click OK.**

   Because SQL Server Enterprise Manager doesn't display the password, you must enter the password twice to make sure you entered the correct password.

9. **Open SQL Server Query Analyzer.**

   You're going to test UserC's SQL login ID by logging in within SQL Server Query Analyzer.

10. **Below Connect Using, select SQL Server authentication. In the Login Name text box, type** UserC. **In the Password text box, type** password, **as shown in Figure 20-4.**

Figure 20-4:
Logging in
with a SQL
login ID.

11. **Click OK to log in to SQL Server as UserC.**

    Notice that your default database is the Northwind database.

12. **Close SQL Server Query Analyzer.**

Managing a SQL login ID

As an administrator, you can change the password for any SQL login ID by using either SQL Server Enterprise Manager or the sp_password stored procedure. To use sp_password to change another login ID's password, use the following syntax:

```
sp_password null, 'new_password', 'login'
```

Notice that you don't need to know the login ID's password. Instead, you can use null for the old password.

Removing a SQL login ID

If you no longer want a user to log in with a SQL login ID, you simply delete that user's login ID. You can do so by using either SQL Server Enterprise Manager or the sp_droplogin stored procedure. Here's the Transact-SQL syntax:

```
sp_droplogin 'login'
```

Prep Test

1 Your network consists of clients running Windows NT Workstation, Windows 2000 Professional, and UNIX. How should you implement login security?

   A ○ Configure the server to use Windows authentication only, and create Windows login IDs for each user.

   B ○ Configure the server to use SQL Server authentication only, and create SQL login IDs for each user.

   C ○ Configure the server to use mixed-mode authentication, and create the necessary Windows and SQL login IDs.

   D ○ Configure a trust relationship between the Windows 2000 domain and UNIX. Use Windows authentication on the SQL Server, and create Windows login IDs for each user.

2 Which of the following server roles enable you to create login IDs on a SQL server? (Choose all that apply.)

   A ❑ Database Owner

   B ❑ Server Administrators

   C ❑ System Administrators

   D ❑ Security Administrators

3 Setup automatically creates login IDs for which of the following users? (Choose all that apply.)

   A ❑ The built-in Users group

   B ❑ The built-in Administrators group

   C ❑ sa

   D ❑ The services account

4 What happens to a user's login ID when you delete the user from the Active Directory?

   A ○ Nothing. Deleting a user from the Active Directory has no effect on the user's login ID in SQL Server.

   B ○ SQL Server disables the user's login ID.

   C ○ SQL Server deletes the user's login ID.

   D ○ You can't delete a user from the Active Directory unless you first delete the user's login ID on the SQL server.

5 You want to make sure that a Windows 2000 user can't log in to SQL Server. Which stored procedure should you use?

A ○ sp_droplogin

B ○ sp_revokelogin

C ○ sp_denylogin

D ○ sp_preventlogin

6 Which stored procedure should you use to remove a Windows login ID from SQL Server?

A ○ sp_revokelogin

B ○ sp_droplogin

C ○ sp_deletelogin

D ○ None. Delete the user or group account in Active Directory Users and Computers.

Answers

1 **C.** Because your environment consists of both Windows-based and UNIX clients, configure your server to support both SQL and Windows authentication. *See "Configuring an Authentication Mode."*

2 **C** and **D.** You must be a member of either the server administrators or system administrators server roles in order to create login IDs. *Review "Creating Login IDs."*

3 **B, C,** and **D.** Setup automatically creates login IDs for the built-in Administrators Windows group, your server's service account, and the sa SQL user. *See "Default login IDs."*

4 **A.** SQL Server does not remove a user's login ID when you delete the user's Active Directory account in order to avoid orphaning objects. *See "Windows login IDs."*

5 **C.** You use the `sp_denylogin` stored procedure to have SQL Server deny access to a specific Windows user or group. *See "Windows login IDs."*

6 **A.** You delete a Windows login ID from SQL Server by using the `sp_revokelogin` stored procedure. (You use `sp_droplogin` to delete a SQL login ID.) *See "Windows login IDs."*

Chapter 21

Implementing Permissions

· ·

Exam Objectives

▶ Creating and managing database users

▶ Creating and managing security roles

▶ Enforcing and managing security by using stored procedures, triggers, views, and user-defined functions

▶ Setting permissions in a database

· ·

SQL Server security consists of two layers. The first layer, login security, controls whether or not a user can log in to SQL Server — but that's it. Login security doesn't enable a user to access any of the databases. The second layer, permissions security, enables you to control which databases a user can access — and what the user can do in those databases. In this chapter, we show you how to add a login ID as a user of a database. We also explore how to assign permissions to users within a database by using roles and direct permissions assignment.

You can expect to see quite a number of questions on permissions security on your exam. Make sure that you spend a lot of time studying the information in this chapter.

Quick Assessment

Creating and managing database users

1 You assign a login ID as a database user by using the _____ stored procedure.

2 By default, SQL Server automatically maps the members of the sysadmin server role to the _____ database user.

3 You can use the _____ stored procedure to have SQL Server attempt to match a database user to a SQL login ID.

Creating and managing security roles

4 The _____ server role enables its members to install and configure replication.

5 Members of the _____ server role can manage server login IDs.

6 You add a login ID to a server role by using the _____ stored procedure.

7 By default, SQL Server adds all database users to the _____ database role.

8 Members of the _____ database role can add, change, or delete database objects.

Enforcing and managing security by using stored procedures, triggers, views, and user-defined functions

9 You must have the _____ statement permission in order to create a user-defined function.

10 You have created a view named SalesView based on the Orders table. In order for a user to use the view, you must you give the user permissions to the following object(s): _____.

Setting permissions in a database

11 You must assign a user the _____ and _____ permissions for a table if you want the user to update only selected rows in the table.

12 _____ a permission prevents a user from ever exercising that permission for the object.

Answers

1 `sp_grantdbaccess`. Review "Creating database users."

2 *dbo.* See "Assigning Database Users."

3 `sp_change_users_login`. Study "Managing database users."

4 *Setupadmin.* See "Fixed server roles."

5 *Securityadmin.* Review "Fixed server roles."

6 `sp_addsrvrolemember`. Study "Fixed server roles."

7 *Public.* See "Fixed database roles."

8 *Db_ddladmin.* Study "Fixed database roles."

9 *CREATE FUNCTION.* See "Using statement permissions."

10 *Only the view.* See "Implementing permissions for views and stored procedures."

11 *SELECT and UPDATE.* Study "Assigning permissions."

12 *Denying.* See "Using Permissions."

Assigning Database Users

After you create your server's login IDs (see Chapter 20), your next task in securing SQL Server is to specify which login IDs can access which databases on your server. You do this by assigning each login ID as a database user. And unless you make a login ID a database user, the login ID can't access any of your server's databases.

SQL Server stores database user information in the sysusers system table within each database.

SQL Server automatically creates a special database user named dbo (short for database owner). SQL Server maps all login IDs that are members of the system administrators server role and the sa SQL login ID to the dbo user when they access a database. This means that although you might log in to SQL Server with your Windows user account (such as your first name), when you access a database, SQL Server identifies you as the dbo user. Microsoft designed SQL Server this way so that objects created by any system administrator, regardless of the login ID, are all owned by the same user (dbo).

You can't delete the dbo user.

Creating database users

You add a user to a database by using either SQL Server Enterprise Manager or the sp_grantdbaccess stored procedure. Here's the syntax for using sp_grantdbaccess:

```
use database_name
exec sp_grantdbaccess 'login', ['db_user_name']
```

Make sure that you use the database for which you want to add the user first, and then replace *login* with the user or group's login ID. By default, SQL Server makes the database user's name the same as the login ID. You can optionally assign the login ID a different database user name using the db_user_name parameter.

You can optionally create a guest user account within a database to permit guest access to the database. Any login ID that isn't already a user of the database can then access that database as the guest user. SQL Server does not create a guest user account in any database by default. You can create a guest user in any database except the tempdb and master databases.

In Lab 21-1, we show you how to add the SQLUsers login ID as a user of the Northwind database. (We show you how to create the SQLUsers login ID in Lab 20-2.)

Lab 21-1   Creating Database Users

1. **If necessary, log in to your server as Administrator and start SQL Server Enterprise Manager.**

2. **In the console tree, expand the database for which you want to create a user (the Northwind database, in our example).**

3. **Right-click the Users object and choose New Database User.**

4. **From the Login Name drop-down list, select the login ID that you want to add as a user of the selected database — for example, SQLUsers.**

   Notice that SQL Server Enterprise Manager automatically assigns the login ID as the user name, as shown in Figure 21-1.

Figure 21-1:
Adding a database user.

5. **Click OK to add the selected login ID as a user of the database.**

You can also assign a login ID as a user of a database by modifying the properties of the login ID.

Managing database users

You can remove a user from a database by using either SQL Server Enterprise Manager or the `sp_revokedbaccess` stored procedure. Of course, if you delete the user's login ID, SQL Server removes the user from the database as well. SQL Server includes the `sp_change_users_login` stored procedure for changing database user properties. For example, you can use this stored procedure to map a database user to a different login ID.

You can use the `sp_change_users_login` stored procedure to have SQL Server attempt to match a database user to one of the server's login IDs. This capability comes in handy if you've moved a database to a different server. Here's the syntax:

```
use database
exec sp_change_users_login 'auto_fix', 'db_user_name'
```

Assigning Users to Roles

In order to make administering SQL Server easier, Microsoft includes server and database roles with predefined permissions. In addition, you can also create your own custom database roles. These roles make administration easy for you because you can give users permissions simply by adding them as members of a role.

Fixed server roles

SQL Server includes a group of server roles that enable you to assign server-wide administrative permissions. Because these permissions are at the server level and not database-specific, you assign users to server roles by using their login IDs. SQL Server keeps track of each login ID's membership in the various roles by updating the login ID's information in the master..sysxlogins table.

Microsoft calls these server roles "fixed" because you can't modify or delete any of the server roles, nor can you modify the permissions associated with the roles. You also can't define custom server roles. We describe the server roles and their nicknames in Table 21-1. Most of Microsoft's documentation refers to these roles by their nicknames.

Make sure that you know the function of each of these roles for the exam.

Table 21-1	Fixed Server Roles	
Server Role	*Nickname*	*Permission*
System Administrators server	sysadmin	Perform any task on the
Security Administrators	securityadmin	Manage the server's login IDs
Server Administrators	serveradmin	Manage server-wide configuration settings
Setup Administrators	setupadmin	Install and configure replication; execute some of the system stored procedures; and configure linked servers
Process Administrators	processadmin	Administer the processes running on a server
Disk Administrators	diskadmin	Manage database and transaction log files
Database Creators	dbcreator	Create and modify databases
Bulk Insert Administrators	bulkadmin	Run the BULK INSERT SQL statement for importing a large amount of data into a table

Any member of a fixed server role can assign other login IDs to that role. For example, if UserA is a member of the dbcreator server role, UserA can add UserB's login ID to that role. By default, SQL Server automatically adds the built-in Administrators Windows 2000 group to the System Administrators (sysadmin) server role. In other words, all members of the local Administrators group on the SQL server are also members of the sysadmin server role.

You add a login ID as a member of a server role by using either SQL Server Enterprise Manager or the sp_addsrvrolemember stored procedure. Likewise, you can remove a user from a server role by using either SQL Server Enterprise Manager or the sp_dropsrvrolemember stored procedure. (The syntax for sp_dropsrvrolemember is the same as that of sp_addsrvrolemember.) Here's the syntax for the sp_addsrvrolemember stored procedure:

```
sp_addsrvrolemember login, role
```

Use the format *domain_name\user_name* if you're adding a Windows login ID as a member of a role.

Know how to add and remove server role members by using stored procedures for the exam.

In Lab 21-2, we show you how to add login IDs to server roles in SQL Server Enterprise Manager.

Lab 21-2   Adding Login IDs to Server Roles

1. **In SQL Server Enterprise Manager, expand your server's Security folder.**

2. **Select the Logins object.**

3. **In the details pane, double-click your login ID.**

   Chapter 20 shows you how to create a login ID.

4. **Select the Server Roles tab.**

   As shown in Figure 21-2, you use this page to add a login ID to one of the fixed server roles.

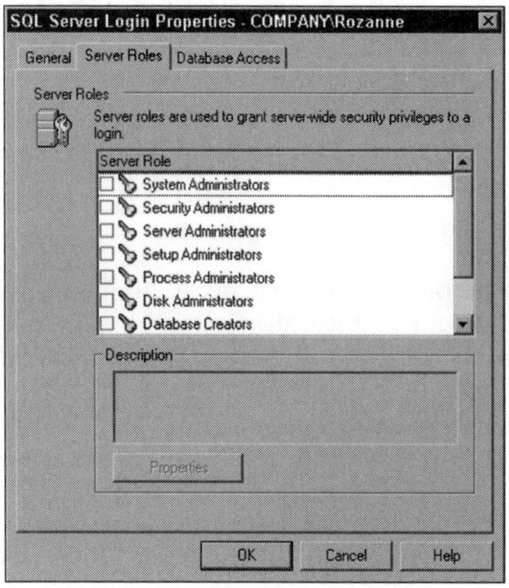

Figure 21-2:
Assigning a login ID to a server role.

5. **Check System Administrators to give your login ID all permissions for managing SQL Server.**

6. **Click OK to save your changes.**

7. **In the Security folder, select the Server Roles object.**

8. **In the details pane, double-click System Administrators.**

   You can also assign login IDs to a server role by double-clicking that role and then clicking on Add.

9. **Click Cancel to close the Server Role Properties dialog box.**

Fixed database roles

Like the server roles, you use database roles to assign users permissions to a database. SQL Server includes a number of fixed server roles with predefined permissions. Unlike server roles, you add database users, not login IDs, to database roles. SQL Server keeps track of each user's membership in the database roles by updating the user's information in the sysusers table within the database.

Although you can create your own custom database roles, the database roles created automatically by SQL Server are also fixed. With the exception of the public role, you can't modify the permissions associated with any of the roles. You can't delete any of the fixed database roles (including public). We describe the fixed database roles in Table 21-2.

We can't stress it enough: Make sure you know the function of each of the database roles for your exam.

Table 21-2	Fixed Database Roles
Database Role	**Permission**
Public	Perform any task permitted by the permissions you've assigned to this role. **Note:** By default, SQL Server automatically adds all database users to the public role; and, in fact, you can't remove users from this role.
Db_owner	Perform any task in the database.
Db_accessadmin	Add or delete database users, groups, and user-defined roles.
Db_securityadmin	Assign permissions.
Db_ddladmin	Add, change, or delete database objects.
Db_backupoperator	Back up and restore the database.
Db_datareader	Read data from any of the database's tables.
Db_datawriter	Add, change, or delete data in any of the database's tables.
Db_denydatareader	Prevent reading data in any of the database's tables.
Db_denydatawriter	Prevent adding, changing, or deleting data in any of the database's tables.

Defining the public role

SQL Server includes the public role in a database as a way to make assigning permissions to all of a database's users easy. Because all the users of a database are automatically members of public, all database users inherit the permissions you assign to the public role. Although the public role is convenient, be careful when assigning permissions to it. In addition, be aware that if you create a guest user in a database, the guest user is also a member of the public role — and thus inherits the permissions you assign to that role.

In Lab 21-3, we show you how to check the permissions for the public role.

Lab 21-3   Checking the Public Role's Permissions

1. **In SQL Server Enterprise Manager, expand the database for which you want to check permissions.**

2. **Select the Roles object.**

3. **In the details pane, double-click public.**

   You now see the members of the public role.

4. **Click Permissions.**

   As shown in Figure 21-3, SQL Server Enterprise Manager displays a list of the objects within the database — and the public role's permissions for those objects.

5. **Click Cancel twice to close the open dialog boxes.**

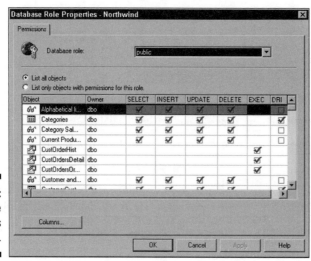

Figure 21-3:
Viewing the public role's permissions.

Determining a user's effective permissions

You can assign a user to multiple database roles. For example, you might assign a user to both the db_datareader and db_datawriter database roles (in addition to the public role). In this scenario, the user's effective permissions are cumulative: The user can both read and write to the tables within the database.

One exception to the rule of permissions being cumulative is that any time you deny a user permissions, those permissions are denied no matter what. For example, if you add a user to both the db_owner and the db_denydatareader roles, that user can't read any of the data in the database's tables.

Make sure you understand the impact of denying a user permissions for the exam. You can expect to see a number of questions prompting you to determine a user's effective permissions.

Adding and removing users from database roles

In order to add a user to a database role, you must be a member of the db_owner role for that database. SQL Server automatically adds the special dbo user to the db_owner role, which means that all members of the system administrators fixed server role are automatically members of the db_owner role in each database.

You add a user to a database role by using either SQL Server Enterprise Manager or the `sp_addrolemember` stored procedure. You remove a user from a role by using either SQL Server Enterprise Manager or the `sp_droprolemember` stored procedure. In Lab 21-4, we show you how to add a login ID to the db_datareader role in SQL Server Enterprise Manager. (Our example is based on the UserC login ID we create in Chapter 20.)

Lab 21-4	Adding Database Users to Database Roles

1. **In SQL Server Enterprise Manager, select your server's Logins object.**

2. **In the details pane, double-click the login ID for the user you want to add to a database role (in our example, we use UserC).**

3. **Select the Database Access tab.**

   You use this page to add a login ID as a database user, and to assign the database user to any of the fixed database roles.

4. **Select the appropriate database (we use Northwind), and then check the database role to which you want to assign the selected user (db_owner, in our example).**

   As shown in Figure 21-4, UserC is now a member of both the public and db_owner database roles. You can also add a user to a database role by double-clicking the specific database role within the database's folder.

5. **Click OK to save your changes.**

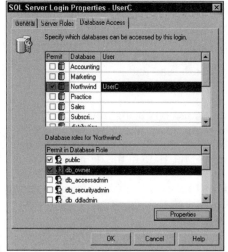

Figure 21-4:
Adding a
user to a
database
role.

User-defined database roles

If you find that the fixed database roles don't meet your needs, you can
create your own database roles with exactly the permissions you want to
assign. Use user-defined database roles whenever you want to assign custom
permissions to a group of users. You also find these roles handy if you aren't
an administrator of the Windows 2000 domain.

You must be a member of either the db_securityadmin or db_owner database
roles before you can create user-defined database roles. Members of the
sysadmin server role, and the db_securityadmin and db_owner database
roles, can add members to user-defined database roles.

You create a user-defined database role and assign permissions and members
to it within SQL Server Enterprise Manager by right-clicking the Roles object
within a database and choosing New Database Role. You can also use stored
procedures and Transact-SQL statements to do the same thing:

- Use `sp_addrole` to create the database role.
- Use the `GRANT` or `DENY` SQL statements to add or deny permissions to
  the role.
- Use `sp_addrolemember` to add database users to the role, and
  `sp_droprolemember` to remove users from the role.
- Use `sp_droprole` to delete the role.

Using Permissions

In addition to the server and database roles, you can also assign permissions for executing specific SQL statements and for accessing database objects. You can assign these permissions to specific database users or to a user-defined database role.

Using statement permissions

Only members of the sysadmin, db_owner, or db_securityadmin roles can assign statement permissions. Statement permissions enable you to permit or deny users the ability to execute the following SQL statements (whether you execute them explicitly in SQL Server Query Analyzer or implicitly by using a utility such as SQL Server Enterprise Manager):

- ✔ CREATE DATABASE
- ✔ CREATE TABLE, CREATE VIEW, CREATE PROCEDURE, CREATE RULE, CREATE DEFAULT, or CREATE FUNCTION
- ✔ BACKUP DATABASE or BACKUP LOG

If a user creates an object (such as a table), the user automatically has all object permissions for that object.

Using object permissions

Members of the sysadmin, db_owner, and db_securityadmin roles, along with the owner of the object, can set object permissions. Object permissions enable you to control access to database objects. These permissions include

- ✔ SELECT, INSERT, UPDATE, DELETE, and REFERENCES for tables and views
- ✔ SELECT, UPDATE, and REFERENCES for columns
- ✔ EXECUTE for stored procedures

The REFERENCES permission controls access to primary key to foreign key relationships. In order for a user to add a row to a table for which you've defined a foreign key, that user must have either the SELECT permission on the primary key table or the REFERENCES permission on the foreign key table.

Assigning a user only the UPDATE permission for a table is possible. However, you should always assign users the SELECT permission when you assign the UPDATE permission. If you don't, the user won't be able to use a WHERE clause with the UPDATE statement.

Assigning permissions

As with just about everything in SQL Server, you can assign permissions for your current database by using either SQL Server Enterprise Manager or the equivalent Transact-SQL statements: GRANT, DENY, and REVOKE. Like database roles, the individual permissions you assign are also cumulative with one exception: If you deny a specific permission for a user, that permission is denied no matter what. For example, if you grant UserC the SELECT, INSERT, UPDATE, and DELETE permissions for the Northwind..customers table, and you deny the public database role the UPDATE permission for that same table, UserC's effective permissions for the table are SELECT, INSERT, and DELETE.

Use the following steps to determine a user's effective permissions for an object:

1. **Check the user's membership in fixed database roles.**

2. **Check the user's membership in user-defined database roles. If the user is a member of a user-defined database role, check the permissions assigned to the role.**

3. **Check to see whether any permissions have been assigned to the individual user.**

Permissions are cumulative unless an assignment denies a permission. A user's effective permissions for an object result from the combination of all permissions assigned through roles and individually, minus any permissions that have been denied.

Denying a permission is not the same as revoking a permission. When you deny a specific permission such as DELETE, you prevent a user from exercising that permission. Revoking a permission simply removes a permission assignment. Make sure you know the effect of denying a permission for the exam.

In Lab 21-5, we show you how to grant, deny, and revoke permissions by using SQL Server Enterprise Manager.

Lab 21-5   Assigning Permissions in SQL Server Enterprise Manager

1. **In SQL Server Enterprise Manager, expand the database for which you want to assign permissions.**

   In our example, we use the Northwind database.

2. **In Tables, right-click a table and choose Properties.**

   Choose one of your own tables, or use the Customers table within the Northwind database.

3. **Click Permissions to open the Object Properties dialog box.**

   You use the Object Properties dialog box to assign permissions to users or roles for a specific database object. Notice that SQL Server configured the public database role for the Northwind database with the SELECT, INSERT, UPDATE, DELETE, and REFERENCES (shown as DRI) permissions for the Customers table.

4. **Select one of your database users (in our example, we use UserC), and then click Delete.**

   As shown in Figure 21-5, SQL Server Enterprise Manager displays a green check mark the first time you check a permission. This check mark indicates that you have granted the user that permission.

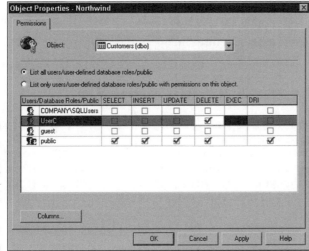

Figure 21-5:
Granting
permissions
in SQL
Server
Enterprise
Manager.

5. **Click Delete again.**

   Notice that the green check mark changes to a red X, as shown in Figure 21-6, to indicate that you've now denied the user's permission. By denying the DELETE permission, you prevent this user's effective permissions from ever including the DELETE permission.

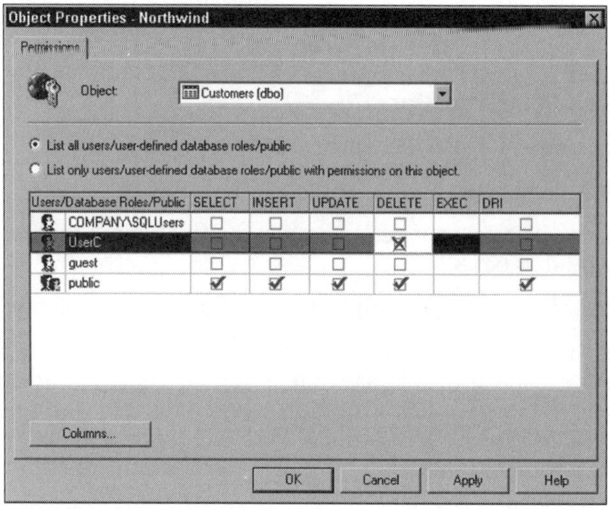

Figure 21-6:
Denying the
DELETE
permission.

6. **Click Delete one more time.**

   When you clear the check box below the DELETE permission, you revoke the permission assignment. Although the user no longer has an explicit DELETE permission assignment, the user's effective permissions can now include the DELETE permission provided you've assigned the DELETE permission to a database role of which the user is a member.

7. **Click Cancel twice to close the open dialog boxes.**

Implementing permissions for views and stored procedures

Because both views and stored procedures can reference one or more tables, you may be worrying about the work involved in managing their security. The good news is that you only have to worry about granting users permissions to the view or stored procedure — and not the underlying tables.

Using Application Roles

Most end-users access SQL Server not through tools such as SQL Server Query Analyzer, but through custom applications. For example, many of the popular e-commerce Web sites use applications that store information such as orders in a SQL database. So how should you design security for such an environment? The solution is through application roles.

Application roles are a special type of role that you can use to define security for an application. These roles enable you to define the permissions you want users to have only when they access SQL Server from within an application — and not when they access SQL Server directly (such as with SQL Server Query Analyzer).

One key difference between an application role and the other types of security roles is that you can't assign members to an application role. Instead, you activate the role from within your application. An application role is database-specific. If your application accesses more than one database on your SQL server, you must create an application role for each database.

Make sure you know the difference between an application role and server, database, and user-defined database roles for the exam.

Creating an application role

Provided you're a member of the sysadmin, db_owner, or db_securityadmin roles, you can create an application role. You create an application role by using either (you guessed it) SQL Server Enterprise Manager or the sp_addapprole stored procedure. When you define the application role, you must specify a password for activating the role. After creating the application role, you can assign permissions to it by using either SQL Server Enterprise Manager or the GRANT, DENY, or REVOKE SQL statements.

Activating an application role

You activate an application role for your users by programming the commands to activate it into your application. One technique you can use is to have your application call the sp_setapprole stored procedure. This stored procedure activates the application role for a user's current connection. Once activated, the user has the permissions you've assigned to the application role. These permissions are in effect until the user disconnects from your server.

Prep Test

1 **Which of the following tasks can you complete for the dbo database user?**

A ○ You can rename the dbo database user.

B ○ You can delete the dbo database user.

C ○ You can change the dbo user's password.

D ○ None of the above.

2 **You plan to detach a database from one SQL server and attach it to a different SQL server. You have defined the same login IDs on both servers. What is the most efficient way to configure security for the database on the new server?**

A ○ Do nothing. SQL Server automatically transfers the necessary security information.

B ○ Execute `sp_change_users_login` with the `auto_fix` parameter to associate each database user with a login ID on the new server.

C ○ Create the necessary database users on the new server.

D ○ Drop and recreate the database users on the new server.

3 **SQL Server keeps track of the members of the various server roles in what table?**

A ○ Master..sysxlogins

B ○ *database_name*..sysxlogins

C ○ Master..sysusers

D ○ *database_name*..sysusers

4 **Who can add login IDs as members of the db_creator server role? (Choose all that apply.)**

A ❏ Members of the sysadmin server role

B ❏ Members of the dbcreator server role

C ❏ Members of the securityadmin server role

D ❏ Members of the setupadmin server role

5 **You have added UserB to the public, db_datareader, and db_datawriter roles for the Northwind database. You have denied UserB the UPDATE permission for the Northwind..employees table. What are UserB's effective permissions for the Northwind..employees table?**

A ○ SELECT, INSERT, UPDATE, and DELETE

B ○ SELECT, INSERT, UPDATE, DELETE, and REFERENCES

C ○ SELECT, INSERT, and DELETE

D ○ SELECT, INSERT, DELETE, and REFERENCES

6 **How do you assign a user to an application role?**

   A ○ By adding the user as a member of the application role.

   B ○ By activating the role within an application.

   C ○ By adding the user's login ID as a member of the application role.

   D ○ By configuring the application role as the user's default role within a database.

7 **You want to delegate creating login IDs and managing their passwords to another user. To what server role should you add the user?**

   A ○ Sysadmin

   B ○ Setupadmin

   C ○ Securityadmin

   D ○ ServerAdmin

8 **You want to delegate the management of database users to another user. To what database role should you add the user?**

   A ○ Db_owner

   B ○ Db_securityadmin

   C ○ Db_ddladmin

   D ○ Db_accessadmin

Answers

1 **D.** You can't delete or change any of the properties of the dbo user. *See "Assigning Database Users."*

2 **B.** You can use the `sp_change_users_login` stored procedure to associate the database's users with login IDs on the new server. *See "Managing database users."*

3 **A.** SQL Server tracks all members of the server roles in the sysxlogins table within the master database. *Study "Fixed server roles."*

4 **A** and **B.** You can add members to a server role if you're a member of the sysadmin server role, or if you're a member of the role to which you want to add members. For example, you can add members to the dbcreator server role as long as you're a member of the dbcreator role. *See "Fixed server roles."*

5 **C.** UserB inherits the SELECT, INSERT, and DELETE permissions through membership in the db_datareader and db_datawriter roles. UserB doesn't inherit the UPDATE permission because you've denied that permission. *See "Assigning permissions."*

6 **B.** You don't add members to application roles. Instead, you activate the application role within your application. *See "Activating an application role."*

7 **C.** You should add the user as a member of the securityadmin server role. *See "Fixed server roles."*

8 **D.** Members of the db_accessadmin database role can add, manage, and delete database users. *See "Fixed database roles."*

Chapter 22

Auditing SQL Server

• •

Exam Objectives

▶ Implementing C2 auditing

▶ Managing security auditing with SQL Server Profiler and SQL Trace

• •

*T*he United States government uses the term *C2 security* to indicate that a system complies with its standards for auditing and discretionary resource protection through actions such as specifying permissions and requiring passwords. SQL Server 2000 includes support for C2 security auditing, which enables you to verify your SQL server's conformance to the government's C2 security standards.

In this chapter, we show you how to implement, manage, and analyze the audit log files generated by C2 auditing. You can expect to see a few questions on implementing C2 auditing on your exam.

Quick Assessment

Implementing
C2 auditing

1 C2 auditing enables you to audit _____, _____, _____, _____, and _____
activities.

2 The C2 audit mode is a(n) _____ server option.

3 You enable the C2 audit mode by using the _____ stored procedure.

4 SQL Server stores the audit log files in the _____ folder.

Managing
security
auditing
with SQL
Server
Profiler and
SQL Trace

5 The audit log files are stored in the _____ format.

6 You analyze an audit log by using _____.

Answers

1 *User, administrator, utility, server, and auditing.* Review "Understanding C2 Auditing."

2 *Advanced.* See "Enabling C2 Auditing."

3 `sp_configure`. **Study "Enabling C2 Auditing."**

4 *\Program Files\Microsoft SQL Server\MSSQL\Data.* Study "Managing the Audit Logs."

5 *Trace file.* See "Managing the Audit Logs."

6 *SQL Server Profiler.* Study "Analyzing the Audit Logs."

Understanding C2 Auditing

One of the new features in SQL Server 2000, C2 auditing, permits you to audit many different events in SQL Server and to record them into an audit log. Events you can audit include

- User activity, such as all SQL commands, logins, and logouts.

- Administrator activity, such as execution of the CREATE, ALTER, and DROP SQL statements, modifying the configuration of the server, and security actions (such as creating or dropping login IDs and changing permissions).

- Utility activity, such as backing up, restoring, bulk copy operations, and DBCC commands.

- Server activity, such as shutdown, pause, and start. (C2 auditing records a shutdown of your server only if it's initiated within a SQL Server utility. It can't record the event if SQL Server is shut down by using a Windows 2000 utility such as the Computer Management MMC.)

- Auditing activity, such as enabling or disabling of auditing.

For each event you audit, SQL Server records information such as the date and time the event occurred, the login ID who initiated the event, the event type, and the success or failure of the event.

Enabling C2 Auditing

By default, Setup doesn't enable C2 auditing when you install SQL Server. You enable C2 auditing by modifying the configuration of your server with the sp_configure stored procedure. You must be a member of the sysadmin server role in order to change your server's configuration.

C2 auditing is considered an advanced configuration option, which means that sp_configure doesn't display its status by default. You can view your server's current C2 auditing status by executing the following statements in SQL Server Query Analyzer:

```
exec sp_configure 'show advanced options', 1
go
reconfigure
go
exec sp_configure 'c2 audit mode'
go
```

You turn any of the configuration options on or off by using a 1 for on, 0 for off. So, to enable C2 auditing, execute the following statement:

```
exec sp_configure 'c2 audit mode', 1
go
reconfigure
go
```

You must stop and restart the MSSQLServer service in order for your server to begin auditing events. Know this for the exam!

In Lab 22-1, we walk you through enabling C2 auditing on your server.

Lab 22-1   Enabling C2 Auditing

1. **If necessary, log on to your server as Administrator.**

2. **Open SQL Server Query Analyzer and connect to your server using Windows Authentication.**

3. **Execute the following query:**

```
exec sp_configure 'show advanced options', 1
go
reconfigure
go
exec sp_configure 'c2 audit mode'
go
```

As shown in Figure 22-1, you should see that C2 auditing isn't currently enabled on your server. (Look at the run_value column. This column indicates the current status of the server option.)

Figure 22-1: Viewing your server's C2 auditing status.

```
SQL Query Analyzer - [Query - SQLSERVER.master.COMPANY\administrator - Untitled4*]
File   Edit   Query   Tools   Window   Help

exec sp_configure 'show advanced options', 1
go
reconfigure
go
exec sp_configure 'c2 audit mode'
go
```

name	minimum	maximum	config_value	run_value
1 c2 audit mode	0	1	0	0

```
Grids  Messages
Query batch complete SQLSERVER (8.0)  COMPANY\administrator master  0:00:01  1 rows Ln 7, Col 1
                                                     Connections: 1           NUM
```

4. **Execute the following query to enable C2 auditing on your server:**

```
exec sp_configure 'c2 audit mode', 1
go
reconfigure
go
exec sp_configure 'c2 audit mode'
go
```

We use the last `sp_configure` statement to confirm that C2 auditing is enabled on your server.

5. **Stop and restart the MSSQLServer service.**

Managing the Audit Logs

After you enable C2 auditing, SQL Server stores the auditing information in audit logs. These files are trace files that you can analyze within SQL Server Profiler. The log files are stored in the \Program Files\Microsoft SQL Server\MSSQL\Data folder. If you've installed multiple named instances of SQL Server, you must enable C2 auditing for each instance. SQL Server stores a named instance's C2 audit logs in the \Program Files\Microsoft SQL Server\MSSQL$*instance_name*\Data folder.

SQL Server automatically names the audit log file audittrace_*YYYYDDMM9999*. trc, where YYYY represents the four-digit year, DD the date, MM the month, and 9999 the time the file was created (in the format MMHH, where MM is the minutes and HH the hour). For example, an audit log filename of audit-trace_200018125612.trc indicates that SQL Server created the file on December 18, 2000, at 12:56.

The log file can grow until it reaches 200MB in size. When it reaches the maximum size, SQL Server automatically creates a new log file. By creating a new log file, SQL Server never overwrites an existing file in order to provide you with a complete audit trail. SQL Server continues to create new log files until you run out of disk space. If your server runs out of available disk space, SQL Server shuts down. You must free up disk space or you won't be able to start SQL Server.

Analyzing the Audit Logs

You analyze the audit logs by using SQL Server Profiler. You can view the audit logs directly by opening them as trace files within SQL Server Profiler. SQL Server can continue to record events in the audit log file even if you have it open in SQL Server Profiler. You can also use SQL Server Profiler to import the data in the audit logs into a table. After you import the data into a table, you can use SQL statements (such as the `SELECT` statement along with `WHERE` clauses) to filter and analyze its contents.

SQL Server includes a command-line utility, `FiletoTable.exe`, which you can use to import a trace file into a table without using SQL Server Profiler.

In Lab 22-2, we show you how to analyze the audit log in SQL Server Profiler.

Lab 22-2   Analyzing an Audit Log File

1. **Generate some server activity that you can examine in SQL Server Profiler. For example, open SQL Server Query Analyzer and log in with Windows Authentication.**

2. **Open SQL Server Profiler.**

3. **Choose File⇨Open⇨Trace File.**

4. **Access the \Program Files\Microsoft SQL Server\MSSQL\Data folder, and then double-click your audit log file.**

   Notice the many rows in your trace file (typically thousands). Keep in mind that C2 auditing records almost everything that occurs on your server, including actions performed by SQL Server itself. We show you how to configure a filter to exclude those events generated by the service account.

5. **Choose File⇨Properties.**

   You can use the Properties dialog box to specify the events and columns you want to view (by default, you see all events and columns), and configure a filter on the data. You can use filters to include or exclude events based on a value.

6. **Select the Filters tab.**

7. **Expand the LoginName category, and then expand Not Like. In the text box, type *your_domain_name*\sqlservice to have SQL Server Profiler filter out those events performed by the service account, as shown in Figure 22-2. Click OK.**

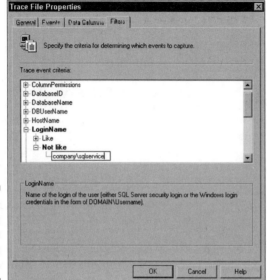

Figure 22-2:
Configuring
a filter on an
audit log
file.

8. **In the Event Class column, look for Audit Logon.**

   SQL Server has recorded your login to SQL Server within SQL Server
   Query Analyzer in the audit log file.

9. **Close SQL Server Profiler.**

10. **Disable the C2 audit mode on your server by executing the following
    statement in SQL Server Query Analyzer:**

```
exec sp_configure 'c2 audit mode', 0
go
reconfigure
go
exec sp_configure 'c2 audit mode'
go
```

   Because C2 auditing consumes a significant amount of disk space on
   your server, don't leave it enabled if you aren't using it.

11. **Stop and restart the MSSQLServer service.**

Prep Test

1 **What happens to the audit log if your server's hard disk is full?**

A ○ SQL Server automatically overwrites old audit log files beginning with the oldest file.

B ○ SQL Server shuts down.

C ○ SQL Server disables C2 auditing.

D ○ SQL Server continues to run but no new users can log in to your server.

2 **What server role(s) permit you to enable C2 auditing?**

A ○ Setupadmin

B ○ Serveradmin

C ○ Diskadmin

D ○ Sysadmin

3 **Which of the following commands can you use to enable C2 auditing on your server?**

A ○ `sp_configure 'show advanced options', 'c2 audit mode', 1`

B ○ `sp_configure 'c2 audit mode', 0`

C ○ `sp_configure 'c2 audit mode', 1`

D ○ `sp_configure 'c2 auditing', 1`

4 **What is the maximum size of an audit log file?**

A ○ 20MB

B ○ 200MB

C ○ 2,000MB

D ○ Whatever value you configure in SQL Server Enterprise Manager

5 **You would like to store the audit log information in a table on your SQL server. What should you do? (Choose all that apply.)**

A ❑ Modify the configuration of the C2 audit mode so that it stores auditing information in a table instead of a log file.

B ❑ Use the FiletoTable command-line utility to import a log file into a table.

C ❑ Nothing. You can't store the log information in a table.

D ❑ Use SQL Server Profiler to import the log file into a table.

6 You would like to view only the actions of a specifio user in the audlt log file. Which of the following actions enable you to do so? (Choose all that apply.)

A ❑ Import the log file's data into a table. Use a WHERE clause on the SELECT statement to view only that user's actions.

B ❑ Use SQL Server Profiler to restrict the event classes displayed in the log file.

C ❑ Use SQL Server Profiler to define the columns you want to view in the log file.

D ❑ Configure a filter in SQL Server Profiler on the user name.

Answers

1 **B.** SQL Server shuts down if your server's hard disk is full. You can't restart your server until you free up disk space. *See "Managing the Audit Logs."*

2 **D.** Only the members of the sysadmin server role can enable C2 auditing. *Study "Enabling C2 Auditing."*

3 **C.** You enable C2 auditing by setting the C2 audit mode option to 1. *Review "Enabling C2 Auditing."*

4 **B.** The maximum log file size is 200MB. *See "Managing the Audit Logs."*

5 **B** and **D.** You can use either the FiletoTable command-line utility or SQL Server Profiler to import log file data into a table. *Study "Managing the Audit Logs."*

6 **A** and **D.** You can use SQL commands such as SELECT to view the information in the log file after you've imported it into a table. You can also configure a filter in SQL Server Profiler to restrict the events it shows based on values such as the user name. *Study "Analyzing the Audit Logs."*

Part VII

Managing, Monitoring, and Troubleshooting SQL Server 2000

The 5th Wave · By Rich Tennant

"You know, this was a situation question on my SQL Server exam, but I always thought it was just hypothetical."

In this part . . .

*A*s a database administrator, one of your more important responsibilities is to make sure that your SQL
server is performing as it should — and to troubleshoot
any problems that arise. In this part, we show you how
you can manage, monitor, and troubleshoot SQL Server
2000 by using a variety of utilities.

In Chapter 23, we show you how you can automate the
administration of SQL Server by creating jobs, alerts, and
operators. We review the steps for analyzing and optimizing
your server's hardware in Chapter 24. And in Chapter 25,
we examine the steps you can take to optimize SQL Server
itself.

Chapter 23

Automating Administrative Tasks and Alerts

Exam Objectives

▶ Creating, managing, and troubleshooting SQLServerAgent jobs

▶ Configuring alerts and operators by using SQLServerAgent

*S*QL Server includes an impressive array of features that you can use to automate many of the administrative tasks on your server. For example, you can configure and schedule jobs for performing anything from backing up your server to performing maintenance checks. You can also create alerts to notify you when a problem arises on your server. You can even have an alert execute a job to resolve the problem.

In this chapter, we explore all the steps for configuring operators, jobs, and alerts. You can expect to see a number of questions on your exam on automating administrative tasks.

Quick Assessment

Creating, managing, and trouble-shooting SQLServer-Agent jobs

1 You can configure a job step to run an .exe file by choosing _____ as the step type.

2 SQL Server executes _____ job steps in the security context of the user who initiated the job.

3 You can optionally assign jobs to _____ in order to organize them.

4 You can use a(n) _____ to set the security context for an ActiveX script job step.

5 SQL Server stores a job's history in the _____ table within the _____ database.

Configuring alerts and operators by using SQLServer-Agent

6 You should define a(n) _____ if you want SQL Server to notify you of a job's status if no other operators are available.

7 You can configure SQL Server to notify an operator by _____, _____, or _____.

8 SQL Server alerts work in conjunction with the Windows 2000 _____.

9 You can define an alert based on _____, _____, or _____.

10 You can check the history of an alert by _____.

Answers

1 *Operating system command.* Study "Defining Jobs."

2 *Transact-SQL.* See "Defining job security."

3 *Categories.* See "Creating a job."

4 *Proxy account.* See "Defining job security."

5 *Sysjobhistory, msdb.* Review "Viewing a job's history."

6 *Fail-safe operator.* Review "Creating Operators."

7 *E-mail, pager, or* `net send`. See "Creating Operators."

8 *Event Log service.* See "Defining Alerts."

9 *Error number, severity level, or performance condition.* Study "Defining Alerts."

10 *Opening its Properties dialog box.* See "Check the history."

Preparing for Automating Jobs and Alerts

Before you define any jobs and alerts, you must configure the SQLServerAgent service properly. In addition, if you want jobs and alerts to notify you by e-mail or pager, you must configure the SQLServerAgent service to send e-mail with SQLAgentMail. We show you how to configure the SQLServerAgent service and SQLAgentMail in Chapter 7.

Creating Operators

Both jobs and alerts have the ability to notify you about their status. You configure SQL Server to notify you (or other users) by defining one or more operators. SQL Server can notify operators by e-mail, pager, or by using the net send command. In Lab 23-1, we show you how to add yourself as an operator. (This lab assumes that you have completed the labs in Chapter 7 for configuring SQLAgentMail and have mailboxes for both the SQLServerAgent service account and the administrator.)

Lab 23-1   Creating an Operator

1. **In SQL Server Enterprise Manager, expand the SQL Server Agent object.**

   The SQL Server Agent object is in the Management folder.

2. **Right-click Operators and choose New Operator.**

3. **In the Name text box, type your first name. In the E-mail Name text box, type** Administrator **to configure SQL Server to notify you via the Administrator's e-mail account, as shown in Figure 23-1.**

4. **Next to the E-mail Name text box, click Test to send a test message to the Administrator's mailbox. Click OK to confirm that you want to send the message.**

   If you open Outlook, you can see the test message in your mailbox. We show you the test message in Figure 23-2.

5. **In SQL Server Enterprise Manager, click OK to save your operator.**

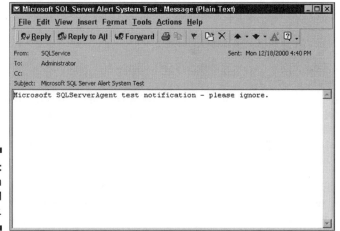

Figure 23-1:
Configuring
an e-mail
operator.

Figure 23-2:
Testing an
e-mail
operator.

You can configure the SQLServerAgent to notify a fail-safe operator. SQL
Server notifies this operator if you have configured an alert to notify opera-
tors by pager and all the operators are off-duty. SQL Server notifies the fail-
safe operator by whatever methods you have configured for the operator.
You configure the fail-safe operator by modifying the properties of the
SQLServerAgent object within SQL Server Enterprise Manager.

Defining Jobs

You create jobs by using either SQL Server Enterprise Manager or the sp_add_job stored procedure. SQL Server stores all jobs within the sysjobs table in the msdb database. Each job is made up of a series of steps; each step can execute only one of four action types:

- ✔ **ActiveX scripts.** A job can execute ActiveX scripts written in VBScript or Microsoft Jscript. Make sure you identify the language in which the script was written.

- ✔ **Operating system commands.** You can have a job run any operating system command that ends in .exe, .bat, .cmd, or .com.

- ✔ **Replication processes.** You can configure a job to execute one of the replication agents.

- ✔ **Transact-SQL statements.** Make sure that you explicitly state the database name for any objects you reference in the statements (for example, use northwind..customers instead of just customers).

Defining job security

Be careful as to how you configure the security context for jobs. If a login ID owns a job but isn't a member of the sysadmin server role, you must make sure that the login ID has the necessary permissions to execute the job's steps. SQL Server executes Transact-SQL job steps in the security context of the user who initiated the job. In other words, if your job executes the SELECT statement for a view, the user who runs the job must have at least SELECT permissions on that view.

In contrast to SQL statements, operating system command and ActiveX script job steps execute in the security context of the SQLServerAgent service account, which means that a user who executes a job within SQL Server may be able to perform Windows 2000 commands for which they have been denied permission in Windows 2000. If you want to avoid this situation, you can configure the SQLServerAgent service to permit only users that are members of the sysadmin server role to perform operating system command and ActiveX script job steps.

Alternatively, you can configure an operating system command or ActiveX script to execute in the context of a specific domain user account. This account is called a proxy account. You can define a proxy account by using either SQL Server Enterprise Manager or the xp_sqlagent_proxy_account extended system stored procedure.

Creating a job

You create a job in SQL Server Enterprise Manager by right-clicking the Jobs icon and choosing New Job. You then define the following properties for the job:

- ✔ Job name.

- ✔ Job category (optional). You use job categories to organize jobs based on the tasks they perform.

- ✔ One or more job steps. A job step can be a Transact-SQL statement, operating system command, ActiveX script, or a replication process.

- ✔ The order in which you want job steps to execute.

- ✔ One or more schedules for the job.

- ✔ Whether or not you want SQL Server to notify you about the status of the job.

In Lab 23-2, you create a job to back up the transaction log for a database. You also configure this job to notify you by e-mail about its status.

Lab 23-2   Creating a Job

1. **In SQL Server Enterprise Manager, right-click Jobs and choose New Job to open the New Job Properties dialog box.**

2. **In the Name text box, type** Backup of *database_name* Transaction Log.

   In our example, we back up the Northwind database's transaction log. As shown in Figure 23-3, you can also define a category for the job and a description.

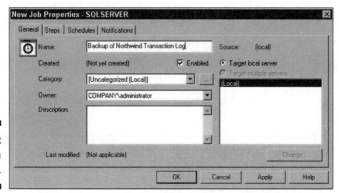

Figure 23-3: Naming a job.

3. **Select the Steps tab.**

As shown in Figure 23-4, you use the Steps page to define the steps you want your job to perform — and the order in which to execute them. Notice that you can specify that you want certain steps to perform only if the preceding step fails or succeeds.

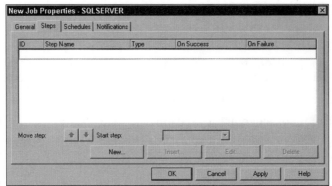

Figure 23-4: Defining job steps.

4. **Click New to add a new step to your job.**

5. **In the Step Name text box, type** Back up transaction log.

6. **Verify that the step type is Transact-SQL.**

You will execute the BACKUP LOG SQL statement to configure the job to back up your database's transaction log.

7. **From the Database drop-down list, select your database (we use Northwind for our example).**

Make sure you choose a database that isn't using the simple recovery model. (You can't back up the transaction log for such a database because SQL Server automatically truncates its transaction log.)

8. **In the Command text box, type the following SQL statement:**

```
BACKUP LOG database_name
TO backup_device_name
WITH INIT
```

Replace *database_name* with the name of the database you're backing up, and *backup_device_name* with the name of a permanent backup device. In our example, we use Northwind for the database name and Northwind_log for the backup device's name. Make sure you create the backup device before you run this job. For more information on creating permanent backup devices, see Chapter 14.

At this point, your screen should look like what you see in Figure 23-5.

Figure 23-5:
Defining a
job step to
back up the
Northwind
database's
transaction
log.

9. **Click OK to save your job step.**

10. **Select the Schedules tab, and then click New Schedule.**

    You use the New Job Schedule dialog box to define a schedule for when
    you want your job to execute. You can configure a job to execute when-
    ever the SQLServerAgent service starts, when your server's CPU is idle,
    once, or on a recurring basis. You can name a schedule so that you can
    reuse it for other jobs.

11. **In the Name text box, type** Daily Backup.

12. **Click Change to configure the backup to occur on a daily basis begin-
    ning at midnight, as shown in Figure 23-6.**

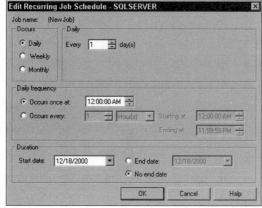

Figure 23-6:
Configuring
a job
schedule.

13. **Click OK to save your recurring schedule.**

14. **Click OK again to save the job schedule.**

15. **Select the Notifications tab.**

    You use the Notifications page to configure SQL Server to notify an operator as to the status of a job.

16. **Check E-mail Operator. From the drop-down list, select your first name (if necessary).**

17. **Take a look at the job status drop-down list, as shown in Figure 23-7.**

Figure 23-7:
You can configure SQL Server to notify you when the job succeeds, fails, or simply completes.

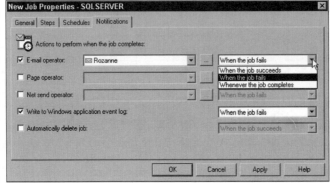

18. **Configure the job to notify you whenever it completes.**

19. **Click OK to save your job.**

20. **Look at the details pane in SQL Server Enterprise Manager.**

    At a minimum, you see your Backup of *database_name* Transaction Log job. You may also see jobs for replication tasks (if you completed the labs in Chapter 19) and performing database maintenance (if you completed the labs in Chapter 16).

If you schedule your job to run whenever your server's CPU is idle, you must define what "idle" is for your server by modifying the properties of the SQLServerAgent service. (You configure this value on the Advanced page of the SQLServerAgent Properties dialog box.) You configure what counts as idle for your server by specifying a CPU usage percentage. The minimum value you can set is 10 percent.

Running a job

Provided the SQLServerAgent service is running on your server, SQL Server executes all jobs based on the schedule you define. You can also force SQL

Server to run a job manually by right-clicking the job and choosing Start Job. In Lab 23-3, we have you run the job you created in the previous lab.

Lab 23-3   Manually Running a Job

1. **In SQL Server Enterprise Manager, select the Jobs object in the console tree.**

2. **In the details pane, right-click the job you created in Lab 23-2 and choose Start Job.**

   In our example, we use the Backup of Northwind Transaction Log job.

3. **If necessary, open Microsoft Outlook. Verify that you received an e-mail message indicating that the job completed.**

   Your e-mail message should look similar to the one we show in Figure 23-8.

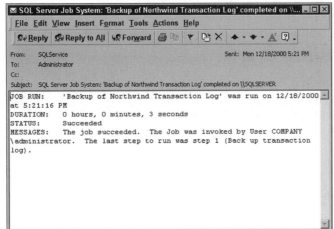

Figure 23-8:
A job status e-mail notification.

Viewing a job's history

You can view the history of a job in SQL Server Enterprise Manager by right-clicking the job and choosing View Job History. We show you the history for the Backup of Northwind Transaction Log job in Figure 23-9. Notice that you can check the Show Step Details option to have SQL Server Enterprise Manager display information about each of the steps performed by the job.

SQL Server stores the job history information in the sysjobhistory table within the msdb database. By default, SQL Server configures the sysjobhistory table to store a maximum of 1,000 rows, of which, each job can use a maximum of 100 rows for its history. When SQL Server reaches the maximum number of rows for all jobs or a specific job, it overwrites rows based on date.

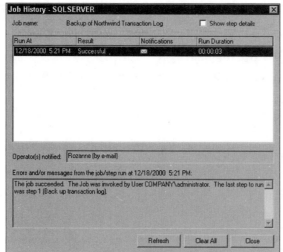

Figure 23-9:
Viewing job
history
information.

Disabling a job

If you want to prevent a job from executing, but you don't want to delete the job altogether, you can disable it within SQL Server Enterprise Manager. To do so, right-click the job and choose Properties. Uncheck the Enabled option, and then click OK.

Defining Alerts

You use SQL Server's alert capability to notify you of problems on your server. SQL Server's alerts work in conjunction with the Windows 2000 Event Log service. Alerts are triggered when SQL Server records an error in the Windows 2000 application log. You can configure SQL Server to both notify you and perform a job in response to an alert.

The following events cause SQL Server to record an event in the application log:

- ✔ SQL Server errors with a severity level between 19 and 25. You can also create your own custom error messages with the same severity levels by using the `sp_addmessage` or `sp_altermessage` stored procedure and call these errors from within stored procedures or an application.

- ✔ Any time you execute the `RAISERROR WITH LOG` SQL statement.

- ✔ Whenever you execute the `xp_logevent` stored procedure.

You create alerts by using either SQL Server Enterprise Manager or the sp_add_alert stored procedure. SQL Server stores the alerts you define in the sysalerts table within the msdb database. You can create alerts to fire based on the following:

- ✔ SQL Server error number.

- ✔ Specific severity level (such as 25).

- ✔ Performance condition. These alerts enable you to choose any of the System Monitor counters. For example, you can configure an alert to notify you if the SQL Server: Databases: Percent Log Used counter for a specific database exceeds 75 percent.

In Lab 23-4, we show you how to create an alert to notify you if the transaction log for the Northwind database is more than 75 percent full.

You can't make changes to a database if its transaction log is full. If the log fills up, you must truncate the log before you will be able to make changes to the database.

Lab 23-4   Creating an Alert

1. **In SQL Server Enterprise Manager, right-click the Alerts object and choose New Alert.**

2. **In the Name text box, type a name for your alert (in our example, we use** Monitor Northwind Log).

3. **From the Type drop-down list, select SQL Server Performance Condition Alert. From the Object drop-down list, select SQL Server: Databases, and then select Percent Log Used from the Counter drop-down list.**

   You can use the Percent Log Used counter to monitor how full a database's transaction log is.

4. **From the Instance drop-down list, select the appropriate database (Northwind in our example). Choose Rises Above from the Alert If Counter drop-down list, and then type** 75 **in the Value text box.**

   Your screen resembles that shown in Figure 23-10.

5. **Select the Response tab.**

   You use the Response page to specify what you want SQL Server to do if the alert condition occurs.

6. **In the Operators list, check E-mail for your operator.**

   This setting configures SQL Server to e-mail you in the event the transaction log for the Northwind database becomes more than 75 percent full. But what if you aren't there to fix the problem? That's where configuring an alert to call a job comes in handy.

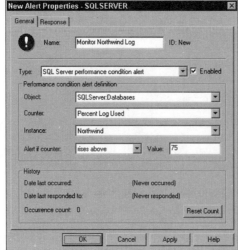

Figure 23-10:
Configuring
an alert to
monitor a
database's
transaction
log.

7. **Check Execute Job. From the drop-down list, select the Backup of** *database_name* **Transaction Log job you created earlier in Lab 23-3, as shown in Figure 23-11.**

   Remember, SQL Server automatically truncates the transaction log whenever you back it up. By configuring the alert to call the backup job for your database's transaction log, you force SQL Server to back up the log and then truncate it whenever it becomes more than 75% full.

8. **Click OK to save the new alert.**

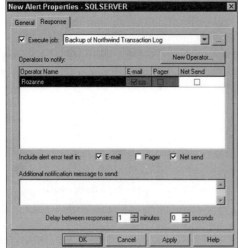

Figure 23-11:
Configuring
SQL
Server's
response to
an alert
condition.

Troubleshooting Jobs, Alerts, and Operator Notifications

You need to consider many factors if any of your jobs, alerts, and operator notifications aren't working. In this section, we look at each of the factors you should examine to SQL Server automation.

Check the SQLServerAgent service

Make sure that the SQLServerAgent service is started. Verify also that you have configured the SQLServerAgent service to log in with a domain user account that is a member of the local Administrators group on your server. Finally, double-check that you have entered the correct password for this user account.

Make sure the component is enabled

Remember, you can enable or disable an operator, job, or alert. You enable or disable each of these components by modifying its properties. Check the Enabled check box to enable a component; clear the check box to disable it.

Check the error logs

SQL Server creates its own error log for the SQLServerAgent service. You can view the SQLServerAgent service's error log by right-clicking the SQLServerAgent object in SQL Server Enterprise Manager and choosing Display Error Log. The SQLServerAgent's error log displays only errors by default. As shown in Figure 23-12, you can use the Type drop-down list to configure it to display only errors, warning messages, or informational messages, or all types of messages.

Another error log you need to check is the error log for SQL Server itself. You can view your server's error logs by expanding the Management folder within SQL Server Enterprise Manager, and then selecting the SQL Server Logs object. SQL server creates a new error log each time your server is started. In addition, it maintains an archive of the last six logs.

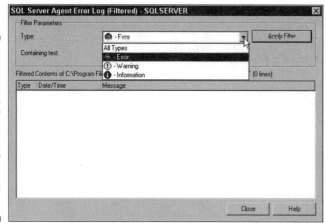

Also double-check the Windows application log for SQL Server errors. You view the application log within the Computer Management MMC, or by choosing Event Viewer from the Administrative Tools menu. If you don't see any SQL Server messages in the application log, you may need to increase the maximum size of the application log. In addition, make a habit of clearing the application log in order to prevent the log from filling up. If the log is full, SQL Server can't process any of your error-based alerts.

Check the history

Another troubleshooting resource is the history SQL Server maintains for alerts, jobs, and operators. You can view the history for each component by right-clicking its object (Alerts, Jobs, or Operators) in SQL Server Enterprise Manager and choosing Properties.

SQL Server stores the history for jobs in the msdb..sysjobhistory table. If this table runs out of space, you may not be able to view a job's history. Make sure that the msdb database file is big enough to accommodate storing the history information.

If the msdb database runs out of disk space, SQL Server can't execute your jobs.

Take steps to prevent a backlog of alerts

You could possibly have a situation on your server that repeatedly generates an alert. In this scenario, even if you have configured the alert to call a job to correct the problems, your server's processor may be so busy generating the alerts that it can't fix the problem. The end result is your server can have a backlog of alerts it can't process. Here are some techniques you can use to help resolve such a situation:

- ✔ Temporarily disable the alert.
- ✔ Clear all events from the Windows application log.
- ✔ Reconfigure the alert to increase the delay between responses. By increasing the time, you reduce how often SQL Server checks to see whether the alert condition has been resolved.
- ✔ Modify the properties of an error to prevent it from generating an error message in the Windows application log. If the error isn't added to the application log, SQL Server doesn't process the alert. You modify the properties of an error by editing it in the Registry.

Make sure you know all of these tips for resolving an alert backlog for the exam.

Prep Test

1 Which of the following tasks must you complete to prepare the SQLServerAgent service for jobs and alerts? (Choose all that apply.)

A ❑ Configure the service to use the System account as its service account.

B ❑ Add the service account to the Setupadmin server role.

C ❑ Configure the service to log in as a domain user.

D ❑ Add the service account to the Administrators local group.

2 What must you configure in order for the SQLServerAgent service to notify an operator by e-mail?

A ○ SQL Mail

B ○ SQLAgentMail

C ○ Microsoft Mail

D ○ SQL Server Mail

3 Which stored procedure enables you to define a job?

A ○ `sp_create_job`

B ○ `sp_job`

C ○ `sp_add_job`

D ○ `xp_add_job`

4 Which of the following job steps execute in the security context of the SQLServerAgent service account? (Choose all that apply.)

A ❑ Transact-SQL statements

B ❑ Operating system commands

C ❑ ActiveX scripts

D ❑ Replication processes

5 What events cause SQL Server to record an event in the application log? (Choose all that apply.)

A ❑ Errors with a severity level between 0 and 5

B ❑ Executing the `RAISERROR WITH LOG` statement

C ❑ Errors with a severity level between 19 and 25

D ❑ Any time you execute the `xp_logevent` stored procedure

6 How can you view the SQLServerAgent service's error log?

A ○ Open the log file with Notepad.

B ○ Edit the Registry.

C ○ View the log information in SQL Server Profiler.

D ○ Open the log in SQL Server Enterprise Manager.

Answers

1 **C** and **D.** The SQLServerAgent service account must be a domain user and a member of the Administrators local group. *See "Preparing for Automating Jobs and Alerts."*

2 **B.** The SQLServerAgent service uses SQLAgentMail to send e-mail messages to operators. *Study "Preparing for Automating Jobs and Alerts."*

3 **C.** Use the `sp_add_job` stored procedure to create a new job. *See "Defining Jobs."*

4 **B** and **C.** Both operating system command and ActiveX script job steps execute in the security context of the SQLServerAgent service account. *See "Defining job security."*

5 **B, C,** and **D.** SQL Server automatically writes errors with a severity level between 19 and 25 to the Windows application log. In addition, you can write an error to the log by using either the `RAISERROR` statement or the xp_logevent stored procedure. *Review "Defining Alerts."*

6 **D.** You view the SQLServerAgent service's log file in SQL Server Enterprise Manager. *Review "Check the error logs."*

Chapter 24

Optimizing Hardware Resources

● ●

Exam Objectives

▶ Optimizing hardware resource usage

▶ Monitoring hardware resource usage by using the Windows System Monitor

▶ Resolving system bottlenecks by using the Windows System Monitor

● ●

*W*indows 2000 includes a wonderful utility, System Monitor, that you can use to analyze both the performance of your server's hardware and its software. In this chapter, we examine all the information you need to monitor for analyzing your server's hardware and its performance. In Chapter 25, we look at how you can monitor the performance of SQL Server itself.

Quick Assessment

Optimizing hardware resource usage

1 You should analyze _____, _____, and _____ hardware components to optimize your server's hardware.

2 You should create a(n) _____ when establishing a baseline for your server's hardware.

3 Use the _____ counter to determine whether your server's CPU can keep up with its workload.

Monitoring hardware resource usage by using the Windows System Monitor

4 The value you see for your server's Memory: Available Bytes counter should be at least _____.

Resolving system bottlenecks by using the Windows System Monitor

5 If both the Processor: %Privileged Time and PhysicalDisk: %Disk Time counters are high, you should upgrade _____.

6 Your server's PhysicalDisk: %Disk Time counter averages 92%. You should _____, _____, or _____.

7 You should be concerned if your server's Memory: Pages/sec has a value of _____.

Answers

1 *Processor, memory, and hard disk subsystem.* Check out "Analyzing Hardware Resources."

2 *Log file.* Study "Designing a Performance Optimizing Strategy."

3 *Processor: %Processor Time.* See "Processor."

4 *5,000KB.* Study "Memory."

5 *Your server's hard disk subsystem.* See "Processor."

6 *Upgrade to a faster hard disk, install a drive array, or add more RAM.* Study "Hard disk subsystem."

7 *0 or higher.* See "Memory."

Designing a Performance Optimizing Strategy

The primary tool in your toolkit for optimizing performance is System Monitor, shown in Figure 24-1. Before we look at the objects and counters you need to monitor to optimize your server's hardware, we want to take a minute to talk about designing your method of attack. Most importantly, begin analyzing your server's hardware now (and not when you suspect you have a problem). By analyzing your hardware now, you develop a feel for what's normal on your computer. In other words, you create a *baseline* for your server's performance. After you have a baseline, you can use it to determine any performance problems that are occurring on your server.

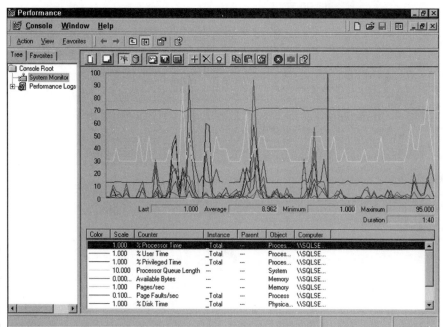

Figure 24-1:
Windows
2000 System
Monitor.

Analyzing Hardware Resources

To develop a baseline for optimizing your SQL server's hardware, focus your attention on the following hardware components:

- Processor
- Memory
- Hard disk subsystem

Each of these hardware resources has an impact on SQL Server's performance. For example, if you don't have enough RAM in your server, you'll see that your server must continually swap (page) information between your computer's RAM and hard disk. And because your computer's hard disk is typically the slowest component in any computer, excessive paging causes a tremendous decrease in your computer's performance.

Make sure that you know the objects and counters we list for each hardware resource, their acceptable values, and what to do to resolve any problems for the exam.

Processor

As you probably already know, the speed of your computer's processor has a big impact on your computer's performance. Table 24-1 describes the counters you need to monitor when developing a baseline for analyzing your processor's performance.

Table 24-1	Counters for Analyzing the Processor
Object: Counter	*What It Shows*
Processor: %Processor Time	The total workload on your server's CPU. If this value consistently exceeds 90 percent, your server's CPU can't keep up with its current workload.
Processor: %Privileged Time	The amount of time your server's CPU is spending performing privileged operating system functions such as servicing SQL Server I/O requests.
Processor: %User Time	The amount of time your server is processing user applications.
System: Processor Queue Length	The number of threads waiting for the processor to process them. This counter should always be less than two.

So what do you do if you analyze the processor in your server, and its values exceed these benchmarks? Here are a few suggestions:

- ✔ If your hardware supports multiple processors, add additional processors to your server.
- ✔ Upgrade to a faster processor.
- ✔ Split your server's workload. For example, if you've configured your server to run both SQL Server 2000 and Internet Information Services, install an additional server and move one of these applications to that server.

✔ Consider upgrading your server's hard disk subsystem if the Processor: %Privileged Time counter along with the physical disk counters are consistently high. A high Processor: %Privileged Time counter indicates that your server's processor is spending a lot of its time performing operating system functions.

Memory

As with your server's processor, the amount of memory in your server is also critical. Without enough memory, your server must continually page information between RAM and its hard disk.

In the Windows NT and Windows 2000 operating systems, your computer uses hard disk space as if it's part of RAM. As demand for memory increases, the operating system can move some of the information that's currently in RAM out to the hard disk. The operating system moves the information in 4KB chunks called *pages*. This process is called *paging*, and the file it uses on your hard disk to store these pages is called a *page file*.

Because memory is so important to your server's overall performance, analyze your server's memory as part of its baseline. We describe the counters you use to monitor memory in Table 24-2.

Table 24-2	Counters for Analyzing Memory
Object: Counter	*What It Shows*
Memory: Available Bytes	The amount of memory available to your server for executing processes. At a minimum, this counter should exceed 5,000KB.
Memory: Pages/sec	How often your server is paging information into and out of RAM as its memory needs increase. This counter shouldn't consistently exceed 0.
Process: Page Faults/sec	How often a program requests information that must be paged into memory. The higher this number, the greater the amount of paging on your computer — and the slower its performance. You can monitor this information for only SQL Server to determine how often it's causing page faults on your server.

If you determine that your server doesn't have enough memory, the solution is simple — add more RAM. If you've already configured your server with the maximum amount of RAM it can support, your only solutions are to move some of your server's workload to another server or upgrade to a new computer altogether.

Hard disk subsystem

SQL Server uses your server's hard disks to read and write to its databases. If your server's hard disk subsystem (made up of the hard disk, its controller, and the system bus) can't keep up with its workload, it degrades your entire server's performance. In Table 24-3, we describe the counters you monitor for analyzing the hard disk subsystem's performance.

Table 24-3	Counters for Analyzing the Hard Disk Subsystem
Object: Counter	*What It Shows*
PhysicalDisk: %Disk Time	The amount of time your server spends servicing hard disk requests. This counter should be less than 90 percent.
PhysicalDisk: Avg. Disk Queue Length	The number of queued hard disk requests that are waiting to be processed. This counter shouldn't exceed two per hard disk in your server.
PhysicalDisk: Disk Reads/sec	The number of read requests your hard disk is servicing per second. The appropriate values for this counter depend on the type of hard disk subsystem you're using. In general, this counter shouldn't exceed the capacity of your hardware.
PhysicalDisk: Disk Writes/sec	The number of write requests your hard disk is servicing per second. Like Disk Reads/sec, this counter's value shouldn't exceed the capacity of your hardware.

If you determine that your server's hard disk subsystem is a bottleneck, here are some steps you can take to fix this problem:

- ✔ Upgrade to a faster hard disk.
- ✔ Install a drive array (RAID).
- ✔ Move some of your server's applications to another server.
- ✔ Add more RAM.

If your server doesn't have enough memory, it pages information between RAM and the hard disk. As a result, your server's hard disk counters may be high simply because you don't have enough memory in your server — and not because your hard disk subsystem can't keep up with its workload. Monitoring both your server's hard disk subsystem and memory together is important so that you can truly determine which resource is causing the bottleneck on your server.

Prep Test

1 Your server's Processor: %User Time counter is consistently high. What should you do?

   A ○ Move some of your server's applications to another server.

   B ○ Add more RAM.

   C ○ Upgrade to a faster hard disk subsystem.

   D ○ Enable the Minimize User Time option for your server in SQL Server Enterprise Manager.

2 You suspect that your server's hard disk subsystem can't keep up with its workload. Which of the following counters should you monitor? (Choose all that apply.)

   A ❑ Processor: %Processor Time

   B ❑ Physical Disk: %Disk Time

   C ❑ Memory: Pages/sec

   D ❑ Memory: Available Bytes

3 Which of the following counters indicate that your server doesn't have enough memory?

   A ○ Processor: %Processor Time = 90%

   B ○ Memory: Pages/sec = 2

   C ○ Memory: Available Bytes = 6,505KB

   D ○ Physical Disk: %Disk Time = 75%

4 If you determine that your server's hard disk is a bottleneck, which of the following techniques can you use to help resolve the problem? (Choose all that apply.)

   A ❑ Upgrade to a faster hard disk subsystem.

   B ❑ Install mirrored hard disks.

   C ❑ Add more RAM.

   D ❑ Install a drive array.

5 Which counter should you use to determine how much time your server is spending processing operating system tasks?

   A ○ Process: Page Faults/sec

   B ○ Memory: Pages/sec

   C ○ Processor: %Privileged Time

   D ○ Processor: %User Time

Answers

1 **A.** Your server's Processor: %User Time counter being high indicates that your server can't keep up with its workload. Your best bet is to upgrade your processor, install an additional processor, or move some of your server's applications to another computer. *Study "Processor."*

2 **B, C,** and **D.** Always monitor both the physical disk and memory counters together. This strategy enables you to determine whether the bottleneck in your server is the hard disk subsystem, memory, or both. *Review " Hard disk subsystem."*

3 **B.** The Memory: Pages/sec counter shouldn't consistently exceed 0. If it does, it's an indication that your server doesn't have enough memory. *See "Memory."*

4 **A, C,** and **D.** Upgrade your hardware, add more RAM, or both if your server's hard disk is a bottleneck. *Study "Hard disk subsystem."*

5 **C.** Operating system tasks are considered "privileged," mostly because they have direct access to your computer's resources. You monitor the amount of time your server spends with these tasks by analyzing the Processor: %Privileged Time counter. *Study "Processor."*

Chapter 25

Monitoring and Troubleshooting SQL Server

Exam Objectives

▶ Optimizing and troubleshooting SQL Server system activity

▶ Monitoring SQL Server system activity by using the Windows System Monitor

▶ Monitoring SQL Server system activity by using traces

*I*n this chapter, we focus on the tools and techniques you can use to optimize and troubleshoot SQL Server itself. As with monitoring your server's hardware resources (see Chapter 24), you can also monitor SQL Server by using its objects and counters in System Monitor. We also show you how to monitor your server by using trace flags and creating a trace in SQL Server Profiler.

Quick Assessment

Optimizing and troubleshooting SQL Server system activity

1 SQL Server uses the _____ cache to store data in memory.

Monitoring SQL Server system activity by using the Windows System Monitor

2 Use the _____ counter to determine how much memory each instance of SQL Server is using.

3 You can use the _____ counter to see how often SQL Server is responding to users' requests with information that's in RAM instead of from the hard disk.

4 You can determine how much of a workload each instance of SQL Server is placing on your server's processors by using the _____ counter.

5 You should enable fiber mode scheduling if the System: Content Switches/sec counter reaches _____ and the Processor: %Processor Time is greater than _____.

6 You turn on a trace flag by using the _____ command.

Monitoring SQL Server system activity by using traces

7 You can save the trace generated in SQL Server Profiler to a(n) _____, _____, or _____.

8 You monitor your server in SQL Server Profiler by selecting _____.

Answers

1 *Data.* Review "Analyzing SQL Server's memory usage."

2 *Process: Working Set.* See "Analyzing SQL Server's memory usage."

3 *SQL Server: Buffer Manager: Buffer Cache Hit Ratio.* Study "Analyzing SQL Server's memory usage."

4 *Process: %Processor Time.* Study "Analyzing SQL Server's processor usage."

5 *8,000 and 90%.* See "Analyzing SQL Server's processor usage."

6 `DBCC TRACEON`. See "Monitoring SQL Server by Using Trace Flags."

7 *Table, file, or SQL script.* Study "Monitoring SQL Server with SQL Server Profiler."

8 *Events.* Study "Monitoring SQL Server with SQL Server Profiler."

Monitoring SQL Server in System Monitor

Microsoft refers to System Monitor as *extensible*, which just means that any application can add its own objects and counters to System Monitor. As a result, you get a whole bunch of new objects and counters when you install SQL Server 2000. You use these objects and their associated counters to monitor things such as how SQL Server is using your server's memory and processor.

Analyzing SQL Server's memory usage

SQL Server uses your server's memory for its data cache. This cache enables SQL Server to respond to users' requests for data from RAM rather than retrieving the data from its hard disk. Because responding to requests with cached data is so much faster than retrieving that same data from the hard disk, making sure that your server has enough memory is very important.

One of the nice things about SQL Server 2000 is that you don't have to assign a fixed amount of memory to its data cache. Beginning with SQL Server version 7.0, Microsoft designed SQL Server to be dynamic — which means that it will add memory to its data cache during period of peak usage, and return that memory to the operating system when it no longer needs it.

If you install multiple instances of SQL Server 2000, keep in mind that each instance has its own data cache. In other words, you need to make sure you have enough memory in your server to handle each instance's memory requirements.

In Table 25-1, we describe the counters that you can use in System Monitor to analyze how well SQL Server is using the memory in your server. And as far as what you do if these counters indicate a problem goes, your only choice is to add more memory!

Table 25-1   Counters for Analyzing SQL Server Memory Usage

Object: Counter	*What It Shows*
Process: Working Set	The amount of memory SQL Server is using for each instance. Can monitor per instance of SQL Server, as shown in Figure 25-1. This counter should be greater than 5,000KB; if less, SQL Server doesn't have enough memory.
SQL Server: Buffer Manager: Buffer Cache Hit Ratio	How often SQL Server is servicing requests for data from RAM rather than the hard disk. This counter should be greater than 90%.

Object: Counter	What It Shows
SQL Server: Buffer Manager: Total Pages	The total amount of pages in the buffer cache. If this counter is low, your server is having to frequently page data into and out of RAM.
SQL Server: Memory Manager: Total Server Memory	The total amount of memory used by SQL Server. If this counter is close to the amount of total RAM in your computer, you don't have enough RAM.

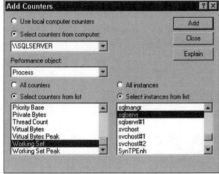

Figure 25-1:
You can monitor each instance of SQL Server individually.

Analyzing SQL Server's processor usage

You can also use System Monitor to analyze how SQL Server is using your server's processors. The first counter you need to monitor is Process: %Processor Time — and monitor it for each instance of SQL Server. You can use this counter to determine the workload each instance is placing on your server. If one of your SQL Server instances is overloading your server, you can then analyze what's happening with that instance to see whether you can optimize it further. For example, can you do anything to optimize the application that you're running in that instance? Or do you need to just upgrade the processors in your server?

Another counter you can monitor is System: Content Switches/sec. This counter enables you to determine how often SQL Server is switching between the current pool of threads. (A thread is a unit of execution for a given process. For a given unit of time, your server must allocate a portion of the CPU's time to each thread in this pool.) If you're running SQL Server on a server with multiple CPUs, always monitor this counter to analyze the performance of the processors.

If the Content Switches/sec counter reaches 8,000 and your server's Processor: %Processor Time is consistently over 90%, then enable fiber mode scheduling. Each thread is made up of smaller units of execution called fibers. With fiber-mode scheduling, SQL Server performs switching between fibers instead of Windows 2000 having to manage switching between threads. By having SQL Server manage fiber switching, you reduce the amount of resources needed for Windows 2000 to manage switching between threads.

You enable fiber-mode scheduling by modifying the properties of your server in SQL Server Enterprise Manager, as follows:

1. **In the contents pane, right-click your server and choose Properties.**
2. **Select the Processor tab.**
3. **Check Use Windows NT Fibers, as shown in Figure 25-2.**

   Although you can check this option on a server with only a single processor, Microsoft recommends that you don't, because the overhead associated with managing fibers can outweigh the benefits on a single processor server.

4. **Click OK to save your changes.**

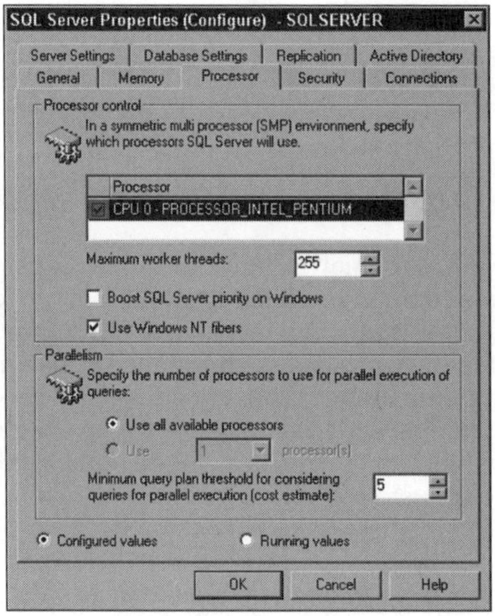

Figure 25-2:
Enabling
fiber-mode
scheduling.

SQL Server Properties (Configure) - SQLSERVER

Server Settings | Database Settings | Replication | Active Directory
General | Memory | Processor | Security | Connections

Processor control
  In a symmetric multi processor (SMP) environment, specify which processors SQL Server will use.

  Processor
  CPU 0 - PROCESSOR_INTEL_PENTIUM

  Maximum worker threads: 255

  ☐ Boost SQL Server priority on Windows
  ☑ Use Windows NT fibers

Parallelism
  Specify the number of processors to use for parallel execution of queries:

  ● Use all available processors
  ○ Use [1] processor(s)

  Minimum query plan threshold for considering queries for parallel execution (cost estimate): 5

● Configured values   ○ Running values

    OK   Cancel   Help

Monitoring SQL Server by Using Trace Flags

SQL Server 2000 includes several trace flags you can use to temporarily change the configuration of SQL Server or to diagnose performance problems. You enable these trace flags by using the following syntax:

```
DBCC TRACEON (trace_number)
```

You can use trace flag 1204 to enable you to view detailed information about the types of locks causing a deadlock, along with the command affected by the deadlock.

You can turn off a trace flag by using the following syntax:

```
DBCC TRACEOFF (trace_number)
```

Monitoring SQL Server with SQL Server Profiler

SQL Server Profiler enables you to trace both server and database activity by creating a trace. You can save the results generated by SQL Server Profiler to a table, file, or a SQL script. SQL Server Profiler enables you to monitor for a variety of problems on your server in a trace, including

- ✔ Actions of specific users or applications
- ✔ Deadlocks
- ✔ Security issues such as successful and failed logins
- ✔ Queries that SQL Server retrieves the result set by performing a table scan instead of using the table's indexes
- ✔ Processor use generated by each SQL statement

You monitor for these problems by expanding the Event Classes in SQL Server Profiler and then selecting and adding the specific events to monitor, as shown in Figure 25-3. We provide in-depth coverage of SQL Server Profiler in Chapter 16.

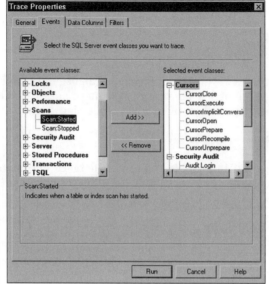

Figure 25-3:
Use SQL
Server
Profiler to
monitor your
server.

You can configure a trace in SQL Server Profiler to monitor the activity on only one server — or only a single instance of SQL Server (if you've installed multiple instances on the same server). If you want to trace activity on multiple servers or SQL Server instances, you must define two separate traces.

Prep Test

1 You used the Processor: %Processor Time to analyze your server's processor usage and found that it consistently exceeds 90%. What counter can you use to determine whether the problem is SQL Server?

A ○ Process: Working Set

B ○ Process: %Processor Time for the SQL Server process

C ○ SQL Server: Buffer Manager: Buffer Cache Hit Ratio

D ○ System: Content Switches/sec

2 By monitoring the Process: Working Set counter, you've determined that the average amount of memory SQL Server is using 8,000KB. What should you do?

A ○ Add more RAM to your server.

B ○ Install a faster hard disk subsystem.

C ○ Reserve more memory for SQL Server by modifying your server's properties.

D ○ Nothing.

3 The SQL Server: Memory Manager: Total Server Memory displays 190,000KB. You've installed 192MB of RAM in your server. What should you do?

A ○ Nothing.

B ○ Upgrade to a faster processor.

C ○ Reconfigure the SQL Server service to use less memory.

D ○ Install more RAM in your server.

4 Your server's SQL Server: Buffer Manager: Buffer Cache Hit Ratio is consistently greater than 90%. What should you do?

A ○ Add more RAM to your server.

B ○ Install a faster processor.

C ○ Nothing.

D ○ Reserve more memory for SQL Server's buffer cache by modifying your server's properties.

5 On what type of server should you enable fiber-mode scheduling?

A ○ A server with a maximum of two hard disks

B ○ A server with multiple processors

C ○ A server on which you're running the Enterprise edition of SQL Server 2000

D ○ A server with a drive array

6 **Which trace flag should you enable for monitoring deadlocks on your server?**

A ○ 260

B ○ 1204

C ○ 2528

D ○ 3205

7 **Which of the following events can you analyze in SQL Server Profiler? (Choose all that apply.)**

A ❑ How SQL Server retrieves a query's result set

B ❑ Successful and failed logins

C ❑ Deadlocks

D ❑ Activities performed by a specific user

Answers

1 **A.** You use the Process: Working Set counter for the SQL Server process to determine the workload it's placing on your computer. If you've configured multiple instances of SQL Server, you can monitor each instance separately in System Monitor. *Study "Analyzing SQL Server's memory usage."*

2 **D.** Microsoft recommends that this counter have a value of 5,000KB or greater. *Study "Analyzing SQL Server's memory usage."*

3 **D.** If the SQL Server: Memory Manager: Total Server Memory counter has a value that's close to the amount of actual RAM in your server, you should install more RAM. *Study "Analyzing SQL Server's memory usage."*

4 **C.** A Cache Hit Ratio of greater than 90% is what you want! *Study "Analyzing SQL Server's memory usage."*

5 **B.** You should enable fiber-mode scheduling only on multiprocessor computers. *Study "Analyzing SQL Server's processor usage."*

6 **B.** Use the 1204 trace flag to monitor for deadlocks. *Review "Monitoring SQL Server by Using Trace Flags."*

7 **A, B, C,** and **D.** You can use SQL Server Profiler to determine whether SQL Server retrieves a query's result set by performing a table scan or by using its indexes; in addition, SQL Server Profiler enables you to identify deadlocks. You can also use SQL Server Profiler to monitor for security events such as successful and failed logins, and the activities performed by a specific user. *Study "Monitoring SQL Server with SQL Server Profiler."*

Part VIII
The Part of Tens

The 5th Wave   By Rich Tennant

"...and it doesn't appear that you'll have much trouble grasping some of the more 'alien' configuration concepts on this MCSE exam."

In this part . . .

*W*elcome to the Part of Tens. Here's where we provide you with our top-ten lists of information that can help you pass your exam. In Chapter 26, we provide you with our best test-taking tips and tricks. And in Chapter 27, we list our favorite online resources for getting information about your exam and improving your knowledge of SQL Server in general!

Chapter 26

Ten Terrific Exam Day Tips

In This Chapter

▶ Preparing for the exam

▶ Practicing with SQL Server before you take the exam

▶ Scheduling your exam

A t long last, you're ready to take the exam! You studied backward and forward, you know this book as well as your ABCs, you passed all the practice exams you can get your hands on, and now you're ready. In this chapter, we offer you ten suggestions to help make sure that everything goes smoothly before you click the Start button for your test.

Write Down Key Concepts as You Study

The best technique you can use to memorize the key concepts about SQL Server is to write them down. Think about it — your mind can wander while you're reading, but it's tougher for your mind to wander while you're writing. Use a clean notepad and write everything down that you can. You'll be surprised at how much easier you can memorize the facts when you write them down.

Work with SQL Server 2000

Microsoft is continually trying to make its exams a more accurate measure of both your knowledge and experience with its products. (In essence, Microsoft is trying to avoid people having "paper" certifications.) As a result, the more you know about using SQL Server 2000, the better you can expect to do on the exam. If at all possible, set up your own SQL server to practice the labs we've provided you with throughout the book. You will definitely find it worth your time!

Schedule Your Exam

When you're ready, schedule your exam. If you live in the United States or Canada, you can do so by calling Prometric at 800-755-EXAM or VUE at 888-837-8616. If you live in other regions, you can find the appropriate phone number for your region on both Prometric and VUE's Web sites. You can also register online (regardless of where you live!) with either testing vendor by going to www.2test.com for Prometric, or www.vue.com for VUE. Be prepared to pay for the exam by credit card; each exam costs $100. You also need your testing ID number to register for the exam.

Choose the Best Time for You

Chances are, you already know that you're at your best at certain times of the day — and not at others. Take advantage of this fact and schedule your exam at the time when you're most alert. Also try to take your exam on a day when you don't have too much going on so that you won't have any distractions.

Bring the Right Stuff

And leave the wrong stuff at home. You can't bring anything like cellular phones, calculators, personal digital assistants (PDAs), and pagers into the testing center. You can't even bring your own scratch paper (but the testing center will provide you with some). But make sure that you bring two forms of ID, one with a photo, to the testing center. You may also want to think about wearing layered clothing just in case the testing center is cold. (We want you to be able to relax when you take your exam!)

Stay Calm

Whatever you do, don't panic! Your test-taking skills will only get worse. Although we understand how frustrating it can be for you to run into questions for which you don't know the answers, the worst thing you can do is panic. Stay calm, take a deep breath, and compose yourself. Who knows? The answer just might come to you if you manage to relax.

Don't Memorize Practice Exams

One of the bigger mistakes you can make is to memorize the answers for the questions on practice exams. Because Microsoft has really cracked down on enforcing the non-disclosure agreement for exams, the likelihood of any practice exam duplicating the actual questions on a real exam is really slim. So if you miss a question on the practice exam, don't look up the answer and memorize it. Instead, take the fact that you missed the question as an indication that you don't know that particular topic's material well enough — and go back and study that concept.

Be Prepared for an Adaptive Exam

As we write this book, the SQL Server 2000 exam isn't adaptive, which means that you can expect to see somewhere in the neighborhood of 50 to 70 exam questions. An adaptive exam tailors its questions to you as you take the exam. For example, if you miss a question on a specific topic, the exam will then ask you other questions about that same topic. Microsoft reserves the right to make any test adaptive (and without announcing it), so make sure you're mentally prepared for an adaptive exam. You can find out more about adaptive exams and download a sample by going to www.microsoft.com/ trainingandservices. When you get to this site, look for the link titled "Testing Innovations."

Watch the Clock

All of Microsoft's exams have a time limit, so make sure you know what it is when you start the exam — and keep track of the time as you go. If your exam isn't adaptive, you can mark the questions you aren't sure of and then come back to them later. And if you spend too much time on a few questions, you can run out of time without answering all the questions.

If at First You Don't Succeed

We know it's a cliché, but it's true even with Microsoft exams: If at first you don't succeed, try, try again. Don't give up if you don't pass the exam on your first try. Many people before you have failed exams — and many will follow in your footsteps. The most important thing is for you to learn from the experience. Although the exam is fresh in your mind, go through your study materials and mark what concepts your exam focused on. Study the areas where you think you are weak — and then take it again.

Chapter 27

Ten MCSE Certification Resources

In This Chapter

▶ Exploring SQL Server Web sites

▶ Finding online resources and help

We know you already know about the bad news (that you have much to learn about SQL Server 2000). But do you know about the good news? The good news is that an absolute ton of information is available to you about SQL Server! In this chapter, we give you our top ten resources for information about SQL Server and MCSE certification.

The Microsoft Training and Services Web Site

Your first stop when touring Web sites for information about the SQL Server 2000 exams is Microsoft's Training and Services Web site. You find it at www.microsoft.com/trainingandservices. This site has information about all of Microsoft's exams and any changes to the exam formats (including new types of questions). It also has links to practice exams that you can download to help you prepare for the exam.

Exam Preparation Guide for Exam 70-228

You find the exam objectives for exam 70-228 in the SQL Server 2000 exam preparation guide at www.microsoft.com/trainingandservices/exams/examasearch.asp?PageID=70-228. Make sure that you add this page to your Favorites because you can keep checking the requirements and objectives for your exam.

The Microsoft SQL Server Web Site

Another site you need to add to your Favorites is Microsoft's Web site for SQL Server. It's at `www.microsoft.com/sql`. From this Web site, you can access links to white papers, find out about Microsoft's training and events (many of which are free!), and get detailed product information. You also can find information about the latest patches and fixes, and download many of the SQL Server 2000 Resource Kit utilities.

The SQL Server Magazine Web Site

In our opinion, one of the better publications on the market for up-to-date information about SQL Server and detailed articles on how to implement its features is *SQL Server Magazine*. You can access many of the magazine's articles for free at `www.sqlmag.com`.

E-Mail Newsletters

Many Web sites have weekly e-mail newsletters to which you can subscribe. These newsletters provide you with the latest and greatest information, along with the convenience of having them delivered directly to your Inbox. Here are a few of our favorite newsletters:

- **SQL Server Magazine Update and Windows 2000 Magazine Update.** You can subscribe to both by going to `www.win2000mag.net/Email`. The weekly SQL Server Magazine Update newsletter provides you with the latest SQL Server news, tips, and tricks for implementing SQL Server, and information about the latest products you can use with SQL Server.

- **The MCP NewsFlash.** You can subscribe to this newsletter by going to `www.microsoft.com/trainingandservices` and clicking the Newsletters link. The MCP NewsFlash provides you with the latest information on the Microsoft Certified Professional (MCP) program, including information about new, beta, and retiring exams; changes to the MCP program; and any special promotions.

- **TechNet Updates.** Subscribe by going to `www.microsoft.com/technet/register/flash.asp`. The TechNet Updates newsletter provides you with the latest technical information and updates for Microsoft products.

- **The Question of the Day.** You can sign up to have Cramsession (at `cramsession.brainbuzz.com`) send you a question of the day for the Microsoft exams by clicking the Newsletters link on the home page.

Microsoft TechNet

TechNet is Microsoft's premier source for technical information about all of its products. Here you find great articles on implementing any product Microsoft makes, along with links to resource kits, service packs, and more. You also find a link to the Microsoft Knowledge Base. This is Microsoft's database of technical support problems with any of their products, the causes of those problems, and how to fix them. If you're having a problem with SQL Server 2000, make this site your first stop.

By the way, after you're an MCP, you can subscribe to TechNet at a reduced rate. You then receive your monthly subscription on CD-ROM. This CD-ROM version really comes in handy when you're troubleshooting a problem at a customer's site and the customer doesn't have Internet access!

The Transcender Web Site

If you find you need more practice exams than the ones we've given you (and the ones you can download from Microsoft's Web site), check out Transcender's Web site at `www.transcender.com`. Transcender offers a full product line of practice exams, along with discounts if you buy packages with practice exams for multiple Microsoft exams. We've included a demo of Transcender's tools on this book's CD-ROM.

The SQL Server Newsgroups

Microsoft has established several newsgroups that you can use to post questions about SQL Server 2000. You can find the complete list of newsgroups by going to `www.microsoft.com/sql/support/Newsgroups.htm`. One of the best things about these newsgroups is that Microsoft has appointed several posters as "SQL Server MVPs." These Most Valuable Professionals are very knowledgeable, and almost always respond to posted questions. If you need help, these newsgroups are a good place to start!

User's Groups

If you want to join a user's group, the Professional Association for SQL Server is a good place to start. You can find out information about the organization by going to its Web site at `www.sqlpass.org`. You can use this Web site to find a user's group in your area. You can find also out about PASS-sponsored events. (One of the best events is the PASS Conference held every year in September.)

The SQL Server Performance Web Site

Last, but definitely not least, the SQL Server Performance Web site has a wealth of good information on tuning and optimizing SQL Server. It also has a glossary, links to other Web sites, tutorials, and book reviews. You can find it at `www.sql-server-performance.com`.

Part IX

Appendix

The 5th Wave   By Rich Tennant

"We sort of have our own way of mentally preparing our people to take the MCSE SQL Server exam."

In this part . . .

*H*ere's where you find the "About the CD" appendix, which gives you complete instructions for installing the software on the CD. The "About the CD" appendix also offers brief descriptions of all the software we've included on the *MCSE SQL Server 2000 Administration For Dummies* CD-ROM.

Appendix

About the CD

You can find the following software on the *MCSE SQL Server 2000 Administration For Dummies* CD-ROM:

- The QuickLearn game, a fun way to study for the test
- Practice and Self-Assessment tests, to make sure you're ready for the real exam
- A full-length Practice Exam — because you can never have too much practice
- Practice test demos from Transcender and Specialized Solutions

System Requirements

Make sure that your computer meets the following minimum system requirements:

- A PC with a 486 or faster processor.
- Microsoft Windows 95 or later.
- At least 16MB of total RAM installed in your computer.
- At least 75MB of free hard disk space for installing the software on this CD. (You won't need as much free space if you don't install every program.)
- A CD-ROM drive — double-speed (2x) or faster.
- A sound card.
- A monitor capable of displaying at least 256 colors or grayscale.
- A modem with a speed of at least 14,400 bps.

If your computer doesn't meet the minimum requirements, you may have problems using the contents of this CD.

Important Note: To play the QuickLearn game, you must have a 166MHz or faster computer running Windows 9x with SVGA graphics. You must also have Microsoft DirectX 5.0 or later installed. If you don't have DirectX, you can install it from the CD. Just run D:\Directx\dxinstall.exe. Unfortunately, DirectX 5.0 does not run on Windows NT 4.0, so you can't play the QuickLearn Game on a computer running Windows NT 4.0 (or any prior version of Windows NT).

Using the CD

To install the items from the CD to your hard drive, follow these steps:

1. **Insert the CD into your computer's CD-ROM drive.**

2. **Choose Start⇨Run.**

3. **In the Open text box, type** D:\SETUP.EXE.

   Replace D with the proper drive letter if your CD-ROM drive uses a different letter.

4. **Click OK.**

   You now see a license agreement.

5. **Read the license agreement, nod your head, and then click the Accept button if you want to use the CD. After you click Accept, you'll never be bothered by the License Agreement window again.**

   You now see the CD interface Welcome screen. The interface is a little program that shows you what's on the CD and coordinates installing the programs and running the demos. The interface basically enables you to click a button or two to make things happen.

6. **Click anywhere on the Welcome screen to enter the interface.**

   The next screen lists categories for the software on the CD.

7. **To view the items within a category, just click the category's name.**

   A list of programs in the category appears.

8. **For more information about a program, click the program's name.**

   Be sure to read the information that appears. Sometimes a program has its own system requirements or requires you to do a few tricks on your computer before you can install or run the program, and this screen tells you what you need to do, if necessary.

9. **If you don't want to install the program, click Go Back to return to the preceding screen.**

   You can always return to the preceding screen by clicking Go Back. This feature enables you to browse the different categories and products and decide what you want to install.

10. **To install a program, click the appropriate Install button.**

    The CD interface drops to the background while the CD installs the program you chose.

11. **To install other items, repeat Steps 7 through 10.**

12. **When you finish installing programs, click the Quit button to close the interface.**

    You can eject the CD now. Carefully place it back in the plastic jacket of the book for safekeeping.

To run some of the programs on the *MCSE SQL Server 2000 Administration For Dummies* CD, you need to keep the CD in your CD-ROM drive.

What You'll Find

This section summarizes the software on the *MCSE SQL Server 2000 Administration For Dummies* CD.

For Dummies test prep tools

This CD contains questions related to SQL Server 2000. Most of the questions are topics that you can expect to see on the test. We've also included some questions on other SQL Server topics that may or may not be on the exam or covered in this book, but that you will need to perform database administration.

QuickLearn Game

The QuickLearn Game is the *For Dummies* way of making studying for the Certification exam fun. Well, okay, less painful. OutPost is a DirectX, high-resolution, fast-paced arcade game.

Answer questions to defuse dimensional disrupters and save the universe from a rift in space-time. (The questions come from the same set of questions that the Self-Assessment and Practice Test use, but isn't this way more fun?) Missing a few questions on the real exam almost never results in a rip in the fabric of the universe, so just think how easy it'll be when you get there!

You need to have DirectX 5.0 or later installed to play the QuickLearn game, and it doesn't run on Windows NT 4.0.

Practice Test

The Practice Test is designed to help you get comfortable with the MCSE testing situation and pinpoint your strengths and weaknesses on the topic. You can accept the default setting of 60 questions in 60 minutes, or you can customize the settings. You can choose the number of questions, the amount of time, and even decide which objectives you want to focus on.

After you answer the questions, the Practice Test gives you plenty of feedback. You can find out which questions you answered correctly and incorrectly, and get statistics on how you did, broken down by objective. Then you can review the questions — all of them, all the ones you missed, all the ones you marked, or a combination of the ones you marked and the ones you missed.

Bonus Chapter: Computerized Adaptive Testing For Dummies

This special CD chapter describes computerized adaptive testing (CAT) — how it works and how it differs from both computerized testing in general and other types of tests. The chapter also includes a FAQ about certification CATs specifically. There is even a section where test takers discuss their reactions to the CATs they have survived. A final section discusses the use of simulations in performance-based testing and shows how such tests are superior to multiple-choice and other types of questioning for certification exams. This chapter is in PDF format, and you will need Adobe Acrobat Reader to view it. If you don't have Acrobat Reader, install it from the CD.

Practice Exam

The CD includes a full-length Practice Exam to help you make sure you are ready for the real thing. Answer 50 questions, check your score, and then decide whether you should continue studying or go ahead and schedule your exam. You need Adobe Acrobat reader to display the PDF file that contains the Practice Exam. If you don't have Acrobat reader, install it from the CD.

Screen Saver

A spiffy little screen saver that the *For Dummies* team created. Screen shots of test questions will fill your screen, so when your computer isn't doing anything else, it can still be quizzing you!

Commercial demos

We've included a few demos on the book's CD to help you prepare for the exam. Practice makes perfect — and these demos help you to get even more practice with taking tests!

Transcender Certification Sampler, from Transcender Corporation

This Certification Sampler offers demos of many of the MCSE practice exams that Transcender offers. Visit www.transcender.com for more information about Transcender's test-prep tools.

QuickCert, from Specialized Solutions, Inc.

This package from Specialized Solutions, Inc., offers practice tests for several of the certification exams. Run the QuickCert IDG Demo to choose the practice test you want to work on. For more information about QuickCert, visit `www.specializedsolutions.com`.

If You Have Problems (Of the CD Kind)

We tried our best to compile programs that work on most computers with the minimum system requirements. Alas, your computer may differ, and some programs may not work properly for some reason.

The two most likely problems are that your computer doesn't have enough memory (RAM) for the programs you want to use, or that you have other programs running that are affecting the installation or running of a program. If you get error messages such as `Not enough memory` or `Setup cannot continue`, try one or more of the following actions and then try using the software again:

- **Turn off any antivirus software that you have on your computer.** Installers sometimes mimic virus activity and may make your computer incorrectly believe that it is being infected by a virus.

- **Close all running programs.** The more programs you're running, the less memory is available to other programs. Installers also typically update files and programs; if you keep other programs running, installation may not work properly.

- **In Windows, close the CD interface and run demos or installations directly from Windows Explorer.** The interface itself can tie up system memory or even conflict with certain kinds of interactive demos. Use Windows Explorer to browse the files on the CD and launch installers or demos.

- **Have your local computer store add more RAM to your computer.** This is, admittedly, a drastic and somewhat expensive step, but adding more memory can really help the speed of your computer and enable more programs to run at the same time.

If you still have trouble installing the items from the CD, please call the Hungry Minds, Inc., Customer Service phone number: 800-762-2974 (outside the U.S.: 317-572-3342).

Index

● ●

• X •

Notes

Hungry Minds, Inc.
End-User License Agreement

5. Limited Warranty.

  (a) HMI warrants that the Software and Software Media are free from defects in materials and workmanship under normal use for a period of sixty (60) days from the date of purchase of this Book. If HMI receives notification within the warranty period of defects in materials or workmanship, HMI will replace the defective Software Media.

  (b) HMI AND THE AUTHOR OF THE BOOK DISCLAIM ALL OTHER WARRANTIES, EXPRESS OR IMPLIED, INCLUDING WITHOUT LIMITATION IMPLIED WARRANTIES OF MERCHANTABILITY AND FITNESS FOR A PARTICULAR PURPOSE, WITH RESPECT TO THE SOFTWARE, THE PROGRAMS, THE SOURCE CODE CONTAINED THEREIN, AND/OR THE TECHNIQUES DESCRIBED IN THIS BOOK. HMI DOES NOT WARRANT THAT THE FUNCTIONS CONTAINED IN THE SOFTWARE WILL MEET YOUR REQUIRE-MENTS OR THAT THE OPERATION OF THE SOFTWARE WILL BE ERROR FREE.

  (c) This limited warranty gives you specific legal rights, and you may have other rights that vary from jurisdiction to jurisdiction.

6. Remedies.

  (a) HMI's entire liability and your exclusive remedy for defects in materials and workmanship shall be limited to replacement of the Software Media, which may be returned to HMI with a copy of your receipt at the following address: Software Media Fulfillment Department, Attn.: *MCSE SQL Server 2000 Administration For Dummies*, Hungry Minds, Inc., 10475 Crosspoint Blvd., Indianapolis, IN 46256, or call 1-800-762-2974. Please allow four to six weeks for delivery. This Limited Warranty is void if failure of the Software Media has resulted from accident, abuse, or misapplication. Any replacement Software Media will be warranted for the remainder of the original warranty period or thirty (30) days, whichever is longer.

  (b) In no event shall HMI or the author be liable for any damages whatsoever (including without limitation damages for loss of business profits, business interruption, loss of business information, or any other pecuniary loss) arising from the use of or inability to use the Book or the Software, even if HMI has been advised of the possibility of such damages.

  (c) Because some jurisdictions do not allow the exclusion or limitation of liability for consequential or incidental damages, the above limitation or exclusion may not apply to you.

7. U.S. Government Restricted Rights. Use, duplication, or disclosure of the Software for or on behalf of the United States of America, its agencies and/or instrumentalities (the "U.S. Government") is subject to restrictions as stated in paragraph (c)(1)(ii) of the Rights in Technical Data and Computer Software clause of DFARS 252.227-7013, or subparagraphs (c) (1) and (2) of the Commercial Computer Software - Restricted Rights clause at FAR 52.227-19, and in similar clauses in the NASA FAR supplement, as applicable.

8. General. This Agreement constitutes the entire understanding of the parties and revokes and supersedes all prior agreements, oral or written, between them and may not be modified or amended except in a writing signed by both parties hereto that specifically refers to this Agreement. This Agreement shall take precedence over any other documents that may be in conflict herewith. If any one or more provisions contained in this Agreement are held by any court or tribunal to be invalid, illegal, or otherwise unenforceable, each and every other provision shall remain in full force and effect.

Installation Instructions

To install the items from the CD to your hard drive, follow these steps:

1. **Insert the CD into your computer's CD-ROM drive.**

2. **Choose Start➪Run.**

3. **In the Open text box, type** D:\SETUP.EXE.

   Replace D with the proper drive letter if your CD-ROM drive uses a different letter.

4. **Click OK.**

5. **Read through the license agreement that's displayed, and then click the Accept button if you want to use the CD.**

   The CD interface Welcome screen appears.

6. **Click anywhere on the Welcome screen to enter the CD interface.**

   The interface displays a list of categories for the software on the CD.

7. **To view the items within a category, just click the category's name.**

   A list of programs in the category appears.

8. **For more information about a program, click the program's name.**

9. **To install a program, click the appropriate Install button. If you don't want to install the program, click the Back button to return to the preceding screen.**

   The CD interface drops to the background while the CD installs the program you chose.

10. **To install other items, repeat Steps 7 through 9.**

11. **After you install the programs you want, click the Quit button and then eject the CD.**

For more information, see the "About the CD" appendix.

FOR DUMMIES
BOOK REGISTRATION

We want to hear from you!

Visit **dummies.com** to register this book and tell us how you liked it!

- Get entered in our monthly prize giveaway.

- Give us feedback about this book — tell us what you like best, what you like least, or maybe what you'd like to ask the author and us to change!

- Let us know any other *For Dummies* topics that interest you.

Your feedback helps us determine what books to publish, tells us what coverage to add as we revise our books, and lets us know whether we're meeting your needs as a *For Dummies* reader. You're our most valuable resource, and what you have to say is important to us!

Not on the Web yet? It's easy to get started with *Dummies 101: The Internet For Windows 98* or *The Internet For Dummies* at local retailers everywhere.

Or let us know what you think by sending us a letter at the following address:

For Dummies Book Registration
Dummies Press
10475 Crosspoint Blvd.
Indianapolis, IN 46256

...FOR DUMMIES™

**BESTSELLING
BOOK SERIES**